THE
NUCLEAR
READER

STRATEGY, WEAPONS, WAR

THE
NUCLEAR
READER

STRATEGY, WEAPONS, WAR

Edited by

Charles W. Kegley, Jr.
University of South Carolina

Eugene R. Wittkopf
University of Florida

St. Martin's Press
New York

For Pamela and Barbara,
Suzanne, Debra, and Jonathan

ISBN 0-312-57982-9
ISBN 0-312-57979-9 (pbk.)

Library of Congress Cataloging in Publication Data

Main entry under title:

The Nuclear Reader.

   Includes bibliographical references.
   1. Nuclear warfare—Addresses, essays, lectures.
2. Nuclear weapons—Addresses, essays, lectures.
I. Kegley, Charles W.   II. Wittkopf, Eugene R.,
1943–
U263.N758 1985   355'.0217   84–51846
ISBN 0-312-57982-9
ISBN 0-312-57979-9 (pbk.)

ACKNOWLEDGMENTS

Part I: Strategy

"Nuclear Temptations: Doctrinal Issues in the Strategic Debate," by Theodore Draper.
   Abridged from Theodore Draper, "Nuclear Temptations," *The New York Review of Books*,
   Vol. 30, Nos. 21 and 22 (January 19, 1984), pp. 42–48. The article is a revised and enlarged
   version of the Walter E. Edge lecture given by Mr. Draper at Princeton University on
   November 15, 1983.
"MAD versus NUTS: Can Doctrine on Weaponry Remedy the Mutual Hostage Relation-
   ship of the Superpowers?", by Spurgeon M. Keeny, Jr., and Wolfgang K. H. Panofsky.
   Excerpted by permission of *Foreign Affairs* (Winter 1981/82). Copyright 1981 by the Coun-
   cil on Foreign Relations, Inc.

Acknowledgments and copyrights continue at the back of the book on pp. 331–
   332, which constitute an extension of the copyright page.

PREFACE

Public opinion polls and the agendas of interest groups in the United States and elsewhere in the Western world have shown repeatedly that issues relating to nuclear weapons and war are a dominant public concern. That concern is rooted in a seemingly intractable predicament: on the one hand, nuclear weapons threaten the destruction of human civilization as we know it; on the other, they are the very instruments relied on to avert the threatened disaster. Under such conditions questions relating to the maintenance of stable deterrence on which world peace seems to rest so precariously, to the utility of nuclear weapons as instruments of foreign policy, to the means of limiting their quantity and quality and perhaps abolishing them altogether, and to the horrors that might befall humanity should nuclear deterrence fail have understandably captivated public attention and become the focal point of policy debates at home and abroad.

The Nuclear Reader: Strategy, Weapons, War is designed to expose the range of opinion and prescription regarding these urgent matters. The perspective is primarily that of the United States, and the focus is primarily the competition between the two nuclear giants, the United States and the Soviet Union. Nonetheless, within these confines the range of opinion is wide and the viewpoints compelling. Our purpose in compiling the essays in this book is to illuminate these opinions and viewpoints while at the same time drawing attention to the complexities of the issues inherent in the nuclear predicament. The urgency of keeping the nuclear genie in its bottle requires such knowledge and understanding.

Many people provided advice and assistance as we developed this volume. We are pleased to acknowledge the contributions of Chester Bain, William A. Clark, Harvey Carpenter, Mark DeHaven, G. Mitchell Evander, Sandra Hall, Lawrence Jackson, Levi Martin, John W. Outland, Lucia Wren Rawls, Gregory A. Raymond, Neil R. Richardson, Joseph Sausnock, Peter Schraeder, Peter Sederberg, Van Sturgeon, Will Van Sant, and Thomas D. White. We also wish to thank Michael Weber of St. Martin's Press for his continued support of our work, and Richard Steins, also of St. Martin's, for his craftsmanship in bringing it to fruition.

C. W. K.
E. R. W.

CONTENTS

Part II   Weapons   111

Part III   War   233

NUCLEAR NOMENCLATURE: A SELECTIVE DICTIONARY OF TERMS

Afterwinds. Wind currents set up in the vicinity of a nuclear explosion directed toward the burst center, resulting from the updraft accompanying the rise of the fireball.

Air burst. The explosion of a nuclear weapon at such a height that the expanding fireball does not touch the earth's surface when the luminosity is at a maximum.

Air-launched cruise missile (ALCM). A cruise missile designed to be launched from an aircraft.

Air-to-surface ballistic missile (ASBM). A ballistic missile launched from an airplane against a target on the earth's surface.

Antiballistic missile (ABM). Any ballistic missile used to intercept and destroy an incoming hostile missile. An antiballistic missile system would include such technology (weapons, targeting devices, guidance and tracking radar, and so on) as needed to provide adequate defense.

ABM Treaty. Formally entitled the "Treaty between the United States of America and the Union of Soviet Socialist Republics on the Limitation of Anti-Ballistic Missile Systems," this Treaty is one of the two agreements signed at Moscow in 1972, known collectively as the SALT I agreements. The ABM Treaty entered into force on October 3, 1972, and is of unlimited duration. Together with a Protocol to the treaty signed in 1974, it restricts the United States and the Soviet Union each to only one ABM deployment site.

Antisatellite system (ASAT). A weapon system designed to destroy enemy surveillance and hunter-killer satellites.

Arms control. Any measure limiting or reducing forces, regulating armaments, and/or restricting the deployment of troops or weapons that is intended to induce restrained behavior or is taken pursuant to an understanding with another state or states.

Atom. The smallest particle of an element that still retains the characteristics of that element. Every atom consists of a postively charged central nucleus, which carries nearly all the mass of the atom, surrounded by a number of negatively charged electrons, so that the whole system is electrically neutral.

Atomic weapon (or bomb). A weapon based on the rapid fissioning of combinations of selected materials, thereby inducing an explosion (along with the emission of radiation) caused by the energy released by reactions involving atomic nuclei.

Ballistic missile. Any missile designed to follow the trajectory that results when it is acted upon predominantly by gravity and aerodynamic drag after thrust is terminated. Ballistic missiles typically operate outside the atmosphere for a substantial portion of their flight path and are unpowered during most of the flight.

Ballistic missile defense (BMD) system. A weapon system designed to destroy offensive strategic ballistic missiles or their warheads before they reach their targets.

Blast wave. A pulse of air in which the pressure increases sharply at the front, accompanied by winds, as a result of an explosion.

Build-down. An arms control strategy whereby more old weapons are retired for each new one that comes on line.

Catalytic war. An unwanted nuclear war between the United States and the Soviet Union provoked by a calculating third party.

Circular error probable (CEP). A measure of the delivery accuracy of a weapon system. It is the radius of a circle around a target of such size that a weapon aimed at the target has a 50 percent probability of falling within the circle.

Civil defense. Passive measures designed to minimize the effects of enemy action on all aspects of civilian life, particularly to protect the population and production base. Civil defense includes emergency steps to repair or restore vital utilities and facilities.

Clean weapon. One in which measures have been taken to reduce the amount of residual radioactivity relative to a "normal" weapon of the same energy yield.

Collateral damage. The damage inflicted on the non-targeted surrounding human and nonhuman resources as a result of military strikes on enemy forces or military resources.

Command/Control/Communication and Intelligence (C³I). The arrangement of facilities, equipment, human personnel, and standardized operating procedures aimed at facilitating the acquisition, processing, and dissemination of information needed by decisionmakers in planning and executing operations.

Contamination. The deposit of radioactive material on the surfaces of structures, areas, objects, or people following a nuclear explosion. This material generally consists of fallout in which fission products and other weapon debris have beome incorporated with particles of dirt and other materials.

Counterforce strategy. A strategy designed to use nuclear weapons to destroy an opponent's nuclear and general military resources. To be credible, a counterforce strategy requires the possession of large numbers of highly accurate nuclear weapons.

Countervalue strategy. A strategy designed to use nuclear weapons to destroy an opponent's population and industrial centers. A countervalue strategy (compared to a counterforce strategy) is more compatible with less accurate and more powerful nuclear weapons.

Crisis stability. The objective of minimizing the risk of war by reducing the incentives for and probability of a preemptive nuclear attack.

Cruise missile (CM). A pilotless, subsonic non-ballistic missile capable of carrying a nuclear or non-nuclear warhead through the atmosphere along a pre-programmed course to its target. A cruise missile's flight path remains within the earth's atmosphere and is usually ground-hugging so as to avoid detection.

Damage limitation. The objective of trying to limit as much as possible the destruction caused by a nuclear exchange should deterrence fail.

Deterrence. The prevention from action by fear of the consequence. Deterrence is a condition resulting from creation of a state of mind brought about by the existence of a credible threat of unacceptable counteraction in response to a contemplated attack on an adversary, thereby inhibiting the temptation to initiate such an attack.

Direct radiation. Exposure to radioactive contamination occurring during a nuclear explosion, which, while intense, is limited in range.

Disarmament. Reduction of military forces or armaments, especially to levels resulting from international agreements.

Electromagnetic pulse (EMP). A sharp pulse of radio frequency (long wavelength) electromagnetic radiation produced by a nuclear explosion. The intense electronic and magnetic fields can damage unprotected electrical and electronic equipment over a large area.

Equivalent megatonnage. The effective destructive power of a nuclear weapon, defined in terms of the size of the area it would destroy.

Escalation. The deliberate or unpremeditated expansion of the scope of violence of a war to a higher level of threat or destruction.

Euromissiles. Missiles with less-than-intercontinental-capability but which are capable of striking the Soviet Union if launched from Western Europe, and vice versa.

Extended deterrence. The goal, usually by a superpower, to prevent not only an attack on itself but also an attack on others, such as allies or clients, usually but not necessarily exclusively through the threat of nuclear retaliation.

Fallout. The process or phenomenon of the descent to the earth's surface of particles contaminated with radioactive material from a radioactive cloud, produced by detonation of a nuclear device above the earth's surface. **Early** or **local fallout** refers to those particles which reach the earth within 24 hours after a nuclear explosion. **Delayed** or **worldwide fallout** consists of the smaller particles which ascend into the upper troposphere and into the stratosphere and are carried by winds to remote parts of the earth. Delayed fallout ultimately returns to nearly all areas of the earth's surface, mainly by rain and snow, over a period of months or years.

Fire ball. The luminous sphere of hot gases which forms a few millionths of a second after a nuclear explosion as the result of the absorption by the surrounding medium of the thermal X rays emitted by the extremely hot (several tens of million degrees) weapon residues.

Firebreak. The psychological barrier separating conventional from nuclear war; an obstacle to the onset of the latter as a result of the existence of the former.

Fire storm. Stationary mass fire, generally in developed urban areas, causing strong, inrushing winds from all sides which prevent such fires from spreading while providing fresh oxygen that increase their intensity.

First strike capability. The capacity to launch a preemptive nuclear strike against an adversary, thereby eliminating its ability to retaliate with an effective second strike.

Fissile isotopes. Varieties of elements able to sustain a chain reaction in nuclear reactors or weapons. Fissile isotopes, in other words, are fissionable.

Fission. The process whereby the nucleus of a particular heavy element splits into (generally) two nuclei of lighter elements, with the release of substantial amounts of energy. The most important fissionable materials are Uranium 235 and Plutonium 239.

Flash burn. A burn caused by excessive exposure of bare skin to thermal radiation.

Flexible response. A shorthand description of NATO's strategy for dealing with a Soviet or Warsaw Pact thrust against Western Europe. Flexible response is a policy referring to the capability to react to a broad spectrum of threats, ranging from infiltration and conventional threats to response to a nuclear initiative by the adversary.

Fusion. The process whereby the nuclei of light elements, especially those of the isotopes of hydrogen (deuterium and tritium), combine to form the nucleus of a heavier element with the release of substantial amounts of energy.

Ground-launched cruise missile (GLCM). A cruise missile launched from ground installations.

Half-life. The time required for the activity of a given radioactive species to decrease to half of its initial value due to radioactive decay.

Hard-target-kill capacity. The ability to destroy a missile protected by a reinforced or "hardened" container, such as an ICBM missile silo, otherwise designed to withstand the blast and radiation effects of a nuclear explosion.

Horizontal proliferation. The spread of nuclear capabilities from nuclear to non-nuclear states and/or nongovernmental political entities.

Intercontinental ballistic missile (ICBM). A rocket-propelled vehicle capable of delivering a nuclear warhead across intercontinental ranges. An ICBM may have single or multiple warheads, may be fixed or mobile, and may be land- or sea-based. An ICBM consists of a booster, one or more re-entry vehicles, possibly penetration aids, and in the case of a MIRVed missile, a post-boost vehicle.

Intermediate-Range Nuclear Force (INF) negotiations. Negotiations between the United States and the Soviet Union begun in 1981 in an effort to limit the deployment of intermediate-range nuclear weapons in Europe. The principal weapons of concern: the so-called Euromissiles consisting of the Soviet SS-20 missile and U.S. ground-launched cruise missiles (GLCMs) and Pershing II intermediate-range ballistic missiles.

International Atomic Energy Agency (IAEA). The UN-affiliated international organization charged, among other objectives, with monitoring the production and use of special fissionable materials.

Isotopes. Forms of the same element having identical chemical properties but differing in their atomic masses (due to different numbers of neutrons in their respective nuclei) and in their nuclear properties (e.g., radioactivity, fission). Both of the common isotopes of uranium, with masses of 235 and 238 units, respectively, are radioactive, emitting alpha particles, but their half-lives are different. Furthermore, uranium-235 is fissionable by neutrons of all energies, but uranium-238 will undergo fission only with neutrons of high energy.

Kiloton. The amount of energy that would be released by the explosion of 1,000 tons of TNT equivalent.

Launcher. The equipment that launches a missile. ICBM launchers are land-based launchers and can be either fixed or mobile. SLBM launchers are the missile tubes on a ballistic missile submarine. An ASBM launcher is the carrier aircraft with associated equipment. Launchers for cruise missiles can be installed on aircraft, ships, or land-based vehicles or installations.

Launch-on-warning. Retaliatory strikes triggered upon notification that an enemy attack is in progress, but before hostile forces or ordnance reach their targets (see also launch-under-attack).

Launch-under-attack. A policy advocated by some military strategists as a solution to the perceived problem of ICBM vulnerability that calls for launching U.S. ICBMs against the U.S.S.R. upon acquiring evidence that a Soviet attack was underway but before its actual effects were felt. This policy is sometimes labelled "launch-on-warning".

Launch-weight. The weight of a fully loaded missile at the time of launch. It includes the aggregate weight of all booster stages, the post-boost vehicle, and the payload.

Medium-range ballistic missile (MRBM). A ballistic missile with a strike range of 600 to 1,500 nautical miles (1,100–2,800 km).

Megaton. The amount of energy that would be released by the explosion of 1,000 kilotons (1,000,000 tons) of TNT equivalent.

Minuteman III. Principal U.S. intercontinental ballistic missile, introduced in 1970, with a potential range of 7,020 nautical miles and a payload consisting of three 160-kiloton independently targetable warheads.

Multiple independently targeted reentry vehicle (MIRV). A ballistic missile payload consisting of two or more nuclear warheads, each of which can be separately assigned different targets.

Mutual assured destruction (MAD). The condition or situation describing the ability of both the United States and the Soviet Union to inflict massive countervalue damage after absorbing a full-scale nuclear strike from the adversary.

Mutual deterrence. The situation that obtains between two powers when each is deterred from attacking the other because the damage expected to result from the victim's retaliation is perceived to be unacceptably high.

National Command Authority (NCA). U.S. political and military leaders designated as members of the chain of command for U.S. military forces.

National technical means (NTM) of verification. National assets for monitoring compliance with an arms control or other agreement. NTM include photographic reconnaissance satellites, aircraft-based systems such as radars and optical systems, and sea- and ground-based systems, such as radars and antennas for collecting telemetry.

Nuclear club. Consists of the states known to possess nuclear weapons: the United States, the Soviet Union, the United Kingdom, France, China, and India.

Nuclear deterrence. A strategic doctrine based on the assumption that a potential aggressor can be dissuaded from provocative action or war by (a) the possession of nuclear forces sufficient to deny the enemy its political-military objectives at any level of conflict (counterforce deterrence), or (b) the possession of nuclear forces sufficient to launch a massive urban-industrial retaliatory strike (countervalue deterrence).

Nuclear non-proliferation. The set of institutions and procedures for the transnational management and restriction of the number of states possessing deployed nuclear weapons capabilities.

Nuclear Non-Proliferation Treaty (NPT). The multilateral agreement officially known as the Treaty on the Non-proliferation of Nuclear Weapons signed in 1968 that prohibits: (a) the transfer by nuclear-weapon states to any recipient whatsoever of nuclear weapons or other nuclear explosive devices or control over them; (b) the assistance, encouragement, or inducement of any non-nuclear weapon state to manufacture or otherwise acquire such weapons or devices; and (c) the receipt, manufacture, or other acquisition by non-nuclear weapon states of nuclear weapons or other nuclear explosive devices.

Nuclear radiation. Particulate and electromagnetic radiation emitted from atomic nuclei through various processes. In terms of nuclear weapons, the most important radiations are alpha and beta particles, gamma rays, and neutrons.

Nuclear terrorism. Terrorism is the systematic use of terror as a means of coercion. Nuclear terrorism involves the use or threatened use of nuclear weapons or radioactive materials by an actor, either state or nonstate, for coercive purposes.

Nuclear utilization theory (NUT). A body of strategic doctrine which imbues nuclear weapons with a war-fighting role. The acronym NUTs is sometimes used to refer to those theorists who advocate preparing to utilize nuclear weapons in war should deterrence fail. NUTs is also sometimes used to refer to nuclear utilization target selection.

Nuclear weapon (or bomb). A general name given to any weapon in which the explosion results from the energy released by reactions involving atomic nuclei, either fission or fusion or both. Thus, the atomic and the hydrogen bombs are both nuclear weapons.

Nuclear winter. The climatic aftermath of a major nuclear war in which vast areas of the earth could be subjected to prolonged darkness, abnormally low temperatures, violent windstorms, toxic smog, and persistent radioactive fallout.

Overkill. A destructive capacity in excess of that required to achieve identified objectives.

Overpressure. The shock or blast caused by a nuclear explosion, usually measured in pounds per square inch.

Partial Test Ban Treaty (PTB). The multilateral agreement officially known as the Treaty Banning Nuclear Weapons Tests in the Atmosphere, in Outer Space and Under Water, signed in 1963. The treaty prohibits "any nuclear weapon test explosion, or any other nuclear explosion" in the atmosphere, in outer space, or under water.

Payload. Weapons and penetration aids carried by a delivery vehicle. In the case of a ballistic missile, the re-entry vehicle or vehicles and anti-ballistic missile penetration aids placed on ballistic trajectories by the main propulsion stages or the post-boost vehicles; in the case of a bomber, the bombs, missiles, or penetration aids carried internally or attached to the wings or fuselage.

Plutonium fuel cycle. A fuel cycle in which separated (reprocessed) plutonium is routinely recycled as fresh fuel for a nuclear power reactor. The reprocessed fuel can either be recycled to light-water reactors or used as fuel for breeder reactors, which produce more plutonium than they consume. Plutonium is readily used in making nuclear weapons.

Preemptive strike. An attack launched by one party in the expectation that an attack from its adversary is imminent. A preemptive strike is designed to forestall or lessen the destructive impact of the expected attack. A preemptive nuclear strike is usually expected to entail a counterforce strategy.

Sea-launched cruise missile (SLCM). A cruise missile launched from a submarine or surface ship.

Second strike capability. The capacity to execute a nuclear attack against an adversary after having already absorbed a first strike. For a deterrent strategy to be credible, any potential adversary must be convinced that its opponent will retain and be willing to utilize a second strike capability, even after absorbing a first strike.

Shock wave. A continuously propagated pressure pulse (or wave) in the air, water, or earth initiated by the expansion of the hot gases produced in an explosion. A shock wave in air is generally referred to as a blast wave, because it resembles and is accompanied by strong, but transient, winds.

Stable deterrence. A situation between two nuclear adversaries in which neither has the capacity or incentive to launch a first-strike against the other.

Strategic Arms Limitations Talks (SALT). A series of negotiations between the U.S. and the U.S.S.R. begun in 1969 in an effort to limit and reduce both offensive and defensive strategic arms. The first round of negotiations, known as SALT I, concluded in 1972 with two agreements, the ABM Treaty and the Interim Agreement on Certain Measures with Respect to the Limitations of Strategic Offensive Arms. SALT II, begun in November 1972, resulted in a treaty signed by the U.S. and the U.S.S.R. in 1979, which has yet to receive ratification by the United States Senate.

Strategic Arms Reduction Talks (START). A series of Soviet-American negotiations begun in 1982 in a effort to reduce offensive strategic weapon arsenals.

Strategic stability. A situation in the overall relation of forces between potential adversaries which leads them to conclude that any attempt to settle their conflict by military means would clearly constitute a risk of calculably unacceptable proportions.

Submarine-launched cruise missile (SLCM). Any cruise missile transported by and launched from a submarine.

Surface burst. The explosion of a nuclear weapon at the surface of land or water at a height above the surface less than the radius of the fireball at maximum luminosity.

Tactical Weapons. Weapons intended for battlefield operations as opposed to those intended for targeting against an adversary's homeland.

Theater nuclear forces. U.S. forward-based systems, primarily in Europe but also in Asia, which provide a tactical nuclear-weapons link between American conventional and strategic nuclear forces, thus coupling American nuclear capabilities to the defense of its allies. Theater nuclear forces are designed for use in specific regional settings.

Thermal radiation. Electromagnetic radiation emitted from a fireball as a consequence of its very high temperature. Essentially, thermal radiation consists of ultraviolet, visible, and infrared radiation.

Thermonuclear weapon. A weapon in which part of the explosive energy results from thermonuclear fusion reactions. The high temperatures required are obtained by means of a fission explosion.

Threshold Test Ban Treaty (TTBT). A treaty between the United States and the Soviet Union on the Limitation of Underground Nuclear Weapon Tests signed in 1974 but not yet in force. The treaty establishes a nuclear "threshold" by prohibiting nuclear tests having a yield exceeding 150 kilotons of TNT equivalent.

Triad. The term used to refer to the three components of the U.S. strategic deterrent capability consisting of ICBMs, SLBMs, and intercontinental bombers.

Throw-weight. The useful weight placed on a trajectory toward the target by the boost stages of a ballistic missile.

Uranium fuel cycle. A "once-through" fuel cycle in which natural uranium containing mostly non-fissile U-238 and less than 1 percent fissile U-235 is enriched for use in generating electrical power. Most nuclear power reactors now in use, known as light-water reactors, depend on the uranium fuel cycle. Unless chemically reprocessed, spent fuel cannot be used directly to make nuclear weapons.

Verification. The process of determining, to the extent necessary to adequately safeguard national security, that a party to an agreement acts in conformity with its stipulations.

Vertical proliferation. The development and enlargement of a state's nuclear capacity in terms of further refinement, accumulation, and deployment of nuclear weapons.

War-fighting strategy. Combat actions, as opposed to deterrence (which theoretically is designed to prevent rather than prosecute wars).

Warhead. That part of a missile, projectile, torpedo, rocket, or other munition which contains either the nuclear or thermonuclear system, the high explosive system, the chemical or biological agents, or the inert materials intended to inflict damage.

Yield. The energy released in an explosion. The energy released in the detonation of a nuclear weapon is generally measured in terms of the kilotons (KT) or megatons (MT) of TNT required to produce the same energy release. The total energy yield is manifested as nuclear radiation, thermal radiation, and shock and blast energy.

STRATEGY, WEAPONS, AND WAR IN THE NUCLEAR AGE

Charles W. Kegley, Jr., and Eugene R. Wittkopf

The invention of nuclear weapons and their continuing proliferation have imposed on humankind a series of momentous—some would say intractable—challenges and policy problems. It is not an exaggeration to assert that by building extensive nuclear arsenals, humankind has devised the potential to extinguish itself as a species.

The awareness of these threats has expanded dramatically in recent years, stimulated in no small part by the attention given to the "nuclear predicament" by scientists, policymakers, politicians, academics, and the mass media. More so than at any time since the aftermath of Hiroshima and the depths of the cold war, the prevention of nuclear war has returned to the top of the global agenda. Indeed, public concern about the causes and consequences of a nuclear war is likely to disappear only if deterrence fails, with a nuclear holocaust perhaps bringing human history to a tragic end. Herein lies the nuclear predicament, one defined by knowledge, hope, and fear: "Atomic fire has become an inescapable part of the human heritage. Wisely controlled, it will remain unused in war and can prevent the reoccurrence of large-scale conventional conflict. Unwisely attended, it will break forth at some unpredictable time and consume much of humanity."[1]

To facilitate an understanding of the issues that underlie this predicament, *The Nuclear Reader* seeks to elucidate the major positions advanced by informed debaters. In order to analyze the many problems associated with the nuclear predicament, *The Nuclear Reader* is organized around three generic concepts central to discussions of nuclear politics, namely, *strategy, weapons,* and *war.*

The first concept (Part I) looks at the various *strategies* that have been constructed either to fight or prevent a nuclear war. The articles selected focus on major political-military doctrines, such as mutual assured destruction, nuclear utilization, and flexible response, and on the major issues that separate debaters on doctrinal problems and strategic policies. These selections offer background information on the historical

1

evolution of strategic theory on which the current global peace precariously rests, as well as proposals to minimize risks by means of nuclear superiority or the maintenance of mutual deterrence. The essays make clear that positions on these strategic issues are often incompatible with one another, and they were purposely chosen to highlight these theoretical controversies.

The second organizing concept, *weapons* (Part II), offers information and opinion regarding appropriate ways to control current nuclear arsenals or those that might be contemplated so as to ensure that weapons serve their intended political purposes. As in Part I, the essays seek to expose the range of ideas and opinion about how best to harness the threat that nuclear weapons pose.

The third and final organizing concept, *war* (Part III), completes the circle of coverage by confronting the problem of peace in the nuclear age. The essays in this part consider how a nuclear war might begin, what it might be like, how it might be conducted, and what its consequences could be. Implicit in their focus is concern for both the causes and the consequences of nuclear war.

These three categories—strategy, weapons, and war—are overlapping and interconnected, perhaps synergistically. A new development or initiative in one area may generate changes in another. For instance, technological changes in weapons' precision have required subsequent changes in strategy. Conversely, new departures in doctrine often rationalize the creation of new weapons systems. Similarly, changes in war-fighting capabilities (may) have modified the probability of war and mobilized efforts to revise doctrine to curtail the probability of a nuclear strike. Thus, change in any one dimension of the nuclear situation may be expected to exert pressure for changes in the other two. This synergy is illustrated by the claim that nuclear weapons led to the concept of deterrence, which led to the nuclear arms race, which generated pressures for both arms control initiatives and new strategic doctrines. Having come full circle, the interactive process continues, feeding on itself as it moves from one dimension to the next.

Despite *The Nuclear Reader*'s three-part organizing scheme, it encourages its readers to decide for themselves how these dimensions of the nuclear problem affect one another. For it is an empirical question if and how developments in one sector influence developments in another. As Keeny and Panofsky observe in our second selection in Part I, "It is not at all clear in the real world of war planning whether declaratory doctrine has generated requirements or whether the availability of weapons for targeting has created doctrine." The direction of causation among the three dimensions (and the influences acting on them) thus requires critical examination.

THE DISUTILITY OF FORCE AND STRUCTURAL TERRORISM

In order to understand current nuclear strategies, weapons, and war, it is necessary also to understand current international politics and to speculate about the impact of nuclear weapons on individual and global security.

In an international system that since its inception in the seventeenth century has given states the sovereign right to use military force to settle disputes, war has been recurrent; understandably, therefore, national preparation for war by acquiring arms has been a nearly universal preoccupation.[2] Indeed, an anarchical international political system provides little incentive for states to reduce their armaments. The strategy underlying most countries' national security policies could be summed up by the classic cliché, "If you want peace, prepare for war."

But with the destruction of Hiroshima in 1945, this pattern was altered, perhaps permanently and irrevocably. In 1981 Pope John Paul II noted: "In the past, it was possible to destroy a village, a town, a region, even a country. Now it is the whole planet that has come under threat."

In "The Absolute Weapon," Bernard Brodie offered in 1946 a now-classic definition of the changes caused by atomic weapons in strategy in world affairs.[3] Recognizing that with the creation of weapons of mass annihilation, "mankind had brought upon itself a deadly peril," Brodie anticipated that it was only a matter of time before these weapons would be possessed by more than one country. And when that time came, the purposes of American strategy would have to be revised:

> The first and most vital step in any American security program for the age of atomic bombs [should be] to take measures to guarantee to ourselves in case of attack the possibility of retaliation in kind. [We no longer need be] concerned about who will *win* the next war in which atomic bombs are used. Thus far the chief purpose of our military establishment has been to win wars. From now on its chief purpose must be to avert them. It can have almost no other useful purpose.[4]

Since Brodie's prophecy and prescription, the destructiveness of the weapons of war has grown enormously. Carl Sagan, the Pulitzer Prize–winning astronomer, describes today's nuclear arsenals:

> There are some 50,000 nuclear weapons in the world, most of them far more powerful than the weapons which utterly devastated Hiroshima in 1945. In fact, the energy equivalent of all the nuclear weapons in the world is enough to annihilate one million cities. There are only 2,300 cities on the planet with populations of more than 100,000 people. Every major city on the planet could be destroyed and there would be 15,000 strategic weapons left over in the arsenals of the United States and the Soviet Union. A single U.S. nuclear submarine could destroy 160 Soviet cities, and of course vice versa. [These

instruments of destruction are] genies of death awaiting the rubbing of the lamp.[5]

Under these conditions, in which expanding nuclear arsenals may have made the use of these weapons suicidal, Brodie's prognosis seems to have been borne out, and thus the "game" of international politics played by the most heavily armed has shifted from waging war to deterring it. Paralyzed by their own power, the superpowers, the United States and the Soviet Union, have for four decades managed their relationships without recourse to war. War *has* been deterred (even if those without nuclear weapons have warred among themselves and with the great powers since World War II). A *pax atomica* has arisen, as Winston Churchill reasoned it might when he envisioned the emergence of an age of superpower peace based on mutual deterrence.[6]

The bases of this precarious superpower peace, sustained now for forty years, are multiple. The simple formulas that "the curse is the cure" and "the menace is the miracle" fail to take into account other contributing factors. But whatever the sources of nuclear peace, it is clear that the environment for the conduct of diplomacy—and the prospects for humankind's future—have been radically transformed by these weapons. A new system has been created. It was Churchill, again, who showed that he understood this when he introduced into the vocabulary the idea of peace resting on "a balance of terror."

Let us extend this metaphor. Can the nuclear age be appropriately characterized as one predicated on *terror*?

To be sure, the destructiveness of nuclear weapons makes for truly terrifying "nuclear nightmares."[7] No one can contemplate the peril in which the entire globe has been placed by the existence of these weapons and the potential for their use without experiencing a true sense of terror. As Churchill warned, "The Stone Age may return on the gleaming wings of science, and what might now shower immeasurable blessings upon mankind, may even bring about its total destruction. Beware, I say; time may be short."

Carl Sagan dramatized the terror of the nuclear age thus:

Imagine a room awash in gasoline, and there are two implacable enemies in that room. One of them has 9,000 matches; the other has 7,000 matches. Each of them is concerned who's ahead, who's stronger. Well, that's the kind of situation we are actually in. The amount of weapons that are available to the United States and the Soviet Union are so bloated, so grossly in excess of what's needed to dissuade the other, that if it weren't so tragic, it would be laughable. What is necessary is to reduce the matches and to clean up the gasoline.[8]

Sagan's metaphor suggests that the nuclear age is terrorizing because it is a situation or set of circumstances from which there is no escape.

And because this situation includes the relationships among nations and peoples, their fears, and their weapons technologies—relationships that color the entire fabric of international politics[9]—it might be described as *structural terrorism*.

Consider, for example, four simple propositions concerning terrorists and terrorism of the sort that the world has witnessed numerous times in recent years:

- Terrorists threaten indiscriminate violence.

- Governments are unable to guarantee their citizens protection from such violence.

- Because there is no protection from such violence, terrorism produces fear and anxiety with which individuals cope psychologically by denying it.

- Terrorists rely on their ability to inflict death and destruction to win compliance with their political objectives.

With but a few changes in words, each of these propositions could be used to describe nuclear weapons or the policies of those states that possess them. No one, it seems, including those countries and peoples that might not be directly involved, would be immune from the immediate or long-term ravages of nuclear war. Indeed, the very threat of death and destruction by one nuclear adversary against another has become a key element in the preventive strategy known as deterrence. But governments cannot provide a foolproof guarantee that deterrence will succeed—which is, in fact, one of the principal elements in the current debate about nuclear weapons that prompted this book. And although some believe we must learn to live with nuclear weapons, the anxiety of life with them seems only to be reduced by sublimation—which is why and how the psychological terror of the nuclear age appears to have dissipated in the years since its inception.

Finally, just as terrorists and those governments (such as the Libyan, Syrian, and Iranian) alleged by others (such as the United States) to engage in "state terrorism" (that is, government-sponsored terrorism directed by one country against the citizens or institutions of another) rely on threats or acts of violence to achieve their goals, so, too, the nuclear states depend on the threatened use of force and mass destruction to achieve their policy objectives. If state terrorism is condemned, why not nuclear terrorism?

Both terrorism and nuclear weapons have become dominant factors in international politics. The power of each is derived from and contingent upon the continuation of a threat-system rather than its elimination. Both demand the legitimization of violence, because both are sustained by the anxiety and fear they inspire. Both are targeted principally on the populations of the most advanced industrial societies, which are the primary hostages of their threat of death and destruction. And both erode the individual and global security for which the world searches.

If the nuclear predicament can be likened to the practice of international terrorism, what makes it distinctive, in the second instance, is that the terror of the nuclear age has also become part of the international system's *structure*. The structure of a social system is conventionally defined as a basic, enduring, and institutionalized organization of things and their relationships. To state that the nuclear age is an age of structural terrorism, therefore, is also to assert that the nuclear threat is an attribute of the international system, affecting many aspects of behavior and patterns of life on earth.

The emergence of this structural attribute has put human existence at risk, and it can be said to dominate, even govern, world affairs. It rules by the force of its terror. Accordingly, structural terrorism has changed the world in many ways; it has given world politics properties that set the contemporary system apart from its historical predecessors.

In addition, structural terrorism has a special importance because, unlike other structures that can be modified to improve or diminish the quality of life, it may have become so entrenched that it cannot be eradicated. There is an irony in this, for, as Norman Cousins has noted, what man has made can unmake man.[10] The insecurities that nuclear weapons produce, the costly worldwide race for arms that these fears provoke, the habits that have been created from thinking about their uses, the industries and military establishments that lobby for their further expansion, and the momentum of history and push of technology all are potent forces within a self-perpetuating, synergistically reinforcing system that encourages its own preservation . . . or destruction.

To characterize current world politics as marked by structural terrorism is to assert that the prevailing levels of armaments pose to the world its most serious threat, a threat that cannot be contained. For structural terrorism deprives the human species of freedom from fear. No one is safe; all, from the most impoverished to the most wealthy, are its potential victims. The material costs to human welfare of preparations for a war that dare not be waged are immeasurable; structural terrorism also diminishes the world's standard of living and compromises its ability to enhance its collective welfare to the extent otherwise possible.

Structural terrorism is a system supported by many states, whose policies and decisions have contributed to its development. But the paradox is that most states have not benefited from the structure they have created. By preparing for war in order to preserve peace, states find themselves competing in an arms race that may culminate in the very disaster that each seeks to avoid. Nuclear arms indeed have protected, if not enhanced, the national security of their possessors, but they have also decreased global security by increasing the probability of national and human obliteration.

To assume that structural terrorism is the international system's most threatening feature is not to deny that the world also suffers from other less serious, but nonetheless extremely costly, structural deficiencies.[11] But because structural terrorism risks the extinction of all humankind, it terrorizes life on a scale heretofore neither experienced nor possible. In short, structural terrorism describes a circumstance unique in human history. What is also unique, therefore, is that for the first time in world history, the choice, borrowing a perceptive phrase from Martin Luther King, Jr., has become "either nonviolence or nonexistence."

It is important to recall that what Churchill first described as a balance of terror is a product of human invention; humankind was not born with it—it had to be created. It may be an invention that, with hindsight, few would prefer. But it has been invented nonetheless and with its invention have come powerful obstacles to its removal, as we have noted. As discomforting as may be its pessimistic viewpoint, the conclusion of the Harvard Nuclear Study Group is compelling: "Humanity has no alternative but to hold [the] threat [of infinitely destructive nuclear war] at bay and to learn to live . . . in the world we know: a world of nuclear weapons, international rivalries, recurring conflicts, and at least some risk of nuclear crisis. . . . Living with nuclear weapons is our only hope."[12]

Because a nuclear-free world is no longer probable, structural terrorism appears destined to continue both to describe and influence world conditions. The purpose of *The Nuclear Reader* is thus to describe this reality. The selections that follow should help the reader understand the developments that led to this reality and to the predicaments and choices it has created, including the choice of living with nuclear weapons or seeking their abolition.

NOTES

1. Albert Carnesale et al. (The Harvard Nuclear Study Group), *Living with Nuclear Weapons* (Toronto: Bantam, 1983), p. 5. Portions of this study are reprinted in Parts II and III of this book.

2. For documentation and summaries of trends in both military capabilities and the incidence of war over time, see Charles W. Kegley, Jr., and Eugene R. Wittkopf, *World Politics: Trend and Transformation*, 2nd ed. (New York: St. Martin's Press, 1985).

3. Bernard Brodie et al., eds., *The Absolute Weapon* (New York: Harcourt, Brace, 1946). Brodie updated and elaborated this statement in *War and Politics* (New York: Macmillan, 1973), especially pp. 375–432.

4. Brodie et al., p. 76.

5. Commencement address, University of South Carolina, Columbia, S.C., May 12, 1984.

6. Churchill stated this thesis in 1953 when he confessed that he occasionally had "the odd thought that the annihilating character of [nuclear] weapons may bring an utterly unforeseeable security to mankind. . . . It may be that when the advance of destructive

weapons enables everyone to kill anybody else no one will want to kill anyone at all." He elaborated on this in 1955, with the speculation that "after a certain point has passed, [things may get so bad that they get better, and] . . . it may be that we shall, by a process of sublime irony, have reached a stage in this story where safety will be the sturdy child of terror, and survival the twin brother of annihilation."

7. See Nigel Calder, *Nuclear Nightmares: An Investigation into Possible Wars* (New York: Penguin, 1979).

8. Quoted by Anne H. Ehrlich and Paul R. Ehrlich, Newsletter, Friends of the Earth, p. 1 (no date).

9. For an examination of the security dilemma of nations, which explores these relationships in depth, see Barry Buzan, *People, States and Fear: The National Security Problem in International Relations* (Chapel Hill: University of North Carolina Press, 1983).

10. Public address delivered at the University of South Carolina, March 15, 1979.

11. Structural terrorism is similar to the concept *structural violence*, which refers to those of the earth's inhabitants "harmed, maimed, or killed by poverty and unjust social, political, and economic institutions, systems, or structures." Thus structural violence is said to inflict two kinds of injury: "it either kills its victims or it harms them in various ways short of killing." Gernot Köhler and Norman Alcock, "An Empirical Table of Structural Violence," *Journal of Peace Research* 13 (1976):343. The concept of structural violence was first developed by Johan Galtung in his article "Violence, Peace, and Peace Research," *Journal of Peace Research* 6 (1969):167–191. See also his *The True Worlds* (New York: Macmillan, 1980) for an elaboration. For estimates of the aggregate damage to life because of structural violence and armed conflict, see Köhler and Alcock, and William Eckhardt and Gernot Köhler, "Structural Violence and Armed Violence in the Twentieth Century: Magnitudes and Trends," *International Interactions* 6 (1980):347–375.

12. Carnesale et al., pp. 19, 255. This conclusion is not without controversy. For an assessment that challenges it and proposes approaches to eliminating the threat of nuclear extinction, see Jonathan Schell, *The Abolition* (New York: Knopf, 1984), as well as some of the thinking expressed in other segments of *The Nuclear Reader*.

Part I: Strategy

To " . . . provide for the common defense." These challenging words of the United States Constitution identify a mission that this country—and for that matter all others—must define as a national priority. To seek to protect one's nation from external threats is the *sine qua non* of every nation's definition of the national interest in an anarchical international arena.

Since the advent of the nuclear age, the ability of the United States and other countries to provide for the common defense has been considerably complicated and compromised. President John F. Kennedy was not engaging in hyperbole when he noted that nuclear weapons "have changed all the answers and all the questions," for nuclear weapons have challenged the validity of traditional approaches and previous doctrines. Because of them, world politics takes place in an environment fraught with unprecedented dangers. It is a world system whose very structure terrorizes its inhabitants and diminishes the ability of its leaders to provide the national security they seek.

Under the emergent conditions of "structural terrorism," as described in the preceding introduction to *The Nuclear Reader*, policymakers have been forced to confront the twin questions of what to do *with* nuclear weapons and what to do *about* them. Traditionally, it has been assumed that national leaders are responsible for forging a strategy that will realize their country's objectives abroad. A national strategy (whether grand or improvisational, calculated or incoherent) presumes the identification of external goals, a plan for realizing them, and guidelines for dealing with the challenges perceived to emanate from abroad.[1] Following the German theoretician Karl von Clausewitz, military force was considered historically to be the most important component of strategy in states' efforts to achieve their political objectives in relation to others. War was thus seen as the continuation of politics by other, albeit extreme, means.

The nuclear age has forced the reevaluation and revision of this conventional conception of national strategy. The capacity of nuclear weapons to cause unprecedented destruction has challenged the traditional view that military might is merely another instrument of foreign policy.

9

Although some, as we shall see, continue to believe that nuclear weapons can be used in the same way that other instruments of policy can to pursue political objectives (that is, to influence others or to get one's way by making others do what they otherwise would not do), many now question the use of force to exercise influence.[2]

Accordingly, opinions regarding strategy in the nuclear era have become divided and discordant. As a consequence, strategic theory is now in a state of arrested ambiguity; its current condition has been labeled a "morass," and the doctrine of deterrence has been described as "now in a state of confusion amounting almost to disintegration."[3]

Without agreement on a conception of strategy to replace the Clausewitzean formula that served the prenuclear era so well, some talk of strategy in terms of ends, and others do so in terms of tactics, procurement policies, targeting doctrines, and weapons deployment. One scholar illustrates the semantic problem by asking that employment, declaratory, acquisition, and deployment policies be distinguished.[4] Similarly, another scholar has asked that *doctrine* be emphasized and that strategic doctrine be defined as "a set of operative beliefs, values, and assertions that in a significant way guide official behavior with respect to strategic research and development (R&D), weapons choice, forces, operational plans, arms control, etc."[5] Apparently, strategy lacks the clear, empirical boundary necessary to separate it from other phenomena associated with it, and there is no clearly defined, widely agreed-upon body of empirical theory of nuclear strategy. As a result, debate concerning strategic issues defies easy characterization, and comparisons of viewpoints are difficult.

To cut into this conceptual thicket requires that some underbrush be removed. In order to give some order to our discussion of strategy and its boundaries, this book presumes that nuclear strategy under conditions of structural terrorism revolves around the question *"For what political purposes can nuclear weapons be used?"*

This query does not, of course, take us very far. But it suggests, as a corollary, another division that further defines thinking about strategic issues. On the one hand, as we shall see shortly in the readings in Part I, one school of thought contends that nuclear weapons can be used to serve the full range of options to which they might be put. These include both war-fighting and war-winning options made possible through the acquisition of preemptive, first-strike capabilities. Opposing this, on the other hand, is a school of thought that assumes that nuclear weapons can be used for only one political purpose, namely, the deterrence of an adversary's attack.

Even this dichotomy breaks down into intermediate positions. Many argue, for example, that the uses to which nuclear weapons can and should be put are conditional, that is, the circumstances of the decision-making environment at any particular decision point should define the range of viable options. (This position is somewhat akin to "situation ethics," which maintains that the principles governing the propriety of conduct depend on the situation and not on irrevocable norms for behavior.) Others support a doctrine that sanctions the use of nuclear weapons, but only for defense. The argument here is that in order to deter attack, one's adversary must believe in one's threat to use nuclear weapons in retaliation. Still others argue that deterrence cannot be condoned morally because it implies the use of weapons that cannot discriminate enemies from innocents, although, they argue, deterrence itself warrants the possession of nuclear weapons and even the creation of plans for targeting them in a retaliatory strike. Opinion on strategic issues can thus be seen as spread along a continuum, with the use of nuclear weapons for purposes of "compellence" and persuasion at one end and for deterrence and dissuasion at the other end.[6]

Thus, preserving peace and deterring a nuclear attack have become preoccupations of theorists in *all* schools of strategic thought. Even those advocating the utility of a war-fighting strategy recognize the dangers of escalation inherent in the actual execution of such a strategy, and *all* dread and seek to guard against an enemy's pursuit of a nuclear warfighting strategy. (In this sense, the superpowers' postures are mirror images—each sees the other's potential to acquire a preemptive capability as a threat to stability.) Thus from either end of this continuum, strategies for preserving stability through deterrence have assumed center stage; all strategists regard the capability to deter as indispensable, even if some doubt that that goal is achievable (and agree with Edward Teller's fear, expressed in 1974, that "reliable deterrents do not exist").

For this reason, deterrence is often regarded as a strategy in itself, rather than one element in a comprehensive strategy. An objective is not a policy, however. To avoid confusing a passion and a program, a position and a policy, it is necessary to understand the meaning of deterrence, which is difficult, as deterrence, like strategy, is a concept that invites confusion.[7] At its core, however, is a rather simple idea: deterrence is a condition created when an aggressor's attack is prevented by threatening retaliation. Or as Rothschild put it, "Deterrence in a more or less pure form consists of the following threat: 'Do not attack me because if you do, something unacceptably horrible will happen to you.'"[8] The doctrine of nuclear deterrence has been summarized by Jonathan Schell as embracing the beliefs

that nuclear weapons offer nations effectively unlimited force; that winning a nuclear war is impossible; that it is imperative, therefore, to stop such a war from ever beginning; that the weapons themselves play a crucial role in that effort; that an invulnerable retaliatory force is of particular importance; that there is a special danger inherent in any capacity, on either side, for destroying the nuclear forces of the other side in a first strike; and that "perceptions" and "psychology" play an essential role in convincing the adversary that any aggression by him will lead only to his annihilation, and so in maintaining the "stability" of the whole arrangement.[9]

Although the foregoing encapsulates the fundamentals of deterrence, ideas become muddled in debates about which policies can best attain the desired condition of deterrence. For example, analysts differ in their evaluation of the advantages and liabilities of military superiority as opposed to parity, launch-on-warning as opposed to launch-on-attack retaliatory policies, counterforce as opposed to countervalue targeting, ballistic missile defense, antisatellite weapons defense, civil defense, and the like. These and other aspects of the current debate are introduced in the readings, which also illuminate the diversity of prevailing positions.

Our first selection is an informed survey of current strategic thinking. Its author, Theodore Draper, describes what he terms *nuclear temptations:* a series of strategic proposals advocating new uses for the new generation of accurate and versatile nuclear weapons. These weapons tend to drive strategy, he argues; they make available new strategic options which in turn invite their actual use. Technological developments in weapons pose new challenges to the maintenance of deterrence, for the new temptations threaten to destroy the foundations on which peace has rested during much of the postwar era.

By framing the discussion of today's strategic thinking, Draper provides the intellectual baggage necessary to evaluate strategic issues. In doing so, Draper discloses his own perspective on the temptations currently being recommended as a basis for defense policy in the United States: he finds them troubling and deficient and rejects their acceptance (a viewpoint that has provoked a strident response from others, including Secretary of Defense Caspar Weinberger).[10] His conclusion that "the main enemy at present is not a nuclear balance that results in mutual deterrence; it is the propaganda about the feasibility of nuclear war by way of precise and discriminating weapons allegedly capable of avoiding mass destruction" some will find reasonable, and others will see as disregarding the strategic options that such weapons make possible. But regardless of one's reaction to his conclusion, one should consider his thesis and warning that

> the main reason nuclear weapons have not been used thus far is precisely the belief that they cannot be launched for any useful political purpose and that mutual mass destruction can be of no conceivable benefit to either side. But now Pied Pipers of a protracted nuclear war are trying to lure us to break through the psychological barriers to nuclear war.

The temptation that Draper finds most threatening is a nuclear war–waging capability. In "MAD Versus NUTS," Spurgeon M. Keeny, Jr., and Wolfgang K. H. Panofsky further explore this proposal. Using the acronym NUTS to characterize various doctrines that seek to utilize nuclear weapons in war, and whose advocates can be described as "nuclear utilization theorists," the authors question the belief that a nuclear utilization targeting strategy can eliminate the essentially MAD character of nuclear war under conditions of mutual assured destruction. Although they find the MAD doctrine inadequate, they find the dangers inherent in NUTS unacceptable. They thus find themselves in company with Draper, and the reasons on which they base their position illuminate the most fundamental issues dividing contemporary strategic theorists. How the MAD-versus-NUTS debate is resolved will affect the prospects for future strategic stability.

Strategic doctrines can be evaluated in terms of their efficacy and practicality. But they also can be evaluated in terms of their moral implications as normative issues in the nuclear predicament. As Jonathan Schell has urged us to think, strategic doctrine allows humankind only two paths, and ultimately "one leads to death, the other to life."[11]

The most comprehensive investigation of the ethical problems of nuclear strategy is the famous pastoral letter drafted by the National Conference of Catholic Bishops under the leadership of Joseph Cardinal Bernardin. Those portions pertaining to the dilemmas posed by nuclear weapons and strategy are reprinted in our third reading, entitled "Nuclear Strategy and the Challenge of Peace: Ethical Principles and Policy Prescriptions."

The pastoral letter compares contemporary strategic doctrine with the principles of Christian doctrine and finds the former largely unacceptable. The plans—or what Draper might call the "temptations"—being constructed or already in place are perceived to violate a number of principles central to the "just-war" tradition in Christian theology. Violated especially are the stipulations that the resort to violence be (1) *discriminate*, by giving noncombatants immunity; (2) *proportionate*, by limiting any collateral harm caused by war to a level commensurate with the good intended or the evil to be avoided; and (3) *reasonable* in its probability of success. As the pastoral letter makes clear, these norms are inadequate to justify many of the strategic plans in place, and they challenge such prominent features of American strategic doctrine as counterpopulation (countervalue) warfare and unrestricted counterforce warfare. The reasoning behind the bishops' conclusion is explicated in a style that serves secondarily as a useful summary of doctrinal positions and issues.

The position adopted in the pastoral letter is controversial. By recommending a strategy for peace that severely limits the uses of nuclear weapons ("never!"), by restricting how the threat of their use can be expressed (only to deter an attack), and by allowing nuclear weapons to be possessed nonetheless, the bishops arrive at what may be described as a "strictly conditioned" acceptance of nuclear weapons, one that comes close to a "you can have them but you can't use them" position.[12]

This prescription brings into focus a series of related issues, including "limited" nuclear war, "no first use," mutual assured destruction, and targeting doctrines. It is thus not surprising that this carefully reasoned position has generated widespread commentary, both for and against it.

Perhaps the most visible critique of the bishops' position is that of the well-known strategic theorist Albert Wohlstetter, in his "Bishops, Statesmen, and Other Strategists on the Bombing of Innocents," which is the fourth selection in *The Nuclear Reader*. Wohlstetter disagrees with the bishops on empirical, normative, and logical grounds, after scrutinizing their position on moral, political, and military issues.

As a point of departure, Wohlstetter places the debate about many of these issues into historical perspective, retracing the evolution of American strategic doctrine from the presidency of Harry Truman to that of Ronald Reagan. His conclusions directly confront those of the pastoral letter; unlike the latter, Wohlstetter advocates a war-fighting nuclear strategy, claiming that it is ethically acceptable to make contingency plans for war in the event that deterrence should fail and to develop the capability to wage it with nuclear weapons. Technological developments, in his view, create opportunities for new departures in strategic doctrine and make limited nuclear war practicable.

Wohlstetter is unmoved by the risks involved. He concludes that deterrence based on a MAD strategy should be jettisoned and that in its place a counterforce strategy should be implemented that would allow the United States to utilize nuclear weapons to pursue political purposes. In assuming this position, Wohlstetter prescribes the very kind of strategy that Draper finds so tempting but objectionable and that Keeny and Panofsky find so unrealistic. It calls for the acquisition of military capabilities that would allow the United States to confront the Soviet Union on the battlefield, to fight, to survive, and to emerge victorious. In embracing this view, Wohlstetter approaches the position of Colin S. Gray and Keith Payne, other strategists who urge that the United States prepare to use its nuclear arsenal, and not necessarily only in response to a nuclear attack; they contend that "victory" from such a strategy "is possible."[13]

In our fifth selection, "MAD Is the Moral Position," Paul M. Kattenburg introduces new facets of the debate by offering a rebuttal to Wohlstetter (and to others who attack the MAD doctrine[14]). Kattenburg attacks the premises of Wohlstetter's convictions regarding the nature of Soviet leaders and their intentions. Moreover, like Keeny and Panofsky, Kattenburg finds Wohlstetter's beliefs concerning waging war through counterforce targeting strategies to be "nuts."[15] In Kattenburg's view, Wohlstetter's strategy would undermine the bases that have enabled deterrence, predicated on MAD principles, to work successfully for forty years.

It is noteworthy that in challenging Wohlstetter's interpretation of strategic issues, Kattenburg does not associate himself with the position of the Catholic bishops which Wohlstetter attacks so vehemently. To the contrary, in recommending a strategy of deterrence predicated on the principle of mutual assured destruction, Kattenburg contends that a countervalue, but not a counterforce, capability is required. The threat of massive retaliation against the targets that the Soviets value most (that is, *not* their military assets) must be preserved and made credible if deterrence is to work. To Kattenburg, the path to maintaining deterrence is one that ensures an adversary's awareness that the United States would answer an attack decisively and without restraint.

This view echos the belief of former Secretary of Defense Robert McNamara that "to the extent that the nuclear threat has deterrent value, it is because it in fact increases the risk of nuclear war."[16] To preserve peace, Kattenburg tells us, we must resist the temptation to pursue a war-waging nuclear strategy but must accept the necessity of going to the brink—even beyond—to counter an adversary's attack with an annihilating counterstrike against its population and industrial centers. Unlike the bishops, who see the means of nuclear weapons as unacceptably disproportionate to the ends, Kattenburg sees the viability of MAD as contingent upon decision makers' willingness to accept the use of nuclear weapons in self-defense: "the morality of the end sought in this case justifies the apparent immorality of the means."

The logic and ethics of this position, intermediate between that of Wohlstetter and that of the bishops, deserve scrutiny. It lends balance by offering another view of the contradictions inherent in the nuclear debate. By looking at these issues from the perspectives of the Catholic bishops, Wohlstetter, and Kattenburg, we are drawn to Jonathan Schell's admonition that we recognize "what a doomsday machine really is, and what it means to intend, in certain circumstances, to use one." And we become better equipped to assess whether a strategy can be justified, which, again in Schell's words, entails the "unresolvable contradiction of 'defending' one's country by threatening to use weapons whose actual use would bring on the annihilation of one's country and possibly of the world as well."[17]

In reviewing the debate about deterrent strategies and war-fighting options, one soon discovers that much of the exchange centers not simply on considerations of the efficacy of policy programs and their ethics but also on the roles and intentions of the superpowers. The strategy of each superpower reflects and is shaped by images of the other's goals, doctrines, and capabilities. Indeed, one of the things that makes the nuclear debate so perplexing is that different observers proceed from different premises regarding superpower strategies, and these premises lead inevitably to incompatible conclusions.

If the superpowers' strategies are to be assessed accurately, their *declared* strategic doctrines must be investigated, especially the postures of the United States and the Soviet Union toward nuclear weapons and the policy options that those weapons presumably create.

The basic outlines and assumptions underlying the nuclear strategy of the United States are open to public scrutiny. The same is not as true of the Soviet Union. Nevertheless, both superpowers have found it prudent to pronounce publicly their doctrinal positions (but not their tactical plans or true military capabilities!), which is why these strategies provoke such debate about their wisdom and morality. Moreover, the weapons systems assembled and the targeting modes they allow or require do much to define their possible strategic uses. Some would even say that the weapons systems' capabilities determine strategy, although others contend that declared doctrine is instrumental because strategic doctrine fuels rather than follows the technological expansion of the arms race.[18]

The two superpowers' general strategic goals and operational plans are discussed in our next three selections. In "The Madness Beyond MAD: Current American Nuclear Strategy," Robert Jervis considers the "countervailing" strategy pursued by the United States. He rejects the logic of Kattenburg's advocacy of MAD, arguing that "a rational strategy for the employment of nuclear weapons is a contradiction in terms."

Jervis finds American policy paradoxically jeopardizing the national security that a nuclear strategy is designed to provide. Why? Because the pursuit of a countervailing strategy—a pursuit made possible by the revolution in weapons technology that affects the military balance—multiplies the vulnerabilities to which the United States is exposed. The temptation (as Draper would term it) to develop a counterforce capability with which to challenge Soviet power, "to engage in wars rather than deter them," would undermine deterrence and expand the risks of escalation. A countervailing strategy that requires the United States to prepare for war at all levels with the Soviets is thus seen as potentially suicidal. These conclusions force us to question whether the current efforts to move American strategy beyond the MAD doctrine are well advised. Moreover, Jervis questions the traditional identification of nuclear destructive power with national security, especially when the use of that power is strategically proposed. How can security be provided, Jervis asks, when security requires reliance on weapons whose use would mean one's own destruction?

Part of the answer depends on how America's principal adversary, the Soviet Union, is likely to respond to a countervailing policy. In "On Russians and Their Views of Nuclear Strategy," Freeman Dyson contrasts two prevailing views of the Soviet strategic perspective: those of Richard Pipes and George F. Kennan.[19] The two differ in fundamental ways, the former picturing the Soviet Union intent on world conquest and willing to use military force to satisfy its expansionist goals and the latter seeing the Soviet Union fearful and dominated by the perceived need to defend itself from foreign attack. As Dyson makes clear, the implications derived from each viewpoint lead to different prescriptions for American strategy. The propriety of American doctrine may finally depend on which view is more accurate. Dyson's approach is useful because it pictures Soviet thinking without imposing American vocabulary and concepts on Soviet attitudes. Because Soviet and American doctrines are seriously "mismatched,"[20] it may be dangerous to interpret the former from a frame of reference peculiar to the latter.

Some will disagree with this reasoning. An argument can in fact be made that just as technology may drive strategy in the United States, the Soviet Union, too, is being "tempted" to revise its strategic thinking concomitantly with the development of highly accurate missiles tipped with lower-yield nuclear warheads that open new strategic options. In this case, however, Pierre Gallois and John Train argue in "When a Nuclear Strike Is Thinkable" that the Soviets purposely moved toward the newer generation of weapons as a means of coping with their peculiar geopolitical and geostrategic needs. Indeed, they assert that "Soviet military practice is quite different from Soviet propaganda, which pushes the idea that no atomic weapons can ever be used because they would escalate immediately to city-for-city exchanges." The reality, they continue, is a sophisticated Soviet military machine able to inflict finely tuned nuclear destruction on a highly vulnerable Western Europe—circumstances that may make a nuclear strike thinkable. The controversial argument has strong implications for a broad range of foreign and national security policy issues among the NATO countries generally and the United States in particular. Moreover, the authors' controversial convictions suggest how emotional the nuclear debate often becomes.

Gallois and Train make clear that the superpowers' allies also have a stake in the nuclear competition. Although the nuclear predicament is defined most succinctly when the superpowers' doctrinal positions are brought into focus, the ability to secure the goal that many prize most—that nuclear weapons not be put to military use, but only to the political purpose of deterring aggression—also depends on other actors. Doctrine and strategy require, on the one hand, the defense of allies who depend on the superpowers' nuclear umbrellas for their protection. On the other hand, the security policies of at least some of these states may help define the global security predicament; what they plan for and how they might execute those plans can significantly affect the superpowers' strategic plans and goals and also the search for national and global security.

In "Strategies for Making a Nuclear Strike Unthinkable," Earl C. Ravenal inspects contemporary United States strategy in light of its allies, the newly emergent weapons capabilities, and the doctrinal debate concerning countervalue and counterforce targeting. Stressing the linkage between deterrence and alliance that has brought into the vocabulary the concept of "extended deterrence," Ravenal concludes that the United States' overriding interest must be to avoid nuclear war on American territory and that to safeguard that objective the United States should insulate itself from the possibility of a conventional war in Europe escalating to an attack on the United States. This neoisolationist approach calls for the removal of America's "protective mantle over Western Europe and other parts of the world." A "firebreak"[21] between a conventional European war and a superpower nuclear war could be constructed, Ravenal contends, by adopting a stringent "no first use of nuclear weapons" policy and by embracing a "countermilitary" (not countervalue or countermissile) targeting strategy.

Although the logic of these proposals seems compelling, they are not without their problems, including the probably vehement disapproval of American allies who would largely be left to fend for themselves. But by illustrating how political and technological factors join to define strategic postures, Ravenal's assessment of the United States' security dilemma demonstrates the difficulties of developing a comprehensive and coherent strategy for the nation's defense.

By emphasizing how weapons capabilities can influence strategic planning, Ravenal's selection also prepares the way for the discussion of weapons in Part II of *The Nuclear Reader*. Recent developments in weapons systems require new strategies to govern their use and to prevent the destruction that they threaten. Strategic innovation seems destined to follow in the wake of the continuing revolution in weapons innovation.[22] The need to somehow control those weapons so that they secure their intended political purposes thus becomes imperative.

NOTES

1. It is, of course, an empirical question whether the processes through which nations formulate foreign policies do, indeed, display the attributes that satisfy the assumptions of rational decision making. For a discussion that draws on the extensive literature on foreign policymaking to analyze the processes through which U.S. policies and strategies are formulated, see Charles W. Kegley, Jr., and Eugene R. Wittkopf, *American Foreign Policy: Pattern and Process*, 2nd ed. (New York: St. Martin's Press, 1982).

2. For a discussion of the limits and uses of military might in the nuclear age, see Klaus Knorr, "On the International Uses of Military Force in the Contemporary World," *Orbis* 21 (Spring 1977): 5–27.

3. The former characterization was voiced by Donald M. Snow in *The Nuclear Future* (University, Ala.: University of Alabama Press, 1983), pp. 1–34. The latter description is offered by Jonathan Schell, *The Abolition* (New York: Knopf, 1984), p. 48.

4. Milton Leitenberg, "NATO and WTO Long Range Nuclear Forces," pp. 9–64 in Karl E. Birnbaum, ed., *Arms Control in Europe* (Laxenburg: Austrian Institute for International Affairs, 1980), p. 10.

5. Fritz W. Ermarth, "Contrasts in American and Soviet Strategic Thought," *International Security* 3 (Fall 1978): 138–155.

6. *Compellence* is a strategy that envisions the use of nuclear weapons to exercise influence, to coerce others to act in ways they would not otherwise behave in the absence of that influence; *Deterrence*, in contrast, threatens retaliation in order to prevent an actor from contemplating an attack. This distinction is analogous to that between persuasion and dissuasion as strategic goals in internation bargaining. For discussions in the context of the evolution of strategic doctrine in the United States, see Kegley and Wittkopf, especially pp. 84–110; Thomas C. Schelling, *Arms and Influence* (New Haven, Conn.: Yale University Press, 1966); and J. David Singer, "Inter-Nation Influence," *American Political Science Review* 57 (June 1963): 420–430.

7. For a useful discussion, see Patrick M. Morgan, *Deterrence: A Conceptual Analysis*, 2nd ed. (Beverly Hills, Calif.: Sage Publications, 1983).

8. Emma Rothschild, "The Delusions of Deterrence," *The New York Review of Books*, April 14, 1983, p. 40.

9. Schell, p. 36.

10. See Draper's debate with Weinberger in the *New York Review of Books*, August 18, 1983, and his subsequent debates with Albert Wohlstetter in "Nuclear Temptations: An Exchange," *The New York Review of Books*, May 31, 1984, pp. 44–50, as well as in the January 19, 1984, issue of the same journal.

11. Jonathan Schell, *The Fate of the Earth* (New York: Knopf, 1982), p. 231.

12. Bruce M. Russett, "Ethical Dilemmas of Nuclear Deterrence," *International Security* 8 (Spring 1984): 36–54. For another assessment of the bishops' statement, see Susan Moller Okin, "Taking the Bishops Seriously," *World Politics* 36 (July 1984):527–554.

13. Colin S. Gray and Keith Payne, "Victory Is Possible," *Foreign Policy* 39 (Summer 1980): 14–27.

14. For an argument that there is no alternative to MAD and that thus anticipates and takes exception to the view advanced by Wohlstetter, see Glenn C. Buchan, "The Anti-MAD Mythology," *The Bulletin of the Atomic Scientists* 37 (April 1981):13–17.

15. The origins of this doctrinal shift is sometimes traced to Henry A. Kissinger's often quoted declaration that "it is necessary that we develop a military purpose for our strategic forces and move away from the senseless and demoralizing strategy of massive civilian extermination." "NATO: The Next Thirty Years," *Survival* 21 (November-December 1979):267.

16. Robert S. McNamara, "The Military Role of Nuclear Weapons," *Foreign Affairs* 62 (Fall 1983): 75. This article is reprinted in Part II of this book.

17. Schell, *The Abolition*, p. 48.

18. For an interpretation that argues the latter thesis, see Jonathan B. Stein, *From H-Bomb to Star Wars: The Politics of Strategic Decision Making* (Lexington, Mass.: Lexington Books, 1984).

19. The numerous available interpretations of Soviet strategic doctrine and goals vary widely, even if the Pipes and Kennan views represent well the basic differences. Pipes' hawkish position is stated in "Why the Soviet Union Thinks It Could Fight and Win a Nuclear War," *Commentary* 64 (July 1977): 21–34. It is joined by Paul H. Nitze, "Strategy in the Decade of the 1980s," *Foreign Affairs* 59 (Fall 1980): 82–101, which essentially agrees with Wohlstetter. George F. Kennan's less-alarmist view, like Kattenburg's, is summarized in "Two Views of the Soviet Problem," in Charles W. Kegley, Jr., and Eugene R. Wittkopf, eds., *Perspectives on American Foreign Policy* (New York: St. Martin's Press, 1983), pp. 40–46. Fred Kaplan agrees with Kennan and Kattenburg and extends the argument in *Dubious*

Specter: A Skeptical Look at the Soviet Nuclear Threat (Washington, D.C.: Institute for Policy Studies, 1980). For balanced reviews that attempt to weigh the contrasting evidence, see Dimitri K. Simes, "Deterrence and Coercion in Soviet Policy," *International Security* 5 (Winter 1981–1982): 123–143; and Daniel Frei, *Risks of Unintentional Nuclear War* (Totowa, N.J.: Allanheld, Osmun, 1983). Also recommended for general discussions are Lawrence Freeman, *The Evolution of Nuclear Strategy* (New York: St. Martin's Press, 1981), and William E. Odom, "The Soviet Approach to Nuclear Weapons," *Annals of the American Academy* 469 (September 1983): 117–135. Also of interest is Edward N. Luttwak, *The Grand Strategy of the Soviet Union* (New York: St. Martin's Press, 1983), which looks apprehensively at Soviet motives but disregards the notion that the Soviets have in mind anything as irrational as a nuclear attack on the United States.

20. See Frei, especially pp. 61–109, for a discussion of the "mismatch" of Soviet and American strategic doctrines and their consequences.

21. The concept of a "firebreak" refers to the psychological barriers designed to keep conventional warfare from escalating to nuclear warfare. For a discussion that stresses the difficulties of maintaining such barriers, see Michael T. Klare's article in Part II of this book.

22. The experience of one strategist is revealing. Lord Zuckerman reports that "during the twenty years or so that I myself was professionally involved in these matters, weapons came first and rationalizations and policies followed." "Nuclear Fantasies," *The New York Review of Books,* June 14, 1984, p. 7.

1 NUCLEAR TEMPTATIONS: DOCTRINAL ISSUES IN THE NUCLEAR DEBATE

Theodore Draper

There are so many aspects of the nuclear war problem that anyone who talks about it, especially in a relatively short span of time, must choose a particular aspect to deal with. It is all too easy to get tangled up in terminology, technicalities, or the controversies of the moment. I am going to discuss what I consider to be the chief danger or threat of nuclear war. It is what I call "nuclear temptations," by which I mean nothing more than the temptations to use nuclear weapons. These temptations have taken various forms, some of which are still with us. But temptations in this field, as in life generally, come with inhibitions, and so one will naturally lead to the other as we go along. . . .

In the Clausewitzian sense, the grand strategy of nuclear war is . . . simple, though that does not mean that everything about it is very easy. Its strategic simplicity is what permits us—non-nuclear experts and non-military professionals—to think seriously about the problem of nuclear war. One such simple conception is that of nuclear "deterrence," and it did not need nuclear experts or military professionals to think of it. . . .

The first atomic bomb was dropped on Hiroshima on August 6, 1945. Only a month later, . . . the University of Chicago [initiated] . . . an "Atomic Energy Control Conference." . . . Two of the participants are of the greatest interest to us.

One was Professor Jacob Viner [who] . . . was, of course, no atomic expert or military professional. But he already knew one thing . . . "A single atomic bomb can reduce a city and its population to dust." From this simple enough premise, . . . Viner made a striking allusion to the strategic military implication of atomic warfare. Though the United States was then the only country to have the bomb, Viner already foresaw that the monopoly could not last and, moreover, that a stage of parity, or equal destructiveness, was bound to come about.

Here is a key sentence in a memorandum he wrote for the conference: "Retaliation in equal terms in unavoidable and in this sense the atomic bomb is a war deterrent, a peace-making force." The term "deterrent"

Note: Footnotes in original have been deleted. Subtitle has been added.

was thus used for the first time in this connection. In his later talk, in November 1945, Viner developed the thought behind his original insight. That thought might be summed up in this way: If one atomic power is capable of retaliating in kind against another atomic power, each is capable of deterring the other from using atomic weapons.

The second pioneer in this field was Bernard Brodie, then at Yale University. Brodie had specialized in the history of naval warfare, but he too was no nuclear expert or military professional. He also attended the Chicago conference, where he spoke directly on "Strategic Consequences of the Atomic Bomb." . . . Brodie's talk contained a mention of "possible deterrent value" in connection with the atomic bomb. The word "deterrent," therefore, had crept into Brodie's thinking at this time, but the summary of his talk on record is too cryptic to reveal fully what he may have meant.

But whereas Viner, as far as I can tell, dropped the subject after 1945, Brodie stayed with it for the rest of his life. In a book published in 1946, Brodie produced the classic formulation of the military consequence of atomic weapons. Three of his sentences have been quoted innumerable times, but I may perhaps be excused for quoting them once again, because they sum up the essence of the matter better than anything else:

> Thus far the chief purpose of our military establishment has been to win wars. From now on its chief purpose must be to avert them. It can have almost no other useful purpose.

Brodie thus hit on the main point—the strategic essence—that this weapon was capable of such mutual destruction that it could have no useful purpose except to make war between atomic or thermonuclear powers irrational and suicidal.

Previous wars had been rational to the extent that they had served some political purpose. . . . [But] what would a nuclear power intend to achieve by waging a nuclear war against another nuclear power? Win the war? But what does victory mean if the enemy has a nuclear force that can retaliate in kind? What is victory worth if the nuclear aggressor must take the risk—at the very least the risk—of mutual devastation? . . .

This question immediately raises another: Do nuclear weapons represent a qualitative rather than a quantitative change in warfare? If the answer is qualitative, as most theorists agree, there is no experience or precedent for conducting it. Armed forces learn how to use new weapons by trial and error. The function of the machine gun, for example, was misconceived at the outset. It took time and failure to learn how to use the machine gun to best advantage. But no one in his senses—to use Clausewitz's language—is going to be able to learn how best to use nuclear weapons, especially those of the greatest destructiveness, by a process of trial and error. The risk and the cost make such experimentation in real combat prohibitive.

Some such reasoning flowed from the fundamental insight first stated by Viner and Brodie. Their analysis has been refined; various distinctions have been introduced; but the central idea of deterrence is still very much with us. It was recently restated by former Secretary of Defense Robert McNamara, who was not always such a firm believer. In an article [*Foreign Affairs* (Fall 1983)] the newspapers played up as if he had said something new and original, McNamara wrote that nuclear weapons *"are totally useless—except only to deter one's opponent from using them."* Viner and Brodie had been there thirty-seven years earlier. For this they should be properly honored.

But the idea of deterrence has peculiar flaws in it. It is by its very nature not a strategy for waging war; it is rather a nonstrategy or an antistrategy. In all previous human history, weapons have been invented to be used; the more effective they were, the more they were used. But nuclear weapons are too effective to be used. This paradox is almost too much for the military mind, and its civilian counterparts, to bear.

This nuclear nonstrategy is also very expensive. It devours untold sums of the national budget, incredible quantities of rare and costly materials, prodigious amounts of human knowledge and ingenuity. And all this for something that cannot or should not be used? All this for something that is merely intended to deter someone else from using it?

Another problem with deterrence is linguistic. In ordinary usage, deterrence is treated as if it were a thing, a doer, an active agent. The question is asked, "If deterrence fails?"—as if deterrence by itself can fail or succeed. This reification of deterrence is natural enough, but it can be grossly misleading and distorting. The concept of deterrence is nothing more than a mode of analysis, a shorthand for a relationship between nuclear weapons and political decision making. The weapons do not make decisions to be used or not to be used; political leaders make the decisions. If nothing can be gained from using these weapons, the political leaders will or could be deterred from using them. If "deterrence" fails, the political leaders—or those who have elected or tolerated them—will have failed. As long as hostility and rivalry persist, weapons will be their instruments, not their causes. The real success or failure of deterrence depends on political thinking, not on unthinking objects that obey the will of men.

Deterrence, then, is not a stockpile of weapons. Just here is the source of the greatest misunderstanding of and discomfort with the whole doctrine of deterrence. Because a stable balance of nuclear weaponry is necessary for the deterrent effect, it is all too common to transfer the hatefulness of those weapons to the balance that inhibits their use. Those weapons will not disappear however much we may fear and detest them; the idea of deterrence cannot be blamed for bringing them into existence or making them continue to exist. To reject deterrence because the weapons are rejected is to give up one of the few—perhaps the only convincing rationale why the weapons cannot be used for any sane, credible purpose. It is the link with politics that is the best hope of deterring the employment of nuclear weapons.

Even here, however, there is a hitch. The same nuclear weapon that can be used for deterring can also be used for fighting. This ambiguity is inherent in nuclear weapons, and we may have to live with it as we live with many lesser ambiguities in our lives. Some people seem to think that they have to be against deterrence because they are against nuclear weapons, as if one has to approve of nuclear weapons because one may favor a policy of deterrence. The real dividing line should be between those who wish to give nuclear weapons a war-deterring and those who wish to give them a war-fighting role. The distinction cannot be determined in practice solely by whether nuclear weapons are involved; they are inevitably involved in both cases. We must draw the line by determining whether the level of nuclear weaponry far exceeds the requirements for deterrence, whether the types of weapons are far more suitable for war fighting than for war deterring, and whether the official strategic doctrine encourages or requires the use of nuclear weapons. In this case as in so many others, policymakers are far more apt to give themselves away by their actions than by their words.

In some sense, then, deterrence is psychological or, better yet, political. It depends on the political calculation of political leaders who might want to use nuclear weapons for political gain. If there could be no gain, there would be no point in their use. Nevertheless, the equation is always going to be made by human beings, not by the weapons themselves. There is something scary about the responsibility of mere human beings for such ultimate decisions. It is for this very reason that rationality is our best hope and guide in this awful predicament. By rationality, I do not mean to suggest the need for any great feat of wisdom or foresight; nothing more is needed than the rational will to survive—and the leaders of even the most aggressive and detestable regimes have that. The worst way of dealing with the problem is to build up an atmosphere of mindless terror, which almost surely leads to fatalism or abdication.

We would be in an even worse position than we are in already if we thought that deterrence worked its wonders automatically and inevitably. Nothing could be more dangerous than taking deterrence for granted. We would then be really vulnerable to accidents and misjudgments; that they *can* happen is what must make us guard against them or at least take the necessary precautions to minimize their damage. The subtlety of Bernard Brodie's mind was never better displayed than in this little-noted observation in his late, great work, *War and Politics*:

> It is the curious paradox of our time that one of the foremost factors making deterrence really work well is the lurking fear that in some massive confrontation crisis it might fail. Under these circumstances one does not tempt fate.

The temptation is to say: Since no conceivable use of nuclear weapons makes sense, let's get rid of them. We don't go on building cars or computers or anything else in order *not* to use them. Why go on building nuclear weapons in order not to use them?

The logic is impeccable; the reality is something else. In the first place, all nations having nuclear weapons would have to get rid of them altogether, simultaneously. There is no serious chance of that happening. More than that, it would be necessary to get rid of the knowledge of how to make nuclear weapons. That is not even worth dreaming about; it is out of the question. There are a great many things in life easier to get rid of than nuclear weapons—cigarettes, for example. No one expects us to get rid of cigarettes—or cigarette smokers—all at once, universally and simultaneously. Probably no one expects us to get rid of them ever.

So we have been left with the nonstrategy of deterrence. It amounts to this: We have nuclear weapons; we are going to have them; but the weapons themselves are of such a nature that we—and other nuclear powers—dare not use them.

It is not the most elegant or satisfying solution—if it can be called a solution. As long as these weapons exist, there is always the danger that they may be used. At best, deterrence belongs to the lesser-evil, or *faute-de-mieux*, variety of human conduct. No one likes to choose the lesser evil—but isn't that what we are doing most of the time in our lives? We rarely get the chance to choose between the perfect good and the ultimate evil. The problem of the lesser evil is not that it is less but just how much less it is. If a lesser evil is infinitely preferable to the greater evil, we are lucky to have it. So let us not scoff at lesser evils, even in the case of nuclear arms.

Nevertheless, the lesser-evil nature of nuclear deterrence makes it vulnerable to pulls from two directions. One is the utopian—simply to do away with these weapons altogether, unilaterally or universally. The utopian program is not my subject, so I do not have to discuss it. The other pull, however, is my subject—it is "nuclear temptations."

It is best to start with a brief history of these temptations.

The original temptation came in with the defense strategy of NATO. The temptation arose from the problem of finding a means of defending Western Europe against what was conceived to be an overwhelming Soviet advantage in conventional, or non-nuclear, forces. NATO adopted a military policy of using atomic weapons to deter or to defeat a conventional attack.

That is still official NATO doctrine. General Bernard Rogers, the Supreme Allied Commander in Europe, recently declared that the alliance, if attacked conventionally, would have to resort to nuclear weapons "fairly quickly," unless its conventional strength were considerably increased, which seems to be unlikely. I do not wish to linger on this—the original—nuclear temptation, because it is an old story. At this point I merely wish to point out that this policy was adopted when the Soviets did not have or were far behind in nuclear weapons; the same policy, however, prevails in a condition of nuclear parity, that is, the "retaliation in equal terms" that Jacob Viner predicted in 1945.

This form of deterrence also has a serious flaw. The most controversial of nuclear weapons are those that can reach the Soviet Union from the United States and the United States from the Soviet Union—the ICBMs, or intercontinental ballistic missiles. They are known as "strategic deterrents"—a misuse of the term "strategic," which, unfortunately, has by now become customary. . . .

It has long been difficult to believe in the efficacy—or, as the current jargon has it, "credibility"—of this deterrent. No president, it has been argued, would risk the devastation of the United States in defense of someone else's territory, even that of Western Europe. The first obligation of an American president is to the safety of the United States, whatever other obligations there may be. The argument goes that the use of the strategic deterrent against the Soviet Union would lead to the use of the Soviets' strategic deterrent against the United States, with the result of mutual devastation. So [Lawrence Freedman], one of the best students of the nuclear war problem—English, not American—has flatly stated: "The United States would be irrational to commit suicide on behalf of Western Europe. . . ." Charles de Gaulle had said more or less the same thing at least two decades ago. It is not a new problem, but no one has yet thought of a good answer.

So now we have at least two serious problems with traditional deterrence—it depends on a huge investment in weapons that will never be used; and it assumes the willingness of an American president to risk the devastation of the United States in behalf of other countries, albeit allies. There are other problems, no doubt, but these two are enough for our present purpose.

For at least three decades now, efforts have been made to get around such problems. It is these efforts that have brought about the most tempting inducements to use nuclear weapons.

First, there were the so-called tactical nuclear weapons, which are still with us. Tactical nuclear weapons, developed in the early 1950s, were small enough to be used on a battlefield. NATO officially decided in

1954 to use tactical nuclear weapons in defense of Europe. The Soviets then introduced tactical weapons on their side. Thus a distinction was created between "strategic" and "tactical" nuclear weapons. In effect, there were now "bad" nuclear weapons—the strategic—because they were most useful against cities and civilian populations, and there were "good" nuclear weapons, because they could be used within a much smaller area by enemy units in combat.

The development of tactical weapons brought with it another temptation—that of "limited nuclear war." A limited war would have to be "controlled," so now we had another tempting proposition—the "controlled" and "limited" nuclear war. If, in effect, the only weapons used were the smaller, less destructive ones, a nuclear exchange could be said to be "controlled" and "limited." The two terms were really interchangeable because a nuclear war would have to be controlled to be limited and limited to be controlled.

Now, in order for a nuclear war to be limited and controlled, it was necessary to fit the technology to the strategy. The new technology was supposed to produce nuclear weapons that were precise enough to be "discriminating." That was the favorite word—"discriminating." The Hiroshima type of weapon had been hopelessly imprecise and undiscriminating. It was effective only against big targets, such as cities. But the smaller, tactical weapons were now touted as precise and discriminating, so that they could avoid mass destructiveness.

For example, Henry Kissinger first attracted widespread attention in 1957 with a book called *Nuclear Weapons and Foreign Policy*. It advocated a policy of waging limited nuclear war, largely based on the new tactical weapons. Kissinger then sought "to break down the atmosphere of special horror which now surrounds the use of nuclear weapons" and "to overcome the trauma which attaches to the use of nuclear weapons." And what kind of weapons were needed to accomplish these goals? They had to be, Kissinger then thought, both "destructive" and "discriminating."

A great fuss was made about the limited-war doctrine in the late 1950s. Its nuclear version was so shaky that Kissinger—to his credit—repudiated his earlier position in another book [*The Necessity for Choice*] in 1961, only four years later. In 1957, he had come out in favor of limited nuclear war and against conventional war; in 1961, he came out against limited nuclear war and in favor of conventional war, with the use of nuclear weapons only as a last resort.

Yet the technological solution to the nuclear dilemma continued to captivate. In 1973, Fred Charles Iklé, the present under secretary of defense for policy, advocated "taking advantage of modern technology" by exploiting "the potential accuracy of 'smart' bombs and missiles." He wanted "assured destruction" of the enemy's "military, industrial and transportation assets" instead of "the killing of vast millions," as if one were the antithesis of the other. This strategy, Iklé admitted, was not an alternative to deterrence; it was nothing more than a change of form, not of substance. Thus the technological nostrum for conducting nuclear war in a way to avoid the destruction of cities and the massacre of civilians is hardly a new idea; it goes back at least a quarter of a century in one form or another, as if we could return to a nuclear version of the premodern art of warfare.

What was wrong with those "discriminating" and "accurate" nuclear weapons? In the first place, they were not discriminating or accurate enough. In June 1955, NATO held an exercise to find out what casualties might result in tactical nuclear warfare. In less than three days, it was found, 1.5 to 1.7 million people could expect to be killed and 3.5 million wounded if only 268 bombs fell on German soil. The rate of German casualties would be five times that suffered in World War II as a whole. In 1960, NATO maneuvers in Schleswig-Holstein showed that between 300,000 and 400,000 civilian deaths were to be expected within forty-eight hours of the initiation of tactical nuclear warfare. These figures did not take into account the effects of radiation and follow-up diseases. At that time the future German Chancellor Helmut Schmidt was moved to protest: That the concept of tactical nuclear warfare "should remain in force is inconceivable."

Something else was even more troublesome and embarrassing. Where was this limited war with tactical nuclear weapons going to be fought? The obvious answer was: in Europe and, primarily, in Germany. On second thought, the Europeans in general and Germans in particular were not enamored of this prospect. A limited nuclear war is a war limited to Europe. That circumstance has always made a limited war more attractive to Americans than to Europeans.

The problem of tactical nuclear weapons was soon compounded by that of so-called intermediate nuclear weapons. Intermediate weapons may be defined as those with a range great enough to reach the Soviet Union from Western Europe and to reach Western Europe from the Soviet Union. They are thus classified somewhere between the tactical nuclear weapons, with a range short enough to be used on a battlefield, and the strategic nuclear weapons, with an intercontinental, or Soviet-American, range. The Soviet SS-20s and the American Pershing IIs, much in dispute today, are typical of the intermediate weapons.

The Pershing IIs illustrate a point that I have previously tried to make about the ambiguity of nuclear weapons. One reason the European members of NATO originally wanted Pershing IIs was that they were supposed to "couple" European and American nuclear weaponry. It was reasoned that a threat to the Pershing IIs would be regarded in the United States as great enough to bring into play the "strategic," or intercontinental, weapons in the United States. But then doubts arose. It was also charged that the Pershing IIs could just as well "decouple," or dissociate, the nuclear defense of Europe from that of the United States. An alarm was raised that an American president was more likely to accept Soviet retaliation against weapons in Europe than against those in the United States.

Which is right? It seems to me that either one may be right—or wrong. The weapons themselves will not couple or decouple; they can be used for either purpose. The decision will be made politically in circumstances we cannot now foresee. Ambiguity and uncertainty hover over almost every aspect of the nuclear question. Anyone who can believe that the United States would passively permit the domination or destruction of Western Europe could be convinced of the decoupling theory: those who find it hard to imagine that the United States would not regard such an attack on Western Europe as a mortal threat to itself will lean over to the coupling side. The irony is, however, that the decision will not be made because there are a few hundred more intermediate-range weapons in Europe; the same decision would be made without them, because the United States is coupled with Western Europe by interest, culture, and geopolitical imperatives, not by any particular weaponry.

In any case, temptations soon came in new guises. Four terms characterize the variations on the old theme—options, escalation, flexible response, and counterforce.

The idea of "options" was brought forward to get rid of the nightmare of all-out nuclear war. It held that the president had to have something between all or nothing to defend against a Soviet attack. The concept of "options" seemingly left everything wide open, from any kind of conventional war to any kind of nuclear war or a combination of both.

The temptation to use nuclear weapons, if necessary, was therefore inherent in the concept of "options." But when might it be necessary? It was hoped that a war could be waged, at least at the outset, at the lowest level of violence, in a conventional manner. But the losing side, it was also realized, was bound to try to overcome some disadvantage by a process of escalation, that is, by bringing new forces or weapons into play.

Thus "options" and "escalation" were intimately related: the process of escalation was bound to result in the optional use of nuclear weapons. Abstractly, one could envisage the process of escalation going from conventional warfare to the use of tactical nuclear weapons, then to intermediate nuclear weapons, and finally to strategic nuclear weapons.

But "options" and "escalation" were really parts or aspects of a more basic doctrine—that of "flexible response." It was officially adopted by NATO, in 1967, at the urging of the United States and after much resistance by the Europeans. The Europeans had always preferred to put their trust in the American strategic nuclear umbrella to deter the Soviets from any kind of war, conventional as well as nuclear. Flexible response, or, as it was also called, graduated deterrence, implied that a war could be fought conventionally or with lesser nuclear weapons in Europe before the United States might be called on to use its strategic nuclear weapons, that is, the very weapons that risked American self-destruction. Nevertheless, flexible response remains official NATO doctrine to this day.

Flexible response has one irresistible attraction. It can be all things to all countries and all people. It does not, in principle, promise to use nuclear weapons; it does not promise not to use them. It is an accordion-like policy; you can stretch it out or pull it in as much as you like.

The reality about flexible response is something else. It has one fatal military defect: it does not tell what kind of war to prepare for. It tells military planners to prepare for any kind of war, which is exactly the same as telling them that they cannot prepare for any particular war. Choices always have to be made, and choices cannot be made if the response is so flexible that it must cover all possible eventualities.

In fact, a choice has been made. That choice has boiled down to one between a conventional war and a nuclear war. In 1982, General Rogers explained: "If flexible response is to be credible, it must be supported by an adequate military capability for each leg of the NATO triad of forces—strategic nuclear, theater nuclear and conventional." In order to keep the nuclear threshold in Europe as high as possible, he advocated an adequate conventional deterrent, which would require an average annual real increase in defense spending of about 4 percent for the six years between 1983 and 1988. The NATO members had previously agreed on an annual 3-percent increase, which had not been met. No one seems to expect a 4-percent increase, and even if it were met, there is much skepticism that it would really be enough, because the putative enemy need only increase his conventional forces to match.

More recently, General Rogers [*Foreign Affairs* (Summer 1982)] has told a rather more somber story: "The record shows that nations in the Alliance have never fully met their commitments to conventional force improvements. As a result NATO, while continuing to proclaim its faith in the declaratory policy of Flexible Response, has in fact mortgaged its defense to the nuclear response." So we are back to the nuclear temptation in the name of Flexible Response.

Of all the nuclear temptations, however, the most seductive and most menacing is still to come; it is the "counterforce" doctrine. It is different in kind from the other three I have just mentioned—options, escalation, and flexible response. These three theoretically leave open the possible use of nuclear weapons and to that extent do not foreclose the issue.

The counterforce doctrine requires the use of nuclear weapons, but in a certain way.

For those not accustomed to nuclear jargon, two terms should be briefly explained. They are countervalue and counterforce. Countervalue means nuclear attacks against cities or civilian populations and industries in highly populated areas. Counterforce refers to nuclear attacks against military targets, such as the enemy's own nuclear weapons, military units, or facilities.

The counterforce doctrine first appeared, in the late 1950s and early 1960s, for two main reasons. It was argued that attacks against cities were not *militarily* productive; they killed the wrong people, namely civilians. And attacks against enemy cities were bound to bring similar attacks against our own cities, with the result that no American president was likely to adopt a countervalue, or city-oriented, strategy.

Counterforce presents a very strong temptation to use nuclear weapons, because it promises to take much of the horror out of nuclear war. No one can contemplate with equanimity a devastating attack on the entire social fabric of any country, let alone our own, but an attack on its nuclear weapons or even military establishment does not arouse quite the same repulsion. In one way or another, all present efforts to make nuclear war more feasible go back to the counterforce doctrine.

Here again, the doctrine needed a technological foundation. It was necessary to make two main assumptions. One was that military targets were physically or geographically separate and distinct from civilian targets. The other was that it was possible to develop nuclear weapons capable of distinguishing between the two. Again, as in the case of tactical weapons, the favorite terms are "precise" and "discriminating," but now they seem to be applied to all kinds of nuclear weapons, even those of greatest range and most destructive power.

The counterforce strategy was actually adopted by Secretary McNamara in 1962 during the Kennedy administration. But he then quickly backed away from it and became a convert to a form of the classical deterrence doctrine, which he called "mutual assured destruction," meaning that if both sides were assured of destruction, they would stay away from it as serving no conceivable political purpose. In effect, the goal again became how not to fight a nuclear war rather than how to fight one.

[It is instructive to note that] McNamara's choice of words invited the unfortunate acronym MAD. Critics of deterrence theory love to ridicule it as if it were a description of the doctrine. Professor Michael Howard has suggested that a better term would be "mutually assured *deterrence*," which would still have permitted the acronym MAD but made it seem less mad.

The reasons for this shift are just as valid today as they were then. In the first place, for counterforce to work, both sides have to adopt the same policy. No one, however, expects the United States and the Soviet Union to agree on how to fight a nuclear war or to guarantee their adherence to the same strategy in advance.

It was also realized that a counterforce policy was likely to cause such great civilian casualties that the line between counterforce—military—and countervalue—civilian—was purely theoretical and largely illusory. A Department of Defense study in the 1960s estimated that between 30 and 150 million Americans and a comparable number of Russians were likely to die in a nuclear war, even if efforts were made to stay away from highly populated areas. In 1981, a group of UN experts found that a minimum of five to six million immediate civilian casualties and 400,000 military casualties would result if 1,500 nuclear artillery shells and 200 nuclear bombs were used by both sides against each other's military targets. In effect, counterforce targeting was no panacea for what ailed countervalue.

Another reason for the shift away from counterforce strategy was somewhat more complicated and takes us some way into the darker recesses of nuclear war theory. It was the threat of a first strike. This threat has always hovered over nuclear war strategy, but it became particularly acute in the case of counterforce planning, which implies in the first place an attack against the enemy's nuclear forces.

The trauma of the first strike comes about in the following way: Basically, there are two ways of conceiving a possible nuclear war. One is that it will resemble a conventional, or non-nuclear, war—only more so. There will be one or more fronts; a development of hostilities with some degree of gradualness; a mixture of weaponry; in general, a protracted, more or less controlled escalation. The other conception is peculiar to nuclear war. It can be conceived as an almost immediately catastrophic exchange, with millions of casualties suffered in one, two, or three days.

Neither of these alternatives is particularly appealing—to put it mildly. The protracted nuclear war would be, at best, a protracted agony. As for the nuclear cataclysm, nothing more need be said about it. So the problem presents itself: how to get around both of these unpleasant alternatives?

The logic of the situation points to a way out—to knock out the enemy's nuclear weapons before they can be fired. If they—or most of them—could be knocked out at the very outset, the enemy would be prevented from waging a cataclysmic or protracted nuclear war. In short, a first strike is, logically, the most effective way to wage a nuclear war. That is what makes it so tempting and dangerous.

But to be successful a first strike must benefit from two preconditions: it must be thorough, and it must come as a surprise. If it is not thorough, it invites retaliation, which would begin a cycle of mutual devastation. If it does not come as a surprise, it would invite a preemptive first strike by the other side.

Of course, no nuclear nation will admit that it has ever contemplated or is even capable of contemplating a surprise attack and an unprovoked first strike. What cannot be denied is that they are inherent in the logic of the nuclear dilemma. That is why both sides fear them so much and charge the other with preparing for them.

But logic does not exhaust reality. The full reality is that a surprise attack and a first strike would be an infinitely risky business. They would have to be totally successful or they would open the aggressor to devastating retaliation and retribution. Without any experience of nuclear warfare, no one knows, and no one can know, what a surprise attack would achieve. It would have to be a go-for-broke operation. In the abstract, the first strike would seem like an attractive proposition. In the real world, it is an almost senseless gamble.

In any case, for these reasons and others, McNamara gave up the counterforce temptation after 1962. But now we are getting it again, and in a worse form than ever before.

The present phase began in 1974, during the Nixon administration. It was sponsored by then Secretary of Defense James Schlesinger. His new policy was basically no more than a variation on an already old theme—that of "options." The argument, still in vogue today, maintained that the president should not be limited to choosing between no nuclear war and all-out nuclear war. He should instead be able to engage in all forms and degrees of conventional and nuclear war. Schlesinger's National Security Study Memorandum of 1974 brought forward the option of threatening Soviet military targets.

After Schlesinger came Harold Brown, secretary of defense in the Carter administration. In 1980, President Carter issued Presidential Directive 59, which played more variations on the theme of "options." This directive has never been made public, so we are dependent on what Mr. Brown and other insiders have said about it.

According to Mr. Brown: "There is a good chance that any US-Soviet nuclear exchange would escalate out of control." Nevertheless, the United States must prepare for just such a nuclear exchange, that is, a limited nuclear exchange that would probably escalate out of control. Why? Because the United States must have a "victory-denying" response—"victory-denying" is typical of the fudging language customary in this field—to a Soviet effort to obtain victory in a limited nuclear war.

Notice: the whole idea is predicated on the assumption that the Soviets may seek some sort of nuclear superiority to obtain victory in a limited nuclear war—the same sort of war that is unlikely to stop short of an all-out exchange. After all this, Mr. Brown also tells us that "superiority is an idle goal." Yet without superiority, victory could not be obtained in a limited nuclear war and it would almost certainly escalate out of control. If Presidential Directive 59 follows Mr. Brown's exposition, it is a mishmash of contradictory premises and prescriptions.

After Brown came Caspar W. Weinberger, the present secretary of defense in the Reagan administration. Mr. Weinberger is another whole-sale options merchant. He has offered the president one of the most treacherous options of all, though the idea may not have originated with him or his advisers. This option is the conduct of a protracted nuclear war in which the United States "must prevail" or out of which it must "emerge" with "terms favorable" to us. This policy was enshrined in a document entitled "Fiscal Year 1984–1988 Defense Guidance," issued in the spring of 1982, which had to be leaked in order for ordinary citizens to know about it.

Ironically, Mr. Weinberger has indirectly criticized his own policy. The idea of a protracted or prolonged nuclear war is so indefensible that he tried to repudiate it in a letter sent to a number of US and foreign publications in August 1982. He also tried to repudiate the concept of a nuclear victory in a letter sent to me in July 1983. What seems to have happened is this: The policy of waging a protracted nuclear war and of prevailing in such a war has been adopted officially but disavowed publicly. The least that can be said of this two-tracked or two-faced policy is that it is a strange way of conducting serious business in a democracy.

Here is Mr. Weinberger on both sides of these issues:

For protracted nuclear war: US forces must be able to maintain "through a protracted conflict period and afterward, the capability to inflict very high levels of damage" on Soviet industry. Should a Soviet attack "nevertheless occur, United States nuclear capabilities must prevail under the condition of a prolonged war."

Against protracted nuclear war: "I am increasingly concerned with news accounts that portray this Administration as planning to wage protracted nuclear war, or seeking to acquire a nuclear 'war-fighting' capability. This is completely inaccurate. . . . "

For winning: " . . . United States nuclear capabilities must prevail. . . . earliest termination of hostilities on terms favorable to the United States"; . . . "to achieve political objectives and secure early war termination on terms favorable to the United States and its allies." "You show me a Secretary of Defense who's planning not to prevail and I'll show you a Secretary of Defense who ought to be impeached."

Against winning: " . . . we do not believe there could be any winners in a nuclear war"; " . . . our belief that there could be no winners in a nuclear war."

Finally, a still greater temptation has recently been put forward by influential nuclear war theorists. Like most temptations, nuclear or otherwise, there is nothing new or original about it; it merely pushes the temptation further than anyone has dared to do in the past. These tempters advocate the development of nuclear weapons that could attack targets so "precisely and discriminately" that they could safely be used against the enemy's weapons "without mass destruction." Their nuclear war would be something like a ping-pong game in which each side would "precisely and discriminately" drop its nuclear warheads on the other side's weapons. Since this scheme holds out the prospect of avoiding mass destruction, it is more tempting than the prospect of repeating the heavy civilian casualties and widespread destruction of the two conventional world wars in this century.

As I have tried to show, we have been through all this before. Targeting the enemy's weapons or military facilities may reduce civilian casualties at the outset, but these will still be so high—somewhere in the millions—that it is irresponsible and heartless to play around with the likelihood of avoiding mass destruction. The Soviets, at least, have clustered many of their nuclear weapons and installations in proximity to their cities, especially Moscow. There would be no way of adequately testing our precise and discriminating weapons, even if—someday—we should have them. There is no reason to believe that both sides would agree to use precise and discriminating weapons only, especially if one side should be put at a disadvantage in the development of such weapons. There is no reason to believe that either side would trust the other, even if they both agreed to use such weapons only. If those precise and discriminating weapons did not knock out all or most of the other side's nuclear weapons at once, retaliation could only take the form of a more indiscriminate counterattack. For one thing, the same type of weapon would no longer be available to both sides; for another, one side's precise and discriminating weapons would already have been shot off, thus no longer offering a useful target to the other.

Thus the technological cure is a form of the disease. It is actually a prescription for a potential first strike, the most dangerous of all nuclear temptations. It is interesting to note that an analysis was made in 1968 to determine the relative number of casualties in the event of a Soviet or an American first strike. The paradoxical result was a finding that there would be more American casualties in the case of an American first strike than in the case of a Soviet first strike. The paradox arose because it was figured that the side striking first would go after military targets, whereas the retaliating side would mainly hit cities. All of which suggests that this is not a subject for weak nerves or soft heads. . . .

But "what if deterrence fails?" This question is often asked, with an air of triumph, as if the possible failure of deterrence were a reason for rejecting it. Such an attitude is comparable to that of rejecting a life-support system in a hospital because it may fail or be inadequate to keep a mortally ill patient alive. Yet the possibility of failure does confront us with the fearful problem of what to do if some sort of nuclear war should break out. Toward the end of his life, Bernard Brodie gave [in 1978] the answer that the main goal should be "to terminate it as quickly as possible and with the least amount of damage possible—on both sides." That was the attitude of one who had thought that almost anything was better for mankind than total nuclear war. I have also been driven ineluctably to this conclusion, without, however, pretending to know how it will be possible to terminate a nuclear war with the least possible damage. Yet Brodie's view is infinitely preferable to [that of Colin S. Gray, *International Security* (Summer 1979)], which calls for a "Nuclear Strategy: The Case for a Theory of Victory" or of another [Robert Jastrow, in *Commentary* (March 1983)] which claims that the Soviet Union has found a theory of victory by way of nuclear "superiority."

To my mind, the obvious answer to the question "What if deterrence fails?" is that we do not know what will happen. We have no experience with the failure of nuclear deterrence, and without experience we have little or nothing to go by. Wars have been notoriously unpredictable, and nuclear wars must surely be the most unpredictable of all. We do not know how, where, by whom, or to what extent deterrence would fail. It would seem to be the most ordinary prudence and elementary common sense to make sure that we are not responsible for its failure, that we do whatever we must to limit the damage to ourselves and our allies, and to induce the other side to terminate the conflict as quickly as possible in its own interest. But all this is so far in the realm of the contingent and unpredictable that no one can be sure what such a war would be like or how the antagonists and the world at large could even survive it in recognizable condition. This very uncertainty is an element of deterrence. If it is any comfort, we know more about how to deter a nuclear war, judging from almost half a century of some sort of deterrence, than we know how to fight one.

I am, therefore, a believer in the lesser evil of nuclear deterrence. I believe in it because it is by far the lesser evil, not because it is good. The main enemy at present is not a nuclear balance that results in mutual deterrence; it is the propaganda about the feasibility of nuclear war by way of precise and discriminating weapons allegedly capable of avoiding mass destruction. The main reason nuclear weapons have not been used thus far is precisely the belief that they cannot be launched for any useful political purpose and that mutual mass destruction can be of no conceivable benefit to either side. But now the Pied Pipers of a protracted nuclear war and of precise and discriminating nuclear weapons are trying to lure us to break through the psychological and political barriers to nuclear war.

Lord Henry Wotton told Dorian Gray that the only way to get rid of a temptation is to yield to it. Clearly that would not do in this case. The only way for us to get rid of this temptation is to know it for what it is and to reject it precisely and discriminatingly.

"To use or not to use"—that is the "to be or not to be" of our time and for as long as we can now foresee.

2   MAD VERSUS NUTS: CAN DOCTRINE OR WEAPONRY REMEDY THE MUTUAL HOSTAGE RELATIONSHIP OF THE SUPERPOWERS?

Spurgeon M. Keeny, Jr., and Wolfgang K. H. Panofsky

Since World War II there has been a continuing debate on military doctrine concerning the actual utility of nuclear weapons in war. This debate, irrespective of the merits of the divergent points of view, tends to create the perception that the outcome and scale of a nuclear conflict could be controlled by the doctrine or the types of nuclear weapons employed. Is this the case?

We believe not. In reality, the unprecedented risks of nuclear conflict are largely independent of doctrine or its application. The principal danger of doctrines that are directed at limiting nuclear conflicts is that they might be believed and form the basis for action without appreciation of the physical facts and uncertainties of nuclear conflict. The failure of policymakers to understand the truly revolutionary nature of nuclear weapons as instruments of war and the staggering size of the nuclear stockpiles of the United States and the Soviet Union could have catastrophic consequences for the entire world.

Military planners and strategic thinkers for 35 years have sought ways to apply the tremendous power of nuclear weapons against target systems that might contribute to the winning of a future war. In fact, as long as the United States held a virtual nuclear monopoly, the targeting of atomic weapons was looked upon essentially as a more effective extension of the strategic bombing concepts of World War II. With the advent in the mid-1950s of a substantial Soviet nuclear capability, including multimegaton thermonuclear weapons, it was soon apparent that the populations and societies of both the United States and the Soviet Union were mutual hostages. A portion of the nuclear stockpile of either side could inflict on the other as many as 100 million fatalities and destroy it as a functioning society. Thus, although the rhetoric of declaratory strategic doctrine has changed over the years, mutual deterrence has in fact remained the central fact of the strategic relationship of the two superpowers and of the NATO and Warsaw Pact alliances.

Most observers would agree that a major conflict between the two hostile blocs on a worldwide scale during this period may well have been prevented by the specter of catastrophic nuclear war. At the same time, few would argue that this state of mutual deterrence is a very reassuring foundation on which to build world peace. In the 1960s the perception of the basic strategic relationship of mutual deterrence came to be characterized as "Mutual Assured Destruction," which critics were quick to note had the acronym of MAD. The notion of MAD has been frequently attacked not only as militarily unacceptable but also as immoral since it holds the entire civilian populations of both countries as hostages.[1]

As an alternative to MAD, critics and strategic innovators have over the years sought to develop various war-fighting targeting doctrines that would somehow retain the use of nuclear weapons on the battlefield or even in controlled strategic war scenarios, while sparing the general civilian population from the devastating consequences of nuclear war. Other critics have found an alternative in a defense-oriented military posture designed to defend the civilian population against the consequences of nuclear war.

These concepts are clearly interrelated since such a defense-oriented strategy would also make a nuclear war-fighting doctrine more credible. But both alternatives depend on the solution of staggering technical problems. A defense-oriented military posture requires a nearly impenetrable air and missile defense over a large portion of the population. And any attempt to have a controlled war-fighting capability during a nuclear exchange places tremendous requirements not only on decisions made under incredible pressure by men in senior positions of responsibility but on the technical performance of command, control, communications and intelligence functions—called in professional circles "C³I" and which for the sake of simplicity we shall hereafter describe as "control mechanisms." It is not sufficient as the basis for defense policy to assert that science will "somehow" find solutions to critical technical problems on which the policy is dependent, when technical solutions are nowhere in sight.

In considering these doctrinal issues, it should be recognized that there tends to be a very major gap between declaratory policy and actual implementation expressed as targeting doctrine. Whatever the declaratory policy might be, those responsible for the strategic forces must generate real target lists and develop procedures under which various combinations of targets could be attacked. In consequence, the perceived need to attack every listed target, even after absorbing the worst imaginable first strike from the adversary, creates procurement "requirements," even though the military or economic importance of many of the targets is small.

In fact, it is not at all clear in the real world of war planning whether declaratory doctrine has generated requirements or whether the availability of weapons for targeting has created doctrine. With an estimated 30,000 warheads at the disposal of the United States, including more than 10,000 avowed to be strategic in character, it is necessary to target redundantly all urban areas and economic targets and to cover a wide range of military targets in order to frame uses for the stockpile. And, once one tries to deal with elusive mobile and secondary military targets, one can always make a case for requirements for more weapons and for more specialized weapon designs.

These doctrinal considerations, combined with the superabundance of nuclear weapons, have led to a conceptual approach to nuclear war which can be described as Nuclear Utilization Target Selection. For convenience, and not in any spirit of trading epithets, we have chosen the acronym of NUTS to characterize the various doctrines that seek to utilize nuclear weapons against specific targets in a complex of nuclear war-fighting situations intended to be limited, as well as the management over an extended period of a general nuclear war between the superpowers.[2]

While some elements of NUTS may be involved in extending the credibility of our nuclear deterrent, this consideration in no way changes the fact that mutual assured destruction, or MAD, is inherent in the existence of large numbers of nuclear weapons in the real world. In promulgating the doctrine of "countervailing strategy" in the summer of 1980, President Carter's Secretary of Defense Harold Brown called for a buildup of nuclear war-fighting capability in order to provide greater deterrence by demonstrating the ability of the United States to respond in a credible fashion without having to escalate immediately to all-out nuclear war. He was very careful, however, to note that he thought that it was "very likely" that the use of nuclear weapons by the superpowers at any level would escalate into general nuclear war.[3] This situation is not peculiar to present force structures or technologies; and, regardless of future technical developments, it will persist as long as substantial nuclear weapon stockpiles remain.

Despite its possible contribution to the deterrence of nuclear war, the NUTS approach to military doctrine and planning can very easily become a serious danger in itself. The availability of increasing numbers of nuclear weapons in a variety of designs and delivery packages at all levels of the military establishment inevitably encourages the illusion that somehow nuclear weapons can be applied in selected circumstances without unleashing a catastrophic series of consequences. . . . [T]he recent uninformed debate on the virtue of the so-called neutron bomb as a selective device to deal with tank attacks is a depressing case in point. NUTS creates its own endless pressure for expanded nuclear stockpiles with increasing danger of accidents, accidental use, diversions to terrorists, etc. But more fundamentally, it tends to obscure the fact that the nuclear world is in fact MAD.

The NUTS approach to nuclear war-fighting will not eliminate the essential MAD character of nuclear war for two basic reasons, which are rooted in the nature of nuclear weapons and the practical limits of technology. First, the destructive power of nuclear weapons, individually and most certainly in the large numbers discussed for even specialized application, is so great that the collateral effects on persons and property would be enormous and, in scenarios which are seriously discussed, would be hard to distinguish from the onset of general nuclear war. But more fundamentally, it does not seem possible, even in the most specialized utilization of nuclear weapons, to envisage any situation where escalation to general nuclear war would probably not occur given the dynamics of the situation and the limits of the control mechanisms that could be made available to manage a limited nuclear war. In the case of a protracted general nuclear war, the control problem becomes completely unmanageable. Finally, there does not appear to be any prospect for the foreseeable future that technology will provide a secure shield behind which the citizens of the two superpowers can safely observe the course of a limited nuclear war on other people's territory. . . .

[The authors continue with a discussion of the horrendous consequences of a nuclear war, consequences that point to the conclusions that a nuclear war would be devastating and that each of the two superpowers is inescapably vulnerable to the capacity of the other to destroy it—regardless of who launches the first missile. They then critique the views of those who support the concept of a nuclear war-fighting capability, and especially those advocating the development of theater nuclear forces (TNF) and the associated doctrine that a nuclear war can remain limited. Contending, finally, that the protection of populations against large-scale attack is impossible, they are driven to the conclusion that nuclear utilization theory is indeed NUTs—that it cannot succeed without imperiling civilization as we know it—eds.]

. . . [W]e are fated to live in a MAD world. This is inherent in the tremendous power of nuclear weapons, the size of nuclear stockpiles, the collateral damage associated with the use of nuclear weapons against military targets, the technical limitations on strategic area defense, and the uncertainties involved in efforts to control the escalation of nuclear war. There is no reason to believe that this situation will change for the foreseeable future since the problem is far too profound and the pace of technical military development far too slow to overcome the fundamental technical considerations that underlie the mutual hostage relationship of the superpowers.

What is clear above all is that the profusion of proposed NUTS approaches has not offered an escape from the MAD world, but rather constitutes a major danger in encouraging the illusion that limited or controlled nuclear war can be waged free from the grim realities of a MAD world. The principal hope at this time will not be found in seeking NUTS doctrines that ignore the MAD realities but rather in recognizing the nuclear world for what it is and seeking to make it more stable and less dangerous.

NOTES

1. See, for example, Fred Charles Iklé, "Can Nuclear Deterrence Last Out the Century?" *Foreign Affairs*, January 1973, pp. 267–85.

2. The acronym NUT for Nuclear Utilization Theory was used by Howard Margolis and Jack Ruina, "SALT II: Notes on Shadow and Substance," *Technology Review*, October 1979, pp. 31–41. We prefer Nuclear Utilization Target Selection, which relates the line of thinking more closely to the operational problem of target selection. Readers not familiar with colloquial American usage may need to be told that "nuts" is an adjective meaning "crazy or demented." For everyday purposes it is a synonym for "mad."

3. See Harold Brown, Speech at the Naval War College, August 20, 1980, the most authoritative public statement on the significance of Presidential Directive 59, which had been approved by President Carter shortly before.

3 NUCLEAR STRATEGY AND THE CHALLENGE OF PEACE: ETHICAL PRINCIPLES AND POLICY PRESCRIPTIONS

National Conference of Catholic Bishops

The Second Vatican Council opened its evaluation of modern warfare with the statement: "The whole human race faces a moment of supreme crisis in its advance toward maturity." We agree with the council's assessment; the crisis of the moment is embodied in the threat which nuclear weapons pose for the world and much that we hold dear in the world. We have seen and felt the effects of the crisis of the nuclear age in the lives of people we serve. Nuclear weaponry has drastically changed the nature of warfare, and the arms race poses a threat to human life and human civilization which is without precedent. . . .

As Catholic bishops we write this letter as an exercise of our teaching ministry. The Catholic tradition on war and peace is a long and complex one; it stretches from the Sermon on the Mount to the statements of Pope John Paul II. We wish to explore and explain the resources of the moral-religious teaching and to apply it to specific questions of our day. . . .

WAR AND PEACE IN THE MODERN WORLD

. . . This must be the starting point of any further moral reflection: nuclear weapons particularly and nuclear warfare as it is planned today, raise new moral questions. No previously conceived moral position escapes the fundamental confrontation posed by contemporary nuclear strategy. Many have noted the similarity of the statements made by eminent scientists and Vatican II's observation that we are forced today "to undertake a completely fresh reappraisal of war." The task before us is not simply to repeat what we have said before; it is first to consider anew whether and how our religious-moral tradition can assess, direct, contain, and, we hope, help to eliminate the threat posed to the human family by the nuclear arsenals of the world. Pope John Paul II captured the essence of the problem during his pilgrimage to Hiroshima: "In the

Note: Footnotes in original have been deleted.

past it was possible to destroy a village, a town, a region, even a country. Now it is the whole planet that has come under threat." . . .

In a striking demonstration of his personal and pastoral concern for preventing nuclear war, Pope John Paul II commissioned a study by the Pontifical Academy of Sciences which reinforced the findings of other scientific bodies. The Holy Father had the study transmitted by personal representative to the leaders of the United States, the Soviet Union, the United Kingdom, and France, and to the president of the General Assembly of the United Nations. One of its conclusions is especially pertinent to the public debate in the United States:

> Recent talk about winning or even surviving a nuclear war must reflect a failure to appreciate a medical reality: Any nuclear war would inevitably cause death, disease and suffering of pandemonic proportions and without the possibility of effective medical intervention. That reality leads to the same conclusion physicians have reached for life-threatening epidemics throughout history. Prevention is essential for control.

This medical conclusion has a moral corollary. Traditionally, the Church's moral teaching sought first to prevent war and then to limit its consequences if it occurred. Today the possibilities for placing political and moral limits on nuclear war are so minimal that the moral task, like the medical, is prevention: as a people, we must refuse to legitimate the idea of nuclear war. Such a refusal will require not only new ideas and new vision, but what the gospel calls conversion of the heart. . . .

Though certain that the dangerous and delicate nuclear relationship the superpowers now maintain should not exist, we understand how it came to exist. In a world of sovereign states, devoid of central authority and possessing the knowledge to produce nuclear weapons, many choices were made, some clearly objectionable, others well-intended with mixed results, which brought the world to its present dangerous situation.

We see with increasing clarity the political folly of a system which threatens mutual suicide, the psychological damage this does to ordinary people, especially the young, the economic distortion of priorities—billions readily spent for destructive instruments while pitched battles are waged daily in our legislatures over much smaller amounts for the homeless, the hungry, and the helpless here and abroad. But it is much less clear how we translate a "no" to nuclear war into the personal and public choices which can move us in a new direction, toward a national policy and an international system which more adequately reflect the values and vision of the kingdom of God. . . .

Precisely because of the destructive nature of nuclear weapons, strategies have been developed which previous generations would have found unintelligible. Today military preparations are undertaken on a vast and sophisticated scale, but the declared purpose is not to use the weapons produced. Threats are made which would be suicidal to implement. The key to security is no longer only military secrets, for in some instances security may best be served by informing one's adversary publicly what weapons one has and what plans exist for their use. The presumption of the nation-state system, that sovereignty implies an ability to protect a nation's territory and population, is precisely the presumption denied by the nuclear capacities of both superpowers. In a sense each is at the mercy of the other's perception of what strategy is "rational," what kind of damage is "unacceptable," how "convincing" one side's threat is to the other.

The political paradox of deterrence has also strained our moral conception. May a nation threaten what it may never do? May it possess what it may never use? Who is involved in the threat each superpower makes: government officials? or military personnel? or the citizenry in whose defense the threat is made?

In brief, the danger of the situation is clear; but how to prevent the use of nuclear weapons, how to assess deterrence, and how to delineate moral responsibility in the nuclear age are less clearly seen or stated. Reflecting the complexity of the nuclear problem, our arguments in this pastoral must be detailed and nuanced; but our "no" to nuclear war must, in the end, be definitive and decisive. . . . The "new moment" which exists in the public debate about nuclear weapons provides a creative opportunity and a moral imperative to examine the relationship between public opinion and public policy. We believe it is necessary, for the sake of prevention, to build a barrier against the concept of nuclear war as a viable strategy for defense. There should be a clear public resistance to the rhetoric of "winnable" nuclear wars, or unrealistic expectations of "surviving" nuclear exchanges, and strategies of "protracted nuclear war." We oppose such rhetoric.

We seek to encourage a public attitude which sets stringent limits on the kind of actions our own government and other governments will take on nuclear policy. We believe religious leaders have a task in concert with public officials, analysts, private organizations, and the media to set the limits beyond which our military policy should not move in word or action. Charting a moral course in a complex public policy debate involves several steps. We will address [two] questions, offering our reflections on them as an invitation to a public moral dialogue: (1) the use of nuclear weapons; [and] (2) the policy of deterrence in principle and in practice. . . .

Establishing moral guidelines in the nuclear debate means addressing first the question of the use of nuclear weapons. That question has several dimensions.

It is clear that those in the Church who interpret the gospel teaching as forbidding all use of violence would oppose any use of nuclear weapons under any conditions. In a sense the existence of these weapons simply confirms and reinforces one of the initial insights of the nonviolent position, namely, that Christians should not use lethal force since the hope of using it selectively and restrictively is so often an illusion. Nuclear weapons seem to prove this point in a way heretofore unknown.

For the tradition which acknowledges some legitimate use of force, some important elements of contemporary nuclear strategies move beyond the limits of moral justification. A justifiable use of force must be both discriminatory and proportionate. Certain aspects of both U.S. and Soviet strategies fail both tests as we shall discuss below. The technical literature and the personal testimony of public officials who have been closely associated with U.S. nuclear strategy have both convinced us of the overwhelming probability that major nuclear exchange would have no limits.

On the more complicated issue of "limited" nuclear war, we are aware of the extensive literature and discussion which this topic has generated. As a general statement, it seems to us that public officials would be unable to refute the following conclusion of the study made by the Pontifical Academy of Sciences:

> Even a nuclear attack directed only at military facilities would be devastating to the country as a whole. This is because military facilities are widespread rather than concentrated at only a few points. Thus, many nuclear weapons would be exploded.
>
> Furthermore, the spread of radiation due to the natural winds and atmospheric mixing would kill vast numbers of people and contaminate large areas. The medical facilities of any nation would be inadequate to care for the survivors. An objective examination of the medical situation that would follow a nuclear war leads to but one conclusion: prevention is our only recourse.

. . . In light of these perspectives we address three questions more explicitly: (1) counter population warfare; (2) initiation of nuclear war; and (3) limited nuclear war.

COUNTER POPULATION WARFARE

Under no circumstances may nuclear weapons or other instruments of mass slaughter be used for the purpose of destroying population centers or other predominantly civilian targets. Popes have repeatedly condemned "total war" which implies such use. For example, as early as 1954 Pope Pius XII condemned nuclear warfare "when it entirely escapes the control of man," and results in "the pure and simple annihilation of all human life within the radius of action." The condemnation was repeated by the Second Vatican Council: "Any act of war aimed indiscriminately at the destruction of entire cities or of extensive areas along with their population is a crime against God and man itself. It merits unequivocal and unhesitating condemnation."

Retaliatory action whether nuclear or conventional which would indiscriminately take many wholly innocent lives, lives of people who are in no way responsible for reckless actions of their government, must also be condemned. This condemnation, in our judgment, applies even to the retaliatory use of weapons striking enemy cities after our own have already been struck. No Christian can rightfully carry out orders or policies deliberately aimed at killing non-combatants. . . .

THE INITIATION OF NUCLEAR WAR

We do not perceive any situation in which the deliberate initiation of nuclear warfare, on however restricted a scale, can be morally justified. Non-nuclear attacks by another state must be resisted by other than nuclear means. Therefore, a serious moral obligation exists to develop non-nuclear defensive strategies as rapidly as possible.

A serious debate is under way on this issue. It is cast in political terms, but it has a significant moral dimension. Some have argued that at the very beginning of a war nuclear weapons might be used, only against military targets, perhaps in limited numbers. Indeed it has long been American and NATO policy that nuclear weapons, especially so-called tactical nuclear weapons, would likely be used if NATO forces in Europe seemed in danger of losing a conflict that until then had been restricted to conventional weapons. Large numbers of tactical nuclear weapons are now deployed in Europe by the NATO forces and about as many by the Soviet Union. Some are substantially smaller than the bomb used on Hiroshima, some are larger. Such weapons, if employed in great numbers, would totally devastate the densely populated countries of Western and Central Europe.

Whether under conditions of war in Europe, parts of Asia or the Middle East, or the exchange of strategic weapons directly between the United States and the Soviet Union, the difficulties of limiting the use of nuclear weapons are immense. A number of expert witnesses advise us that commanders operating under conditions of battle probably would not be able to exercise strict control; the number of weapons used would rapidly increase, the targets would be expanded beyond the military, and the level of civilian casualties would rise enormously. No one can be certain that this escalation would not occur, even in the face of political efforts to keep such an exchange "limited." The chances of keeping use limited seem remote, and the consequences of escalation to mass destruction would be appalling. Former public officials have testified that it is improbable that any nuclear war could actually be kept limited. Their testimony and the consequences involved in this problem lead us to conclude that the danger of escalation is so great that it would be morally unjustifiable to initiate nuclear war in any form. The danger is rooted not only in the technology of our weapons systems but in the weakness and sinfulness of human communities. We find the moral responsibility of beginning nuclear war not justified by rational political objectives.

This judgment affirms that the willingness to initiate nuclear war entails a distinct, weighty moral responsibility; it involves transgressing a fragile barrier—political, psychological, and moral—which has been constructed since 1945. We express repeatedly in this letter our extreme skepticism about the prospects for controlling a nuclear exchange, however limited the first use might be. Precisely because of this skepticism, we judge resort to nuclear weapons to counter a conventional attack to be morally unjustifiable. Consequently we seek to reinforce the barrier against any use of nuclear weapons. Our support of a "no first use" policy must be seen in this light.

At the same time we recognize the responsibility the United States has had and continues to have in assisting allied nations in their defense against either a conventional or a nuclear attack. Especially in the European theater, the deterrence of a *nuclear* attack may require nuclear weapons for a time, even though their possession and deployment must be subject to rigid restrictions.

The need to defend against a conventional attack in Europe imposes the political and moral burden of developing adequate, alternative modes of defense to present reliance on nuclear weapons. Even with the best coordinated effort—hardly likely in view of contemporary political division on this question—development of an alternative defense position will still take time.

In the interim, deterrence against a conventional attack relies upon two factors: the not inconsiderable conventional forces at the disposal of NATO and the recognition by a potential attacker that the outbreak of large scale conventional war could escalate to the nuclear level through accident or miscalculation by either side. We are aware that NATO's refusal to adopt a "no first use" pledge is to some extent linked to the deterrent effect of this inherent ambiguity. Nonetheless, in light of the probable effects of initiating nuclear war, we urge NATO to move rapidly toward the adoption of a "no first use" policy, but doing so in tandem with development of an adequate alternative defense posture.

LIMITED NUCLEAR WAR

It would be possible to agree with our first two conclusions and still not be sure about retaliatory use of nuclear weapons in what is called a "limited exchange." The issue at stake is the *real* as opposed to the *theoretical* possibility of a "limited nuclear exchange."

We recognize that the policy debate on this question is inconclusive and that all participants are left with hypothetical projections about probable reactions in a nuclear exchange. While not trying to adjudicate the technical debate, we are aware of it and wish to raise a series of questions which challenge the actual meaning of "limited" in this discussion.

- Would leaders have sufficient information to know what is happening in a nuclear exchange?
- Would they be able under the conditions of stress, time pressures, and fragmentary information to make the extraordinarily precise decision needed to keep the exchange limited if this were technically possible?
- Would military commanders be able, in the midst of the destruction and confusion of a nuclear exchange, to maintain a policy of "discriminate targeting"? Can this be done in modern warfare, waged across great distances by aircraft and missiles?
- Given the accidents we know about in peacetime conditions, what assurances are there that computer errors could be avoided in the midst of a nuclear exchange?
- Would not the casualties, even in a war defined as limited by strategists, still run in the millions?
- How "limited" would be the long-term effects of radiation, famine, social fragmentation, and economic dislocation?

Unless these questions can be answered satisfactorily, we will continue to be highly skeptical about the real meaning of "limited." One of the criteria of the just-war tradition is a reasonable hope of success in bringing about justice and peace. We must ask whether such a reasonable hope can exist once nuclear weapons have been exchanged. The burden of proof remains on those who assert that meaningful limitation is possible.

A nuclear response to either conventional or nuclear attack can cause destruction which goes far beyond "legitimate defense." Such use of nuclear weapons would not be justified.

In the face of this frightening and highly speculative debate on a matter involving millions of human lives, we believe the most effective contribution or moral judgment is to introduce perspectives by which we can assess the empirical debate. Moral perspective should be sensitive not only to the quantitative dimensions of a question but to its psychological, human, and religious characteristics as well. The issue of limited war is not simply the size of weapons contemplated or the strategies projected. The debate should include the psychological and political significance of crossing the boundary from the conventional to the nuclear arena in any form. To cross this divide is to enter a world where we have no experience of control, much testimony against its possibility, and therefore no moral justification for submitting the human community to this risk. We therefore express our view that the first imperative is to prevent any use of nuclear weapons and our hope that leaders will resist the notion that nuclear conflict can be limited, contained, or won in any traditional sense.

The moral challenge posed by nuclear weapons is not exhausted by an analysis of their possible uses. Much of the political and moral debate of the nuclear age has concerned the strategy of deterrence. Deterrence is at the heart of the U.S.-Soviet relationship, currently the most dangerous dimension of the nuclear arms race.

THE CONCEPT AND DEVELOPMENT OF DETERRENCE POLICY

The concept of deterrence existed in military strategy long before the nuclear age, but it has taken on a new meaning and significance since 1945. Essentially, deterrence means "dissuasion of a potential adversary from initiating an attack or conflict, often by the threat of unacceptable retaliatory damage." In the nuclear age, deterrence has become the centerpiece of both U.S. and Soviet policy. Both superpowers have for many years now been able to promise a retaliatory response which can inflict "unacceptable damage." A situation of stable deterrence depends on the ability of each side to deploy its retaliatory forces in ways that are not vulnerable to an attack (i.e., protected against a "first strike"); preserving stability requires a willingness by both sides to refrain from deploying weapons which appear to have a first strike capability.

This general definition of deterrence does not explain either the elements of a deterrence strategy or the evolution of deterrence policy since 1945. A detailed description of either of these subjects would require an extensive essay, using materials which can be found in abundance in the technical literature on the subject of deterrence. Particularly significant is the relationship between "declaratory policy" (the public explanation of our strategic intentions and capabilities) and "action policy" (the actual planning and targeting policies to be followed in a nuclear attack).

The evolution of deterrence strategy has passed through several stages of declaratory policy. Using the U.S. case as an example, there is a significant difference between "massive retaliation" and "flexible response," and between "mutual assured destruction" and "countervailing strategy." It is also possible to distinguish between "counterforce" and "countervalue" targeting policies; and to contrast a posture of "minimum deterrence" with "extended deterrence." These terms are well known in the technical debate on nuclear policy; they are less well known and sometimes loosely used in the wider public debate. It is important to recognize that there has been substantial continuity in U.S. action policy in spite of real changes in declaratory policy.

The recognition of these different elements in the deterrent and the evolution of policy means that moral assessment of deterrence requires a series of distinct judgments. They include: an analysis of the factual character of the deterrent (e.g., what is involved in targeting doctrine); analysis of the historical development of the policy (e.g., whether changes have occurred which are significant for moral analysis of the policy); the relationship of deterrence policy and other aspects of U.S.-Soviet affairs; and determination of the key moral questions involved in deterrence policy.

THE MORAL ASSESSMENT OF DETERRENCE

The distinctively new dimensions of nuclear deterrence were recognized by policymakers and strategists only after much reflection. Similarly, the moral challenge posed by nuclear deterrence was grasped only after careful deliberation. The moral and political paradox posed by deterrence was concisely stated by Vatican II:

> Undoubtedly, armaments are not amassed merely for use in wartime. Since the defensive strength of any nation is thought to depend on its capacity for immediate retaliation, the stockpiling of arms which grows from year to year serves, in a way hitherto unthought of, as a deterrent to potential attackers. Many people look upon this as the most effective way known at the present time for maintaining some sort of peace among nations. Whatever one may think of this form of deterrent, people are convinced that the arms race, which quite a few countries have entered, is no infallible way of maintaining real peace and that the resulting so-called balance of power is no sure genuine path to achieving it. Rather than eliminate the causes of war, the arms race serves only to aggravate the position. As long as extravagant sums of money are poured into the development of new weapons, it is impossible to devote adequate aid in tackling the misery which prevails at the present day in the world. Instead of eradicating international conflict once and for all, the contagion is spreading to other parts of the world. New approaches, based on reformed attitudes, will have to be chosen in order to remove this stumbling

block, to free the earth from its pressing anxieties, and give back to the world a genuine peace.

Without making a specific moral judgment on deterrence, the council clearly designated the elements of the arms race: the tension between "peace of a sort" preserved by deterrence and "genuine peace" required for a stable international life; the contradiction between what is spent for destructive capacity and what is needed for constructive development.

In the post-conciliar assessment of war and peace, and specifically of deterrence, different parties to the political-moral debate within the Church and in civil society have focused on one aspect or another of the problem. For some, the fact that nuclear weapons have not been used since 1945 means that deterrence has worked, and this fact satisfies the demands of both the political and the moral order. Others contest this assessment by highlighting the risk of failure involved in continued reliance on deterrence and pointing out how politically and morally catastrophic even a single failure would be. Still others note that the absence of nuclear war is not necessarily proof that the policy of deterrence has prevented it. Indeed, some would find in the policy of deterrence the driving force in the superpower arms race. Still other observers, many of them Catholic moralists, have stressed that deterrence may not morally include the intention of deliberately attacking civilian populations or non-combatants. . . .

In June 1982, Pope John Paul II provided new impetus and insight to the moral analysis with his statement to the United Nations Second Special Session on Disarmament. The pope first situated the problem of deterrence within the context of world politics. No power, he observes, will admit to wishing to start a war, but each distrusts others and considers it necessary to mount a strong defense against attack. He then discusses the notion of deterrence:

> Many even think that such preparations constitute the way—even the only way—to safeguard peace in some fashion or at least to impede to the utmost in an efficacious way the outbreak of wars, especially major conflicts which might lead to the ultimate holocaust of humanity and the destruction of the civilization that man has constructed so laboriously over the centuries.
>
> In this approach one can see the "philosophy of peace" which was proclaimed in the ancient Roman principle: *Si vis pacem, para bellum.* Put in modern terms, this "philosophy" has the label of "deterrence" and one can find it in various guises of the search for a "balance of forces" which sometimes has been called, and not without reason, the "balance of terror."

Having offered this analysis of the general concept of deterrence, the Holy Father introduces his considerations on disarmament, especially, but not only, nuclear disarmament. Pope John Paul II makes this statement about the morality of deterrence:

In current conditions "deterrence" based on balance, certainly not as an end in itself but as a step on the way toward a progressive disarmament, may still be judged morally acceptable. Nonetheless in order to ensure peace, it is indispensable not to be satisfied with this minimum which is always susceptible to the real danger of explosion.

. . . The moral duty today is to prevent nuclear war from ever occurring *and* to protect and preserve those key values of justice, freedom and independence which are necessary for personal dignity and national integrity. In reference to these issues, Pope John Paul II judges that deterrence may still be judged morally acceptable, "certainly not as an end in itself but as a step on the way toward a progressive disarmament."

On more than one occasion the Holy Father has demonstrated his awareness of the fragility and complexity of the deterrence relationship among nations. Speaking to UNESCO in June 1980, he said: "Up to the present, we are told that nuclear arms are a force of dissuasion which have prevented the eruption of a major war. And that is probably true. Still, we must ask if it will always be this way."

In a more recent and more specific assessment Pope John Paul II told an international meeting of scientists on August 23, 1982: "You can more easily ascertain that the logic of nuclear deterrence cannot be considered a final goal or an appropriate and secure means for safeguarding international peace."

Relating Pope John Paul's general statements to the specific policies of the U.S. deterrent requires both judgments of fact and an application of moral principles. In preparing this letter we have tried, through a number of sources, to determine as precisely as possible the factual character of U.S. deterrence strategy. Two questions have particularly concerned us: (1) the targeting doctrine and strategic plans for the use of the deterrent, particularly their impact on civilian casualties; and (2) the relationship of deterrence strategy and nuclear war-fighting capability to the likelihood that war will in fact be prevented.

. . . Targeting doctrine raises significant moral questions because it is a significant determinant of what would occur if nuclear weapons were ever to be used. Although we acknowledge the need for deterrent, not all forms of deterrence are morally acceptable. There are moral limits to deterrence policy as well as to policy regarding use. Specifically, it is not morally acceptable to intend to kill the innocent as part of a strategy of deterring nuclear war. The question of whether U.S. policy involves an intention to strike civilian centers (directly targeting civilian populations) has been one of our factual concerns.

This complex question has always produced a variety of responses, official and unofficial in character. The NCCB Committee has received a series of statements of clarification of policy from U.S. government officials. Essentially these statements declare that it is not U.S. strategic policy to target the Soviet civilian population as such or to use nuclear weapons deliberately for the purpose of destroying population centers. These statements respond, in principle at least, to one moral criterion for assessing deterrence policy: the immunity of non-combatants from direct attack either by conventional or nuclear weapons.

These statements do not address or resolve another very troublesome moral problem, namely, that an attack on military targets or militarily significant industrial targets could involve "indirect" (i.e., unintended) but massive civilian casualties. We are advised, for example, that the United States strategic nuclear targeting plan (SIOP—Single Integrated Operational Plan) has identified 60 "military" targets within the city of Moscow alone, and that 40,000 "military" targets for nuclear weapons have been identified in the whole of the Soviet Union. It is important to recognize that Soviet policy is subject to the same moral judgment; attacks on several "industrial targets" or politically significant targets in the United States could produce massive civilian casualties. The number of civilians who would necessarily be killed by such strikes is horrendous. This problem is unavoidable because of the way modern military facilities and production centers are so thoroughly interspersed with civilian living and working areas. It is aggravated if one side deliberately positions military targets in the midst of a civilian population. In our consultations, administration officials readily admitted that, while they hoped any nuclear exchange could be kept limited, they were prepared to retaliate in a massive way if necessary. They also agreed that once any substantial numbers of weapons were used, the civilian casualty levels would quickly become truly catastrophic, and that even with attacks limited to "military" targets, the number of deaths in a substantial exchange would be almost indistinguishable from what might occur if civilian centers had been deliberately and directly struck. These possibilities pose a different moral question and are to be judged by a different moral criterion: the principle of proportionality.

While any judgment of proportionality is always open to differing evaluations, there are actions which can be decisively judged to be disproportionate. A narrow adherence exclusively to the principle of non-combatant immunity as a criterion for policy is an inadequate moral posture for it ignores some evil and unacceptable consequences. Hence, we cannot be satisfied that the assertion of an intention not to strike civilians directly, or even the most honest effort to implement that intention, by itself constitutes a "moral policy" for the use of nuclear weapons.

The location of industrial or militarily significant economic targets within heavily populated areas or in those areas affected by radioactive fallout could well involve such massive civilian casualties that, in our judgment, such a strike would be deemed morally disproportionate, even though not intentionally indiscriminate.

The problem is not simply one of producing highly accurate weapons that might minimize civilian casualties in any single explosion, but one of increasing the likelihood of escalation at a level where many, even "discriminating," weapons would cumulatively kill very large numbers of civilians. Those civilian deaths would occur both immediately and from the long-term effects of social and economic devastation.

A second issue of concern to us is the relationship of deterrence doctrine to war-fighting strategies. We are aware of the argument that war-fighting capabilities enhance the credibility of the deterrent, particularly the strategy of extended deterrence. But the development of such capabilities raises other strategic and moral questions. The relationship of war-fighting capabilities and targeting doctrine exemplifies the difficult choices in this area of policy. Targeting civilian populations would violate the principle of discrimination—one of the central moral principles of a Christian ethic of war. But "counterforce targeting," while preferable from the perspective of protecting civilians, is often joined with a declaratory policy which conveys the notion that nuclear war is subject to precise rational and moral limits. We have already expressed our severe doubts about such a concept. Furthermore, a purely counterforce strategy may seem to threaten the viability of other nations' retaliatory forces, making deterrence unstable in a crisis and war more likely.

While we welcome any effort to protect civilian populations, we do not want to legitimize or encourage moves which extend deterrence beyond the specific objective of preventing the use of nuclear weapons or other actions which could lead directly to a nuclear exchange.

These considerations of concrete elements of nuclear deterrence policy, made in light of John Paul II's evaluation, but applying it through our own prudential judgments, lead us to a strictly conditioned moral acceptance of nuclear deterrence. We cannot consider it adequate as a long-term basis for peace.

This strictly conditioned judgment yields criteria for morally assessing the elements of deterrence strategy. Clearly, these criteria demonstrate that we cannot approve of every weapons system, strategic doctrine, or policy initiative advanced in the name of strengthening deterrence. On the contrary, these criteria require continual public scrutiny of what our government proposes to do with the deterrent.

On the basis of these criteria we wish now to make some specific evaluations:

1. If nuclear deterrence exists only to prevent the *use* of nuclear weapons by others, then proposals to go beyond this to planning for prolonged periods of repeated nuclear strikes and counterstrikes, or "prevailing" in nuclear war, are not acceptable. They encourage notions that

nuclear war can be engaged in with tolerable human and moral consequences. Rather, we must continually say "no" to the idea of nuclear war.

2. If nuclear deterrence is our goal, "sufficiency" to deter is an adequate strategy; the quest for nuclear superiority must be rejected.

3. Nuclear deterrence should be used as a step on the way toward progressive disarmament. Each proposed addition to our strategic system or change in strategic doctrine must be assessed precisely in light of whether it will render steps toward "progressive disarmament" more or less likely.

Moreover, these criteria provide us with the means to make some judgments and recommendations about the present direction of U.S. strategic policy. Progress toward a world freed of dependence on nuclear deterrence must be carefully carried out. But it must not be delayed. There is an urgent moral and political responsibility to use the "peace of a sort" we have as a framework to move toward authentic peace through nuclear arms control, reductions, and disarmament. Of primary importance in this process is the need to prevent the development and deployment of destabilizing weapons systems on either side; a second requirement is to insure that the more sophisticated command and control systems do not become mere hair triggers for automatic launch on warning; a third is the need to prevent the proliferation of nuclear weapons in the international system.

In light of these general judgments *we oppose* some specific proposals in respect to our present deterrence posture:

1. The addition of weapons which are likely to be vulnerable to attack, yet also possess a "prompt hard-target kill" capability that threatens to make the other side's retaliatory forces vulnerable. (Several experts in strategic theory would place both the MX missile and Pershing II missiles in this category.) Such weapons may seem to be useful primarily in a first strike; we resist such weapons for this reason and we oppose Soviet deployment of such weapons which generate fear of a first strike against U.S. forces.

2. The willingness to foster strategic planning which seeks a nuclear war-fighting capability that goes beyond the limited function of deterrence outlined in this letter.

3. Proposals which have the effect of lowering the nuclear threshold and blurring the difference between nuclear and conventional weapons. . . .

. . . [T]here must be no misunderstanding of our profound skepticism about the moral acceptability of any use of nuclear weapons. It is obvious that the use of any weapons which violate the principle of discrimination merits unequivocal condemnation. We are told that some weapons are designed for purely "counterforce" use against military forces and targets. The moral issue, however, is not resolved by the design of weapons or the planned intention for use; there are also consequences which must be assessed. It would be a perverted political policy or moral casuistry which tried to justify using a weapon which "indirectly" or "unintentionally" killed a million innocent people because they happened to live near a "militarily significant target."

Even the "indirect effects" of initiating nuclear war are sufficient to make it an unjustifiable moral risk in any form. It is not sufficient, for example, to contend that "our" side has plans for "limited" or "discriminate" use. Modern warfare is not readily contained by good intentions or technological designs. The psychological climate of the world is such that mention of the term "nuclear" generates uneasiness. Many contend that the use of one tactical nuclear weapon could produce panic, with completely unpredictable consequences. It is precisely this mix of political, psychological, and technological uncertainty which has moved us in this letter to reinforce with moral prohibitions and prescriptions the prevailing political barrier against resort to nuclear weapons. Our support for enhanced command and control facilities, for major reductions in strategic and tactical nuclear forces, and for a "no first use" policy (as set forth in this letter) is meant to be seen as a complement to our desire to draw a moral line against nuclear war.

Any claim by any government that is pursuing a morally acceptable policy of deterrence must be scrutinized with the greatest care. We are prepared and eager to participate in our country in the ongoing public debate on moral grounds.

The need to rethink the deterrence policy of our nation, to make the revisions necessary to reduce the possibility of nuclear war, and to move toward a more stable system of national and international security will demand a substantial intellectual, political, and moral effort. It also will require, we believe, the willingness to open ourselves to the providential care, power and word of God, which call us to recognize our common humanity and the bonds of mutual responsibility which exist in the international community in spite of political differences and nuclear arsenals. . . .

4 BISHOPS, STATESMEN, AND OTHER STRATEGISTS ON THE BOMBING OF INNOCENTS

Albert Wohlstetter

Must the West threaten to bomb innocent bystanders in order to deter nuclear war? Does the West itself need to be threatened with annihilation of its civil society in order to be deterred? President Reagan's speech of March 23 [1983] proposing a decades-long research program to protect civilians against ballistic-missile attack revived these questions. The instant hoots of ridicule and references to *Star Wars* from many Senators and Congressmen suggest that holding out the nightmare vision of last things, the apocalypse, is now part of the nature of things; that the need to threaten the end of the earth must dominate earthly policy.

In fact, the West has for years used apocalyptic threats as a substitute for improving our capacity for discriminate response and in particular for a conventional reply to conventional attack. (The media hardly noticed the more immediate technical effort urged in the President's speech—to improve conventional technology.) Reckless nuclear threats and the intimidating growth of both Soviet conventional and nuclear strength have had much to do with the rise of the anti-nuclear movement here and in Protestant Northern Europe. By revising many times in public their pastoral letter on war and peace, American Catholic bishops have dramatized the moral issues which statesmen, using empty threats to end the world, neglect or evade. For the bishops stand in a long moral tradition which condemns the threat to destroy innocents as well as their actual destruction. They try but do not escape reliance on threatening bystanders. Ironically, the view dominating all their revisions reflects an evasive secular extreme which, instead of speeding improvements in the ability to avoid bystanders, has tried to halt or curb them. But because the bishops must take threats seriously, they make more visible the essential evasions of Western statesmen. That, however, is a kind of virtue. The letter offers a unique opportunity to examine the moral, political, and military issues together, and to show that, as the President suggests, threatening to bomb innocents is not part of the nature of things. Nor has it been, as is now widely claimed, an essential of deterrence from the beginning. Nor is it the inevitable result of "modern technology." It may be that our Senators and even some of our younger Congressmen haven't watched *Star Wars* closely enough.

The bishops have been sending a message to strategists in Western foreign-policy establishments—and to strategists in Western anti-nuclear counter-establishments. It seems unequivocal: "Under no circumstances may nuclear weapons or other instruments of mass slaughter be used for the purpose of destroying population centers or other predominantly civilian targets." Though that only restates an exemplary part of Vatican II two decades earlier, it is far from commonplace. Nonetheless it should be obvious to Catholics and non-Catholics alike. Informed realists in foreign-policy establishments as well as pacifists should oppose aiming to kill bystanders with nuclear or conventional weapons: indiscriminate Western threats paralyze the West, not the East. We have urgent political and military as well as moral grounds for improving our ability to answer an attack on Western military forces with less unintended killing, not to mention deliberate mass slaughter.

The bishops *seem* to be countering the perverse dogma which, after the Cuban missile crisis, came increasingly to be used by Western statesmen eager to spend less on defense: that the West should rely for deterring the Soviets on the ability to answer a nuclear military attack by assuring the deliberate destruction of tens or even hundreds of millions of Soviet civilians; and that the United States should also, for the supposed sake of "stability," give up any defense of its own civilians and any attack on military targets in order to assure the Soviets that they could, in response, destroy a comparable number of American civilians. The long humanist as well as the religious tradition on "just war" stresses especially the need to avoid attacks on "open," that is undefended, cities. The new doctrine exactly reversed this; it called both for leaving cities undefended and threatening to annihilate them. John Newhouse succinctly stated this dogma, to which he was sympathetic, in the "frosty apothegm": "Offense is defense, defense is offense. Killing people is good, killing weapons is bad." The late Donald Brennan, a long-term advocate of arms control to defend people and restrain offense from killing innocents, was not sympathetic. He noted that the acronym for Mutual Assured Destruction—MAD—described that Orwellian dogma.

Having observed long ago that not even Genghis Khan avoided combatants in order to focus solely on destroying noncombatants, I was grateful, on a first look at this issue in the evolving pastoral letter, to find the bishops on the side of the angels. Unfortunately, a closer reading suggested that they were also on the other side. For, while they sometimes say that we should not threaten to destroy civilians, they say too that we may continue to maintain nuclear weapons—and so implicitly threaten their use as a deterrent—while moving toward permanent verifiable nuclear and general disarmament; *yet we may not meanwhile plan to be able to fight a nuclear war even in response to a nuclear attack.*

Before that distant millennial day when all the world disarms totally, verifiably, and irrevocably—at least in nuclear weapons—if we should not intend to attack noncombatants, as the letter says, what alternative is there to deter nuclear attack or coercion? Plainly only to be able to aim at the combatants attacking us, or at their equipment, facilities, or direct sources of combat supply. That, however, is what is meant by planning to be able to fight a nuclear war—which the letter rejects.

Perhaps the bishops can work this out in later statements. But a close reading of their changing text, their congressional testimony, and the writings of their associates suggests that this is unlikely. For their struggle with conscience has led them to make only more explicit the widespread confusions and evasions of many secular strategists—including many statesmen, scientists, Senators, editors, and business leaders. Take John Cardinal Krol and Father Brian Hehir, who was staff adviser to the ad-hoc committee drafting the pastoral letter. Cardinal Krol repeated in a sermon at the White House in 1979 what he and his associates had been saying in recent years: in brief, "possession, yes, for deterrence . . . but use, never." It is all right for the United States implicitly to threaten the use of nuclear weapons, but "at the point of such decisions, . . . political and military authorities are responsible to a higher set of values" and so "must reject the actual use of such weapons, whatever the consequences." Any consequence "whatever" includes giving up military resistance. But "the history of certain countries under Communist rule today shows that not only are human means of resistance available and effective but also that human life does not lose all meaning with replacement of one political system by another."

Father Hehir elaborates this view: (A) We should not get or keep an ability to attack combatants. (B) We may maintain an ability to attack noncombatants while waiting for nuclear disarmament, and (C) We may use that ability implicitly (though not explicitly) to threaten retaliation against noncombatants. (D) Indeed, to deter nuclear attack, we must *convince* other nations that our "determination to use nuclear weapons is beyond question." (E) We should never intend to use nuclear weapons. (F) Nor (to make the deception harder) *declare* an intent to use them even in reply to a nuclear attack. (G) We should never actually use them; that is to say, we shouldn't retaliate at all.

Precisely how this volubly revealed deception is to fool allies and adversaries "beyond question" has not itself been revealed. (Future sermons at the White House might have to be classified.) If the bishops could transmit that revelation, it would fortify a good many strategists in our foreign-affairs establishment who want fervently to believe that we can safely deter an adversary solely by threatening the nuclear extermination of his cities while making clear to the entire world that we would never use nuclear weapons at all; and who also want firmly to believe we needn't spend much money on a less reckless defense. In sending that message to Western elites the letter only relays, amplifies, and broadcasts signals our elites have themselves been sending for years. The troubling obscurity of the letter reflects that establishment ambivalence and incoherence. On many matters of technical military and political fact the bishops derive their views not from sacred authority but from a more doubtful range of secular strategists than they realize. Much of the letter, for example, stems from the strategists who hold that defense is offense and that killing people is good and killing weapons bad—the very strategists who would rely exclusively on threatening to destroy cities.

In invoking divine authority to sustain such lay strategies, the bishops' power seems dangerous to many Catholics who disagree. But their moral prestige alone gives weight to the bishops' strategic views with non-Catholics and Catholics. They reinforce the impassioned pacifist and neutralist movements that have been growing in Europe and in the United States, as well as the establishment strategies which helped to generate these protest movements.

For the bishops pass lightly over or further confound many already muddled and controversial questions of fact and policy. In a world where so many intense, deep, and sometimes mutually reinforcing antagonisms divide regional as well as superpowers, are there serious early prospects for negotiating the complete, verifiable, and permanent elimination of nuclear or conventional arms? If antagonists don't agree, should we disarm unilaterally? If we keep nuclear arms, how should we use them to deter their use against us or an ally? Might an adversary in some plausible circumstance make a nuclear attack on an element (perhaps a key non-nuclear element) of our military power or that of an ally to whom we have issued a nuclear guarantee? Might such an enemy nuclear attack (for example, one generated in the course of allied conventional resistance to a conventional invasion of NATO's center or of a critical country on NATO's northern or southern flank) have decisive military effects yet restrict side effects enough to leave us, and possibly our ally, a very large stake in avoiding "mutual mass slaughter"? Could some selective but militarily useful Western response to such a restricted nuclear attack destroy substantially fewer innocent bystanders than a direct attack on population centers? Would any discriminate Western response to a restricted nuclear attack—even one in an isolated area on a flank—inevitably (or more likely than not, or just possibly, or with some intermediate probability) lead to the destruction of humanity, or "something little better"? Or at least to an unprecedented catastrophe? Would it be less or more likely than an attack on population to lead to unrestricted attacks on populations? Can we deter a restricted nuclear attack better by threatening an "unlimited," frankly suicidal, and therefore improbable attack on the aggressor's cities, or by a limited but much more probable response suited to the circumstance?

The bishops' authorities slip by or confuse almost all these questions. The bishops sometimes seem only to be saying that the extent of direct collateral harm done by a particular restricted attack is uncertain, quite apart from the possibilities of "escalation." At other times they are certain that restricted attacks will lead to an entirely unrestricted war. And they then suggest that the chance is "so infinitesimal" that any Western nuclear response to a restricted attack would end short of ending humanity itself, that we might better threaten directly to bring on the apocalypse. The bishops cite experts as authority for their judgment that any use whatever of nuclear weapons would with an overwhelming probability lead to unlimited destruction. And some of their experts do seem to say just that. But some they cite appear only to say that we cannot be quite sure (that is, the probability is not equal to one) that any use of nuclear weapons would stay limited. If any response other than our surrender is to be believed, it makes a difference whether we talk of a probability that is not quite zero or a probability that is not quite equal to one that any nuclear response would bring on a suicidally total disaster. Yet two successive paragraphs in the 1982 *Foreign Affairs* article by McGeorge Bundy, George F. Kennan, Robert S. McNamara, and Gerard Smith proposing "no first use" of nuclear weapons, which the bishops cite, assert each of a wide range of such differing possibilities without distinction. Most authorities relied on by the bishops are themselves not very discriminating about which point they are trying to make.

Some important components of conventional military power vulnerable to nuclear attack are close to population centers. Others, however, may be very far from them—for example, naval forces at sea; or satellites in orbit hundreds or even a hundred thousand miles above the earth, that may be expected to perform the essential tasks during a conventional war of reconnaissance, surveillance, navigation, guidance, and communications. These are more vulnerable to nuclear than conventional attack. If we have no way of discouraging a limited nuclear attack except by extracting a promise from an adversary that he will not attack, or by threatening that we will respond to such isolated attacks with a suicidal retaliation on his cities, an adversary might, in the course of a conventional war, chance a small but effective nuclear attack against such isolated military targets. Such an attack would do incomparably less damage to civilians in the West than any of the "limited" attacks discussed by the bishops' authorities. Is it really so evident that a similarly restricted Western nuclear response to such a nuclear attack would be nearly certain to escalate to the end of humanity? Wouldn't a restricted response doing minimal damage to civilians on either side be much less likely to escalate than an attack on cities? And wouldn't the ability to respond in a proportionate way be a better deterrent to an adversary's crossing the gap between nuclear and conventional weapons? The bishops' lay experts tend to see the Soviets as mirror images of themselves, but sometimes diabolize them. They argue as if the Soviets would not continue during a war to have the strongest possible incentives to keep escalation within bounds; and as if the Soviets would love every killing of a Western bystander exactly as much as the West values his survival; as if the Soviet interest were in annihilating rather than dominating Western society.

In fact, calculations cited by the bishops' authorities hardly probe the issue as to whether an adversary might use nuclear weapons that would destroy key components of a military force discriminately, leaving us a very large stake in making either a discriminate response or no response at all. The calculations published in 1979 by the Office of Technology Assessment (OTA), in answer to an inquiry by supporters of MAD on the Senate Foreign Relations Committee, deal with hypothetical "small" and supposedly "limited" attacks. However, OTA's "limitations" were not seriously designed to test the feasibility, now or in the future, of destroying military targets and *not* population. One of their "limited" cases involves direct attacks on the populations of Detroit and Leningrad. And OTA's most "limited" Soviet attack directed 100 one-megaton nuclear warheads at oil refineries, including some inside Philadelphia and Los Angeles, in order "to inflict as much economic damage as possible" and "without any effort to maximize or *minimize* human casualties" (emphasis added). No one should be surprised that such a "limited" attack might kill about 5 million bystanders; or that a similar attack on Soviet oil refineries might kill 840,000—a result which the influential English military historian, Michael Howard, describes as "little better" than "a genocidal pact" killing up to 160 million in each country and leaving the rest "to envy the dead."

The bishops rely heavily on a three-and-a-half page study embodying the views of fourteen scientists who seem mainly to be specialists in public health. The Papal Academy of Sciences convened this group from several countries, including the Soviet Union, "to examine the consequences of the use of nuclear weapons on the survival and the health of humanity." Like the Physicians for Social Responsibility in this country, the group considers (except for one paragraph) only the effects of intentionally bombing cities. It says that the consequences of such an attack on the survival and health of humanity "appear obvious." Indeed they have always been. That is the principal reason to reject MAD and avoid threatening cities.

The papal study devotes one paragraph to "a nuclear attack directed only at military facilities." Like the pastoral letter, that paragraph assumes that any nuclear attack by an aggressor anywhere or any response by his victim would be directed at *all* the adversary's military facilities, however minor or irrelevant to the immediate outcome of the conflict that generated the use of nuclear weapons. It also assumes there would be no attempt to explode the weapons at altitudes that avoided fallout and no attempt in any other way to confine destruction to targets critical to the conflict's outcome.

But such analyses dodge all the serious issues as to whether an adversary might, in the course of a conventional war, use some nuclear weapons with substantial military effect and yet deliberately leave us and our allies with very strong incentives to avoid mutual mass slaughter; and as to whether we should have no response to such an attack except bringing on the mass slaughter or surrendering; and no better way of deterring it than promising one or the other or even, like the bishops' strategists, *both* of these two incompatible bad alternatives.

Yet the problem of deterring nuclear coercion or attack on an ally will persist. Despite lip-service at Geneva and the United Nations, hardly anyone seriously expects that each and every one of the six or seven or eight nations that have made nuclear explosives will destroy all their nuclear arms irretrievably and verifiably in a future near enough to govern our present actions. (The uncertainty as to the number of *present* nuclear powers suggests some of the difficulty we would have in getting actionable evidence that all of the existing nuclear powers had destroyed all of their weapons.) Nor are all prospective nuclear powers likely or even able to surrender the possibility of making the bomb. Moreover, the harm that these weapons can do is so great that merely reducing them to the numbers talked of by "minimum deterrers," who would use the remainder to threaten the mass slaughter of populations, would not remove and might increase the probability of an enormous catastrophe. And it would not prevent the potent use of threats of mass slaughter for coercing those who have disarmed. Pope John Paul II has observed that "a totally and permanently peaceful human society is unfortunately a utopia"; and that "pacifist declarations" frequently cloak plans for "aggression, domination, and manipulation of others" and could "lead straight to the false peace of totalitarian regimes." (The Pope has known that false peace personally.)

It has been obvious since the 1950's that the West needs to: rely less on threats of nuclear destruction and much more on improving conventional defenses; discourage the spread of nuclear weapons; and continue making nuclear weapons less vulnerable to attack, safer from "accidental" detonation, and more secure against seizure and unauthorized or mistaken use. The Soviet Union has its own reasons, as have we, for undertaking such measures unilaterally, with or without formal agreements or even "understandings." Formal agreements on these matters, in fact, have frequently defeated their overt purpose. Agreements, for example, that were supposed to encourage exclusively peaceful uses and research on nuclear energy have spread plutonium usable in explosives. The bishops call for "strengthening command and control over nuclear weapons" to make them more secure against unauthorized or inadvertent use, but call more strongly for agreement on a freeze—which would halt all current programs to replace aging nuclear weapons with ones that are not only more secure against seizure but safer against accidents, more discriminate, and less susceptible to attack.

What is more, the West has many excellent reasons for reducing the numbers and destructiveness of its nuclear weapons quite apart from any agreement. The indiscriminate destructiveness of the American stockpile (as measured in numbers of megatons) was four times higher in 1960 than in 1980. The number of weapons was one-third higher in 1967. The persistent failure of the bishops and other strategists who make a fetish of bilateral agreements to observe the unilateral decline in destructiveness and numbers in American nuclear stockpiles shows, at the very least, a certain lack of seriousness. In any case, if a freeze doesn't stop it from doing so, the U.S. can reduce further and drastically the numbers and destructiveness of its nuclear stockpile by exploiting the improved accuracies possible today. Improved accuracies make feasible greater discrimination as well as effectiveness in the use of nuclear weapons, and they also make possible more extensive replacement of nuclear with conventional weapons.

My own research and that of others has for many years pointed to the need for a much higher priority on improving our ability to hit what we aim at and only what we aim at. That would mean, in particular, that effective conventional weapons could drastically reduce the West's reliance on nuclear force. Moreover, for years now, the thrust of technology, as in the electronics revolution, has been to improve the possibilities of discrimination and control. It can increasingly provide us with just such intelligent choices between using conventional or nuclear weapons, and between killing innocent bystanders with nuclear weapons or attacking means of aggression and domination.

The danger of Soviet aggression is more likely to be lessened by a Western ability to threaten the military means of domination than by a Western ability to threaten bystanders. First, the Soviets value their military power, on the evidence, more than the lives of bystanders. Second, Western nonsuicidal threats against legitimate military targets are more credible than threats to bring about the destruction of civil society on both sides. The latter have a negligible likelihood of being carried out by Western leaders, and therefore cannot be relied on to dissuade Soviet

intimidation or aggression. Finally, it is even more absurd and dangerous to suppose that the only way to dissuade the U.S. from unleashing
aggression is to help the Soviets threaten our civilians by leaving them
defenseless and by leaving us no choices other than capitulation or an
uncontrollably destructive offense against Soviet cities that would invite
the reciprocal destruction of our own civil society.

Only some widely prevalent but shallow evasions and self-befuddle-
ments, and not any deep moral dilemma or basic paradox, force us to
threaten the annihilation of civilians in order to prevent nuclear or conventional war. The bishops are clear about rejecting the actual use of
nuclear weapons to kill innocents. About *threats* to kill innocents, they
are much less clear. Their obscurity mirrors an uneasy area of darkness
at the core of establishment views.

Precisely because the bishops' views do not come from on high but
are shared by many in the establishment, and also in the anti-nuclear
and pacifist movements that shake the establishment, it is worth looking
at their arguments on the morality of nuclear deterrence in the context
of changing defense policies. Anti-nuclear arguments proceed from
premises about the inevitable dependence of deterrence on threats deliberately or uncontrollably to kill innocents. To some degree, bluffs
about bringing on the nuclear apocalypse helped generate the rise of
the unilateral nuclear disarmers; and continuing reliance on such bluffs
helps to disarm the establishment from answering the unilateral disarmers. The arguments of both undermine deterrence.

Many recent accounts of defense policy in the nuclear age rewrite
history to lend an aura of inevitability to the extreme view that we can
reliably deter a nuclear attack in any plausible circumstance solely by
threats to kill innocents on both sides, threats which we plainly should
never and would never carry out. Advocates of that dangerous self-
paralyzing bluff claim that this extreme has been the essential base of
Western defense policy since Hiroshima. It wasn't at the beginning. Nor
was it the meaning of the second-strike theory of deterrence that originated near the start of the 1950's. The second-strike theory did not hold
that we had to choose between deterring and being ready and willing
to fight if deterrence failed. Americans who oppose unilateral disarmament have never split into a "party of deterrence" as distinct from
a "war party" that prefers fighting to deterring a nuclear war. Advocates
of MAD suggest as much. But MAD was not declaratory policy before
the mid-1960's. And it has never been operational policy. Yet many
liberal and conservative critics of the bishops, like the bishops themselves, are under the impression that it always has been. Many believe
that MAD has kept the nuclear peace and is therefore necessary, at least
as myth. But the evolution of doctrines and policies of deterrence needs

to be seen in relation to the changing technologies of discriminateness and control as well as the technologies of nuclear brute force. . . .

[Wohlstetter reviews the development and evolution of American strategic doctrine and policy, a review that challenges the version and interpretation depicted by the pastoral letter and others. He also discusses the problems of having deterrence rest on a targeting policy of massive destruction, analyzes the second-strike theory, and assesses the strategic consequences of the now greater precision of weapons delivery systems. The last ends with the conclusion that improvements in guidance capability render conventional warfare feasible without undue risk of collateral damage to innocent noncombatants—*eds.* This, Wohlstetter contends] . . . would permit a conventional weapon to replace nuclear bombs in a wide variety of missions with an essentially equal probability of destroying a fixed military target. It would drastically raise the threshold beyond which one would have to resort to nuclear weapons in order to be effective. It would mean a much smaller likelihood of "escalation" and incomparably smaller side effects.

Destroying ground targets that might decide a conventional conflict could have much more troubling side effects even in relatively isolated areas than the destruction of equally decisive naval forces at sea or key satellites deep in space. Yet the situation has altered greatly here too. Most such land targets are less blast-resistant than ICBM silos. Yet attacking them effectively with the huge inaccuracies expected in the late 1950's would have meant filling an enormous area of uncertainty with destruction. That might typically have subjected an area of 1000 square miles or so to unintended lethal effects. By contrast, a current cruise missile, with midcourse guidance and a small nuclear warhead, could be equally effective against a military target while confining lethal damage to less than one square mile. Most important, improved terminal guidance in the next few years could enable a cruise missile with a suitable *non*-nuclear warhead to destroy a military target and reduce the area of fatal collateral damage to about one-thousandth of a square mile—an enormous contrast with World War II.

Some conservative critics counter the bishops' strictures against a nuclear response to conventional attack by suggesting that any "conventional war in Western Europe would almost certainly mean terror and destruction far in excess of World War II"—with perhaps 100 million dead; that, in short, any conventional conflict in Europe would bring on horrors hardly less terrible than nuclear war. Such expectations lead many Europeans to feel that even a conventional war would destroy Europe and end Western civilization. For the bishops, a policy of No-First-Use follows from the broader nuclear policy of "Use, Never." And both are only part of Cardinal Krol's injunction in his White House sermon against all war. ("No more war, war never again.") Through all the political compromises in various drafts, the bishops support conventional alternatives only grudgingly. But estimates of conventional damage by the bishops' critics have even less basis in evidence than those the bishops cite to show that nuclear damage would be unlimited. It is plain that the increasing advances in precision and control can be most fully exploited by suitably designed conventional weapons.

It is essential to emphasize that advances in our ability to reduce collateral damage and increase the effectiveness of conventional weapons do not blur the distinction between nuclear and conventional force. On the contrary, that remains vital. But these revolutionary changes make it much more feasible to avoid crossing the divide between nuclear and conventional weapons. They give us choices.

Discussions of the morality of bombing and deterrence today often proceed as if "the technical realities" foreclose choice (as one eminent physicist, Wolfgang Panofsky, suggests), as if "the mutual hostage relation" were not at all a "consequence of policy and therefore . . . subject to change," but a matter of physics—permanently determined by the technology for releasing nuclear energy. Yet the evolution since the 1950's of technologies other than the release of nuclear energy has altered the possibilities of discrimination and will not excuse us from the responsibility for preparing to keep violence from mounting without bounds. . . .

[Wohlstetter next describes the historical evolution of strategic thinking in the United States, from the end of the 1950s through the Kennedy administration. He discusses the relationships between terror and technology and deterrence and counterforce doctrines in the context of the "just war" theory. Then he continues with an evaluation of the shifting foundation of strategic doctrine, as follows—eds.]

One difficulty in getting the evolution straight of both official doctrines and operational policies on nuclear weapons is that the two have often diverged, and the statements of doctrine have often been designed for political combat within domestic bureaucracies rather than potential combat with the Soviets. McNamara in his first two years as Secretary of Defense sought options between suicide and surrender, according to Stewart Alsop, "as Parsifal sought the Grail." Out of office, he has ended ironically by foreclosing all such options. With an intensity that dims his memory as well as his understanding, he doubts that any nuclear response to nuclear attack can limit destruction.

After the missile crisis, McNamara often talked of Assured Destruction—and later Mutual Assured Destruction—as if they were serious operational policies. Neither was. While Secretary, he never abandoned the goal of using strategic forces against Soviet military forces or the goal of limiting harm to American civilians. Even as declaratory doctrine he never stated MAD in the unqualified and brutal Orwellian form of the aphorism "killing weapons is bad, killing people is good." When he talked about a capability for assured destruction of 20–25 percent of the Soviet population, he was thinking of deterring the Joint Chiefs of Staff from asking for higher budgets rather than the Soviets from attacking the U.S. It was his way, if not the best way, of winning a budget battle and putting a lower ceiling on the size of our strategic forces. He stressed that we would have the capability for destroying the Soviet population—and he expected that capacity to deter the Soviets; but if deterrence failed, we would use our strategic forces to destroy Soviet forces attacking the United States. Later, when he drifted toward regarding it as desirable for the Soviets to deter us, he was still talking about capabilities.

In short, the form of MAD doctrine he introduced can best be described by the acronym MADCAP rather than MAD. McNamara said we would use a MAD *capability* for deterrence without seriously intending to assure the destruction of enemy noncombatants. Nor was he entirely serious about attacks on combatants. MADCAP did not lead to any persistent thought about how to improve the force to make it increasingly discriminating, and it discouraged thinking about the selection of various theater and other military targets suited to proportionate responses. It led to slowing or stopping various programs that would have increased our ability to discriminate between military and civilian targets. It made us less serious about the problems of nuclear targeting of combatants *or* noncombatants: it avoided some of the obloquy of *seriously* threatening to do the cheap and easy job of killing large "soft" concentrations of civilians without forcing thought about the harder job of carefully selecting and, if necessary, destroying military targets without killing bystanders; or about the hard but feasible and necessary job of keeping violence under control.

The bishops, their defenders, and the strategists on whom they rely all talk of the uncontrollability of nuclear weapons as a deplorable but unavoidable fact of life. However, they make a virtue of this supposed necessity. John Garvey, columnist for the Catholic *Commonweal*, knows that one may not threaten what one does not intend to do, and grants that "if your enemy knows that you will absolutely refuse to use a weapon, what you have is no longer a weapon and is therefore useless"; but he claims that "it would be naive to think that we are so fully in control of ourselves that in the event of an attack we would not say, 'What the hell,' and hit them with everything we've got." Which apparently would give the threat, however immoral, some use as a deterrent.

However, it would be naive or worse to suppose that we cannot impose controls over both initial and subsequent uses of nuclear weapons. "Permissive action links," which we place on all our weapons overseas

and which microchips and other electronic advances are constantly improving, can make it essentially infeasible for military commanders to
use nuclear weapons without release by a remote political authority.
Moreover, if we really thought political authority were reckless, we
could make this release mechanism as elaborate as we liked and even
divide the releasing codes so that they would require the agreement of
many parties. But the processes of consultation in the Alliance are now
complex, and would affect not only the initial, but also subsequent re-
leases. It is most unlikely that we would simply say "Whee!" and let
everything go. In Europe the problem is quite the opposite. We should
not and do not rely on the threat of losing control to deter either nuclear
or conventional attack. But MAD and the fictions of uncontrollability it
has propagated encourage us to rely on the threat of losing control as
a substitute for dealing with the dangers of conventional conflicts. In
short, they have led us to be less serious about conventional war as well.

The bishops' strategists, who believe that one can deter even if one is
plainly committed never to use nuclear weapons, first, second, or ever,
would maintain a capability but never use nuclear weapons at all.
McNamara, when he changed from the doctrine of his first two years
to talk of capabilities for mutual assured destruction, said he would
maintain the capability to kill Russian civilians but would actually use
nuclear weapons against certain military targets. That's rather different.
Nonetheless it was a long step on the way to the present absurdities
and evasions of the moral and prudential problems of discouraging a
nuclear attack on the U.S. or one of its allies. Or a conventional attack.

Michael Walzer writes perceptively about the use of terror by guerrillas
to provoke counterterror against innocents. But when it comes to nuclear
weapons, he accepts the MAD stereotype about the use of threats of terror
against innocents to deter attack. He doesn't question the technical de-
terminism of the nuclear technologists that limiting harm to civilians on
either side is impossible. He advances comfortably the familiar paradox
about "the monstrous immorality that our policy contemplates" but
thinks it inevitable. "The unavoidable truth is that all of these policies
rest ultimately on immoral threats." Like [Robert W.] Tucker, Walzer is
unwilling to give up immoral threats because he thinks they are necessary for deterrence. Here he rests on the baseless judgment that the
only thing that will deter Soviet aggression is the prospect that Russian
bystanders will be killed.

To reject that view one need not assume that Soviet values are the
same as our own; nor that the Soviets are simply monsters who don't
care or even like to see civilians killed. We need only observe that the
Soviets value military power and the means of domination at least as
much and possibly more than the lives of Russian civilians. This is surely
evidenced by a long history documented by careful scholars like Adam

Ulam, Robert Conquest, Nikolai Tolstoy, and many others, in which the Soviets have sacrificed civilian lives for the sake of Soviet power. Their collectivization program in the 1920's gained control over the peasants at the expense of slaughtering some 12–15 million of them. (Stalin told Churchill that the great bulk of 10 million kulaks had to be wiped out or transferred to Siberia.) The Soviet government sharply increased grain exports during the famine year of 1933, when 5 million Ukrainian peasants were dying. If Robert Conquest is right, the Great Purge of the late 1930's killed several million more Soviet citizens. If Nikolai Tolstoy is right, Stalin and the NKVD were responsible for more than half of the 20–30 million deaths suffered by the Soviets during World War II. Soviet refusal to abide by the Geneva Convention on Prisoners of War doomed many additional Soviet as well as German prisoners.

Whatever else one may say of these actions, they do not suggest that Soviet leaders value the life of Russian citizens above political and military power. If the West responded to Soviet military attack by destroying military targets, it would affect something on which Soviet leaders continue to lavish a huge part of their painfully scarce resources and which they appear to cherish quite as much as they do Russian citizens; and the prospects of such a Western response would be the best deterrent to their initiating war. Moreover, continued attacks during a war on elements of their military power and means of domination would appear to be the best way to bring the war to a rapid close. Prudence does not force us to rely for deterrence on even *unintended* damage done to civilians. Discrimination remains an important goal during the war— and an important capability to achieve in advance of the war. It helps deter the war or bring it to an end.

But Walzer believes that "counterpopulation deterrence" is basic. He also believes it is perfectly effective. It "rules out" (i.e., makes so unlikely as to be negligible) any nuclear war between the great powers; even though the Soviets know we believe that nuclear attacks on populations would be suicidal, our threat would be sure to deter them. And, typical of his time, he is also quite comfortable about the effectiveness of counterpopulation deterrence for forestalling a conventional invasion. His complacency here parallels that expressed in various British and American magisterial writings of the late 1960's and 1970's. He quotes with approval a passage from Bernard Brodie: "The spectacle of a large Soviet field army crashing across the line into Western Europe in the hope and expectation that nuclear weapons would not be used against it—thereby putting itself and the USSR totally at risk while leaving the choice of weapons to us—would seem to be hardly worth a second thought. . . . " One may surmise that if Brodie were alive he would be having second thoughts. Many who wrote that way in the late 1960's and 1970's are less comfortable today, in particular about threatening mutual annihilation as a way of deterring a conventional attack on Western Europe.

McGeorge Bundy illustrates the change in the American establishment. He had chided Henry Kissinger for expressing public doubts on the credibility of American strategy for the protection of West Europe at Brussels in 1979. "American strategy for the protection of West Europe," he was satisfied, was "a classic case of doctrinal confusion and pragmatic success." (He inserted the two words "so far," suggesting he was not completely satisfied.) I cautioned at the time that it would be a great mistake to attribute the pragmatic success to the doctrinal confusion; and Bundy did not disagree. The protest movements in Europe were already visible, for one thing; for another, there were the Soviets, and they might not be confused just because we were. We cannot count on a Mutual Assured Confusion. In any case, Bundy, less confident now about MAD threats to deter conventional invasion, has joined Robert McNamara, George Kennan, and Gerard Smith in proposing that we exchange pledges with the Soviets that neither would be the first to use nuclear weapons. The four stress the No-First-Use pledge much more than any serious and extensive program to improve the size or quality of NATO conventional forces, so that NATO could depend less on nuclear threats to overcome Soviet advantages in the use of conventional force. These advantages have to do not only with the massive and increasing size and quality of the Soviet force, but with the Soviets' geographical position and their relatively improving access to air space and bases near critical areas. Japan and Korea as well as all our European allies are within immediate range of Soviet, but far from the center of American, conventional power. So is Persian Gulf oil on which they all have come to depend.

Indeed, it seems that Bundy and his three coauthors have not really abandoned an implicit threat of the first use of nuclear weapons to make up for our conventional disadvantage. For while the four may *mean* the Western pledge, they rely on the Soviets not trusting us to live up to our pledge and so continuing to keep their ground forces dispersed and less effective for conventional attack and defense. In short, the policy they advocate resembles the pastoral letter in *explicitly* abandoning a nuclear threat, while implicitly continuing to rely on it. In their case, the threat is implicit in NATO's continued capability to use nuclear weapons first. If their policy led each side to believe the *other's* pledge, the Soviet Union would be more likely to concentrate its conventional force effectively—and safely since, on their recommendation, we would keep our pledge. On the other hand, if we trusted the Soviet pledge, we might concentrate our defenses at the likely points of attack. That would *not* be safe since NATO has no way of enforcing such a Soviet pledge. It seems that the four want neither side to believe the other's pledge. In sum, recommendations for exchanging unenforceable pledges about the first use of nuclear weapons in Europe do not reduce the doctrinal confusion that has been troubling NATO even on the subject of nuclear deterrence of conventional attack. They only alarm West European leaders who continue to rely excessively on nuclear weapons.

Many have observed that the four are rather perfunctory about a program to improve NATO conventional forces—in size, quality, method of deployment, or strategy—which would make it less necessary for European leaders to rely on nuclear weapons by making it more likely we could defeat by conventional means any of several plausible Soviet conventional attacks. They do talk of "maintaining and improving the specifically American conventional forces in Europe" but claim, in the face of much evidence of an unanticipated worsening in our ability to defend Europe's interests in more than one critical area near the Soviet periphery, that we tend to exaggerate Soviet relative conventional strength. And they say we underestimate "Soviet awareness of the enormous costs and risks of any form of aggression against NATO"—which is to rely covertly on the threat of first use of nuclear weapons that they overtly abjure. . . .

If the anti-nuclear movement in West Europe has served any useful function at all, it has done so by making responsible West Europeans more aware of the recklessness of depending on apocalyptic nuclear threats to meet conventional attacks. And given Europe's economic problems, key Western leaders are forced to think not merely of multiplying brute numbers but also of exploiting the new intelligent technologies to increase the effectiveness of the resources used. Such an effort has been hampered up to now by a kind of Luddite and moralistic resistance to qualitative improvement and by a particular antipathy to technologies that improve the possibility of discrimination and choice.

Moralists who have chosen to emphasize the shallow paradoxes associated with deterrence by immoral threats against population have been at their worst when they have opposed any attempts to improve the capability to attack targets precisely and discriminately. While they have thought of themselves as aiming their opposition at the dangers of bringing on nuclear mass destruction, they have often stopped research and engineering on ways to destroy military targets without mass destruction; and they have done collateral damage to the development of precise, long-range conventional weapons. (Junior Congressmen like Thomas Downey and Edward Markey, who had their fun with talk of *Star Wars* in March, might have benefited from observing that Luke Skywalker used one accurately placed weapon to destroy the indiscriminately destructive Death Star. And with advanced terminal guidance we need not rely on "The Force.") They have tried to stop, and have slowed, the development of technologies which can free us from the loose and wishful paradoxes involved in efforts to save the peace with unstable threats to terrorize our own as well as adversary civilians. . . .

Declaratory doctrine for the American defense of Europe started in the 1950's with the belief that strategic and tactical nuclear weapons could replace the conventional firepower which our NATO allies hesitated to supply against conventional invasion. It went through a phase in which many of the present advocates of MAD entertained exaggerated hopes for limiting the harm done by the large-scale use of tactical nuclear weapons on European battlefields; and for using massive active and civil defense, limiting to quite small amounts the damage done by a large raid on U.S. cities. When their hopes began to seem excessive, they switched to the view that the *threat* of unlimited mutual destruction was actually good, Soviet Union to avoid altering the division of power in Europe, even if unintentionally, if it seized some future opportunity to satisfy its long expressed interest in expanding toward the Persian Gulf and the Eastern Mediterranean. (England is said to have acquired its empire in a fit of absentmindedness.) Moreover, from the Soviet point of view, the destruction of the Western alliance that would result would surely be a bonus in defense of Soviet Western borders. George Kennan draws rather more satisfaction than is warranted from Soviet paranoid defensiveness. Paranoids can be dangerous.

But Michael Howard isn't terribly worried about the Soviets beginning a war. He worries about Americans. Though he has been subject to attack by E.P. Thompson and the nuclear disarmers, he sometimes sounds a little like them. He says: "Whether I could encounter the same phenomenon in the Soviet Union, I do not know. But wars begin in the minds of men, and in many American minds the flames of war seem already to have taken a very firm hold." And: "When I hear some of my American friends speak of that country [the Soviet Union], when I note how their eyes glaze over, their voices drop an octave, and they grind out the words *'the Soviets'* in tones of gravelly hatred, I become really frightened; far more frightened than I am by the nuclear arsenals themselves or the various proposals for their use." I know some of Howard's American friends (indeed have counted myself as one), but none resembling that description. If such glazed-eyed monsters controlled the U.S. arsenal, instead of planning proportionate Western responses that might credibly discourage Soviet attack, the West might focus its attention entirely on stopping us and let the credibility of U.S. guarantees erode.

Unfortunately, the reactions to the President's speech of March 23 [1983] on protecting civilians showed that the view of some Americans, indeed of some former Cabinet officers firmly attached to MAD doctrine, resembles that of Michael Howard. These Americans, like their British counterparts, may deplore the "oversimple" view of Soviet leaders which they attribute to American "hawks." But when seized by MAD dogmas their view of U.S. leaders is more outrageously simple. They suppose American leaders to be so wantonly unconcerned about the unprecedented catastrophe of nuclear war that they are very likely to start one in any grave crisis. Anyone professing to believe that finds it even easier to believe that an American President would casually unleash nuclear war if he thought that American civil society had some substantial protection. But it is absurd to think that American *or Soviet* leaders are straining at the nuclear leash.

Former Defense Secretary Harold Brown answered the President with a variant of the fantasy that American hawks are likely to unleash nuclear war if they think the U.S. has a fair chance of coming out gravely but not totally ruined. The bishops cite him in support of their view that there is "an overwhelming probability that a nuclear exchange would have no limits." While in office, Brown was torn between, on the one hand, the view forced upon him by evidence that Soviet arms had been going up while ours went down and, on the other hand, the view that *both* superpowers are engaged in a spiraling buildup incapable of yielding either side the ability to fight, to coerce, or even to gain some political advantage. Thus "the Soviets have as great an interest and should have as great an interest in strategic arms limitations as we do." And he oscillated between the MAD dogma that all either side needs is to be able to destroy the other as a "functioning modern society"—an implicit pact for mutual suicide—and the recognition embodied in Presidential Directive 59 that the Soviets have made no such pact and shown no desire to make any possible Soviet attack an act of suicide. Like Hamlet (and McNamara) he is "but MAD north-northwest; when the wind is southerly, he knows a hawk from a handsaw." But now the political winds blow more from the north and Brown's American leaders are amazingly susceptible to clever briefers:

> Deterrence must leave no doubt that an all-out nuclear war would destroy the nation—and the leadership—that launched it. Realistically we must contemplate deployments by both superpowers, investing huge amounts in such defensive systems. If a clever military briefer, in a time of grave crisis, with such systems in place, can persuade the political decision-makers that the defensive systems, operating together with other strategic forces, had a reasonable chance to function well enough to result in even a severely damaged "victor," the scene will have been set for the ultimate disaster.

One might suppose that leaders on either side might be given pause if they thought that *they* would be completely destroyed even if the nation were not. But evidently the American leaders Brown contemplates wouldn't mind that and would be easily swayed by a military briefer who told them that the nation would have a reasonable chance of coming out only "severely damaged."

The United States could have launched a nuclear attack on the Soviet Union during any of several crises that came up while we had nuclear weapons and they did not. For example, we had 50 nuclear weapons and they had none in 1948 at the time of the Berlin crisis. It would not have taken a very clever military briefer to convince our leadership that the United States would not be destroyed by a nuclear attack in 1948. Yet since McNamara introduced the notion that it was very important for the U.S. that the Soviets be able to threaten the U.S. with annihilation of its cities, the absurdities implicit in MAD have become gospel even with intelligent men like Harold Brown.

The United States never seriously considered an attack on the Soviets when it had a nuclear monopoly; nor for many years after, while Soviet nuclear forces were extremely vulnerable. The idea that it would launch nuclear aggression now is a fantasy worthy only of the conspiracy theorists in the disarmament movement. Nor should we take seriously the idea that the Soviets tremble in fear that the United States might launch a nuclear attack simply because it had deployed some defense of innocent bystanders.

Many analyses in the 1960's related the use of our strategic forces to the objective of limiting harm done to ourselves and our allies in case deterrence should fail; and they related deterring an adversary to the ability to harm him *if* we responded. McNamara's Annual Posture Statements after the missile crisis, for example, tended to treat these two aims as independent. However, the separation misconstrues the problem of deterring. In a war, when all alternatives may be extremely risky to an adversary, we may not convince him that the alternative of nuclear attack is riskier than the others if we have persuaded him also that it can be done safely because we won't retaliate for fear of the unlimited harm we would bring on ourselves. We only complete the absurdity and undermining of deterrence when we *say* that we have no intention to fight, that is, to use nuclear weapons if deterrence fails. Unfortunately, the principle of deterrence and the principle of "Use, Never" mutually annihilate each other. . . .

5 MAD IS THE MORAL POSITION

Paul M. Kattenburg

As innovations in weapons technology have increased the capacity of weapons to inflict damage, they have stimulated reevaluations of the existing strategies and proposals for new strategic departures. Among these, the deterrent strategy of mutual assured destruction (MAD) has been the subject of intense scrutiny.

Thus, an anti-MAD mentality has developed, which includes a variety of viewpoints.[1] But essentially those opposing MAD have two main arguments. These were forcefully stated by Albert Wohlstetter in "Bishops, Statesmen, and Other Strategists on the Bombing of Innocents" [reprinted as selection 4 in this book] and in his dialogue with his readers.[2] Wohlstetter's eloquent, if pernicious, article deserves special attention because it has already become recognized as a major contribution challenging the premises on which American strategic thinking has been based for several decades.

Wohlstetter's attack pursues two lines of reasoning. First, he argues that our usual mirror image of the Soviets is mistaken and that the Soviets are so different from us that regardless of the loss of civilian lives, they will not shy away from a war-waging, first-strike use of nuclear weapons in order to prevent the loss of their military assets. Accordingly, because the doctrine of mutual assured destruction requires the cooperation and restraint of the Soviets and because they are not willing to provide these, the doctrine is invalid. Second, Wohlstetter argues that the threat of devastating retaliation, which underlies MAD, is an ineffective threat because, knowing that to do so would mean our own suicide, we have no real intention of carrying it out. Associated with this view and contained in the position of the Catholic bishops' pastoral letter,[3] which Wohlstetter otherwise finds so objectionable, is the idea that to threaten devastating retaliation is in itself immoral, as to threaten to destroy large numbers of innocent noncombatants cannot be sanctioned ethically under any circumstances.

Let us first consider the argument regarding the Soviets. Wohlstetter's contention is that in the jungle of world politics, the Soviets are a unique beast: in the arena of nuclear confrontation as in others, their values are completely different from ours, and their priorities are ranked in an entirely different order.

The crux of this point of view, shared by many distinguished analysts and policymakers such as Richard Pipes, Fred Iklé, and Ernest Lefever, is still probably best summed up by Wohlstetter: "We need only observe that the Soviets value military power and the means of domination at least as much and probably more than the lives of Russian civilians." He adds that this is "evidenced by a long history documented by careful scholars like Adam Ulam, Robert Conquest, Nikolai Tolstoy, and many others, in which the Soviets have sacrificed civilian lives for the sake of Soviet power." "Whatever else one may say of these actions," Wohlstetter states, "they do not suggest that Soviet leaders value the life of Russian citizens above political and military power." The prospects, he adds, of a Western response that would destroy military targets would "affect something which . . . Soviet leaders appear to cherish quite as much as they do Russian citizens"; thus the prospects of such a Western response would be "the best deterrent to their initiating war."

What is the Soviets' declaratory policy on nuclear weapons? Officially, Soviet doctrine maintains that nuclear weapons "are like others," a Soviet diplomat observed,[4] but he added quickly that this "doesn't mean the Soviet leaders really accept such nonsense." According to the available evidence, this statement may capture the reality of Soviet strategic thinking. It may be sufficient to show how far the views of Wohlstetter stray from those of George F. Kennan, for example, who certainly is as great an authority on Russia and the Soviets as are the glass-cage think-tank analysts at Rand. Kennan stated:

> This endless series of distortions and oversimplifications . . . this routine exaggeration of Moscow's military capabilities and of the supposed iniquity of Soviet intentions . . . this reckless application of the double standard to the judgment of Soviet conduct and our own; this failure to recognize, finally, the communality of many of their problems and ours as we both move inexorably into the modern technological age . . . ; these, believe me, are not the marks of the maturity and discrimination one expects of the diplomacy of a great power; they are the marks of an intellectual primitivism and naivety unpardonable in a great government. I use the word naivety because there is a naivety of cynicism and suspicion just as there is a naivety of innocence.[5]

Without going quite as far as Kennan did in recognizing a communality between the Soviets and ourselves, the assumption that the Soviets would be more willing than we would to sacrifice innocent lives—not even for the sake of some presumed military triumph, but simply for the apparent sake of preserving the military assets presently protecting the regime—is rubbish. It is not only nonsensical but is also completely denied by the experience of the past thirty-five years. Whatever else may be said of the cold war, the period was undoubtedly one during which we and the Soviets indeed tangoed together to the same tune, that of mutual assured destruction and the balance of terror. Without this record of Soviet willingness to play by the rules of mutual deterrence, it seems clear that there would have been no nuclear test ban and threshold treaties in 1963 and 1974; no SALT [Strategic Arms Limitation Talks] I in 1972, with its ban on the development of ballistic missile defense systems; no Antarctic, seabed, or outer space denuclearization treaties; or any of the related arms control accords reached in the sixties and seventies and cumulating in the post-Helsinki SALT II accords of 1979, which we and they have been carefully observing (despite the United States', not the Soviet Union's, failure to ratify the treaty).

Western policies such as those recommended by Wohlstetter and other believers in deterrence based on nuclear war–waging doctrine, policies based on the faulty premise of the Soviet willingness to risk civilian lives in order to preserve military assets, are not only unwise but also unethical and immoral. Those who believe in nuclear war waging must be willing to state an acceptable damage level, whether that level is ten million or "only" one million or fewer deaths, on the presumption that the Soviets are capable and willing to state a similar and presumably higher acceptable damage level. On so presuming, these believers fail to distinguish between the doctrines and arguments that may be debated and advanced by Soviet analysts and commentators in their military journals (which, in this respect, are not so different from our own) and the responsible and, in the end, clearly authoritative views of the Soviet political leadership in the government as well as in the party's central committee and politburo.

These leaders have certainly never been guilty, at any responsible level, of stating an acceptable damage level. And they must, much as one hopes our own leaders would, fail to see in an inevitably escalating nuclear war *any* political stake or objective worth the horrendous cost. The assumption that a nuclear war would inevitably escalate is correct because the possibilities of settling such a conflict once initiated, at however low a threshold, and once either party or both had incurred military and the inevitably accompanying collateral civilian damages must be regarded as infinitesimal. One must, of course, assume a basic rationality on the part of the actors involved, at least before the eruption of any nuclear scenario. After that, any appropriate analysis should assume their fundamental irrationality. In fact, it may be that those who believe in war waging and who propound its doctrine proceed on exactly opposite assumptions, namely, irrationality before a nuclear outbreak and rationality thereafter. In this respect, as in others, their logic is inverted.

Moreover, the assumptions and recommended policies of those who would deter by adopting a nuclear war–waging doctrine fail to take into account, much less to resist, the driving force and momentum of unbridled, advancing technology. That is what is carrying these doctrinal war wagers, American as well as Soviet, on its wings; and the only possible ethical posture toward it is to stop it dead by considering and judging its potentially disastrous consequences. Just as delays in the development of genetic engineering have been sought in order to allow mature consideration and debate, so we can, and should, delay advancing weapons technology rather than rush its development and then ride the wave, as the U.S. and Soviet governments appear to be doing by espousing and building weapons systems ranging from MIRVs to cruise, SS-20, Pershing, MX, and other missiles, all the way to Star Wars. Ethical imperatives impose the same policy prescriptions on the Soviets, and they impose on both parties the obligation to continue consulting mutually about the policies, and accordingly the weapons systems, that should and should not be developed. It is difficult to find ethical grounds for rejecting a freeze on the continuation of nuclear technology development. Mutual deterrence requires not military superiority through a technological breakthrough but, instead, symmetry or the essential equivalence of weapons systems. Mutual deterrence works only when each side knows that the other can respond in kind to a nuclear attack.

Let us now move to the second and perhaps the more credible argument of the doctrinal war wagers: that even if at least a portion (namely, the underwater portion) of our second-strike retaliatory force maintains a sufficient degree of invulnerability—as it must if it is to deter—its credibility will nonetheless have been lost and, with it, its deterrent value. In other words, the doctrinal war wagers seem to aver, the Soviets do not believe that we would in fact *ever* use our nuclear might in a countervalue retaliatory strike. Even some Americans—the National Council of Catholic Bishops included—do not believe that the use of nuclear weapons in retaliation can be justified. Therefore, our deterrent no longer deters. And because everyone knows that we would never carry out our threat of retaliation against innocent civilians (and which would put the nation's own survival at risk), we had better (according to the counterforce advocates) prepare ourselves, arsenal and morale both, to inflict maximum counterforce/minimum countervalue damage in response to a counterforce-targeted first strike or preemptive strike—and thereby restore our effective deterrence capability and credibility.

This argument is most pernicious. First, it is a self-fulfilling prophecy, guaranteeing the predicted outcome. If our leaders and commentators continue to assert that nuclear weapons are never really going to be used in a retaliatory countervalue strike, either because it will not be worth it after the cost of the first-strike damage against us has been absorbed or because our Western civilized and humane leadership would never have the fortitude or the immorality to push the button, then indeed we shall succeed in convincing the Soviets that our threat is meaningless. In other words, if we, ourselves, make the threat incredible by continuously denying its validity, we shall indeed suffer the consequences of losing our capacity to deter.

But arguing that the balance of terror is not credible is unethical because it substitutes the near certainties of escalating a counterforce nuclear war for the uncertainties and ambiguities of countervalue nuclear deterrence threats. Counterforce targeting leads logically to first-strike capabilities and thus to the temptation of preemption. For the sake of a presumed higher morality, we would be escaping from a deterrence mode that has served us, and the Russians, effectively for nearly forty years in favor of the reasonable certainty that preemption would occur the minute that one side felt it had gained even a slight, but vital, technological breakthrough in the counterforce war–waging capabilities it would have been striving to acquire. If that is not the height of immorality, what is? And yet it is being presented as a moral substitute for the alleged horrors of the balance of terror that holds city populations hostage to the vagaries and vicissitudes of the superpower relations. Rather, it is precisely the balance of terror that provides effective mutual deterrence. In an imperfect world, the balance of terror resting on mutual assured destruction, however precarious, may be the best possible basis for stability.

Second, the belief that a countervalue response to this threat is invalid, or incredible, is based on a fallacious analysis of tactical nuclear war–waging scenarios. Those advocating tactical nuclear war in response to a massive conventional attack in Europe have always believed in the acceptance by both sides of a given, though ill-defined, maximum damage level, beyond which threats of further escalation would cease and the limited nuclear war would accordingly terminate. If they did not believe this, advocates could not recommend tactical nuclear responses to massive conventional attack. Even the installation by the Soviets of powerful medium-range ballistic missiles (MRBMs) to counter NATO's nuclear capabilities (including cruise missiles), followed then by the counterinstallation of Western MRBMs—in other words, the whole process of gradual but apparently unremitting escalation in the so-called INF (intermediate nuclear force) arena—has failed to dissuade the war-waging advocates of the fallacy of their belief in the possibility of limiting a tactical nuclear counterforce war.

This erroneous reasoning has been rather simplistically extended to intercontinental dimensions. It has been postulated that because (as in tactical nuclear warfare) the acceptable damage level on both sides is low or at least limited, then large threats, that is, threats of massive countervalue destruction, are regarded as inoperative, incredible, and invalid as deterrents to superpower nuclear war. Thus, the only effectively deterring threats are those contained in small-scale, low-level damage-producing weapons. Policy, then, must seek to obtain steadily rising but commensurate (countervailing) counterforce capabilities, to devise appropriate nuclear war–waging doctrine, and to enter (because that must follow) the area of first-strike and thus preemptive capabilities.

It is not true, however, that low-level damage, tactical nuclear threats necessarily deter anything. They have certainly not deterred the Soviets over their twenty-five years of existence in NATO Europe from enlarging their conventional capabilities and from seeking larger and more devastating nuclear forces. Second, it is even less true that the possession of such weapons leaves political leaders (who, in the end, as opposed to military leaders, are the determinant players) in an easier position to make war-waging decisions than if all they had at their disposal were holocaust arsenals. This is so because political leaders, contrary to think-tank analysts, constantly sense the reality that *any* real war-waging use of nuclear capabilities will inevitably escalate. Instead of settling the war, the desire of one side or the other not to submit would redouble, not dwindle, after the infliction of so-called acceptable damage. Moreover, one of the key tactics in war-waging doctrine is the early "decapitation" of the enemy's system of Command, Control, Communication, and Intelligence (C^3I). Who then would settle the war?

The fact is that no one—not the Soviet Union, not the United States, not Wohlstetter or Pipes—can dare to state what an acceptable so-called collateral damage level would be in a nuclear war. Obviously, no politician can make such choices. Abandoning MAD and slipping into counterforce and nuclear war–waging doctrine resembles the slippery-slope process that in the past resulted in situations like Vietnam. The flesh-and-blood politicians will remain uncomprehending and, when the baby is thrown out with the bathwater, will abandon the crumbling edifice— as they did with Vietnam. But unlike a conventional war, once a nuclear war has started, and at however "low" a level of destruction, no one will be able to escape.

MAD is the moral position. Its efficacy is suggested by the fact that for a third of a century it has worked. Moreover, the MAD strategy remains the most reliable foundation for stability because, unsatisfactory as it is, it is the best that can be achieved at the lowest cost, given the current human condition. That is what makes moral, not immoral, the threat strategy contained in MAD to cause irreparable destruction if the other party starts nuclear war. It is disingenuous on the part of the supposed moralists to attack the balance of terror on the ground that we would not in fact respond to a nuclear attack with a nuclear counterattack. Actually, our strategy in NATO has long demanded a response to even a conventional attack by a mix of both means. Furthermore, when one faces the reality of a possible nuclear holocaust rather than the abstractions of textbook moralizing, the argument that one should not threaten what one will probably in fact not be able to do acquires a wholly different dimension. We are not engaged in classroom theological debate. In such debates, it may be immoral to threaten what one cannot morally perform; in the face of unprecedented danger to the human race, one has not only the right but also the moral obligation to threaten the unthinkable if that is what is required in order to avoid its happening. In other words (the position of the Catholic bishops notwithstanding), in this case, the morality of the end justifies the apparent immorality of the means.

In addition, MAD is the moral position because the risks of escalation are just too great to adopt any portion of the war-waging reasoning.[6] Let us recall that it was the posing by the strategic analyst Fred Iklé in 1973[7] of the alleged moral dilemma of accepting the ethics of the balance of terror that helped set the nuclear war wagers on their current doctrinal path. This dangerous path led through Secretary of Defense James Schlesinger's 1975 counterforce-oriented defense posture statement, through the failure of SALT II, through the adoption of Presidential Directive 59 (leaked at the Democratic National Convention in 1980), through the loose nuclear war–waging talk of the early Reagan administration, to the present impasse with the Soviets in INF (Intermediate Nuclear Force) and in START (Strategic Arms Reduction Talks) and to Europe's present apprehension of the United States' intentions in general and President Ronald Reagan's in particular. Therefore the posing of false moral dilemmas can lead to radical and faulty policy suggestions at both ends of the political spectrum. Nuclear war waging and unilateral nuclear disarmament should be jettisoned and a deterrence strategy embraced because the latter is the only position that can be taken that is politically realistic as well as essentially humane.

There is nothing unethical about the balance of terror and the threat to end life as we know it, what Wohlstetter and the pastoral letter call "the bombing of innocents," if that is the only effective, feasible, understandable, practical, and proven way to prevent nuclear war. Today, as in the past, the prevention of that horror has rested on three requirements: (1) that no responsible political leader, in any country on the globe including the Soviet Union, be enabled (by development of breakthrough defensive systems) to state an "acceptable damage level" of nuclear destruction; consequently that nuclear war remain unacceptable in any form as an instrument of policy; (2) that each side possess an invulnerable capability with which to retaliate against a first strike by the other, a condition that continues to prevail, despite all the chatter about "windows of vulnerability" to land-based U.S. nuclear forces or the Soviet concern about U.S. underwater tracking capabilities; and (3) that the threat of each side to devastate the other—not in small pieces but once and for all—if the other side attacks it, remain mutually credible or at least sufficiently likely to be implemented, so that inhibiting uncertainty is instilled in the minds of the top decision makers. The only purpose of nuclear weapons must remain, as former Defense Secretary Robert S. McNamara recently reiterated, "to prevent their use."

Any plans, moves, or policies that weaken these desiderata are themselves immoral and unethical and serve the passions of the hour, the personal pride of unthoughtful people, or the selfish motives of new "merchants of death." They do not serve the cause of humanity. In conclusion we can agree with George Kennan's recognition that

> there is no issue at stake . . . no hope, no fear, nothing to which we aspire, nothing we would like to avoid which can conceivably be worth a nuclear war . . . and there is no way in which nuclear weapons could conceivably be employed in combat that would not involve the possibility—and indeed the prohibitively high probability—of escalation into a general nuclear disaster.[8]

NOTES

1. For instance, among the critics of mutual assured destruction are those favoring unilateral disarmament. Similarly, there are those who base their objection to MAD on their rejection of deterrence generally. For a sample of the latter, see James A. Stegenga, "Nuclear Deterrence: Bankrupt Ideology," *Policy Sciences* 16 (1983): 127–145. The arguments made from either of these schools of thought are complicated and lie outside the boundaries of this inquiry.

2. See especially his response to his critics in the December 1983 issue of *Commentary* magazine. Also to be consulted are Theodore Draper's critique of Wohlstetter's position in "Nuclear Temptations: A Postscript," *The New York Review of Books*, January 19, 1984, pp. 49–50; and their subsequent retorts in "'Nuclear Temptations': An Exchange," *The New York Review of Books*, May 31, 1984, pp. 44–50.

3. Selection 3 of this book.

4. Raymond Aron records this statement in *Committed Observer* (p. 191) but says that he does not necessarily give it credence.

5. George F. Kennan, *The Nuclear Delusion: Soviet-American Relations in the Atomic Age* (New York: Pantheon, 1982), p. 197.

6. And at the other end of the scale, there continue to be political values worth fighting for, thus making it futile to advocate unilateral disarmament schemes or to abandon deterrence, as some would have us do. To deter by threatening annihilation may be ethically uncomfortable, but it remains less immoral than are the unilateral disarmament or "no-use" doctrines that can invite attack or subjugation.

7. See Fred Charles Iklé, "Can Nuclear Deterrence Last Out the Century?" *Foreign Affairs* 51(January 1973): 267–285.

8. Kennan, pp. 194–195.

6 THE MADNESS BEYOND MAD: CURRENT AMERICAN NUCLEAR STRATEGY

Robert Jervis

A rational strategy for the employment of nuclear weapons is a contradiction in terms. The enormity of the destruction, either executed or
threatened, severs the nexus of proportionality between means and ends
which used to characterize the threat and use of force. This does not
mean, however, that all nuclear strategies are equally irrational. The
nuclear policy of the Reagan administration—which is essentially the
same as that of the Carter administration and which has its roots in
developments initiated by even earlier administrations—is particularly
ill-formed. As I will demonstrate, the basic reason for this is that the
strategy rests on a profound underestimation of the impact of nuclear
weapons on military strategy and attempts to understand the current
situation with intellectual tools appropriate only in the pre-nuclear era.

American strategy for the past several years—the "countervailing
strategy"—has been based on the assumption that what is crucial is the
ability of American and allied military forces to deny the Soviets military
advantage from any aggression they might contemplate. The U.S. must
be prepared to meet and block any level of Soviet force. The strategy is
then one of counterforce—blocking and seeking to destroy Soviet military power. The goal is deterrence. Although it is concerned with how
the U.S. would fight many different kinds of wars, both nuclear and
non-nuclear, it is not correct to claim that the strategy seeks to engage
in wars rather than deter them. Instead, it argues that the best way to
deter wars and aggression is to be prepared to fight if need be; the
Russians are unlikely to start or risk a war if they know that they cannot
win. To a significant extent, current strategy fits with common sense,
but I will argue that nuclear weapons do not conform to our traditional
ways of thinking.

Whether one accepts this kind of strategy is largely determined by
two factors which are correlated more closely than logic would suggest:
one's image of the Soviet Union and one's analysis of the extent to which
nuclear weapons have brought about a revolution in strategy. I have
discussed the former factor elsewhere[1] and here just want to note that
the policy one advocates is and should be influenced by how aggressive
one thinks the adversary is and what sort of posture is necessary to

deter it. Also crucial, and what will be discussed in this article, are beliefs about nuclear weapons. Some analysts, starting with Bernard Brodie, have argued that mutual second-strike capability makes many military "truths" wrong or irrelevant. In the past, military advantage allowed the state to harm an enemy and to protect itself. Now protection is possible only with the other's cooperation. Seeing mutual vulnerability before and throughout any war as central, these analysts conclude that it is the fear of uncontrolled violence rather than the details of the military balance which influences political outcomes. Other analysts, while realizing that nuclear bombs are more than larger explosives, see the changes as less far-reaching. This logic leads to the countervailing strategy. Thus, Paul Nitze argues:

> It is a copybook principle in strategy that, in actual war, advantage tends to go to the side in a better position to raise the stakes by expanding the scope, duration or destructive intensity of the conflict. By the same token, at junctures of high conflict short of war, the side better able to cope with the potential consequences of raising the stakes has the advantage. The other side is the one under greater pressure to scramble for a peaceful way out. To have the advantage at the utmost level of violence helps at every lesser level.[2]

ESCALATION DOMINANCE VERSUS COMPETITION IN RISK-TAKING[3]

Nitze's view and the countervailing strategy rest on what is called escalation dominance—i.e., the claim that deterrence requires that the U.S. be able to contain or defeat Soviet attacks on all levels of violence with the possible exception of the highest.[4] (The last phrase is needed because in an unrestrained nuclear war it is hard to talk of one side having an advantage.) Those who stress the importance of this capacity argue that in the hands of an aggressor, it is a strong tool for expansion and in the hands of a defender it greatly eases the task of maintaining the status quo. If the Soviets had escalation dominance in Europe, they could launch a war in relative safety because no matter what the West did it would lose. If NATO did not escalate, it would be defeated. If it employed tactical nuclear weapons, it would only create more casualties on both sides, not alter the outcome. Escalation to limited strategic nuclear war would similarly fail because the Soviets would have superior capability on this level also. The West would be in a very weak position because not only would it have to bear the onus of escalating at each stage but doing so could not prevent a Soviet conquest of Europe. Thus Georgia Democratic Senator Sam Nunn concluded, "Under conditions of strategic parity and theater nuclear inferiority, a NATO nuclear response to non-nuclear Soviet aggression in Europe would be a questionable strategy at best, a self-defeating one at worst."[5]

The other side of this coin is that if the West had escalation dominance the Soviets would be stymied. They would not be able to conquer Western Europe with any level of violence, assuming (and, as we will see, this apparently straightforward assumption is troublesome) that the West matched the Soviet behavior—i.e., used conventional forces against their conventional army, employed tactical nuclear weapons if they did, and responded to their intiation of limited strategic nuclear strikes with similar moves.

These arguments rest on the beliefs that what matters most is what is happening on the battlefield, that deterrence without defense is difficult if not impossible, and that the threat to escalate lacks credibility unless the state can defeat the other side on the level of violence which it is threatening. After all, if the escalation cannot stop the aggression but raises costs on both sides, it would not make sense to escalate. The threat to do so, therefore, would not be credible.

The first problem with the escalation dominance logic is that a state confident of winning at a given level of violence may be deterred because it judges the cost of fighting at that level to be excessive. On the other hand, even if defense cannot succeed, the threat to defend can deter if the other side thinks that the status quo power is sufficiently strongly motivated to be willing to fight for a losing cause. Nuclear weapons have not changed the fact that defeating an enemy is not worthwhile if the costs entailed are greater than the gains.

ESCALATION IN A LOSING CAUSE

But what credibility is there in the threat to fight a losing battle? Often, there is quite a bit: such behavior is common—states usually resist conquest. Assuming the state knows it will lose if the adversary persists, the reasons for fighting are several. National honor is one. The desire to harm and weaken the enemy is another. Finally, and most important here, if the state can raise the cost of conquest higher than the value the other side will gain in victory, it can make the contest into a game of Chicken. That is, although war will lead to the state's defeat, the adversary would also rather make concessions than fight. So, while war would damage the state more than the adversary, this does not mean the latter could be sure that the former would not fight; the game of Chicken does not have a determinative solution.

INCREASING THE COSTS TO THE OTHER SIDE

The second and third lines of rebuttal to the escalation dominance position stress that the focus on the battlefield is misleading. The second argument is that in order to increase the cost that the other side will have to pay, the side that is losing can move to a higher level of violence even if it does not think it can win there. A state which realizes this fact can be deterred even if it thinks it can win the war. It is not correct to claim that the threat to escalate will be credible only if it is believed the action will bring a military victory; one must consider the price that both sides would have to pay. Thus, the U.S. might deter a Soviet invasion of Western Europe by threatening to use tactical nuclear weapons even if the Soviets believed that they could win such a war. To gain Europe at the cost of destruction of much of Eastern Europe and the Red Army might not be a good bargain.

But why would the state be willing to escalate if doing so would not bring victory? In the case of the American use of tactical nuclear weapons, such escalation would make a great deal of sense if the American decision-makers believed that war could be kept to this level of violence. For in this event it would be the Soviet Union (and the Europeans) who would pay most of the price. Even without this added incentive, however, escalation could be rational for the same reason that fighting in a losing cause would be—national honor, the desire to harm and weaken those who represent abhorred values, and the belief that the other side will retreat rather than pay the price which can be exacted for its victory.

The third and most important reason that it is incorrect to concentrate on who is winning on the battlefield is that the war may spread even if no one wants it to. The use of force involves a significant but hard to measure possibility of mutually undesired escalation. This means that a state which could not win on the battlefield could rationally enter into a conflict in the belief that the other side would rather concede than engage in a struggle which could escalate. Similarly, a state which had escalation dominance could avoid a confrontation in the knowledge that while it would win a limited war, the risk that the conflict would expand was excessive. The common claim that options which are militarily effective are needed is not correct.

RISK-TAKING AND MILITARY ADVANTAGE

What is crucial is that the ability to tolerate and raise the level of risk is not closely tied to military superiority. Because the credibility of the threat to escalate is not determined by the military effectiveness of the action, escalation dominance does not give the state a great advantage.

If NATO leaders were willing to tolerate increased destruction and an increased risk of all-out war, they could escalate from conventional to tactical nuclear warfare even if they did not expect this action to turn the tide of battle. On the other hand, if they believed escalation could halt a Soviet invasion, but only at an intolerable risk of all-out war, their position would be weak. (The perceived risk of escalation depends in part on the state's estimate of the risks the other side is willing to take. If NATO leaders thought the Soviet Union would back down quickly in the face of NATO's use of tactical nuclear weapons, they would see using them as less risky. If the Soviet Union were seen as willing to tolerate a high level of danger, then escalation would appear as more dangerous since the U.S.S.R. would be believed to be ready to maintain or increase the level of violence, with the attendant risk that the war could spread further. In other words, the dynamics of the Chicken game come into play.)

The links between military power—local and global—and states' behavior in crisis are thus tenuous. Escalation dominance does not make it safe to stand firm. The exact location of the battle lines and the question of whether American troops are pushing back Soviet forces or vice versa matters much less than each side's beliefs about whether the war can be kept limited. This is true not only for warfare in Europe or the Persian Gulf but also for nuclear counterforce wars.

Imagine a situation in which the Soviets believe that they could gain advantages over the U.S. in a missile duel in terms of residual strategic forces. What would they gain? As Warner Schilling has noted, "the strategic debate has focused on numbers of missiles and warheads as if they were living creatures whose survival was of value in their own right, to the near exclusion of any effort to relate these military means to potential differences in the war outcomes among which statesmen might actually be able to discriminate in terms of the values about which they do care."[6] Since destroying many of the other side's weapons cannot protect oneself, an advantage in remaining warheads could help the state terminate the war under acceptable conditions only if its adversary were persuaded or coerced into sparing cities.

The crucial point is that each side's hold over the other's civilization is not affected by who is "ahead" in the counterforce exchange. It is hard to imagine the Soviets thinking "that in the aftermath of a Soviet nuclear strike . . . an American president [would] tote up the residual megatonnage or [warheads] of both sides and sue for peace or even surrender if his side came up short."[7] Unless escalation dominance can be translated into a strategy for terminating war under acceptable conditions—which of course would have to include keeping one's society intact—it would not produce the results analysts like Nitze and Nunn attribute to it. It worked in the pre-nuclear age because even if the war expanded, the state which was losing could not do overwhelming damage to the superior power. Once this is no longer true, escalation dominance is not controlling.

Resolve and Threats That Leave Something to Chance

The threat of escalation implicit in the limited use of force acts through two related mechanisms, neither of which is linked to the local military balance. First, the use of force demonstrates the state's resolve, its willingness to run high risks rather than retreat. It provides evidence that the state will continue to fight and even escalate unless a satisfactory settlement can be arranged.

The second mechanism involves the threat of unintended, as opposed to intended, escalation. As Bernard Brodie points out, "violence between great opponents is inherently difficult to control. . . ."[8] The implications are best discussed by Thomas Schelling:

> The idea . . . that a country cannot plausibly threaten to engage in a general war over anything but a mortal assault on itself unless it has an appreciable capacity to blunt the other side's attack seems to depend on the clean-cut notion that war results—or is expected to result—only from a deliberate yes-no decision. But if war tends to result from a process, a dynamic process in which both sides get more and more concerned not to be a slow second in case the war starts, it is not a "credible first strike" that one threatens, but just plain war. The Soviet Union can indeed threaten us with war: they can even threaten us with a war that we eventually start, by threatening to get involved with us in a process that blows up into war. And some of the arguments about "superiority" and "inferiority" seem to imply that one of the two sides, being weaker, must absolutely fear war and concede while the other, being stronger, may confidently expect the other to yield. There is undoubtedly a good deal to the notion that the country with the less impressive military capability may be less feared, and the other may run the riskier course in a crisis; other things being equal, one anticipates that the strategically "superior" country has some advantage. But this is a far cry from the notion that the two sides just measure up to each other and one bows before the other's superiority and acknowledges that he was only bluffing. Any situation that scares one side will scare both sides with the danger of a war that neither wants, and both will have to pick their way carefully through the crisis, never quite sure that the other knows how to avoid stumbling over the brink.[9]

Schelling's concept of the threat that leaves something to chance is crucial to understanding this process.[10] This is the threat to do something which could lead to escalation undesired by either side. Any time military forces are set into motion, there is a danger that things will get out of control. Statesmen cannot be sure that they will—if they could be sure, then the threat to take the initial action would be no more credible than the threat to wage all-out war. But no one can be sure that they will not; the workings of machines and the reaction of humans in time of stress cannot be predicted with high confidence.

Because confrontations and the use of violence unleash forces of uncertain trajectory, states can deter a wide range of transgressions without making specific threats about what they will do in the event that the other takes the forbidden actions. The deterrent may be effective even if the threat to respond, when viewed as an isolated act, is not. This point is missed by the frequently expressed view that the American "threat of nuclear response has . . . lost credibility with respect to Western Europe and has virtually none at all as a deterrent to Soviet action in China, Southwest Asia or Eastern Europe."[11] This claim is probably valid for the likelihood that the U.S. would use nuclear weapons as an immediate response to a Soviet invasion of China or Iran. But the common phrase, "the credibility of the American threat," is misleading. The problem the Soviets face is not only that the U.S. might fulfill commitments but also that their action might lead to disaster. Could the Soviets be confident that a major attack on China would not lead to the involvement of U.S. strategic forces, especially if Chinese and Soviet nuclear weapons were employed? Could they be certain that the use of military force in the Persian Gulf would not lead to general war?

It is in the wider context of the possible chain of effect which the violent change in the status quo could set off that the influence of nuclear weapons must be seen. A state may then be deterred even if it is sure that its adversary's initial response will not be to carry out its threat. If the Soviets attacked Europe and NATO resisted, nuclear war could readily result even if the U.S. did not immediately launch its bombers. The processes set in motion by the fighting cannot be easily controlled by the participants. States cannot carefully calibrate the risks that they are running. They cannot be sure how close they are to the brink of war. (Indeed, during the Cuban missile crisis Robert Kennedy suggested that enforcing the blockade might be too dangerous and that "it was better to knock out the missiles by air attack than to stop a Soviet ship on the high seas."[12]) Deterrence does not require that states which face aggression begin by using all-out violence; states contemplating expansion must be concerned not with how their efforts would begin, but how they would end. As statesmen understand, the two are often very different.

Competition in Risk-Taking

Because the threat that leaves something to chance exerts pressure on both sides, it is not an automatic way to protect the status quo. Instead, the process involves what Schelling called "competition in risk-taking."[13] The state more willing to run the danger of undesired escalation is likely to prevail; the state which feels that the situation is intolerably dangerous, that the stakes are not sufficiently high to justify a significant level of risk, or that the adversary is apt to continue the confrontation in spite of the dangers is likely to retreat. As Brodie argued soon after the Cuban missile crisis, the fact that states can take actions which create "'some' risk [of nuclear war] is what makes [crisis bargaining] possible. We rarely have to threaten general war. We threaten instead the next in a series of moves that seems to tend in that direction. The opponent has the choice of making the situation more dangerous or less so. This is all pretty obvious when stated, but so much of the theorizing . . . about the inapplicability of the nuclear deterrent to the future overlooks this simple fact."[14]

Indeed, it is missed by those who stress the importance of escalation dominance. As we saw, these analysts imply that local military superiority is crucial for deterring or prevailing in limited conflicts. But if confrontations and crises can get out of hand and lead to total war, advantages on the battlefield may not be of great importance. Such advantages are hard to translate into a successful termination of war. And as long as the conflict continues, both sides will be primarily concerned with the danger of all-out war. Thus, crises and limited wars involving both superpowers are competitions in risk-taking. A state which has gained battlefield victories but finds the risks implicit in continued fighting intolerable will be likely to make concessions; a state which is losing on the ground but finds this verdict so painful that it is willing to undergo higher levels of pain and danger is likely to prevail.[15]

CONCLUSION

As long as decision-makers realize that things can get out of hand, crises and the limited use of force will have most of their impact by generating risks even if neither side explicitly affirms this view. In other words, I am not arguing that the U.S. is facing a choice between escalation dominance and competition in risk-taking as alternative ways of bringing pressure to bear. Even though the U.S. can choose the former as the basis for declaratory and procurement policy, it cannot escape from the fact that in tense situations, decision-makers are going to be preoccupied with the danger of all-out war. Since military advantage cannot control the risk of escalation, the attempt to banish this element cannot succeed no matter what Western policy is.

Similarly, mutual assured destruction exists as a fact, irrespective of policy. No amount of flexibility, no degree of military superiority at levels less than all-out war, can change this fundamental attribute of the nuclear age. Not only can each side destroy the other if it chooses, but that outcome can grow out of conflict even if no one wants it to. Most of the dilemmas of U.S. defense policy stem from this fact, not from policies which might permit the Soviets marginal military advantages in unlikely and terribly risky contingencies. Once each side can destroy the other, any crisis brings up the possibility of this disastrous outcome. Standing firm, although often necessary, has a significant degree of risk which cannot be much reduced by the development of a wider range of military options. Carrying out actions which are militarily effective does not take one's society out of hostage; what undercuts the credibility of American threats is not that they cannot deny the Soviets any gain but that carrying them out may lead to disaster.

NOTES

1. See *Perception and Misperception in International Politics* (Princeton: Princeton University Press, 1976), pp. 58–113; "Why Nuclear Superiority Doesn't Matter," *Political Science Quarterly*, Vol. 94, Winter 1979-80, pp. 620–622; "Beliefs About Soviet Behavior," in Robert Osgood et al., *Containment, Soviet Behavior, and Grand Strategy* (Berkeley Institute of International Studies, 1981), Policy Papers in International Affairs No. 16, pp. 55–59. Also see the pathbreaking study by Robert Levine, *The Arms Debate* (Cambridge: Harvard University Press, 1963).

2. "Is SALT II a Fair Deal for the United States?" (Washington, D.C.: Committee on the Present Danger, 1979), p. 6.

3. The discussion in this section is greatly influenced by James King, "The New Strategy" (unpublished manuscript).

4. Herman Kahn, *On Escalation* (Baltimore: Penguin Books, 1968), p. 290.

5. "NATO: Saving the Alliance," *Washington Quarterly*, Vol. 5, Summer 1982, p. 21.

6. "U.S. Strategic Nuclear Concepts in the 1970s: The Search for Sufficient Equivalent Countervailing Parity," *International Security*, Vol. 6, Fall 1981, p. 72.

7. Richard Ned Lebow, "Misconceptions in American Strategic Assessment," *Political Science Quarterly*, Vol. 97, Summer 1982, p. 196; also see Jervis, "Why Nuclear Superiority Doesn't Matter," pp. 617–634; Bernard Brodie, *War and Politics* (New York: Macmillan, 1973), pp. 363–364; and Patrick Morgan, *Deterrence* (Beverly Hills, CA: Sage, 1977), pp. 136–143.

8. "What Price Conventional Capabilities in Europe," *The Reporter*, Vol. 28, May 23, 1963, p. 32.

9. *Arms and Influence* (New Haven: Yale University Press, 1966), pp. 98–99. Schelling provides no supporting arguments for the claim that military superiority provides any assistance in this process and, in an era of nuclear plenty, I do not think the claim is correct. Indeed, a little later Schelling notes that "If the clash of a squad with a division can lead to unintended war, . . . their potencies are equal in respect of the threats that count" (*ibid.*, p. 103). Stephen Peter Rosen argues that military advantage was vital to determining each side's resolve in Vietnam, but this was a long and costly struggle for what was to the U.S. a relatively minor objective. Furthermore, after U.S. involvement reached a high level, the fear of escalation could exert pressure only on the U.S., and even here it was not the major consideration. (See Rosen, "Vietnam and the American Theory of Limited War," *International Security*, Vol. 7, Fall 1982, pp. 83–113.)

10. *The Strategy of Conflict* (Cambridge, Mass.: Harvard University Press, 1960), pp. 187–204.

11. Samuel Huntington, "The Renewal of Strategy," in Huntington, ed., *The Strategic Imperative: New Policies for American Security* (Cambridge: Ballinger, 1982), p. 13; also see p. 33. Kissinger's view is similar, if more dramatically put: "I have sat around the NATO Council table . . . and have uttered the magic words [reassuring NATO of the American

nuclear commitment] . . . and yet if my analysis is correct these words cannot be true, and . . . we must face the fact that it is absurd to base the strategy of the West on the credibility of the threat of mutual suicide" ("NATO: The Next Thirty Years," *Survival*, Vol. 21, November/December 1979, p. 266). Although disputing most of Kissinger's ideas on strategy, McNamara agrees on this point. See his "The Military Role of Nuclear Weapons," *Foreign Affairs*, Vol. 62, Fall 1983, p. 73.

12. Bromley Smith, "Summary Record of NSC Executive Committee Meeting No. 5, October 25, 1962, 5:00 PM," p. 3. In retrospect, this judgment seems bizarre. But in many areas the relative riskiness of various actions is still hard to determine. For example, Brodie argues: "I see no basis in experience or logic for assuming that the increase in level of violence from one division to thirty [in a conventional war in Europe] is a less shocking and less dangerous form of escalation than the introduction of [tactical] nuclear weapons" ("What Price Conventional Capabilities in Europe?" p. 32). Most analysts would disagree (and so would I), but in reaching our conclusions we must all rely heavily on intuition.

13. *Arms and Influence*, pp. 166–168.

14. "AFAG Talk: Political Impact of U.S. Force Postures," May 28, 1963, p. 7, in *Fourteen Informal Writings from the Unpublished Works of Bernard Brodie, 1952–65* (Santa Monica, CA: RAND Corporation). Also see Schelling, *Arms and Influence*, p. 96.

15. Henry Kissinger made this point in *Nuclear Weapons and Foreign Policy* (New York: Harper, 1957), pp. 144, 188–189, although his later views have been very different.

7 ON RUSSIANS AND THEIR VIEWS OF NUCLEAR STRATEGY

Freeman Dyson

. . . The Russian warriors are now armed with nuclear weapons on a vast scale. The strategic rocket forces of the Soviet Union are comparable in size and quality with those of the United States. The Soviet rocket commanders could, if they were ordered to do so, obliterate the cities of the United States within thirty minutes. It has therefore become a matter of some importance for us in the United States to understand what may be in the Soviet commanders' minds. If we can read their intentions correctly, we may improve our chances of avoiding fatal misunderstanding at moments of crisis. Nobody outside the Soviet government can know with certainty the purposes of Soviet deployments. The American experts who study the Soviet armed forces and analyze the Soviet literature devoted to military questions have reached diverse conclusions concerning Soviet strategy. Some say that Soviet intentions are predominantly defensive, others that they are aggressive. But the disagreements among the experts concern words more than substance. To a large extent, the disagreements arise from attempts to define Soviet policies in a language derived from the American experience. The language of American strategic analysis is alien and inappropriate to the Russian experience of war. If we make the intellectual effort to understand the strategy of the Russians in their terms rather than ours—as a product of Russian history and military tradition—we shall find that it is usually possible to reconcile the conflicting conclusions of the experts. An awareness of the Russian historical experience leads us to a consistent picture of Soviet policies, stripped of the distorting jargon of American strategic theory.

The two experts on whom I mostly rely for information about Soviet strategy are George Kennan and Richard Pipes. Their views of the Soviet Union are generally supposed to be sharply divergent. Kennan has a reputation for diplomatic moderation; Pipes has a reputation for belligerence. Kennan recently summarized his impressions of the Soviet leadership as follows:

> This is an aging, highly experienced, and very steady leadership, itself not given to rash or adventuristic policies. It commands, and is deeply involved

with, a structure of power, and particularly a higher bureaucracy, that would not easily lend itself to the implementation of policies of that nature. It faces serious internal problems, which constitute its main preoccupation.

As this leadership looks abroad, it sees more dangers than inviting opportunities. Its reactions and purposes are therefore much more defensive than aggressive. It has no desire for any major war, least of all for a nuclear one. It fears and respects American military power even as it tries to match it, and hopes to avoid a conflict with it. Plotting an attack on Western Europe would be, in the circumstances, the last thing that would come into its head.

Pipes is a Harvard professor who has been on the staff of the National Security Council in the Reagan Administration. He stated his view of Soviet strategy in a recent article with a provocative title: "Why the Soviet Union Thinks It Could Fight and Win a Nuclear War." Here are a couple of salient passages:

The classic dictum of Clausewitz, that war is politics pursued by other means, is widely believed in the United States to have lost its validity after Hiroshima and Nagasaki. Soviet doctrine, by contrast, emphatically asserts that while an all-out nuclear war would indeed prove extremely destructive to both parties, its outcome would not be mutual suicide: the country better prepared for it and in possession of a superior strategy could win and emerge a viable society. . . . Clausewitz, buried in the United States, seems to be alive and prospering in the Soviet Union. . . .

For Soviet generals the decisive influence in the formulation of nuclear doctrine were the lessons of World War II with which, for understandable reasons, they are virtually obsessed. This experience they seem to have supplemented with knowledge gained from professional scrutiny of the record of Nazi and Japanese offensive operations, as well as the balance sheet of British and American strategic-bombing campaigns. More recently, the lessons of the Is-raeli-Arab wars of 1967 and 1973 in which they indirectly participated seem also to have impressed Soviet strategists, reinforcing previously held convictions. They also follow the Western literature, tending to side with the critics of mutual deterrence. The result of all these diverse influences is a nuclear doctrine which assimilates into the main body of the Soviet military tradition the technical implications of nuclear warfare without surrendering any of the fundamentals of this tradition. The strategic doctrine adopted by the U.S.S.R. over the past two decades calls for a policy diametrically opposite to that adopted in the United States by the predominant community of civilian strategists: not deterrence but victory, not sufficiency in weapons but superiority, not retaliation but offensive action.

These remarks of Pipes were intended to be frightening, whereas Kennan's remarks were intended to be soothing. And yet, if one looks at the substance of the remarks rather than at the intentions of the writers, there is no incompatibility between them. I myself have little doubt that both Kennan's and Pipes' statements are substantially true. Kennan is describing the state of mind of political leaders who have to deal with the day-to-day problems of managing a large and unwieldy empire. Pipes is describing the state of mind of professional soldiers who have accepted responsibility for defending their country against nuclear-armed enemies. It is perhaps a virtue of the Soviet system that the problems of everyday politics and the problems of preparation for a supreme military crisis are kept apart and are handled by separate groups of specialists. The Soviet military authorities themselves insist vehemently on the necessity of this separation of powers. They know that Stalin's mingling of the two powers in 1941, when for political reasons he forbade his generals to mobilize the Army in preparation for Hitler's attack, caused enormous and unnecessary Soviet losses and almost resulted in total defeat. Kennan's picture of the Soviet political power structure is quite consistent with the central conclusion of Pipes' analysis—that Soviet military doctrines are based on the assumption that the war for which the Soviet Union must be prepared is a nuclear version of the Second World War. We should be relieved rather than frightened when we hear that Soviet generals are still obsessed with the Second World War. The Second World War was from the Soviet point of view no light-hearted adventure. One thing of which we can be quite sure is that nobody in the Soviet Union looks forward with enthusiasm to fighting the Second World War over again, with or without nuclear weapons.

The words with which Pipes intends to scare us—"victory," "superiority," "offensive action"—are precisely the goals that the Russians achieved, after immense efforts and sacrifices, at the end of the Second World War. If, as Pipes states, Soviet strategy is still dominated by the lessons learned in the Second World War, it is difficult to see what other goals than these the Soviet armed forces should be expected to pursue. Pipes makes these goals sound frightening by placing them in a misleading juxtaposition with American strategic concepts taken from a different context: "not deterrence but victory, not sufficiency in weapons but superiority, not retaliation but offensive action." The American strategy of deterrence, sufficiency, and retaliation is a purely nuclear strategy, having nothing to do with war as it has been waged in the past. The Soviet strategy of victory, superiority, and offensive action is a continuation of the historical process by which Russia over the centuries repelled invaders from its territory. Both strategies have advantages and disadvantages. Neither is aggressive in intention. The two are to me equally frightening, because they make the survival of civilization depend on people's behaving reasonably.

The central problem for the Soviet military leadership is to preserve the heritage of the Second World War against oblivion, to transmit that heritage intact to future generations of soldiers, who never saw the invader's boot tramping over Russian soil. Soviet strategists know well what nuclear weapons can do. They are familiar with the American style of nuclear strategic calculus, which treats nuclear war as a mathematical exercise, the result depending only on the numbers and capacities of weapons on each side. Soviet generals can do such calculations as well as we can. But they do not believe the answers. The heritage of the Second World War tells them that wars are fought by people, not by weapons; that morale is in the end more important than equipment; that it is easy to calculate how a war will begin but impossible to calculate how it will end. The primary concern of all Soviet strategic writing that I have seen is to make sure that the lessons of the Second World War are well learned and never forgotten by the rising generation of Soviet citizens. These lessons that the agonies of the Second World War stamped indelibly upon Russian minds were confirmed by the later experience of the United States in Vietnam. A Russian acquaintance once asked me how it was that American nuclear strategists appeared to have learned nothing from the lessons of Vietnam. I had to reply that the reason they learned nothing was probably that they did not fight in Vietnam themselves. If they had fought in Vietnam, they would have learned to distrust any strategic theory that only counts weapons, and discounts human courage and tenacity.

Tolstoy's *War and Peace* is the classic statement of the Russian view of war. Tolstoy understood, perhaps more deeply than anyone else, the nature of war as Russia had experienced it. He fought with the Russian Army at Sevastopol. He spent some of his happiest years as an artillery cadet on garrison duty in the Caucasus. In *War and Peace* he honored the courage and steadfastness of the ordinary Russian soldiers who defeated Napoleon in spite of the squabbles and blunders of their commanders. He drew from the campaign of 1812 the same lessons that a later generation of soldiers drew from the campaigns of the Second World War: he saw war as a desperate improvisation, in which nothing goes according to plan and the historical causes of victory and defeat remain incalculable. . . .

The fundamental divergence between American and Soviet strategic concepts lies in the fact that American strategy demands certainty, while Soviet strategy accepts uncertainty as inherent in the nature of war. The American objectives—deterrence, sufficiency, and retaliation—are supposed to be guaranteed by the deployment of a suitable variety of invulnerable weapons. The name of the American nuclear strategy is Assured Destruction, with emphasis upon the word "assured." Any hint of doubt concerning the assurance of retaliation creates consternation in the minds of American strategists, and even in the minds of ordinary American citizens. This demand for absolute assurance of retaliation is the main driving force on the American side of the nuclear-arms race. Soviet strategists, on the other hand, consider the quest for certainty in war a childish delusion. The Soviet strategic objectives—victory, superiority, and offensive action—are goals to be striven for, not conditions to be guaranteed. These objectives cannot be assured by any fixed quantity of weapons, and they remain valid even when they are not assured. Soviet strategy sees war as essentially unpredictable, and the objectives as dimly visible through chaos and fog.

Richard Pipes' statement "The Soviet Union thinks it could fight and win a nuclear war," while it is literally true, does not have the dire implications that Americans are inclined to impute to it. It does not mean that the Soviet high command has a plan for attacking the United States with a calculable assurance of victory. It means that the Soviet leaders have an intuitive confidence, based on their historical experience, in the ability of the Soviet armed forces and population to withstand whatever devastation may be inflicted upon them and ultimately to defeat and destroy whoever attacks them. This confidence of the Soviet leaders in the superior endurance and discipline of their own people is not based upon calculation. It is not a threat to American security. Hard as it may be for Americans to accept, the confidence of the Russian people in their ability to survive the worst that we can do to them is a stabilizing influence, which it is to our advantage to preserve. The demand for survival is the main driving force on the Soviet side of the arms race. Insofar as we undermine the confidence of the Soviet leaders in the ability of their people to endure and survive, we are forcing them to drive their side of the arms race harder.

Because of the divergent views of American and Soviet strategists concerning the nature of nuclear war and the possibility of technical assurance, American and Soviet strategic objectives are strictly incommensurable. It is natural for Americans to believe that the American objective of deterrence is more reasonable or more modest than the Soviet objective of victory. But the objective of deterrence comes with a demand for absolute assurance, while the objective of victory comes, if at all, at the end of a long road of incalculable chances and immense suffering. From a Soviet viewpoint, the objective of victory may be considered the more modest, since it is based only on hope and faith, while the objective of deterrence is based on calculated threats. It is futile to expect that we can convert the Soviet military leaders to our way of thinking or that they can convert us to theirs. The two different ways of thinking are deeply rooted in two different historical experiences. We and they do not need to think alike in order to survive together on this planet. We and they need only to understand that it is possible to think differently and to respect each other's points of view. . . .

8 WHEN A NUCLEAR STRIKE IS THINKABLE

Pierre Gallois and John Train

Thanks to the amazing increase in missile accuracy of recent years and the corresponding reduction in warhead yields, the real nature of deterrence today is drastically different from the public perception. The Jonathan Schell scenario of massive exchanges against cities may be obsolete: Neither side would dare.

A future war in Europe instead could start with a crippling Soviet nuclear strike against North Atlantic Treaty Organization conventional military objectives so precisely targeted that there would be little civilian damage, either directly or through subsequent fallout. In the past 20 years, the accuracy of Russian missiles has increased by a factor of 10, and American missiles, which were much more accurate to begin with, by a factor of five.

In 1964, a Soviet SS-8, because of its low accuracy, might have needed a five-megaton warhead to knock out a two-acre ammunition depot protected by a concrete revetment. Today, the improved Soviet SS-20s could do the same job with a warhead in the low kilotons, a thousandth of the previous power; and in the near future even more accurate versions, with still lower-yield warheads, could be deployed.

18TH-CENTURY WARFARE?

Both sides are rapidly shrinking their missiles' explosive force in order to be able to attack military targets without causing extensive collateral damage that would invite reprisals against cities. Specifically, the megatonnage of the U.S. missile arsenal has shrunk by about half since 1970 and by about three-quarters since the late 1950s. It has become so dangerous—and indeed useless—to attack cities in the World War II style, that war once again may become professionalized, the way it was in the 18th century: uniformed forces vs. uniformed forces, with the noncombatants on the sidelines.

The Soviets are way ahead of NATO in deploying the high-accuracy low-yield and medium-yield missiles that actually could be used in an attack. We shrank from "thinking about the unthinkable" in the 1950s and 1960s, and indeed belittled Herman Kahn as a "Dr. Strangelove" when he dared to consider it. Instead, by our simplistic policy of "staying ahead" through Mutual Assured Destruction, via endless reciprocal escalation, we let the world drift into its current plight.

Most people still think about nuclear strategy on the basis of what was true between 1945 and 1975. But the Russians realized in due course that they couldn't use their huge SS-4s and SS-5s against NATO without showering fallout over the Soviet bloc, since the jet stream blows from West to East, in the same direction as the Earth's rotation. Fallout is created by a ground-level burst that digs a crater: The debris, thrown into the air, lands downwind. So as soon as they could, the Soviets scrapped these weapons and switched to more accurate missiles with much lower explosive force. The new SS-21s, 22s and 23s have a 100-meter "circular error probable," which implies only one-kiloton or two-kiloton air bursts for a soft target, with negligible fallout. Radiation from an air burst extends no farther than the heat and blast. They, in turn, are no more extensive than is needed for the military mission: as little as 500 yards out from the target.

The U.S. is working to catch up: The first American Atlas missiles, with a five-mile circular error probable, carried a 10-megaton warhead, while the MX, with a 100-meter CEP, will use perhaps a 20th of that for a hardened silo, or several one-kiloton warheads for soft-surface targets. Indeed, the Trident II missile may be used with a cluster of conventional warheads.

The Soviets can disable NATO using low-yield air bursts only. Every NATO military target is on the surface: all the airfields, radar antennas and ammunition dumps. The oil pipelines can be cut where they run through open fields. Cities near these targets could be left virtually unscathed.

Soviet military practice is quite different from Soviet propaganda, which pushes the idea that no atomic weapons can ever be used because they would escalate immediately to city-for-city exchanges. The hope is to discourage the deployment of counters to their new, accurate missiles.

What about a defense based on the buildup of our conventional forces? NATO commander Bernard Rogers wants to increase NATO's conventional strength, but does not, as one sometimes hears, believe that NATO can be defended only with conventional weapons. He does have considerable confidence in the effectiveness of the "strike deep" strategy, using conventional "smart" munitions (the "assault breaker" technology) to destroy an invader's rear echelons once the fight has started.

But this assumes that the Soviets are obliging enough to conduct a World War II-style campaign. In fact, however, any war in Europe would start with a surprise attack on the 400 or so NATO military targets—again, by low-yield air bursts that would produce little injury to civilians.

Very few Americans would be killed if the American zone in Europe were avoided. Yet NATO in Europe would be crippled, regardless of the number of conventional divisions it had in place, since it does not have an invulnerable theater-based ability to inflict a corresponding riposte against Soviet conventional forces.

The Pershing II and cruise missiles will partly close this gap, but not for a number of years. Submarine-launched missiles, while they have survivability, are, for now, less accurate. Yet this forward-looking weaponry remains the West's best hope for dealing with the new European reality.

The Soviets will not start a war in Europe with either the conventional tank attack we have prepared for or by launching a strategic attack with high-yield missiles against civilian populations, which would be mutual suicide. Even if it weren't, the Soviets would want to take over a Europe that still works, not a Europe in ruins: Since the Soviet economy is a mess, to control and exploit Western Europe's economy remains attractive. As to a conventional attack, it is far less effective and far more risky than a pinpointed, disabling blow against military targets. One doesn't gain total surprise with a tank assault, with its necessary air and artillery preparation, and in a conventional war the loyalty of the Soviet vassals in Eastern Europe would be uncertain.

All of this describes how a general war in Europe probably would start, if it were to happen, which is possible, not probable. But the description is not academic, because without a clear understanding of Soviet capabilities, the West will remain susceptible to fear propaganda about mass annihilation. That line, in turn, serves the Soviets in their more predictable approach to overcoming Europe and the West: weakening the will to resist, like Hitler's use of *Schrecklichkeit*—the war-of-nerves.

The Soviets will probably avoid applying pressure all at once, which might drive the West together. Instead, like lions stalking zebras, they will continue to pull down each isolated victim in turn. Not whole regions, just specific countries. Not Africa, Angola. Not the Americas, Nicaragua. Not Asia, Afghanistan. They may soon be in a position to grab Baluchistan: Can anybody do more than protest? Or suppose they intervene in eastern Turkey. Would the Norwegians, the Dutch or the Danes send troops to Turkey to fight the Red Army? Hardly. It would be the same if they claim some real estate in the top of Norway, to protect the Kola Peninsula. Would the Greeks send troops to fight in the Arctic? Blackmailed by Soviet military superiority in the European theater, the NATO parliaments would doubtless call for "dialogue" or "a diplomatic solution." And the strategic balance would continue to shift, as it has with Soviet airfields in Afghanistan, which significantly undermine our position in both the Middle East and Southwest Asia.

One should not pin too much faith on arms-control discussions, however optimistic one would like to be. The Soviets do not sign an agreement that doesn't give them an advantage. Even if it can be verified, they will break it, and we will have no method of enforcement. SALT I gave them 62 missile submarines to 41 for America. In fact, the U.S. has only 35, but the Soviets have gone right on to 70 or so—more, if you count some older ones. The huge phased-array radar they've built at Krasnoyarsk is forbidden because it's for an ABM defense. We complain, but there's nothing we can do about it.

IMPROVING SECURITY

So how, then, can NATO improve its security?

To deter a pinpointed nuclear attack on its key European war-making targets, NATO must possess weapons that the Soviets know could survive attack and be used with precision against their military targets in turn. That requires a missile force with four characteristics: First, it must be highly accurate. Second, low-yield warheads must be available to destroy military targets with air bursts creating minimum fallout. Third, the missile supply must be adequate. And finally, it must be fully mobile, so that it can't be destroyed by the Soviet surprise attack with which a future war would start. The U.S. is on the right track toward meeting these objectives with its European missile-deployment program.

Such a defense would improve stability in the region by cutting the rewards of a sudden attack, would reduce our dependence on huge, inaccurate weapons and would diminish Europe's vulnerability to blackmail while its periphery is undermined.

9 STRATEGIES FOR MAKING A NUCLEAR STRIKE UNTHINKABLE

Earl C. Ravenal

The German military historian Clausewitz remarked on the "fog of war," which obscured and frustrated the best calculations of strategists. There is also such a thing as the fog of peace. We are seeing it now in the cloud of proposals to reduce the threat of nuclear war and curtail the buildup of nuclear weapons. But peace movements, on either side of the Atlantic, have not always been helpful. To be "concerned" about war is not necessarily to be serious about peace. Most of those in the peace movement, for instance, think that the more nukes, the worse. It doesn't matter what kind they are, where they are, or even who has them. There may be some limited truth in this, if you are hung up on the fear of a nuclear accident that might trigger a general holocaust. But the most likely case (insofar as any case is really likely) is deliberate escalation to nuclear weapons by the leaders of one country against the territory and forces of another. If you keep your eye on this case, you will be less concerned about numbers and more concerned about incentives—particularly the incentives that are built into the concrete dispositions and characteristics of the nuclear forces and doctrines of the contestants.

It's something like the slogan of the National Rifle Association—that guns don't kill people, people kill people. In this case, nukes don't make wars, governments make wars. To have a nuclear war, someone must start it. With this bit of self-evident, though widely overlooked, wisdom, we come to the question of the first use of nuclear weapons. Given the moral and strategic importance of this question, it would be surprising if the no-first-use initiative of the "Gang of Four," McGeorge Bundy, Robert McNamara, George Kennan, and Gerard Smith, in their article "Nuclear Weapons and the Atlantic Alliance," (*Foreign Affairs*, Spring 1982) were entirely novel. In fact, the proposal has been around as long as nuclear weapons themselves, though mostly in think tanks or institutes of applied ethics.

What is important is the logic, or absence of logic, of the argument. You might excuse some of Bundy, McNamara, Kennan, and Smith's deficiencies and contradictions as no more than the expected results of joint authorship—somewhat like the shape of the camel, which is said to be the horse designed by a committee. But the flaws are more serious. They stem from the foreign policies that the authors still espouse— extended deterrence and even collective defense—policies that have grave deficiencies now that they are projected against a background of nuclear parity and nuclear plenty. These problems are not superficial and accidental; they are central to America's defense of Europe.

The critical question underlying the problem of first use is: Can we continue to defend Europe in a way that is consistent with other, over-riding values, such as avoiding our own physical destruction in a nuclear war? If you are committed, as are Bundy and his fellow authors, both to defending Europe and to avoiding the extension of conflict to our own homeland, you must try to reconcile these awkward objectives. The way they try to do this is by making the renunciation of the first use of nuclear weapons *conditional* on the acquisition of an adequate conventional defense.

The exhortation to enhanced conventional defense has become a ritual incantation. It is a pseudo-strategic reflex. But those who opt for con-ventional defense cannot mean just any conventional effort. They must mean the high-confidence defense of Europe with conventional arms. To determine its feasibility, we must have a bill of costs. Certainly, that bill is nowhere set forth in the Bundy article; and I have never seen an articulate and ample accounting anywhere else, though the journals are full of invocations of various *dei ex machina*, consisting mostly of anti-tank weapons, shot from guns, dropped from planes, and worn off-the-shoulder by infantrymen. Whatever the virtuosity of these pieces of hardware, none will be decisive, and none is cheap.

In fact, our present share of the conventional defense of Europe— and this is not even designed to be a self-contained defense—is about $115 billion for 1984, 42 percent of the $274 billion requested for defense by the Reagan administration. Given a reasonable projection of current cost growth, over the next ten years Europe will cost us almost $2 trillion. Will even those resources be forthcoming, let alone the greater ones required for self-sufficient conventional defense?

If these critical conditions of conventional defense cannot be attained, should we accept conventional defeat or should we relapse into the first use of nuclear weapons? Bundy and company *appear* to be concerned primarily with avoiding the extension of conflict to our own homeland, even if this means possible defeat in Europe and the decoupling of Amer-ica from the fate of our European allies. And so they first indulge themselves in an *apparently* unqualified statement of no first use of nu-clear weapons. But near the end of their article, they hedge: "As long as [nuclear] weapons themselves exist, the possibility of their use will remain." Well, now. Because they cannot guarantee the conventional defense of Europe, they eventually smuggle in the last-ditch threat of our desperate, perhaps even unauthorized, first use of nuclear weapons. These authors—like so many others—would have the deterrent effect of first nuclear use without the opprobrium and the moral agony.

But, for the most part, their primary fear is of the uncontrolled spread of nuclear war if we were to initiate it in Europe; what we need, they deduce, is a "firebreak" between conventional and nuclear war. Unfortunately, however, it is the very fear of inevitable escalation up to the ultimate strategic weapon that constitutes the essential element in the "coupling" of America's strategic nuclear arsenal to the local defense of its allies. This is what is called "extended deterrence." Firebreaks are the antithesis of coupling.

Because our first use of nuclear weapons may be a necessary condition for our defense of Europe, the proposal of no first use inevitably raises deeper questions about deterrence and alliance—the two pillars of the strategic "paradigm" that has governed America's foreign and military policies for three and a half decades, since the beginning of the Cold War. Deterrence and alliance come together in the notion of extended deterrence—that is, the extension of America's nuclear weapons to deter challenges to objects less than vital and nations other than ourselves, in this case, Western Europe.

If we contemplate escalation to the first use of nuclear weapons in the midst of a European war, we must also stand ready to execute a preemptive counterforce strike at the strategic level, since we would be inviting a Soviet retaliation that quite plausibly would not be confined to the European theater. Counterforce and first nuclear strike are mutually dependent. A first strike implies counterforce targeting, since the only initial attack that makes sense is a damage-limiting strike—in the theater, a countermilitary attack that disrupts or destroys dangerous enemy capabilities; at the strategic level, the destruction of as much of the enemy's nuclear force as possible. In return, counterforce targeting implies, at the strategic level though not necessarily at the theater level, a first strike—indeed, a preemptive attack—because a second strike against the enemy's missiles is useless to the extent that our missiles would hit empty holes.

We saw how our commitment to defend Europe might occasion our first use of nuclear weapons in the theater. And we see how using nukes in Europe might force us to unleash a counterforce nuclear strike on the strategic plane against Soviet missiles. Now we begin to see how counterforce fits into our grand strategic design. Our extended deterrence of threats to Europe requires the practical invulnerability of American society itself to Soviet attack—that is, the ability to limit damage to "tolerable" levels of casualties and destruction. Otherwise, how could an American president persuade others that he would risk an attack on our homeland, or that he could face down a threat to attack our homeland, in the act of spreading our protective mantle over Western Europe and other parts of the world?

The trouble is that pursuing invulnerability is prohibitively expensive, and probably risky, too. First, we would need a shield of advanced space weapons, and probably also a vast program of shelters and evacuation. Then, we would require an expanded arsenal of redundant missiles to wage a multistage "protracted" nuclear conflict, dominating each stage; and this might also accelerate an arms race that could cancel out any momentary advantage we attained. And finally, we would have to acquire a "hard-target kill" capability against Soviet missiles in their silos (that is, counterforce); this would also be very demanding, and provocative, since no basing mode would allow our missiles to ride out a Soviet attack, and so such a posture would have to be—and would correctly be construed as—a first-strike posture.

This analysis suggests that the attempt to implement extended nuclear deterrence requires conditions that, if they can be fulfilled at all, are expensive or dangerous or counterproductive. The analysis also tends to demonstrate that conventional defense of Europe is a dead end, too. The only relief lies in abandoning the overarching requirement that demands both nuclear and conventional defense: America's commitment to defend Western Europe.

If we would avoid nuclear danger to our own country, what would be the appropriate policy? In a nuclear age, crisis stability is the key to central peace and relative safety. Indeed, it is all we can prudently seek, and the most we can expect to achieve. Crisis stability consists of the pattern of incentives, for both sides, to initiate or not to initiate nuclear war under a variety of circumstances, especially crisis situations.

The United States can strengthen crisis stability by designing the elements of its nuclear strategy—its posture and doctrine—to discourage either side's first use of nuclear weapons. First, by changing the posture we can dissuade the other side from striking first and starting a nuclear war. Since an enemy's first strike must logically be a damage-limiting attack against our nuclear forces, we can eliminate our fixed land-based systems as they become even theoretically vulnerable to a Soviet preemptive strike; we cannot afford to tempt an enemy at any stage in an unfolding confrontation by offering him attractive, and *necessary*, targets. Furthermore, we should not replace our fixed land-based systems with such devices as the mobile or multi-based MX missiles, or the now disparaged dense-pack configuration, or the now fashionable single-warhead "Midgetman" missiles. These only displace or postpone the incidence of vulnerability. The abandonment of the land-based leg of the nuclear triad would leave a dyad consisting of nuclear submarines and stand-off bombers armed with medium-range, air-launched cruise missiles.

Nuclear doctrine has two aspects: targeting and precedence of use. As for targeting, to discourage a Soviet first strike, we should not aim at enemy missiles in their silos, and thereby provoke the Soviets, in a crisis, to launch preemptively. Rather, we should adopt countermilitary targeting, developing a list of some 3000 military targets such as naval and air bases, concentrations of conventional forces, military logistical complexes, and the arms industry that is relatively far from large civilian population centers. We should also not deliberately target Soviet cities, a conclusion derived from moral reasons, but also from strategic reasons. If we avoid the enemy's cities, he has no incentive to strike our cities. Even if our cities were reached by an enemy's nuclear attack, striking "enemy" populations would make no more strategic sense than it ever did, and no moral sense at all.

As for precedence of use, we should seal off the temptation for us to be the side that starts a nuclear war. That is why I said we should not design our forces to execute a preemptive strike. But we should go further: Since a move to the first use of nuclear weapons by the United States could hardly occur unless we were to escalate in the midst of a conventional war, we can express our overriding interest in avoiding the spread of nuclear war to our homeland by imposing on ourselves a stringent doctrine of no first use of nuclear weapons.

A nuclear policy cannot be just a string of discrete prescriptions for quantities or qualities of forces. It must implement some national strategy and in turn express some foreign-policy design. There can hardly be "middle positions"—certainly not positions that borrow and cobble together the "attractive" features of several other schemes. We must either satisfy the requisites of extended deterrence or move to a nuclear stance compatible with strategic disengagement.

That stance would support and implement a policy of nonintervention, consisting of war-avoidance and self-reliance. Our security would depend on abstention from regional quarrels and, in the strategic nuclear dimension, on what I call "finite essential deterrence." In this context of disengagement, a policy of no first use of nuclear weapons would enhance crisis stability, discouraging escalation to nuclear war—indeed, obviating it, for us.

Reaching that point is essentially a matter of accepting the consequences. Of course, deterrence of conventional war, particularly in Europe, would be diminished. In other words, "deterrent stability" would suffer. It suffers also, however, in the Bundy proposal, which glosses over the contradiction between crisis stability and deterrent stability. But there is an essential tension, not an easy complementarity, between achieving safety for ourselves through crisis stability and achieving safety for the objects of our protection in the world through deterrent stability. The only way we can lessen this tension is by diminishing our obligations to extend defensive protection. Crisis stability more closely coincides with deterrent stability as we shed external commitments and concentrate on our own defense.

This logical conclusion never fails to stir the NATO loyalists, who grump that we could not "tolerate" the "loss" of Western Europe and the shared values that form the basis of our attachment. But no one has a monopoly of values. If, on one side, there is a minuscule risk of losing part of Western Europe to an opportunistic Soviet attack that we seemed unlikely to stop, there is, on the other side, the equally minuscule—but not fictitious—risk of the nuclear destruction of our own country, and possibly of civilization, if we continued to deter and deterrence were to fail. Indeed, only absolute faith in the perfect efficacy of deterrence allows the NATO loyalists to deny their implicit preference for nuclear annihilation.

Any serious discussion of nuclear strategy must lead to the consideration of moral theories. The discussion of morality in the use of nuclear weapons has recently been monopolized by the American Catholic bishops. But, useful and welcome as it is, the Catholic discussion should not set the boundaries of the debate. The pastoral letter suffers from its dependence on, and derivation from, the Church's tradition of the "just war," even though the letter has been criticized by more militant Catholics for ignoring the just-war strictures. It still trails that faint scent of permissiveness about war. That is because it affirms, beyond the core values of the integrity of our own life, lawful property, and freedom of choice (including the choice of our governance), additional values that could be "honored" by military moves that lead to nuclear war. Not the least of such values is the political integrity of Western Europe. But the essential question is whether, and how, such extensive values can be safely preserved. In an age of long-range nuclear weapons, and in a world of quasi anarchy, we must avoid conflict. There are no good wars any more, and few, if any, just ones. . . .

Part II: Weapons

During the late 1970s and early 1980s a "peace movement" began first in Western Europe and then spread to the United States and elsewhere. Those in the forefront of the European movement sought to prevent NATO's deployment of new intermediate-range Euromissiles as part of the Atlantic alliance's force modernization program agreed upon some years earlier. In the United States the call for a "nuclear freeze" united diverse public interest groups.[1] Public opinion polls repeatedly showed overwhelming support for the idea, which was also endorsed by candidates in numerous state and local elections (a mark of the salience of the issue, because foreign and national security policy issues do not normally find their way onto subnational electoral ballots). The freeze was debated and voted on in Congress and eventually was made a plank in the 1984 Democratic party's presidential campaign platform.

The common thread uniting the groups within the United States and across the Atlantic behind the cause of peace seems to have been the threat of nuclear war and efforts to avoid it. More specifically, the elements underlying the peace movement seemed to include

> the large buildup of nuclear arms by the Soviet Union in the last two decades, which has brought it up to the level of nuclear parity with the United States; the breakdown of the Strategic Arms Limitation Talks [SALT] and the stalemate of the Strategic Arms Reduction Talks [START] that succeeded them; the collapse of the mood of "détente" between the United States and the Soviet Union; the growing deployment by both the Soviet Union and the United States of missiles with the power to achieve a first strike against at least some missiles of the other side; the decision by the North Atlantic Treaty Organization to deploy intermediate-range nuclear missiles in Europe; and many provocative or ignorant-seeming statements regarding nuclear arms by officials of the Reagan administration.[2]

The selections in Part II of *The Nuclear Reader* are concerned primarily with the *control* of nuclear weapons. If, as suggested in the essays in Part I, nuclear weapons are to serve political purposes, then policymakers—much like those supporting the peace movement—must ensure that the mere existence of weapons of mass destruction does not become threatening, with the weapons themselves becoming the causes of instability and the irritants leading to their use. In other words, policymakers must make sure that they control the weapons and that the weapons do not control them.

The first essay in Part II, "The Nuclear Balance, East and West," by the Harvard Nuclear Study Group, discusses the numbers making up the nuclear balance. The United States has fewer strategic launchers than the Soviet Union does, but more deliverable warheads; the Soviet Union is ahead of the United States in the destructive power of their nuclear warheads and ICBM payload capacity or throw-weight, but the United States has a far greater capacity to deliver nuclear warheads via bombers. At the tactical level, the Warsaw Pact far outstrips the NATO alliance in numbers of both warheads and launchers (missiles and bombers).

By themselves these facts are comparatively meaningless and noncontentious. They are important only in their interpretation, and on this point, the authors observe, there is wide disagreement among analysts. Apart from real or imagined strategic asymmetries, what is beyond dispute is that the destructive capacity of today's weapons of war is enormous, a point to which we shall return in Part III.

How are nuclear weapons to be managed so that they serve rather than thwart the political objectives of deterrence they presumably are designed to achieve? More broadly, is it possible to control nuclear weapons—indeed, perhaps eliminate them—so that they never are used unintentionally or, one hopes, intentionally?

Complete nuclear disarmament would eliminate both threats, but it is not a realistic policy objective. The reason is simple: nuclear weapons are a consequence, not a cause, of the conflicts of interest that divide states. States will therefore never willingly agree to dispose of the means of defense under prevailing global conditions. To do so unilaterally would be tantamount to admitting that the causes of conflict, for which men and women have been willing to die for millennia, are trivial. They are not. Nor is it reasonable to expect that states will agree to disarm, for this presupposes precisely the kind of trust that is lacking, as evidenced by the presence of arms.

But states have been willing to engage in *arms control* negotiations. Recent examples involving the United States and the Soviet Union include the *Strategic Arms Limitations Talks* (SALT), the *Strategic Arms Reduction Talks* (START), the *Intermediate Nuclear Force* (INF) negotiations, the *Antisatellite* (ASAT) *and Space Weapons Negotiations*, and the efforts to conclude a *Comprehensive Test Ban Treaty* and a *Threshold Test Ban Treaty*.

Arms control is distinguished from disarmament in that "it accepts conflict among nations as an inevitable part of contemporary international politics and views military force as a necessary (and legitimate) instrument of national policy.³ Accordingly, it seeks more modest objectives than disarmament does.

> The theory of "arms control" is based on the rather modest notion that decisions to acquire certain types or quantities of weapons can aggravate political conflicts and thereby *in themselves contribute to the risk of war*. This is not to say that weapons decisions are a primary or even secondary cause of conflict; only that such decisions are one factor which influence the relative probabilities that political conflicts are resolved peacefully, remain unsettled, or result in war. . . . [A]dverse effects can be reduced, or at least contained, both through unilateral decisions to avoid deployments of "destabilizing" weapons and, more important, through international negotiations on agreements to mutually avoid deploying certain types of weapons or to place other types of agreed mutual limitations on weaponry.⁴

If the objectives of arms control are so modest, then the record of its accomplishments should be long and rich—but it is neither. In our next selection, "Arms Control in American Domestic Politics: Impediments to Progress," Steven E. Miller considers this record against the theory of arms control and the expectations of its early advocates. Miller concedes that the Soviet Union is an actor with whom it is difficult to deal and that the problem of verification is a real one. He argues further, however, that the explanation for the dismal Soviet-American arms control record is not found in the political and technical differences between the two superpowers but in the differences among American political factions and interests with a stake in arms control. Miller concludes that the politics of policy formation and ratification "intersect in a complicated way with the larger domestic political process of which they are a part," with the result that "any agreement that successfully runs the gauntlet of impediments will necessarily be modest in impact—otherwise it would not have survived." And although Miller's analysis is confined to the United States, he suggests that domestic politics in the Soviet Union must surely affect the arms control process there as well.

Even though the arms control record has not been good, its recent support in the United States has been promising. Indeed, a nuclear freeze is only one of several proposals to curb the nuclear arms race that have been advanced.⁵ In many of these, the question of verification has been a central issue, suggesting that verification may be a less tractable arms control issue than Miller suggests in his analysis of the domestic impediments to progress. An important issue separating freeze advocates and opponents is whether Soviet compliance could be ensured. Verification—inspection, as it was called earlier in the history of arms control—has often been a point of contention between East and West. Electronic surveillance via satellites and other so-called national technical means permitted verification of compliance with the 1963 partial test-ban treaty, for example, but is arguably inadequate to monitor recent technological innovations in weaponry and its testing. This is one reason that the Reagan administration opposed a nuclear freeze. The administration contends that a freeze would, *inter alia*, preserve an unequal balance of nuclear forces alleged to favor the Soviet Union, thereby removing incentives that it would have for concluding significant arms control agreements with a verification regime that would guarantee compliance.[6]

Certainly some freeze advocates envision a verifiable system of compliance, but the freeze movement is by no means unified by its objectives.[7] Generally, however, freeze advocates seek a ban on the testing, production, and deployment of all new missiles and aircraft for which nuclear weapons are the main payload. The *raison d'être* of this stand is to halt any further improvements in counterforce capabilities, which are perceived as the most threatening.[8]

The critics of a nuclear freeze do not necessarily dispute this point. But as Harold W. Lewis points out in "The Irrelevance of a Nuclear Freeze," the proposed freeze on nuclear weapons

> appears to rest on the assumption that it is somehow the availability of weapons that leads to war, rather than international conflict over national interests, perceived as important by at least one side to the dispute. To prevent wars, we need a peaceful means of resolving genuine and difficult international questions. . . . The inventory of nuclear weapons has nothing to do with that.[9]

In the spring of 1982 four eminent, former high officials of the United States government—McGeorge Bundy, George F. Kennan, Robert S. McNamara, and Gerard Smith—called for a declaratory policy of "no first use" of nuclear weapons.[10] No first use challenges the long-standing doctrine of the United States and its NATO allies, which says that the common defense rests on the strategy of initiating the use of nuclear weapons should their conventional or non-nuclear forces be threatened with defeat in Europe or elsewhere. Bundy, Kennan, McNamara, and Smith urged instead that a no-first-use policy be adopted in Europe, which would also require that NATO's conventional forces be built up to the level necessary to balance the Warsaw Pact forces.

For all the political acumen and prestige of the no-first-use advocates, the proposal was alternately criticized and ignored by others in policymaking circles. In part, at least, this was because of NATO's perceived weak conventional forces relative to those of the Warsaw Pact, coupled with NATO's apparent unwillingness to pay the cost of meeting the conventional challenge.[11] Moreover, no first use lacks credibility. As Jonathan Schell observed,

> Conventional defeat is the Achilles' heel of no first use. A policy of no first use thus can never really live up to its name. There is always an invisible asterisk attached, referring us to a footnote that reads, "Unless we start to

lose." Without this qualification, a policy of no first use would really be a form of unilateral nuclear disarmament by verbal means, in which the foe was invited to take what he could, provided only that he did it with conventional forces.[12]

Indeed, one of the criticisms of the no-first-use proposal is that nuclear weapons are believed to retain their military value, as they may provide the decisive deterrent to a Soviet attack on Western Europe. To abandon the first-use strategy would also decouple the United States from the defense of Europe (recall Ravenal's essay in Part I), because it would prevent the United States from using strategic nuclear weapons against the Soviet Union. "This linkage is considered the ultimate deterrent to Soviet attack against Western Europe."[13]

In our fourth selection in Part II, "The Military Role of Nuclear Weapons: Perceptions and Misperceptions," by Robert S. McNamara, the former American secretary of defense, addresses the question of whether nuclear weapons in Europe serve a military purpose. McNamara surveys the development of NATO's doctrine of *flexible response*, to which he contributed, and concludes that the force posture necessary to support it was never developed. Hence, NATO came to rely on the threatened first use of nuclear weapons. McNamara argues that the threat is no longer credible militarily or politically, and concludes:

> I do not believe we can avoid serious and unacceptable risk of nuclear war until we recognize—and until we base all our military plans, defense budgets, weapon deployments, and arms negotiations on the recognition—that *nuclear weapons serve no military purpose whatsoever. They are totally useless—except only to deter one's opponent from using them.*

Because McNamara disagrees with the logic of both the deployment of nuclear weapons and the conditions under which they might be used, the article might be viewed as a sequel to his earlier advocacy of no first use, for he challenges the proposition that nuclear weapons may represent the decisive obstacle to a Soviet invasion of Western Europe.

McNamara's prescription for shoring up Western defenses and maintaing the link between European and American security through a credible posture of extended deterrence is the familiar one of placing greater reliance on conventional military forces, including reliance on a new generation of high-tech weapons and acceptance of accompanying strategies that such a reliance would require. However, such weapons might increase rather than diminish the risk of conventional war—and ultimately nuclear war. This is the thesis of Michael T. Klare's "Leaping the Firebreak." The *firebreak* in this context refers to the psychological barrier separating conventional from nuclear war. The term comes from the firebreaks that fire fighters build to keep forest fires from racing out of control. Klare worries that the firebreak between nuclear and conventional war is being crossed from both sides—by a new generation of "near-nuclear" conventional weapons capable of "levels of violence approximating those of a limited nuclear conflict" and by a new generation of "near-conventional" nuclear weapons able "to inflict damage not much greater than that of the most powerful conventional weapons." Once the firebreak between conventional and nuclear warfare is breached, "there will be little opportunity to control the process of retaliation and escalation." The fear is that the new generation of weapons make this more likely. It follows logically, if ironically, that reliance on conventional weapons to enhance extended deterrence in Europe may hasten rather than avert a nuclear Armageddon.

As an alternative to no first use, it has been proposed that the United States and the Soviet Union destroy one or more of their existing weapons for each new one they build. Known as *build-down*, this proposal "seeks to apply a relatively simple principle to the complex realities of international competition in the development and deployment of weapons." With these words Alton Frye introduces his "Strategic Build-Down: A Context for Restraint," a proposal that has become part of the Reagan administration's strategic arms negotiation posture toward the Soviet Union.

As with other arms control proposals, build-down also has had critics. The proposal became an issue in the 1984 Democratic party primary campaign for the presidential nomination, during which build-down was alleged to condone and encourage a technological arms race between the superpowers. The allegation derives from the fact that although build-down requires that more old weapons be retired for each new one that comes on line, there is every likelihood—even incentive—that the new weapons will be more deadly than are the old ones. Consider, for example, the effect of retiring old missile launchers in return for new, more sophisticated, multiple-missile warheads known as MIRVs (multiple independently targetable reentry vehicles). Critics argue that such a development is inherently destabilizing because, by changing the ratio of warheads to missiles, there is an increase in the (potential) number of warheads targeted at fixed missiles sitting defensively in their silos. And because fixed, land-based missiles are already the most vulnerable of the strategic weapons, build-down would encourage rather than discourage the temptation to "use 'em or lose 'em."

The growing vulnerability of land-based ICBMs is central to much of the current strategic debate. President Reagan's bipartisan Commission on Strategic Forces (popularly known as the Scowcroft commission) issued a report in 1983 that responded to this issue by recommending the development of a new, single-warhead Midgetman missile able to enhance the invulnerability of America's strategic forces by deterring counterforce attacks on its land-based missile systems. Frye embraces the idea. He also refutes the argument that build-down amounts to an endorsement of a technological arms race; he suggests that it may contain the seeds of a proposal that could control even those third-generation nuclear weapons capable of crossing, from at least the nuclear side, the firebreak between nuclear and conventional war. Perhaps most importantly, he acknowledges that build-down "is not a magic panacea for all the problems that have piled up in the last 20 years" but argues that the proposal is moderate in that "it seeks to mold a consensus among those who have campaigned for a nuclear freeze and those who have opposed it." At the same time it places on Moscow the onus of proving that it has "any genuine interest in the reductions it professes to want."

Managing the superpowers' arms race is one approach to the control of nuclear weapons; preventing their spread to other countries is another. Today only six countries are known to have a nuclear weapons capability: the United Kingdom, France, China, India, and the two superpowers. Thus the spread of nuclear capability has clearly not been rapid; yet preventing the proliferation of nuclear weapons has been on the global agenda since the 1950s when, following successful Soviet and British atomic tests, it became apparent that the United States could not retain a monopoly over nuclear know-how and that other states would seek to acquire, either clandestinely or openly, a nuclear weapons capability. As many as thirty countries now are believed to be on the threshold of joining the nuclear club.

How threatening is nuclear proliferation? Some analysts see *horizontal proliferation*, that is, the spread of weapons to non-nuclear states, as less threatening than *vertical proliferation*, the continued improvement and stockpiling of weapons by the now-nuclear states. This view is premised on the assumption that the nuclear stalemate between the United States and the Soviet Union, captured in the concept of deterrence, explains the absence of war between the great powers since 1945. The lesson seems clear: the possession of nuclear weapons could induce the same degree of caution and restraint in others, thus having a stabilizing effect on world politics that would reduce rather than increase the probability of violent international conflict.[14]

Others disagree with this conclusion. Joseph S. Nye, a deputy to the under secretary of state during the Carter administration responsible for its nonproliferation policies, shows in our next selection, "Sustaining the Non-Proliferation Regime" that the conditions that produce stability in the U.S.-Soviet relationship are not similar elsewhere.

[T]he transferability of prudence [of the sort that nuclear weapons created in U.S.-Soviet relations] assumes governments with stable command and control systems; the absence of serious civil wars; the absence of strong destabilizing motivations, such as irredentist passions; and discipline over the temptation for pre-emptive strikes during the early stages when new nuclear weapons capabilities are soft and vulnerable. Such assumptions are unrealistic in many parts of the world.

The drive for security—often buttressed by a concern for status and prestige—in an otherwise anarchical and insecure world is a primary motivation that may lead others to seek to acquire nuclear weapons. Thus the nature of world politics alone complicates efforts to halt nuclear proliferation. Moreover, there is an inherent element of discrimination in a world that completely denies nuclear capability to most while permitting its expansion by a few. The nonproliferation issue is further complicated by the fact that the knowledge necessary to generate electricity from nuclear energy can be transferred to the production of bombs. In a world where the principal source of energy is a finite reserve of fossil fuels, nuclear energy is often an attractive energy alternative. The danger is that a country may surreptitiously divert nuclear resources from peaceful to military purposes. This is precisely how India became a member of the nuclear club in 1974. It is a danger likely to grow in the future as new nuclear technologies come into their own, such as reliance on the plutonium fuel cycle, which permits an easier conversion of nuclear fuels into explosives.[15]

Today, the International Atomic Energy Agency (IAEA), created in 1957 as part of the United Nations family of organizations, and the Nuclear Non-Proliferation Treaty (NPT), signed in 1968 and now observed by over 120 states, are the cornerstones of an international nuclear nonproliferation regime. Their purpose is to prevent the spread of a nuclear weapons capability from those who have it to those who do not while simultaneously ensuring access to nuclear know-how for legitimate peaceful purposes. The regime—that is, the set of institutions and procedures for the transnational management of the proliferation issue area—is fragile; yet its ability to adapt to the forces that both challenge and sustain it may well influence the shape and membership of tomorrow's nuclear club. Nye describes the nonproliferation regime, how past challenges to it have been met, and what must be done in the future if the proliferation of nuclear weapons is to be contained.

To this point our discussion has focused on arms control and war prevention insofar as they relate to offensive weapons. Defensive weapons have commanded little attention since 1972, when the United States and the Soviet Union agreed to limit their deployment of antiballistic missile (ABM) systems. That accord effectively legitimized mutual assured destruction as an approach to strategic stability, as it proscribed the superpower's ability to mount an effective defense against an adversary's second-strike capability. Since then, as our previous selections make clear, technological developments may nonetheless have eroded the foundations of stable deterrence, based on the principle of assured destruction.

Proponents of ballistic missile defense (BMD) see in these same technological developments the possibility of shifting from an offensively oriented conception of deterrence to a defensively oriented one that promises a far greater measure of national security. President Reagan committed the United States to the search for such a "star wars" approach to defense in 1983, when he called upon the scientific community to devise defensive means of rendering the "awesome Soviet missile threat" "impotent and obsolete."

In our next selection, "Toward Ballistic Missile Defense," Keith B. Payne and Colin S. Gray, long-time critics of mutual assured destruction, contend that the transition from an offensively to a defensively oriented deterrent strategy will be long and difficult—but warranted and practicable. They are undaunted by the limitations of the 1972 ABM treaty and by the impediments to arms control that the pursuit of BMD might pose. Indeed, their conviction that arms control cannot guarantee security leads them to support unilateral efforts to prevent a nuclear holocaust.

The Union of Concerned Scientists offers a strong antidote to Payne and Gray's optimism. In "Star Wars: A Critique," the scientists argue that an effective BMD system depends on technology that will never be available. These scientists join others[16] who attack the assumption that BMD would not disrupt the current, delicate balance of terror that presumably prevents the massive destruction that both superpowers are capable of unleashing, and that might, in addition, trigger a major expansion of the arms race.

Who is right?

NOTES

1. The case for a nuclear freeze is made by one of its early advocates in Randall Forsberg, "A Bilateral Nuclear-Weapon Freeze," *Scientific American* 247 (November 1982): 52–61. A brief history of the international peace movement can be found in *The Nuclear Age: Power, Proliferation and the Arms Race* (Washington, D.C.: Congressional Quarterly, 1984), pp. 207–235.

2. Jonathan Schell, *The Abolition* (New York: Knopf, 1984), p. 9.

3. Barry M. Blechman, "Do Negotiated Arms Limitations Have a Future?" in Charles W. Kegley, Jr., and Eugene R. Wittkopf, eds., *The Global Agenda: Issues and Perspectives* (New York: Random House, 1984), p. 126.

4. Blechman, pp. 125–126.

5. Useful discussions of a number of both official and unofficial arms control proposals can be found in Adam Yarmolinsky and Gregory D. Foster, *Paradoxes of Power* (Bloomington: Indiana University Press, 1983), pp. 129–149; and Harold Brown and Lynn E. Davis, "Nuclear Arms Control: Where Do We Stand?" *Foreign Affairs* 62 (Summer 1984): 1145–1160.

6. Richard R. Burt, "Implications of a Nuclear Freeze," *Department of State Bulletin* 83 (June 1983):29.

7. See *The Nuclear Age: Power, Proliferation and the Arms Race*; and Colin S. Gray, "Nuclear Freeze?" *Parameters* 13 (June 1983): 78–79.

8. Forsberg; Brown and Davis.

9. A counterpoint to Lewis's position appears in Harold Feiveson and Frank von Hippel, "Freeze on Nuclear Weapons Development and Deployment: The Freeze and the Counterforce Race," *Physics Today* 36 (January 1983): 36–49.

10. "Nuclear Weapons and the Atlantic Alliance," *Foreign Affairs* 60 (Spring 1982): 753–768. See also the recommendation of the Union of Concerned Scientists in Kurt Gottfried, Henry W. Kendall, and John M. Lee, "'No First Use' of Nuclear Weapons," *Scientific American* 250 (March 1984): 33–41. Michael Carver, former chief of the defense staff in the United Kingdom, argues in favor of a no-first-use declaration from a European viewpoint in "No First Use: A View from Europe," *Bulletin of the Atomic Scientists* 39 (March 1983): 23–26.

11. P. Terrence Hopmann, "The Path to No-First-Use: Conventional Arms Control," *World Policy Journal* 1 (Winter 1984): 319–337.

12. Schell, pp. 53–54.

13. Jonathan Dean, "Beyond First Use," *Foreign Policy*, Fall 1982, p. 37. See also Henry A. Kissinger, "Nuclear Weapons and the Peace Movement," *Washington Quarterly* 5 (Summer 1982): 31–39.

14. For an elaboration of this argument, see Kenneth N. Waltz, "Toward Nuclear Peace," pp. 573–601 in Robert J. Art and Kenneth N. Waltz, eds., *The Use of Force* (Lanham, Md.: University Press of America, 1983).

15. For a useful discussion of the uranium and plutonium fuel cycles and their relation to weapons production, see Ann Florini, *Nuclear Proliferation: A Citizen's Guide to Policy Choices* (New York: United Nations Association of the United States of America, 1983), pp. 18–21.

16. See, for instance, Kosta Tsipis and Eric Raiten, "Antisatellite Weapons: The Present Danger," *Technology Review* 87 (August-September 1984): 54–63, and Hans A. Bethe, Richard L. Garwin, Kurt Gottfried, and Henry W. Kendall, "Space-based Ballistic-Missile Defense," *Scientific American* 251 (October 1984): 39–49.

10   THE NUCLEAR BALANCE, EAST AND WEST

The Harvard Nuclear Study Group: Albert Carnesale, Paul Doty, Stanley Hoffmann, Samuel P. Huntington, Joseph S. Nye, Jr., Scott D. Sagan

What is the balance between the American and the Soviet nuclear arsenals? Who is ahead?

When the question is asked in this manner, it might appear easy to give a definitive and objective answer. Unfortunately, this is not the case. No definitive answer is possible. . . .

. . . [A]s long as nuclear peace is maintained, it is impossible to measure the complex balance between two nuclear arsenals with any certainty. Given this fortunate uncertainty, different individuals can hold very different beliefs about the nuclear balance. Such differences are usually not about what numbers of weapons exist in the arsenals of the two superpowers, but about how to interpret the differences between the arsenals and the importance of certain kinds of nuclear advantages and disadvantages. The purpose of this selection is both to present the "facts" about the current arsenals and to examine various opinions on how to interpret them.

Some attention to detail is required for at least two reasons. Only by taking a trip through the inventories of the arsenals of the U.S. and USSR can the complexities and differences between the two arsenals be grasped. And only then can the dimensions of the physical threat be appreciated. This inventory check can also help explain the difficulty in deciding who is ahead. It also underlines the magnitude and complexity of the task of bringing these arsenals under control.

A second reason for a close look at the arsenals is that these weapons with their differing numbers and characteristics are the basis of defense budget arguments and votes, and of arms control negotiations. Decisions about nuclear weapons policy can be improved by a better understanding of the complex arsenals. Knowing the numbers of weapons involved is not enough, however; their characteristics, accuracy, and basing modes are equally important.

HOW TO BEGIN

Although defense specialists may disagree on the current nuclear balance, they agree on one major point about how to judge the arsenals: looking at total numbers of weapons in peacetime may tell one little about what would be the outcome of a war. If one side could destroy the other's weapons in a first strike, for example, then a balance in numbers would not produce stable deterrence. Thus it is necessary to examine the vulnerability of weapons as well as their numbers.

Measuring the balance of the nuclear arsenals must therefore include not only the numbers of weapons, but an assessment of what the weapons are aimed at. Both sides' weapons—their numbers and their ability to destroy other weapons—must be assessed.

How many nuclear weapons exist in the superpowers' arsenals? What are they aimed at?

The number of nuclear weapons in the U.S. inventory is near 26,000, down from 30,000 in the mid-1960s. There are no reliable public figures on weapons total in the Soviet nuclear arsenal: it may be as high as ours, but is probably somewhat lower. Only a little more than a third of the U.S. total are strategic weapons capable of hitting the USSR from the U.S. or from submarines; the others have shorter ranges. Clearly the strategic weapons, if even a small percentage could escape destruction in a Soviet first strike, would be more than enough for retaliation against Soviet cities. The great majority of American weapons, however, are aimed at Soviet military and industrial targets.

What targets? The answer is known in some detail, after congressional testimony by the Department of Defense in 1980:[1]

1. *Nuclear forces*
    ICBM and IRBM launcher facilities
    Strategic command and control centers
    Nuclear weapon storage sites
    Strategic air bases
    Submarine bases
2. *Command and control facilities*
    Command posts
    Key communication facilities
3. *Conventional military forces*
    Supply depots
    Airfields
    Tank and vehicle storage yards
    Rail and road systems used by military
4. *War-supporting industry*
    Ammunition factories
    Military vehicle factories
    Refineries
    Railyards and repair facilities
5. *Industries that contribute to economic recovery*
    Coal

Steel and aluminum
Cement
Electric power

This list, which is far from complete, shows a wide range of targets. Are all these military and industrial targets of nearly equal value? Of course not, as all strategists stress.

Some targets would be more important in trying to stop a Soviet attack against Western Europe, others to counter the Soviet nuclear war-fighting ability, and still others to slow Soviet recovery from a nuclear war. If targeting enemy missile silos has high priority, then many weapons will be assigned for this purpose. Other high-priority targets may include bomber bases, submarine bases, and military command centers. But with so many weapons in the arsenal, eventually the military value of adding a new target to the war plan declines. Indeed, at some point there will be little need to be able to destroy new targets. It is a matter of some dispute whether this point has been reached, but the diminished value of new targets is not in doubt.

How similar are nuclear weapons in terms of destructive power? Weapons now in inventory have yields that cover an enormous range, from less than a kiloton to more than 10,000 kilotons, and it may be believed that they cannot be compared. However, most of them are in the relatively narrow range of 40 to 1,000 kilotons. Both the U.S. and the USSR maintain a few very large weapons as well. Most strategic weapons are approximately equivalent for destroying unprotected targets; very large or very accurate weapons are required to destroy specially hardened targets.

The next generation of strategic weapons will be capable of extraordinary accuracy, on the order of a few hundred yards or less, well within the circle of total destruction. Before, high-yield weapons were planned to compensate for larger miss distances. As accuracy improved, the explosive power of modern weapons aimed at soft targets diminished. For example, 25 years ago the U.S. and Soviet bombers carried bombs of 5 to 20 megatons. These have largely been replaced by bombs of 1 megaton and missiles with smaller yields. In 1962 the average yield of ICBM warheads was 1 megaton for the U.S. and 2 megatons for the USSR. Today the average yields are one-fourth as large. As concern about hardened targets increased, the U.S. is again increasing the size of some of its warheads.

AN OVERVIEW OF THE STRATEGIC ARSENALS

Both sides deploy their strategic arsenals in three ways: on land-based missiles (ICBMs), submarine-based missiles (SLBMs), and long-range bombers. Each side emphasizes different weapons. This can be understood by comparing (1) number of launchers, (2) number of warheads, including bombs on bombers, (3) destructive power of warheads, and (4) launcher payload.

The current strategic nuclear capabilities of the two sides are displayed in the figure:

1. *Launchers.* For both sides, ICBM launchers are most numerous, followed by SLBM launchers and then bombers. Soviet launchers exceed U.S. launchers by about 25%. (Had the SALT II Treaty been ratified the Soviet force would have had to reduce the difference by half; the U.S. could have closed the gap to a common ceiling of 2,250 launchers. Since launchers are large and easily detected, arms control agreements have focused on controlling nuclear capability by restricting numbers of launchers.) In 1982 the number of U.S. SLBM launchers is lower than usual by 136, due to early decommissioning of old Polaris submarines. Otherwise the total numbers of U.S. and Soviet launchers have remained essentially the same since 1974.

2. *Warhead numbers.* The Soviets have three to four weapons per launcher for all three types of launchers. The U.S. has fewer weapons per ICBM and considerably more per SLBM or bomber. Indeed, the loading of our heavy bombers accounts for the 25% more warheads the U.S. has. If bomber weapons are excluded, the number of warheads is about the same for the two sides.

3. *Destructive power.* A more direct index of nuclear capability which is related to the estimated area the weaponry would destroy, which is called equivalent megatonnage (EMT).[2] The third panel shows that the Soviet force has about 6,000 EMT and the U.S. force nearly 4,000 EMT. This index displays great differences among the three components of the strategic forces. For the Soviets, 75% of the destructive power is carried by ICBMs, 20% by SLBMs, and only 5% by long-range bombers. U.S. destructive power is much more evenly divided.

4. *Payload.* Another measure of nuclear capability is the weight that each side's strategic force can direct toward the other's targets. This is known as payload: it includes not only the weight of the warheads but also the guidance systems. To the extent that U.S. and Soviet warheads of equal yield have different weights, the interpretation of this index is uncertain. The U.S. has a substantial advantage in overall payload because of its bomber force. But the Soviets are far ahead of the U.S. in ICBM payload.

In sum, the Soviet forces emphasize missile delivery and neglect the bomber component; the U.S. forces are more evenly balanced. The U.S. leads in warheads and payload, the Soviets in launchers and destructive power.

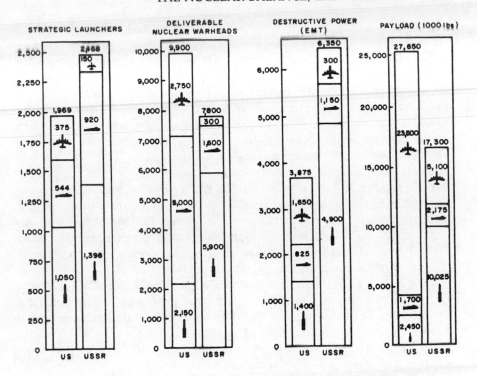

LOOKING AT THE STRATEGIC FORCES IN MORE DETAIL

Other aspects of the nuclear forces must also be examined. Some of the indexes may be more important than others. If destructive power and number of launchers are the crucial indexes, or if the contributions made by heavy bombers should be discounted because of their vulnerability to air defenses, then the Soviet forces are ahead. This position has been argued by conservative military analysts for some time and it is a central tenet of Reagan administration policy. It stresses that the momentum of force improvement lies with the Soviets and that the apparent balance shown in our overview will be lost if an active U.S. buildup is not undertaken.

U.S. forces are being improved. The larger destructive power of Soviet weaponry is a diminishing asset as high accuracy takes over. Indeed a much larger fraction of their destructive capabilities would become vulnerable if the Americans continue to deploy highly accurate missiles, because the Soviet missiles are too big to be made mobile. The superior U.S. bomber force is becoming more effective as it is equipped with air-launched cruise missiles (ALCMs) which permit bombardment from well outside the Soviet homeland, far from Soviet air defenses. As for the

Soviet lead in launchers, it could have been corrected by ratifying SALT II.

The claim of greater Soviet momentum in maintaining and improving strategic forces deserves a closer look. The strategic forces of the U.S. were modernized during the 1960s and faced the 1970s without much need for replacement. The improvements of the 1970s were on existing missiles and launchers: MIRVing and adding short-range attack missiles to the bombers. More recently, the U.S. is replacing 300 Minuteman III warheads with more accurate, more powerful ones.

The Soviet forces at the beginning of the 1970s were in substantial need of modernization: this the Soviets carried out with gusto, replacing their missile systems with at least 16 new types or modifications and deploying their new bomber, the Backfire, as well. By 1980 it was obvious that the U.S. forces had begun to age and required another cycle of replacement and modernization over the next decade or so if parity was to be maintained (as the Carter administration claimed) or restored (as the Reagan administration claimed). For the Carter administration this meant an 18% real increase in the strategic forces budget for fiscal 1982; for the Reagan administration it meant a 34% real increase for fiscal 1983. Thus, without arms control, it was evident that the U.S. would be quickening its pace of military spending in the 1980s if the challenge of the continuing Soviet buildup was to be met. . . .

OTHER FACTORS AFFECTING THE STRATEGIC BALANCE

Other factors, besides these four indexes, must be considered in any judgment of the strategic balance. For the most part, however, these factors are not expressible in numbers.

1. The Soviet Union is at the center of the world's largest landmass and has very poor access to the oceans. The ports it does have require passage through narrow waterways, and in consequence its submarines cannot easily go and come without detection. The USSR has been unable to obtain bases for its submarines at advantageous ports abroad, as the U.S. has. Consequently, even if its strategic submarines were technically the equal of those of the U.S. they would have to be judged more vulnerable, less reliable. In an effort to compensate for this geographical disadvantage, the Soviets are deploying long-range submarine-based missiles. With a dozen neighbors, some with considerable grievances, the USSR, unlike the U.S., has potential border problems. These geographical disadvantages are only partly compensated by the Soviet Union's advantage of short supply lines in wars fought on its periphery.

2. Contrary to widespread opinion, the industrial activities of the Soviet Union are more concentrated than those of the U.S. and therefore far fewer weapons would be needed for equivalent destruction. Moreover, the Soviet transportation system has far less capacity than ours and consequently is more vulnerable and less readily restored.

3. If nuclear war between the two superpowers escalated beyond the exchange of a few weapons, the efficient, controlled use of the vast remainder would depend on the survivability of the network of command, control, communications, and intelligence facilities that serve as the eyes, ears, and nervous systems of each strategic force. No one can know if these facilities, which number only in the low hundreds, would be destroyed early in such an encounter. If they were, each side would be blinded and the effectiveness of the weapons counted in the overview above would be greatly and unpredictably diminished.

4. Throughout the nuclear age the U.S. has been more inventive and technologically advanced than the USSR and has used this to make up for some numerical disadvantages. However, as the Soviet Union concentrates more of its technical ability in the military sphere and learns how to incorporate new technology from abroad into its military design, the gap is narrowing. It is a matter of active dispute whether the technological gap is nearly closed or not. In any event, technological ferment in new weaponry is evident on both sides. As a result, static judgments on nuclear balance may be more subject to change than in the recent past. Meanwhile, the U.S. will continue to benefit from some of its past technological triumphs, such as having much quieter, less detectable submarines, an antisubmarine capability widely recognized as superior, and a head start on modern cruise missiles.

5. The United States has two allies with modest nuclear capabilities; the Soviet Union has none. As France and the United Kingdom shift to MIRVed weapons in the late 1980s their forces will become more destructive. While still only a few percent of the U.S. force, these forces provide a significant deterrent in their own right.

Judgment of the balance of nuclear forces is often carried out in an obsolete framework, reminiscent of judging the likely outcome of a 19th-century artillery duel where each shell was of equal value. The most important task for deterrence is to deter the initial use of strategic weapons, and this is unlikely to be influenced by the total inventory. And in an all-out nuclear exchange the last half of the weapons fired would most likely be used against targets of relatively little military value. Numbers taken alone fall short of measuring the balance; but this does not reject or negate all the ground covered above. Weapons remain the coin of the nuclear realm, even if the exchange rate is not clear.

DIFFERING INTERPRETATIONS OF THE STRATEGIC BALANCE

Assessment of the strategic balance is complicated and uncertain; it is not surprising that different views are expressed by knowledgeable persons well acquainted with the facts just presented. Even a full examination of the state of the strategic balance leads different specialists to quite different interpretations and prescriptions for nuclear policy.

Some defense analysts find the emerging state of balance dangerously off center in favor of the Soviet Union. They stress that the apparent state of near-balance is deceptive. It overestimates the contribution of the American lead in strategic bombers and numbers of warheads because Soviet air defenses would prevent most U.S. bombers from reaching their targets and many of our warheads are too small for their intended targets. The superior Soviet payload also allows for future growth in their warhead numbers. More important, these defense analysts view American land-based missiles as totally vulnerable. These analysts argue that counting missiles on each side in peacetime is the wrong way to measure the balance; instead, one must imagine what the balance would look like if the Soviets struck first. After this first stage of war the Soviet Union would have more weapons left that would be capable of striking hardened targets than we would have.

Other specialists interpret the balance quite differently. They believe that the problem of land-based missile vulnerability is exaggerated and that the strategic forces of both sides are vastly larger than any rational military needs. Arms control negotiations, these specialists argue, deserve high priority and speedy execution in order to draw down the two arsenals at a substantial rate. If this should fail, many urge that U.S. strategic forces should be restructured and reduced so as to provide a robust but smaller deterrent. This would allow for a wide range of options that have in common a leaner strategic force, or at least one that is under no compulsion to mimic all Soviet deployments.

THEATER NUCLEAR WEAPONS

In the U.S. the term "strategic" refers to weapons that can hit the USSR from the United States or from American submarines at sea and vice versa. Other weapons, which are deliverable only at shorter ranges, are often referred to as "theater" weapons. The theater category contains most U.S. nuclear weapons, covering a wide spectrum from intermediate- and medium-range ballistic missiles and medium bombers, with ranges of 1,000–4,000 miles, to shorter-range systems, both missile and bomber, with ranges of 100–1,000 miles, to battlefield weapons of less than 100-mile range, to demolition mines. A large number of theater weapons are deployed in naval forces for sea combat and land attack.

U.S. non-strategic weapons number about 16,000 and are deployed at home, in Western Europe, in South Korea, at one or more Pacific bases, and on shipboard. Nearly half of them are in Western Europe. In the interests of brevity we will examine only these, analyzing the theater nuclear arsenals of Britain, France, and the USSR.

NUCLEAR WEAPONS IN EUROPE

In reviewing the strategic balance we find a rough parity between the forces of the two superpowers and a manageable number of weapons systems.[3] In the European theater we find a striking Soviet superiority in numbers, a larger array of weapon systems, and additional complications such as dual purpose bombers which can deliver nuclear or conventional bombs and thus resist simple counting procedures.

Long-range theater systems have ranges of 1,000–4,000 miles. In Table 1 the relevant inventories for the Warsaw Pact Organization and NATO are listed as of mid-1982. All of the Warsaw Pact weapons are Soviet weapons under Soviet control. The nuclear weapons of Britain and France are included under NATO even though this is not precisely correct. Britain has assigned its submarine-based weapons to NATO command permanently but its bomber-delivered weapons remain under its own command until released to NATO at time of war. France, having separated from the NATO military organization in 1966, keeps its forces entirely under its command and is not obligated to release them to NATO command in time of war. Nevertheless, there is close practical cooperation between the French force and NATO and it seems more appropriate to include French weapons than to exclude them.

The first entries in Table 1 are of Soviet missiles, beginning with the SS-20 carrying three MIRVed warheads and deployed over the last five years in large numbers, about two-thirds in the western Soviet Union and one-third in the Far East. The second column shows the number of launchers, and the third the maximum number of weapons that can be carried by the launchers. The Soviet SS-5 and SS-4 missiles are quite old, large-yield missiles of low accuracy. They are being slowly phased out and are unlikely to be usable after a few more years. Next the medium bombers are listed. The Backfire is currently being deployed; the Badger and Blinder are quite old.

The NATO missiles are British and French, mostly submarine-based. There are only two entries for medium bombers: the British Vulcan which is nearing obsolescence and the U.S. F-111 which is aging. In

Table 1. Warsaw Pact–NATO Nuclear Weapons in Europe (ranges greater than 1,000 miles)

Type	Launchers	Warheads/Bombs
Warsaw Pact:		
SS-20	345	1,035
SS-5	16	16
SS-4	275	275
Missiles	636	1,326
Backfire	100	400
Badger	310	620
Blinder	125	250
Bombers	535	1,270
Total	1,171	2,596
NATO:		
Polaris A-3 (UK)	64	64
M-20 (France)	80	80
SSBS S-2 (France)	18	18
Missiles	162	162
Vulcan B-2	48	96
F-111 E/F	156	312
Bombers	204	408
Total	366	570
Warsaw Pact/NATO ratio:	3.2 to 1	4.6 to 1

Source: *The Military Balance, 1982–83* (International Institute for Strategic Studies, 1982). The figure for SS-20s has been updated to November 1, 1982. The 60 U.S. FB-111A bombers based in the U.S. but designated for deployment to Europe in a crisis have not been included. The 400 warheads in the U.S. strategic forces assigned to NATO have not been included here, since they are counted in SALT/START and the corresponding Soviet assignment is unknown. However, French forces have been included.

long-range nuclear systems, the Warsaw Pact deployments greatly exceed those of NATO both in launchers and in warhead totals.

As for medium-range weapons systems (100–1,000 miles) in Europe, there are more types, larger numbers, and more uncertainty due to dual capable aircraft and varying estimates of aircraft ranges. The Warsaw Pact missiles are present in impressive numbers (Table 2), and there are numerous medium-range bombers and fighter-bombers. For NATO the only missile is the Pershing I with a range of about 400 miles. A variety of aircraft make up the major NATO force. The A-6E and A-7E are planes on two aircraft carriers normally assigned to the Mediterranean. Whether these would be withdrawn in an emergency or others brought in is unpredictable. But this item would surely be larger in a Soviet version of the table.

Table 2. Warsaw Pact–NATO Nuclear Weapons in Europe (ranges 100–1,000 miles)

Type	Launchers	Warheads/Bombs
Warsaw Pact:		
SS-12	70	70
Scud	593	593
SS-22	100	100
SS-23	10	10
SS-N-5	57	57
Missiles	820	820
Fencer	550	1,100
Flogger	550	550
Fitter C/D	688	688
Fitter A	265	265
Fishbed	100	100
Bombers	2,153	2,703
Total	2,973	3,523
NATO:		
Pershing IA	180	180
Missiles	180	180
Mirage IVA	34	34
Buccaneer	50	100
F-104	290	290
F-4	424	424
F-16	68	68
Mirage IIIE	30	30
A-6E	20	40
A-7E	48	96
Super Étendard	16	32
Bombers	980	1,114
Total	1,160	1,294
Warsaw Pact/NATO ratio:	2.6 to 1	2.7 to 1

Again, Soviet superiority in numbers of medium-range systems is clearly evident: 2.6 times as many launchers, and 2.7 times as many weapons in maximum loading.

There can be no comparable tabulation of battlefield nuclear weapons because the relevant Warsaw Pact and NATO data are not publicly known. Some observers believe that most battlefield weapons for the Warsaw Pact would be flown from the Soviet Union at time of crisis. All that can be said is that presumably several thousand battlefield weapons would be available to each side in the form of artillery shells, bombs, air defense missiles, short-range missiles, and mines.

The remarkable disparity between the two sides has its origins in the force deployments of the 1960s, when the U.S. had a substantial lead over the Soviet Union in strategic weapons and the local unbalance in Europe was therefore of little concern. But since rough strategic parity was reached in the 1970s the compensation no longer exists. Whether this should become a cause for alarm and action should be taken to redress the situation has divided NATO and defense specialists in the West for nearly a decade. The issue was crystallized by West German chancellor Helmut Schmidt in 1977, who advocated action to redress the balance. By the end of 1979 NATO governments had agreed to modernize their long-range theater systems by replacing other nuclear weapons with 108 Pershing II missiles with a range of 1,100 miles and 464 ground-launched cruise missiles with a range of 1,500 miles. It was agreed to make serious, parallel efforts to obtain arms control agreements with the Soviet Union on limiting long-range weapons so that only a reduced deployment, or perhaps no deployment of new NATO weapons, would be necessary.

CONCLUSION

Even this brief discussion of the superpower arsenals illustrates the complexity of the subject and the reasons why specialists disagree about the nuclear balance. It is worth repeating that the actual numbers involved are rarely in dispute. The meaning of the numbers is the prime source of disagreement.

Despite deep disagreements between specialists, two important points of consensus exist. First, the current arsenals are so large that the nuclear balance between the U.S. and the USSR is insensitive to minor changes in numbers of weapons. A *minor* advantage in one of the many weapons systems is unlikely to influence the probability of war or its outcome.

Second, specialists agree that the nuclear balance is not cast in iron, even at these high numbers. *Major* imbalances in particular nuclear systems can be destabilizing. To understand why this is so, we must move beyond focusing on the sheer numbers of weapons in the superpower arsenals to analyze the purposes which the weapons are meant to serve. We must ask not only "What is the balance?" but "What do we want from nuclear weapons?" . . .

NOTES

1. Testimony of William J. Perry, Under Secretary of Defense for Research and Engineering, before the U.S. Senate Committee on Armed Services, *Department of Defense Authorization for Appropriations, Fiscal Year 1981, Part 5: Research and Development*. 96th Congress, 2d session, March 1980, p. 2721.

2. The equivalent megatonnage (EMT) is related to the megatonnage (MT) of a weapon by EMT $= (MT)^a$, where $a = \frac{2}{3}$ for MT ≤ 1, and $a = \frac{1}{2}$ for MT > 1. Thus five weapons of 100 KT would have an EMT of about 1.08, a destructive power roughly equal to that of a single 1000-KT (1-MT) weapon.

3. For the U.S.: 3 ICBMs, 2 SLBMs, and 2 bombers. For the USSR: 5 ICBMs, 4 SLBMs, and 2 bombers. *The Military Balance, 1982–83*, p. 140.

11 ARMS CONTROL IN AMERICAN DOMESTIC POLITICS: IMPEDIMENTS TO PROGRESS

Steven E. Miller

Disappointment with negotiated arms control as it has been practiced over the past two decades is widespread and is found as much among proponents as among critics. This disappointment, caused largely by the decade-long failure to achieve telling limitations on strategic offensive nuclear forces, has spawned a veritable cottage industry of writings on the future of arms control, writings which seek new, more fruitful approaches to arms control or new recipes for success in given negotiations. Lavish attention has been given to the problem of rethinking, restructuring, restarting, fixing, or otherwise improving the prospects for and the effectiveness of negotiated arms control. . . .

A common premise of this outpouring of effort and ideas is that further attention to the substantive issues of arms control will yield answers that will somehow make possible significant progress. But the arms control process has never wanted for ideas and proposals, only for success and impact. New ideas and new proposals are unlikely to change that fact.

Largely unconfronted in any systematic way in the current disarray with respect to arms control is one overriding, fundamentally important reality: that the promise of arms control as an instrument of national security policy has been stunted as much by domestic political factors as by any other. Indeed, the lesson that emerges most strongly from the record of the past twenty-five years is that domestic political impediments to negotiated arms control regularly triumph over its substantive possibilities.[1] There are, of course, other serious obstacles: the Soviet Union is a notoriously difficult negotiating partner, obstinate, opaque, and inflexible; the asymmetric forces possessed by the two sides complicate negotiations; the march of technology raises hard, sometimes seemingly intractable negotiating problems; and, on the American side, at least, the sensibilities of allies must be taken into account. But these have not proven insurmountable. . . .

Note: Some footnotes have been deleted, and others have been renumbered to appear in consecutive order.

THE MODERN THEORY OF ARMS CONTROL

The intellectual foundations of arms control in the nuclear age were laid more than twenty years ago and have scarcely been modified since.[2] . . .

Much of this early work on arms control was devoted to demonstrating its potential benefits by showing that there existed plausible arms control solutions to pressing security concerns. Arms control, it was said, could reduce, if not eliminate, the incentives to strike first and so rid the strategic relationship of dangerous fears of surprise attack. It could diminish the chances of accidental or inadvertent war. It would inhibit the spread of nuclear weapons. In general, arms control was offered as a potential means of enhancing the stability, and thereby increasing the safety, of the nuclear balance, and the early theorists of nuclear arms control were keen to explain how it was that it could be so. It is a measure of how far we have come that these notions now seem commonplace. . . .

But to be persuasive, arms control proponents had to do more than just prove that arms control could be useful; they also had to show that it was feasible. This, in the late 1950s and early 1960s, was a harder task. It entailed addressing the two major obstacles to arms control: the difficulty in achieving an effective means of monitoring compliance and the daunting prospect of dealing with the Soviet Union as a negotiating partner. . . .

In sum, three questions troubled those who struggled with these issues during the formative period of 1958 to 1961 when arms control was beginning to emerge as a truly substantive component of national policy: (1) Could arms control be accepted as an instrument of security policy with a role to play in helping to address important security problems? (2) Would it be possible to monitor compliance with arms control treaties? and (3) Would the Soviet Union be willing to play a constructive role in arms control negotiations?

In subsequent years, each of these questions has been answered in the affirmative. It is widely accepted, even by those who have doubts about the particulars of a given treaty, that arms control is, in theory and often in practice, a legitimate and useful activity that can contribute to national security. The rapid improvement of satellite reconnaissance technologies has made verification a far more tractable problem than anyone could have expected twenty-five years ago; the development of national technical means (NTM) of verification has obviated the need for on-site inspection that was once assumed a prerequisite of negotiated agreements. Finally, in the course of a number of negotiations, the Soviets have shown themselves to be tough but serious negotiators with whom it is possible to reach agreement. These points should not be overstated: some still doubt the value of arms control; verification is still a major stumbling block; and some still doubt Soviet seriousness and trustworthiness. But, nevertheless, the main conditions identified by the early theorists as necessary for progress in arms control have been met.

Given this development, it might be expected that arms control had entered its heyday. Certainly the early arms control theorists were quite optimistic about its prospects. But has there been great progress?

GAINS AND DISAPPOINTMENTS FOR ARMS CONTROL

Although negotiated arms control has some significant accomplishments to its credit, the net record is sufficiently disappointing to indicate that simply meeting the conditions of the early theorists was not enough to usher in a new age of negotiated restraint. While the achievements of arms control should not be belittled, it seems fair to say that it has not lived up to the hopes invested in it; the plus side of the arms control ledger is accompanied by a substantial slate of minuses.

On the plus side, there has been, first, a tremendous amount of arms control activity. A fairly steady stream of treaties has been negotiated, beginning with the Antarctic Treaty of 1959 and including the Hot Line Agreement (1963), the Limited Test Ban Treaty (1963), the Outer Space Treaty (1967), the Non-Proliferation Treaty (1968), the Seabed Arms Control Treaty (1971), the Biological Weapons Convention (1972), the SALT I Agreements (1972), the Threshold Test Ban Treaty (1974), as well as the SALT II Treaty (signed in 1979 but never ratified)—and there are others. These treaties are the product of a huge investment in the preparation for and the participation in arms control negotiations. Formal discussion of a ban on nuclear testing began in 1958 and has continued, with occasional interruptions, into the 1980s. The question of non-proliferation occupied statesmen throughout much of the 1960s, and recurred on the arms control agenda of the 1970s in such guises as the Nuclear Suppliers Club discussions of the mid-1970s and the International Nuclear Fuel Cycle Evaluation of the late 1970s. The confrontation of conventional military forces in Central Europe has been the subject of more than a decade of continuous (albeit fruitless) negotiations. And setting aside an occasional hiatus, strategic nuclear arms negotiations have been underway more or less continuously since 1969.

Even during the Reagan Administration, at a time of great acrimony in U.S.–Soviet relations and with an American administration that is unenthusiastic about arms control, three separate negotiations were conducted—the Strategic Arms Reduction Talks (START); the negotiations on intermediate-range nuclear forces (INF) in Europe; and the Mutual and Balanced Force Reduction talks (MBFR)—until the Soviets suspended them in the late fall of 1983. Moreover, arms control is well established as high-level policy, which attracts the attention of presidents, secretaries of state, national security advisers, and of the general public as well.

Second, and much more important than the mere fact of activity, several of the agreements impose restraints on central aspects of the arms competition. The Limited Test Ban Treaty prohibits atmospheric testing of nuclear weapons. The Non-Proliferation Treaty has established a regime which inhibits the spread of nuclear weapons to additional states. And in strategic arms control, the ABM Treaty succeeded in bringing the testing and deployment of defensive systems under stringent control, thereby restraining one large area of weapons technology and closing off, for the time being, the possibility of an interaction between offensive and defensive systems that has the potential to lead to huge increases in the cost and size of the strategic forces of the superpowers. With respect to offensive forces, SALT I did place a ceiling on numbers of delivery systems, and SALT II added to this constraints on numbers of warheads and some modest restrictions on modernization. These were constructive developments and represent considerable improvement over a completely unconstrained environment whose possible costs and dangers make it undesirable compared to the moderately limited environment of today.

Set against these achievements, however, are the disappointing aspects of arms control diplomacy. Surveying the record of the past twenty-five years, one cannot avoid three negative conclusions. First, the recent history of arms control is littered with as many failures as successes. In this, the two conferences of 1958 which initiated the era of serious arms negotiations (the Surprise Attack Conference and the Geneva Conference on the Discontinuance of Nuclear Weapons Tests) were unfortunately symptomatic: both ended unsuccessfully. But beyond those first false starts have been many other failed efforts. There is still no comprehensive test ban treaty. MBFR has to date produced no agreement, despite years of endless discussion. The conventional arms transfer talks were unsuccessful. Discussion of anti-satellite arms control proved abortive. Negotiations on naval limitations in the Indian Ocean led nowhere. The Threshold Test Ban Treaty and the SALT II agreement remain unratified. Even in cases where agreement was eventually reached, progress was often painfully slow.

Second, and more importantly, the impact of arms control has been modest, especially relative to the level of effort invested in it. As one exceptionally cynical commentator put it, "Arms control negotiations have served as a long-term source of employment for diplomats and of copy for journalists and academics but they have had little military impact."[3] Many of the agreements that have been reached have prohibited weapons from being put in places where there were none anyway—

such as Antarctica, the sea-bed, or outer space—or have constrained weapons that nobody had much incentive to use—such as biological weapons. Such agreements are not without value, but they do not address the central problems and dangers that confront us.

In the cases where arms control agreements have confronted major aspects of the arms race, their effect has generally been limited. The Limited Test Ban Treaty has safeguarded the environment but has not proven especially constraining to the nuclear weapons programs of the superpowers (and several of the smaller nuclear powers are not signatories of the treaty). The Non-Proliferation Treaty has contributed to a regime of restraints that has probably slowed the spread of nuclear weapons, but the most worrisome cases remain outside the treaty or seek to elude its constraints.

And strategic arms control, the centerpiece of arms control in the past fifteen years and the primary interest of most defense and arms control analysts, has produced results that have disappointed supporters and critics alike. For in the 1970s, the decade of SALT, there occurred an enormous buildup of strategic nuclear forces *on both sides*. Both the United States and the Soviet Union added thousands of nuclear weapons to their arsenals during this period; between 1971 and 1980 the American stockpile of deployed nuclear warheads doubled while the Soviet Union's tripled. In addition, modernization proceeded apace. The United States deployed the Minuteman III MIRVed ICBM during the first half of the decade, and spent the latter part of the decade upgrading it with a new warhead and guidance system. Poseidon and later Trident I submarine-launched missiles (SLBMs) were added to the strategic submarine force. The B-52 force was steadily modernized and provided with new armament—the short range attack missile (SRAM)—designed to improve its ability to penetrate Soviet air defenses. And throughout the decade, a whole new generation of strategic weapons—the MX, the Trident submarine, the B-1 bomber, and the air-launched cruise missile—was developed, most of which will likely be deployed during the next few years. On the Soviet side, the modernization effort was even more energetic, resulting in the tiresomely familiar litany of "the Soviet buildup": several new, modern, accurate, multiple-warhead ICBMs (including the SS-18 "heavy" missile), several new strategic submarines and SLBMs, deployment of the Backfire bomber and hints of the development of a new strategic bomber, and indications of more systems on the way. In the face of all this, many liberals concluded in despair that strategic arms control simply legitimized the continuing arms race while many conservatives concluded with alarm that it served merely to camouflage an unrelenting Soviet buildup.

And what about the risk of war? Did SALT help to reduce it? Has it contributed to the stability of the strategic balance? As the Oppenheimer

Panel on disarmament thirty years ago commented in one of the first serious efforts to analyze arms control, "the basic objective of any scheme of arms regulation should be to eliminate" the capacity for what the Panel then called a "surprise knockout blow."[4] But strategic arms control has not prevented the emergence of disturbing vulnerabilities, in particular the problem of ICBM vulnerability and the less widely appreciated vulnerability of command and control facilities—both borne of the great accuracy of contemporary ballistic missiles combined with the advent of multiple warheads. Of course, a significant fraction of both superpower strategic arsenals remain survivable and would be available for retaliation, so the fundamental deterrence relationship is not presently jeopardized by this development. But if there is some degree of safety against the possibility of a disarming first strike, it is because of a multiplication of weapons and delivery systems rather than the result of negotiated arms control. Measured by this standard, then, strategic arms control must be judged insignificant if not deficient.

The third negative conclusion that emerges—along with the failures of arms control and its modest impact—is that these twenty-five years of efforts to bring the arms competition under some form of limitation have had the effect of tarnishing the arms control process. The failures, the inadequacies, the sluggishness, the occasional irrelevance of arms control have understandably harmed its image. If the writings on and the successes of arms control in the early 1960s resulted in the legitimizing of arms control, the experiences of more recent years have gone far toward discrediting it. This is reflected in several arresting facts: it has been more than ten years since the last major arms control treaty was signed and ratified. It has been more than five years since the SALT I Interim Agreement on Offensive Weapons expired, since which time there has been no legally binding strategic arms control agreement in place. The last two arms control treaties placed before the Senate (the Threshold Test Ban Treaty and SALT II) have not been ratified. And the fate of SALT II is instructive: it failed to find enthusiasm in the Senate or with the public. Even the nuclear freeze movement, which has attracted such strong public support, is a reaction against the way in which arms control has been practiced in the past decade or two, and is an expression of frustration with the propensity of the "experts" simply to *manage* the arms race rather than truly *control* it. . . .

In short, arms control has not lived up to its promise. Those who took up the cause of arms control in the early 1960s felt that it offered the prospect of substantial benefits in the form of a more stable nuclear balance and a more restrained arms competition. But, as former Secretary of Defense Harold Brown has written, "Measured against these glittering possibilities, the achievements of arms negotiations to date have been modest indeed, as are their immediate prospects. . . . In all, not much to show for thirty-five years of negotiations and twenty years of treaties."[5] But why has this been the case? It is certainly possible for arms control to provide more benefit than it has. There are fairly straightforward arms control solutions to many of the strategic problems that most trouble us. The main obstacles—verification and negotiability—seem more manageable than anyone expected them to be. And yet great exertions have not yielded great results. What has gone wrong?

THE DOMESTIC POLITICAL IMPEDIMENTS TO ARMS CONTROL

A major part of the answer lies in the ability of internal politics to shape and limit the results of arms negotiations. Each of the two main phases of arms control policymaking—the politics of policy formulation and the politics of ratification—is fraught with possibilities for preventing ambitious proposals or resisting agreements. These two phases in turn intersect in a complicated way with the larger domestic political process of which they are a part. In this way, electoral and Congressional politics, as well as public opinion, come to play a role in determining the possibilities of arms control.

The origin of U.S. arms control policy lies, obviously, in the policy formulation phase—in the negotiation primarily within the executive branch of the U.S. government. Here lurk several potential impediments to arms control. It is necessary to get all the many relevant parties within the government to agree on what should or should not be proposed and to get them to support whatever agreement is achieved. This may be the most difficult part of arms control. President Carter has observed, for example, that SALT II required as much negotiation in the United States as it did with the Soviet Union.[6] These internal negotiations can be fully as difficult as the international ones.

The players in the internal game are many: the White House, which often has its own agenda of political, budgetary, and foreign policy concerns; the State Department, with its concern for the international political relationships involved; the Arms Control and Disarmament Agency, a weak player in its own game; the various divisions and subdivisions of the Defense Department, which often have the most directly at stake; and occasionally key individuals from Congress. . . . The goal of the game is to produce an arms control proposal or position that is essentially acceptable to all. The structure of the game is simple: each of the organizations involved will seek, within the limits of its influence and effectiveness in the bureaucratic politics of the situation, to preserve its own interests or, at the least, to avoid having them badly violated.

Here lies the crux of the problem. For while it is commonly said that arms control and military policy are compatible and indeed ought to be integrated, the fact is that the *practice* of arms control, whether as a process or in the particulars of a given agreement, can and usually does affront the interests of some of the players in the game. In particular, few offices in the Pentagon have their interests furthered by arms control, and the wariness of the military toward arms control is evident to participants in the process and is sometimes remarked upon by the military itself. And because military support for agreements is thought to be, and probably is, crucial to the *ratification* process, as well as because military programs are directly affected, the military voice is a powerful one in the *policy formulation process.* . . . The strength of the military hand in shaping arms control policy and in safeguarding its interests against the intrusions of negotiated restraints explains why the JCS [Joint Chiefs of Staff] has, in general, consistently supported ratification of agreements that are reached, for having been satisfied in the policy formulation phase, it is free to take the high ground in the ratification process—as it did with SALT II. In short, although arms control and military policy share many of the same goals, they seek to achieve those goals through different, often incompatible means.

After all, arms control is an effort to interfere with the defense policy process, to constrain certain kinds of weapons, options, and practices for the larger good of national security. But this engages the interests of a large, powerful, complex, and not well understood process of defense decision-making and weapons acquisition, a process that generally seeks security not by constraining or eliminating weapons and military options but by providing them; this, it should not be forgotten, is the job that the Pentagon is hired to do, and it should come as no surprise that it seeks to fulfill that responsibility. But, as William Hyland (himself a long-time participant in the process) has written, "Arms control lends itself well to infringements on defense policy," and further, it creates "an environment for bureaucratic guerilla warfare against military programs. . . ."[7] As the modest impact of arms control agreements to date attests, proponents of defense programs and weapons systems are far from helpless in this particular form of warfare. And given the size and complexity of the defense policy process and the potential for antagonism between military policy and arms control, it is very difficult to coordinate the two and to manage the bureaucratic and organizational politics effectively.

Several important points flow from this analysis. First, arms control proposals are usually the result of internal bargaining. Consequently, deliberations are slow and changing proposals can be difficult. Considerable time and effort must be spent overcoming bureaucratic standoffs and adjudicating internal disputes. Second, in these internal negotiations, some participants often have to be bought off—their positions accommodated or their sacrifices in one area made up in another. Third, losers in the process need not give up. They can oppose or circumvent restrictions, take their case to the public, or air their disagreements before Congress—in short, broaden the fight to the ratification phase, having lost it internally. Such tactics will inevitably obstruct the smooth passage to a signed and ratified agreement. Fourth, internal critics will usually have to be paid for their public support of the treaty, as was the case, for example, with SALT I, where Secretary of Defense Laird and the Joint Chiefs of Staff made Administration support of a broad program of strategic modernization the fairly explicit condition of their support of the treaty. Finally, policy formulation is the President's game if he and his advisers in the White House have the will and the skill to seize control of the process. This John Kennedy did in 1963; Nixon and Kissinger did likewise during SALT I—with some important decisions being made by the two of them in the Kremlin during the Moscow summit; and Carter attempted the same in formulating his bold March 1977 comprehensive proposal. Unlike the ratification process, which can elude presidential control, policy formulation can be marked by decisive presidential interventions. Even if this happens, problems remain, for the Soviets still must agree and the Senate must still ratify. But the President does at least possess substantial power to shape the policy formulation process, and when that power has been exercised, progress has often ensued.

With respect to the politics of ratification, the second dimension of the domestic process of arms control, it is the Senate, rather than the President, that can be the decisive player in the game. In the Senate is vested the authority to ratify treaties, and so the Senate can determine the fate of an agreement even if it is only a marginal influence on the formulation of arms control policy. And the key fact, as *The New Republic*'s Richard Strout has recently commented, is that, "In a Congress of 535 members, 33 Senators plus one can block a treaty." This may be, as Strout remarks, "a queer system."[8] But it is the system nevertheless, and it requires that the politics of ratification be tended to rather carefully so that a minority is not able to gather sufficient strength to defeat an agreement. This can involve a significant amount of cajolery and appeasement of key Senators, the involvement of Senators in policy formulation, permitting Senators to observe the negotiations first-hand, and political logrolling on military programs (or on other unrelated issues) to secure or assure the support of important votes, as well as an effort to mobilize public opinion. . . . SALT I showed that ratification can be easy . . . ; the Threshold Test Ban Treaty showed that ratification cannot be taken for granted; and SALT II showed that ratification can be a major hurdle, not easily overcome even with great effort.

Both the formulation of arms control policy and the ratification of treaties take place in the larger domestic arena, and are affected by the general political process normally at work. One substantial domestic political impediment is the electoral process, especially at the presidential level. The quadrennial electoral cycle has several possible disruptive consequences for the arms control process. For one thing, arms control policy tends to get caught up in partisan politics, with one party attacking the approach of the other, and often unsubstantiated charges and countercharges flung about in public debate. This clearly occurred in the 1980 election, and President Carter strove to paint Reagan as a warmonger while Reagan accused Carter of following policies of weakness, with distinct tendencies toward unilateral disarmament. . . .

A second way that electoral politics can disrupt the arms control process is that administrations that are taking heat on this issue and perceive themselves to be on the political defensive may backpedal from arms control. Thus President Ford, in the midst of his struggle with Ronald Reagan for the 1976 Republican nomination, banished the word "detente" from his political vocabulary and placed SALT II, then nearly completed, on hold. This was a decision that Ford came to regret, but in the event it contributed to a several year delay in the signing of the SALT II agreement. Of course, this phenomenon can cut the other direction as well: when Richard Nixon sought in 1972 to bolster his image as peacemaker aginst the attacks of critics of the Vietnam War, the SALT I agreement became politically useful to him. But the potential for disruption remains.

Third, elections often result, as they are intended to do, in changes of government. It seems to be a rule of thumb, if past experience is any guide, that roughly a year is lost in the transition from one administration to the next. Those new to power generally need time to overcome the instinct to substantially repudiate the policies of their predecessors, to study the issues anew from their own perspectives, to organize the policy machinery, and to formulate their own policies. Thus when the Nixon Administration inherited the incipient SALT process from the Johnson Administration in 1969, its first impulse was to slow the momentum toward negotiations so that it could review the situation. The Carter Administration sought to avoid delay but nevertheless derailed the SALT II negotiations for a time with its impulsive March 1977 comprehensive proposal, which was a substantial departure from the negotiating record with which the Soviets were familiar and comfortable. And more recently, of course, the Reagan Administration held arms control in abeyance for nearly a year before embarking first on the INF and then the START negotiations. This recurrent pattern is not necessarily negative. Indeed, it is probably preferable that new administrations be cautious and careful as they begin to formulate arms control policy. But, when combined with the risk that election years may also be disruptive, this means that as many as two years out of every four may be bad ones from the perspective of furthering arms control. This represents a substantial constraint on the process, one that helps to account for the slowness of many negotiations.

The accountability of members of Congress to the public is yet another way that the electoral process can influence the fate of arms control. Congressmen especially tend to be quite sensitive to public opinion, and so will reflect the favorable (as at present) or unfavorable political mood of the country about arms control. But the politician's finely honed instinct for self-preservation causes many to be ever-ready to duck a hot issue or to avoid taking a clear stand on a controversial one. This rule does not apply equally to all Congressmen and Senators at all times on all issues—obviously much depends on the specific circumstances in each case. But it is clear, for example, that when the strength of public opposition to SALT II became evident in 1979, even Senators sympathetic to the treaty were glad to avoid a vote. And the behavior of key figures—for example, Senator Frank Church—seems to be explained by concern over electoral considerations.

In politics, of course, public opinion counts, although not in any easily traceable way. Because it has often been supportive of arms control, it may seem curious or even incorrect to label it an impediment. But, as we have seen in the recent, rapid reversal of public opinion from supporting to doubting the Reagan defense buildup, it is volatile. And, moreover, it is at the same time manipulable—up to a point—and yet to a considerable extent uncontrollable. This means that it is vulnerable to the blandishments of sellers and opposers of strategic arms control (with success going to the side that most effectively mounts its public relations campaign) but that the efforts of both can be overwhelmed by events—usually to the benefit of one side or the other, depending on whether the event is the Soviet invasion of a neighboring country or slips of the tongue by high-level American officials about fighting limited nuclear war.

In addition, public attitudes towards defense and arms control are schizophrenic. Put most simply, the public fears both nuclear war and the Soviet Union, and the political climate of the moment is determined by which of these fears is predominant. The contradictions in public opinion are manifest in a number of ways. It supports arms control in the abstract but is often lukewarm or negative about specific agreements. It often favors both arms control and American military superiority, both negotiated restraint and military buildup. The public seems to believe in negotiating with the Russians but is mistrustful of Soviet power. Moreover, as the Committee on the Present Danger found in its polls (and demonstrated by its success), there is a sizable anti-arms control constituency that can be mobilized to oppose arms agreements. What all this suggests is that, while public opinion can occasionally be a supporting, or even, as at present, a driving force in the arms control process, it does not provide consistent backing for arms negotiations and agreements. For politicians, this means that support of an arms agreement can be a political liability as well as (and perhaps as often as) a strength.

Public opinion, moreover, is the medium through which international politics reverberates in the American body politic. Indeed, the linkage of arms control with international politics or, more specifically, with Soviet behavior, is the most frequently remarked upon political impediment to successful negotiation. At least twice, the strategic arms control process has been disrupted by provocative Soviet behavior, once in 1968 when it invaded Czechoslovakia and again in the fall of 1979 when first the Cuban brigade episode and then the invasion of Afghanistan proved to be the death of SALT II. Allegations about Soviet use of chemical weapons in Cambodia and Afghanistan, which though not proven have not been conclusively disproven, have caused doubts about Soviet willingness to comply with treaties. And more generally, the absence of restraint in Soviet activity in the Third World—in Indochina, the Horn of Africa, Angola, and Afghanistan—have eaten away at what little trust and good will existed toward the Soviet Union in the United States. It has also destroyed the tentative cooperation in the political relationship between the two powers that was partially created by, but which also sustained, the strategic arms control process.

There are some who welcome this linkage, and indeed urge that it be American policy. The reasoning is that the conduct of arms control with the U.S.S.R. can be a reward for Soviet restraint (thereby providing an incentive for restraint if the Soviets are genuinely interested in arms control) and the abandonment of arms negotiations can be, if not punishment, then at least an appropriate gesture of disapproval of Soviet misbehavior. For others, however, the aim should be to isolate strategic arms control as much as possible from international relations so that it is not constantly buffeted by the vicissitudes of what will continue to be a stormy superpower relationship. . . .

The problem is, however, that, whether or not linkage is policy, it is an unavoidable political fact. This is so because of the way that global politics are refracted by the American polity. The Soviet Union is not likely to modify its interests and the general lines of its foreign policy simply to avoid violating American sensibilities. This means there will be crises and problems in the future just as there have been in the past. And international developments that grab headlines and attract coverage on the evening news will inevitably have an impact on public opinion and therefore on the political fortunes of those in the public arena. Consequently, they will as well help to define the realm of the possible in American politics with respect to foreign policy. So it is not simply the linkage of strategic arms control to Soviet international behavior that must be addressed, but also the linkage between international developments and American politics.

CONCLUSION: RUNNING THE GAUNTLET OF POLITICAL IMPEDIMENTS

In summary, then, the disappointing results of arms control seem to be a consequence of the effects of an imposing set of political impediments: policy formulation, the ratification process, electoral politics, congressional politics, bureaucratic politics, public opinion, even international politics have to be aligned properly or managed effectively if arms control is to be pursued successfully. And it is not enough to have only some pieces of the puzzle in place. In 1979, for example, the White House was eager for SALT II ratification, but public and congressional enthusiasm was lacking and Soviet foreign policy behavior was uncooperative. Today, there is passionate public support for arms control, but the White House is more interested in deployments than limitations. Hence, arms control progress requires that all the internal political factors be brought into positive alignment; any agreement will have to run the gauntlet of these potential impediments. Several implications follow from this fact.

First, because the whole of this political process is so slow, it raises another problem: a technological impediment. The pace of technological improvement is sufficiently rapid and the rate of modernization sufficiently fast that force postures change dramatically during the course of negotiations, raising new issues and problems before old ones are completely resolved. During the course of SALT II (1972–1979), for example, both U.S. and Soviet forces changed markedly and some of the more difficult issues—cruise missiles, Backfire bombers, MIRVed heavy missiles—were not in view when the negotiations began.

Second, any agreement that successfully runs the gauntlet of impediments will necessarily be modest in impact—otherwise it would not have survived. Consequently, the failure of arms control to fully live up to its promise is perfectly understandable. But it has led to disillusionment with arms control at both ends of the spectrum: hawks because it has not solved U.S. strategic problems (for example, ICBM vulnerability), doves because it has not ended the arms race.

Third, the strong and direct commitment of the President and his close associates in the White House seems to be a decisive element in determining whether and how much arms control can succeed. John Kennedy, for example, played an important role in pushing the Limited Test

Ban Treaty to completion. Nixon and Kissinger played pivotal roles in the achievement of SALT I. And Jimmy Carter's personal determination helped to make the SALT II agreement possible. The President is the one player in the game who is powerful enough to override many of the political impediments to agreement. But, as the experience of the Carter Administration demonstrates, it is possible for the impediments to defeat even the President.

Fourth, it must be recognized that the effective pursuit of arms control is incompatible with a number of strategic worlds. For arms control to be a significant constraint on the arms competition and for it to contribute to strategic stability, it must preclude many counterforce systems and render impossible many if not all nuclear war-fighting options; in short, it must close off the paths toward a more heavily armed and heavily counterforce world. But that world appears to be preferable to the Soviet military and desirable to a significant portion of the American strategic community, military and civilian. Others disagree with this direction and attempt to use arms control to stop it. But because we cannot agree among ourselves on the strategic environment toward which we should be moving, it is virtually impossible for arms control to play a constructive role in shaping that environment. . . .

Finally, it is worth noting that some of these domestic impediments can be avoided by pursuing the aims of arms control in a different fashion. An arms control strategy that placed less emphasis on formal treaties and negotiations and more on routinized, less public consultations, such as those of the SALT Standing Consultative Commission, would bring these domestic factors much less into play. Moreover, as the early arms control theorists emphatically pointed out, there are many unilateral steps that can be taken in defense policy that further the objectives of arms control, and much more effort could be invested in these. It is often said that the goals of arms control are no different from those of sound military policy. But the latter is not easy to achieve either, and is necessary whether or not there is great success in arms control.

NOTES

1. This may well be as true for the Soviet Union as for the United States. Because little is known about the politics of arms control within the Soviet Union, however, this essay will focus on the American political scene. For some evidence on the Soviet side of the equation, see David Holloway, *War, Militarism, and the Soviet State*, World Order Models Project, Working Paper Number 17 (1981), which examines obstacles to disarmament in the Soviet system; and Rose Gottemoeller, "Decisionmaking for Arms Limitation in the Soviet Union," in Hans Guenter Brauch and Duncan L. Clarke, eds., *Decisionmaking for Arms Limitation: Assessment and Prospects* (Cambridge, Mass.: Ballinger, 1983), pp. 53–80. Suggestive on this point is the Soviet claim, made privately to the Carter Administration, that Brezhnev has "spilled political blood" in order to achieve the Vladivostok Accord and consequently could not easily depart from it, as the Carter Administration had proposed

in March 1977. See Strobe Talbott, *Endgame: The Inside Story of SALT II* (New York: Harper and Row, 1980), p. 73.

2. In one extraordinary year, 1961, there were published four books which still constitute the basic core of thought on arms control. The discussion which follows is based primarily on a reading of them. The books are: Thomas C. Schelling and Morton H. Halperin, *Strategy and Arms Control* (New York: Twentieth Century Fund, 1969); Hedley Bull, *The Control of the Arms Race: Disarmament and Arms Control in the Missile Age* (New York: Praeger Publishers, for the International Institute for Strategic Studies, 1961); Donald G. Brennan, *Arms Control, Disarmament, and National Security* (New York: George Braziller, 1961); and Arthur T. Hadley, *The Nation's Safety and Arms Control* (New York: Viking Press, 1961). . . .

3. Trevor Taylor, "Arms Control: The Bankruptcy of the Strategist's Approach," in David Carlton and Carlo Schaerf, eds., *The Arms Race in the 1980s* (New York: St. Martin's Press, 1982), p. 59. . . .

4. McGeorge Bundy, "Early Thoughts on Controlling the Nuclear Arms Race: A Report to the Secretary of State, January 1953," *International Security*, Vol. 7, No. 2 (Fall 1982), p. 25.

5. Harold Brown, *Thinking About National Security: Defense and Foreign Policy in a Dangerous World* (Boulder, Colo.: Westview Press, 1983), p. 185.

6. Jimmy Carter, *Keeping Faith* (New York: Bantam Books, 1982), p. 218.

7. Hyland, "Institutional Impediments," [in Richard Burt, ed., *Arms Control and Defense Postures in the 1980s* (Boulder, Colo.: Westview Press, 1983)] pp. 100–101.

8. "Views from Backstage," *The New Republic*, April 18, 1983, p. 39.

12 THE IRRELEVANCE OF A NUCLEAR FREEZE

Harold W. Lewis

The trouble with trite and banal sayings is that they are sometimes painfully to the point. In the case of the freeze, the observation that comes to mind is that to every complex problem there exists a solution that is simple, appealing, and wrong. Wrong may be too strong a term for the freeze proposal—it is wrong only in the sense that it is wrong to give laetrile to a cancer patient. In both cases there is little intrinsic harm done, *unless* the patient really believes the treatment will contribute to the cure of his disease, and thereby substitutes wishful thinking for therapy.

And the disease is all too real. Andrei Sakharov was right when he said that the prevention of nuclear war is the central problem for mankind. Yet it is equally true that no one wants it. That is the dilemma—how to forestall the occurrence of something no one wishes to occur, but that cannot be prevented by oversimplifying the issues. Some of the freeze advocates seem to think that there is a back-burner constituency for nuclear war, that there is a military–industrial complex that lusts after destruction, and that all that is necessary is to "send them a message" that we feel differently. Would that it were so—that would be an easy problem. Any serious discussion of these matters has to begin with the recognition that nuclear war is dreaded by everyone—hawks and doves, Russians and Americans, French and British, Japanese and Germans, and so on—and is yet possible.

WHAT CAUSES WAR?

What on Earth has this to do with the freeze? Simply that the connection between a freeze on nuclear weapons (not a reduction to zero by all nations, which *would* help but would probably make conventional war more likely) and the prevention of nuclear war is tenuous indeed. It appears to rest on the assumption that it is somehow the availability of weapons that leads to war, rather than international conflict over national interests, perceived as important by at least one side to the dispute. To prevent wars, we need a peaceful means of resolving genuine

and difficult international questions, including questions that are regarded as threatening the existence or integrity of a nation. We are inch-
ing our way toward such a capability through international organization,
but it is whimsical to believe we are yet there. The inventory of nuclear
weapons has nothing to do with that. In fact, distasteful though the
thought may be to some, these appalling weapons have probably contributed mightily to preserving the peace among the great powers for
the last 35 years. The realistic course for the prevention of nuclear war
lies first and foremost in the prevention of war among the nuclear powers, and, failing that, making the nuclear threshold high enough to deter
a resort to nuclear weapons by a losing side. The freeze proposals are
not directed to either of these.

In fact, as I listen to arguments for the freeze, the common theme I
find is revulsion against nuclear weapons *per se*, with a strong under-
current of antitechnology sentiment. Rarely is there anything resembling
a considered effort to assess the probable impact of a freeze on the
prospects for world peace. It is not too unlike the arguments against
nuclear power (indeed, many of the same people are among the leaders
of the freeze movement), which are often derived from an emotional
and Luddite base, not from any expert assessment of whether nuclear
power is or is not the cleanest, safest and cheapest way we know to
make electricity. In both cases we find ourselves dealing with issues of
symbolism, where the substance has become subordinated to the "message." In both cases that makes it possible to concentrate on the horrors
of failure, rather than on the tools of success. Is that a good way to run
a country?

But let's get back to what the various freeze initiatives say, and what
they would really do if they were to pass. They vary somewhat among
themselves, but the common theme (for example, in the California initiative and in the Senate Joint Resolution introduced by Senators Edward Kennedy and Mark Hatfield) is to call on the US government to
propose to the Soviets a mutually verifiable freeze on the testing, production and further deployment of nuclear "warheads, missiles and
other delivery systems." They do not call for any of these actions to be
taken unilaterally (though there seems to be an underlying assumption
that we are the impediments to progress), but view a freeze as a step
toward halting "nuclear madness." (I have to express a particular resentment here about the tendency to brand anyone who may hold a
different view as "mad." It makes a reasoned debate difficult. Of course
two can play at that game. . . .) In any case, the apparent objective is
solid—the two major nuclear powers do have in their arsenals enough
firepower to destroy each other many times over, in part at least because
each wants to have enough reserve to provide a credible deterrent in
the event of an attack by the other.

Soviet Buildup

We (the US) have actually not increased our firepower in many years, though the same can not be said of the Soviets. We are frozen at a little over a thousand land-based missiles, somewhat over five hundred sea-based missiles, and some aircraft of debatable penetration capability. We have, on the other hand, been converting to multiple independently targeted reentry vehicles. To the extent that one "MIRVs" a missile, the number of warheads goes up while the total firepower goes down; the destructive capability is a relatively complicated function of those two and of the missile's accuracy and reliability. It is, in particular, not true that we have been madly building missiles. The Soviets *have* been increasing their arsenal, for reasons I have yet to understand—maybe their military–industrial complex is responsible, or whatever. It is true that, whatever the reason, they spend nearly twice as large a fraction of their substance on defense as we. Just as in our case, of course, the actual expenditures for strategic offensive weapons are only a small fraction of defense expenditures, the vast bulk of the budget going to maintain conventional forces. However, in their case, there is an expansion of the strategic forces, particularly those directed against our European friends. To negotiate a "mutual and verifiable" freeze, we have to deal with all that.

We also have to deal with the last point—verifiability—which has been a persistent roadblock for decades of negotiations about arms control and nuclear testing. The ABM and SALT negotiations finessed that question by agreeing that each nation was free to use its own intelligence resources, the so-called "national technical means," to verify compliance with the agreements, while each side undertook not to deliberately interfere with the process. This has come to mean satellite and other forms of remote surveillance, which are reasonably comprehensive with respect to deployment and testing, except for low-yield underground testing of nuclear weapons. Production is another matter.

PRESSURE OUR OWN GOVERNMENT?

Presumably the intent of a freeze—in this case a ban—on the testing of nuclear weapons is to prevent a technology "breakthrough" that might disturb the rough parity that now exists between the Soviets and us. It is, in fact, hard to imagine either country depending upon untested weapons, so that a testing freeze is indeed very likely a technology freeze, and stabilizing. However, a ban on nuclear testing already exists, with the exception of low-yield underground testing, and the exception is there precisely because the verification problem has turned out to be technically very difficult in that regime. I don't want to sound overly pessimistic on this point, but one can always conduct a test too small to be detected by *any* system. The real question is whether the threshold for detection can be made low enough to make the rewards for the violator unequal to the risk. Perhaps the freeze advocates know how. Failing that, the only solution is relatively unconstrained on-site inspection, something we have offered and the Soviets have consistently rejected for decades. The leader of the California freeze movement, a real-estate developer, was quoted recently as having said that he expects the Soviets to eventually change their minds on this point, but he didn't explain why "sending a message" to *our* Government, or "changing *our* political climate" (his words, my emphasis) will accomplish this. This low-yield underground testing is the only nuclear testing we or the Soviets have done in years, so this is all the proposed testing ban refers to.

From all the above, it would probably be possible to conclude that I am opposed to the freeze proposals, but that is not so. Nor am I in favor. Nor do I feel that I even care enough to take a position on an issue that is so disjoint from the prospects for avoiding nuclear war, an objective I regard as paramount. . . . To be sure, the freeze movement is likely to provide somewhat more incentive for the negotiators in our Government, and that is good. It cannot provide any guidance in a formal sense, because a "mutual, verifiable freeze" is just one of many possible objectives for arms-control negotiations, and, while the desire for arms control and reduction is a proper subject for political influence, the form of any putative agreement is not a matter for bumper-sticker or rock-concert politics. Finally, one can ask whether political pressure on our Government by dissenting people on our side is likely to increase the Soviet incentive to strike a mutually satisfactory bargain. . . .

Many good songs end by repeating the refrain. I can't think of a better final paragraph for this article than the first. Please reread it.

13 THE MILITARY ROLE OF NUCLEAR WEAPONS: PERCEPTIONS AND MISPERCEPTIONS

Robert S. McNamara

The public, on both sides of the Atlantic, is engaged in debate on controversial questions relating to nuclear weapons: the desirability of a nuclear freeze; the deployment of Pershing II and cruise missiles to Western Europe; the production of the MX missile and the B-1 bomber; the development of the neutron bomb; and proposals to reduce the risk of nuclear war by such measures as the withdrawal of tactical nuclear weapons from forward areas and the declaration of a strategy of "no launch on warning."

These questions, however, cannot be thoughtfully discussed, and certainly not adequately answered, until there has been general agreement on the military role of nuclear weapons. If there is confusion in the public mind on this matter, it only mirrors the disagreement among those most familiar with such weapons and their implications. . . .

[T]here are three quite contradictory and mutually exclusive views of the military role of nuclear weapons:

- Such weapons can be used in a controlled or selective way, i.e., they have a war-fighting role in defense of the NATO nations. Therefore, a strategy of "flexible response," which has been the foundation of NATO's war plans since 1967, including possible "early first use of nuclear weapons," should be continued. Underlying this policy is the belief that NATO can achieve "escalation dominance"—i.e., NATO can prevent the Warsaw Pact from extending the use of nuclear weapons beyond the level NATO chooses, with the implication that a nuclear war once started can remain limited.

- Any use of nuclear weapons by the United States or the Soviet Union is likely to lead to uncontrolled escalation with unacceptable damage to both sides. Therefore, nuclear weapons have no military use other than to deter first use of such weapons by one's adversary.

- Although initiating the use of nuclear weapons is likely to lead to uncontrolled escalation, with devastation of both societies, the

Note: Some footnotes have been deleted, and others have been renumbered to appear in consecutive order.

threat of such use by NATO acts as a deterrent to both Soviet conventional and nuclear aggression. It is not practical to build up an equivalent deterrent in the form of conventional forces; therefore the threat of early use of nuclear weapons should never be withdrawn.

I propose to examine these views by exploring four questions:

- What is NATO's present nuclear strategy and how did it evolve?
- Can NATO initiate the use of nuclear weapons, in response to a Soviet attack, with benefit to the Alliance?
- Even if the "first use" of nuclear weapons is not to NATO's advantage, does not the threat of such use add to the deterrent and would not the removal of the threat increase the risk of war?
- If it is not to NATO's advantage to respond to a Soviet conventional attack by the use of nuclear weapons, can NATO's conventional forces, within realistic political and financial constraints, be strengthened sufficiently to substitute for the nuclear threat as a deterrent to Soviet aggression?

II

Questions of the military utility of nuclear weapons are addressed most realistically in the context of the possibility of warfare in Europe. Throughout the postwar period the security of Europe has been the centerpiece of U.S. foreign policy; it is likely to remain so indefinitely. In no other region have the two great powers deployed so many nuclear weapons. In no other part of the world are military doctrines which specify the use of nuclear weapons granted such wide-ranging credibility.

The use of nuclear weapons has been an integral part of NATO's military strategy since virtually the inception of the Alliance.

Shortly after the North Atlantic Treaty was ratified in 1949, estimates were made of the size of the Soviet military threat as a basis for developing NATO's military strategy and force structure. Believing that the U.S.S.R. could muster as many as 175 divisions against Western Europe, NATO military planners concluded that the Alliance would require 96 of its own divisions—which were larger than those of the Soviet Union—in order to mount an adequate defense. This estimate was accepted by the NATO ministers in February 1952 at their annual meeting in Lisbon.

It soon became clear, however, that the member nations were not willing to meet these so-called Lisbon force goals. Instead, the Alliance turned consciously to nuclear weapons as a substitute for the financial and manpower sacrifices which would have been necessary to mount an adequate conventional defense. . . .

Nor was this new emphasis only rhetorical. A Presidential Directive (NSC-162/2) ordered the Joint Chiefs of Staff to plan on using nuclear armaments whenever it would be to the U.S. advantage to do so. Changes were made in the organization and plans of the U.S. Army so that it would be better able to fight on nuclear battlefields. By late 1953, substantial numbers of tactical nuclear weapons—artillery shells, bombs, short-range missiles, nuclear mines, and others—were beginning to be deployed in Europe. The buildup of NATO tactical nuclear weapons continued steadily, peaking in the mid-1960s at around 7,000. Although large numbers of conventional forces were retained on the continent, until the early 1960s their only purpose was seen to be to contain an attack long enough for nuclear strikes to defeat the aggressor. . . .

By December 1954, the NATO ministers felt comfortable enough with the nuclear strategy to reduce the force level objective from 96 to 30 active divisions. Two years later, the Alliance formally adopted the policy of "massive retaliation" in a document known as MC 14/2.

Whether the balance of nuclear forces between the Warsaw Pact and NATO, as it was developing during the mid-1950s, justified adoption of NATO's nuclear strategy is arguable. But its merit had become questionable to many by the early 1960s. Soon after taking office in January 1961, the Kennedy Administration began a detailed analysis of the policy's strengths and weaknesses.

These studies revealed two major deficiencies in the reasoning that had led to the adoption of MC 14/2: first, the relative balance of NATO and Warsaw Pact conventional forces was far less unfavorable from a Western perspective than had been assumed (the power of Soviet forces had been overestimated and that of NATO forces underestimated); and second, there was great uncertainty as to whether and, if so, how nuclear weapons could be used to NATO's advantage.

President Kennedy, therefore, authorized me as Secretary of Defense to propose, at a meeting of the NATO ministers in Athens in May 1962, to substitute a strategy of "flexible response" for the existing doctrine of "massive retaliation."

The new strategy required a buildup of NATO's conventional forces, but on a scale that we believed to be practical on both financial and political grounds. Instead of the early massive use of nuclear weapons, it permitted a substantial raising of the nuclear threshold by planning for the critical initial responses to Soviet aggression to be made by conventional forces alone. The strategy was based on the expectation that NATO's conventional capabilities could be improved sufficiently so that the use of nuclear weapons would be unnecessary. But, under the new doctrine, even if this expectation turned out to be false, any use of nuclear weapons would be "late and limited."

Our proposal of the new strategy was the result of the recognition by U.S. civilian and military officials that NATO's vastly superior nuclear capabilities, measured in terms of numbers of weapons, did not translate into usable military power. Moreover, we understood that the initial use of even a small number of strategic or tactical nuclear weapons implied risks which could threaten the very survival of the nation. Consequently, we, in effect, proposed confining nuclear weapons to only two roles in the NATO context:

- deterring the Soviets' initiation of nuclear war;
- as a weapon of last resort, if conventional defense failed, to persuade the aggressor to terminate the conflict on acceptable terms. . . .

The revised strategy proposed to deter aggression by maintaining forces adequate to counter an attack at whatever level the aggressor chose to fight. Should such a direct confrontation not prove successful, the strategy proposed to escalate as necessary, including the initial use of nuclear weapons, forcing the aggressor to confront costs and risks disproportionate to his initial objectives. At all times, however, the flexible response strategy specified that efforts should be made to control the scope and intensity of combat. Thus, for example, initial nuclear attacks presumably would be made by short-range tactical systems in an attempt to confine the effects of nuclear warfare to the battlefield. Even so, the strategy retained the ultimate escalatory threat of a strategic exchange between U.S. and Soviet homelands to make clear the final magnitude of the dangers being contemplated.

"Flexible response" has remained NATO's official doctrine for more than 15 years. Its essential element, however—building sufficient conventional capabilities to offset those of the Warsaw Pact—has never been achieved. Indeed, during the late 1960s and early 1970s, the Alliance may have fallen farther behind its opponent. Although NATO has made considerable strides in improving its conventional posture in more recent years, most military experts believe that the conventional balance continues to favor the Warsaw Pact; they thus conclude that an attack by Soviet conventional forces would require the use of nuclear weapons, most likely within a matter of hours. NATO's operational war plans reflect this belief. The substantial raising of the "nuclear threshold," as was envisioned when "flexible response" was first conceived, has not become a reality. . . .

III

Doubts about the wisdom of NATO's strategy of flexible response, never far from the surface, emerged as a major issue in the late 1970s; debate has intensified in the ensuing years. The debate hinges on assessments of the military value of nuclear weapons.

The nuclear balance has changed substantially since the Kennedy Administration first proposed a strategy of flexible response. Both sides have virtually completely refurbished their inventories, increasing the number of weapons of all three different types—battlefield, intermediate-range and strategic—and vastly improving the performance characteristics of both the weapons themselves and their delivery systems. Because the Soviet Union was so far behind the United States in the early 1960s, the quantitative changes, at least, appear to have been more favorable for the U.S.S.R. The ratio of warheads on strategic and intermediate-range launchers, for example, has shifted from a very great U.S. advantage in 1962 to a far more modest advantage at present.

As the Soviet Union moved toward and then achieved rough parity in strategic and intermediate-range forces, a crucial element of the flexible response strategy became less and less credible.

It will be recalled that the strategy calls for the Alliance to initiate nuclear war with battlefield weapons if conventional defenses fail, and to escalate the type of nuclear weapons used (and therefore the targets of those weapons), as necessary, up to and including the use of strategic forces against targets in the U.S.S.R. itself. Given the tremendous devastation which those Soviet strategic forces that survived a U.S. first strike would now be able to inflict on this country, it is difficult to imagine any U.S. President, under any circumstances, initiating a strategic strike except in retaliation against a Soviet nuclear strike. . . .

In short, a key element of the flexible response strategy has been overtaken by a change in the physical realities of the nuclear balance. With huge survivable arsenals on both sides, strategic nuclear weapons have lost whatever military utility may once have been attributed to them. Their sole purpose, at present, is to deter the other side's first use of its strategic forces.

Thus, given that NATO would not be the first to use strategic nuclear weapons, is it conceivable that the first use of tactical weapons would be to its military advantage?

The roughly 6,000 NATO nuclear weapons now deployed in Europe consist of warheads for air-defense missiles, nuclear mines (known as atomic demolition munitions), warheads for shorter-range missiles, nuclear bombs, and nuclear-armed artillery shells. . . . [N]uclear artillery shells comprise the largest portion of the stockpile, about one-third of the total. They are also the weapons which cause the greatest worry.

There are two types of nuclear artillery shells in the NATO inventory: those for 155mm howitzers and those for 203mm cannons. Both the howitzers and cannons are dual-capable: they can be used to fire shells containing conventional explosives as well as nuclear weapons. The precise ranges of these systems are classified, but most accounts put them at around ten miles. Because of the short range of nuclear artillery, the guns and their nuclear shells tend to be deployed close to the potential front lines of any conflict in Europe—there are, in effect, approximately 2,000 short-range nuclear warheads concentrated at a few sites close to the German border.

Atomic demolition munitions (ADMs) also raise particular concerns. These weapons are about 25 years old and probably no longer reliable. Intended to block mountain passes and other "choke points" on potential Soviet invasion routes, their effects would be felt on NATO territory. Moreover, to be effective they would have to be emplaced before a war actually began. Such an action could aggravate a crisis and would probably contribute to the likelihood of the war starting. At the same time, because ADMs would have to be used at the very onset of the conflict, their use would mean that NATO had not tested the ability of its conventional forces to contain a Warsaw Pact invasion.

Similar problems beset nuclear-armed air defense systems. They are old and probably unreliable. And they are intended for use at the onset of a conflict—to disrupt the large-scale air attacks that would accompany a Warsaw Pact invasion—thus negating the strategy of "flexible response."

In an acute crisis in which the risk of war seemed to be rising, these characteristics of nuclear artillery, mines, and air defense systems would be likely to lead to pressures on NATO's political leaders, particularly the U.S. President, to delegate the authority to release these weapons to the military commanders on the scene. Whether such authority were delegated or not, it is these characteristics—most importantly the vulnerability of NATO's nuclear artillery—which lead many observers to predict that the Alliance would use tactical nuclear weapons within hours of the start of a war in Europe. In effect, whether its military or civilian leaders retained decision authority, NATO would be likely to face the choice of either using its battlefield nuclear weapons or seeing them overrun or destroyed by the enemy.

In terms of their military utility, NATO has not found it possible to develop plans for the use of nuclear artillery which would both assure a clear advantage to the Alliance and at the same time avoid the very high risk of escalating to all-out nuclear war. . . .

Two problems stand in the way.

First, since the assumption is made that NATO will be responding to a Warsaw Pact invasion of Western Europe, and since the artillery has short range, the nuclear explosions would occur on NATO's own territory. If a substantial portion of the 2,000 nuclear artillery shells were fired, not only would the Warsaw Pact likely suffer heavy casualties among its military personnel, but large numbers of NATO's civilian and military personnel also would likely be killed and injured. There also would be considerable damage to property, farmland and urbanized areas.[1]

Moreover, there is no reason to believe that the Warsaw Pact, now possessing tactical and intermediate-range nuclear forces at least comparable to those of NATO, would not respond to NATO's initiation of nuclear war with major nuclear attacks of its own. These attacks would probably seek most importantly to reduce NATO's ability to fight a nuclear war by destroying command and control facilities, nuclear weapon storage sites, and the aircraft, missiles, and artillery which would deliver NATO's nuclear weapons. Direct support facilities like ports and airfields would likely also be attacked in the initial Warsaw Pact nuclear offensive. Thus the war would escalate from the battlefield to the rest of Western Europe (and probably to Eastern Europe as well, as NATO retaliated).

What would be the consequences of such a conflict? In 1955 an exercise called "Carte Blanche" simulated the use of 335 nuclear weapons, 80 percent of which were assumed to detonate on German territory. In terms of immediate casualties (ignoring the victims of radiation, disease, and so forth), it was estimated that between 1.5 and 1.7 million people would die and another 3.5 million would be wounded—more than five times the German civilian casualties in World War II—in the first two days. This exercise prompted Helmut Schmidt to remark that the use of tactical nuclear weapons "will not defend Europe, but destroy it."[2] . . .

Have the more modern weapons deployed on both sides in the 1970s changed the likely results of nuclear war in Europe? Not at all! A group of experts were assembled recently by the U.N. Secretary General to study nuclear war. They simulated a conflict in which 1,500 nuclear artillery shells and 200 nuclear bombs were used by the two sides against each other's military targets. The experts concluded that as a result of such a conflict there would be a minimum of five to six million immediate civilian casualties and 400,000 military casualties, and that at least an additional 1.1 million civilians would suffer from radiation disease.[3]

It should be remembered that all these scenarios, as horrible as they would be, involve the use of only a small portion of the tactical nuclear weapons deployed in Europe, and assume further that none of the roughly 20,000 nuclear warheads in the U.S. and U.S.S.R.'s central strategic arsenals would be used. Yet portions of those central forces are intended for European contingencies: the United States has allocated 400 of its submarine-based Poseidon warheads for use by NATO; the

Soviet Union, it is believed, envisions as many as several hundred of its ICBMs being used against targets in Europe.

Is it realistic to expect that a nuclear war could be limited to the detonation of tens or even hundreds of nuclear weapons, even though each side would have tens of thousands of weapons remaining available for use?

The answer is clearly no. Such an expectation requires the assumption that even though the initial strikes would have inflicted large-scale casualties and damage to both sides, one or the other—feeling disadvantaged—would give in. But under such circumstances, leaders on both sides would be under unimaginable pressure to avenge their losses and secure the interests being challenged. And each would fear that the opponent might launch a larger attack at any moment. Moreover, they would both be operating with only partial information because of the disruption to communications caused by the chaos on the battlefield (to say nothing of possible strikes against communications facilities). Under such conditions, it is highly likely that rather than surrender, each side would launch a larger attack, hoping that this step would bring the action to a halt by causing the opponent to capitulate. . . .

It is inconceivable to me, as it has been to others who have studied the matter, that "limited" nuclear wars would remain limited—any decision to use nuclear weapons would imply a high probability of the same cataclysmic consequences as a total nuclear exchange. In sum, I know of no plan which gives reasonable assurance that nuclear weapons can be used beneficially in NATO's defense.

I do not believe the Soviet Union wishes war with the West. And certainly the West will not attack the U.S.S.R. or its allies. But dangerous frictions between the Warsaw Pact and NATO have developed in the past and are likely to do so in the future. If deterrence fails and conflict develops, the present NATO strategy carries with it a high risk that Western civilization, as we know it, will be destroyed.

If there is a case for NATO retaining its present strategy, that case must rest on the strategy's contribution to the deterrence of Soviet aggression being worth the risk of nuclear war in the event deterrence fails.

IV

The question of what deters Soviet aggression is an extremely difficult one. To answer it, we must put ourselves in the minds of several individuals who would make the decision to initiate war. We must ask what their objectives are for themselves and their nation, what they value and what they fear. We must assess their proclivity to take risks, to bluff, or to be bluffed. We must guess at how they see us—our will and our capabilities—and determine what we can do to strengthen their belief in the sincerity of our threats and our promises.

But most difficult of all, we must evaluate all these factors in the context of an acute international crisis. Our problem is not to persuade the Soviets not to initiate war today. It is to cause them to reach the same decision at some future time when, for whatever reason—for example, an uprising in Eastern Europe that is getting out of control, or a U.S.-Soviet clash in Iran, or conflict in the Middle East—they may be tempted to gamble and try to end what they see as a great threat to their own security.

In such a crisis, perceptions of risks and stakes may change substantially. What may look like a reckless gamble in more tranquil times might then be seen merely as a reasonable risk. This will be the case particularly if the crisis deteriorates so that war begins to appear more and more likely. In such a situation, the advantages of achieving tactical surprise by going first can appear to be more and more important.

As I have indicated, the launch of strategic nuclear weapons against the Soviet homeland would lead almost certainly to a response in kind which would inflict unacceptable damage on Europe and the United States—it would be an act of suicide. The threat of such an action, therefore, has lost all credibility as a deterrent to Soviet conventional aggression. The ultimate sanction in the flexible response strategy is thus no longer operative. One cannot build a credible deterrent on an incredible action.

Many sophisticated observers in both the United States and Europe, however, believe that the threat to use tactical nuclear weapons in response to Warsaw Pact aggression increases the perceived likelihood of such an action, despite its absolute irrationality. They believe that by maintaining battlefield weapons near the front lines, along with the requisite plans and doctrines to implement the strategy that calls for their use, NATO confronts the Warsaw Pact with a dangerous possibility which cannot be ignored.

In contemplating the prospect of war, they argue, Soviet leaders must perceive a risk that NATO would implement its doctrine and use nuclear weapons on the battlefield, thus initiating an escalatory process which could easily get out of control, leading ultimately to a devastating strategic exchange between the two homelands. It is not that NATO would coolly and deliberately calculate that a strategic exchange made sense, they explain, but rather that the dynamics of the crisis would literally force such an action—or so Soviet leaders would have to fear.

Each step of the escalation would create a new reality, altering each side's calculation of the risks and benefits of alternative courses of action. Once U.S. and Soviet military units clashed, perceptions of the likelihood of more intense conflicts would be changed radically. Once any nuclear weapon had been used operationally, assessments of other potential nuclear attacks would be radically altered.

In short, those who assert that the nuclear first use threat serves to strengthen NATO's deterrent believe that, regardless of objective assessments of the irrationality of any such action, Soviet decision-makers must pay attention to the realities of the battlefield and the dangers of the escalatory process. And, in so doing, they maintain, the Soviets will perceive a considerable risk that conventional conflict will lead to the use of battlefield weapons, which will lead in turn to theater-wide nuclear conflict, which will inevitably spread to the homelands of the superpowers.

In fact, it was a desire to strengthen the perception of such a likely escalation that led NATO to its December 1979 decision to deploy the new intermediate-range Pershing II and the nuclear-armed cruise missiles in Europe. The key element in that decision was that the new missiles would be capable of striking Soviet territory, thus presumably precipitating a Soviet attack on U.S. territory and a U.S. retaliation against the whole of the Soviet homeland. The new weapons thus "couple" U.S. strategic forces with the forces deployed in Europe, easing concerns that the Soviets might perceive a firebreak in the escalatory process. So long as the escalation is perceived to be likely to proceed smoothly, the logic continues, then the Warsaw Pact will be deterred from taking the first step—the conventional aggression—which might start the process.

But for the same reason that led Henry Kissinger to recognize that a U.S. President is unlikely to initiate the use of U.S.-based strategic nuclear weapons against the U.S.S.R. [because, in Kissinger's words, "we risk the destruction of civilization"—eds.], so a President would be unlikely to launch missiles from European soil against Soviet territory.

And, as I have indicated, more and more Western political and military leaders are coming to recognize, and publicly avowing, that even the use of battlefield nuclear weapons in Europe would bring greater destruction to NATO than any conceivable contribution they might make to NATO's defense.

There is less and less likelihood, therefore, that NATO would authorize the use of any nuclear weapons except in response to a Soviet nuclear attack. As this diminishing prospect becomes more and more widely perceived—and it will—whatever deterrent value still resides in NATO's nuclear strategy will diminish still further.

There are additional factors to be considered. Whether it contributes to deterrence or not, NATO's threat of "first use" is not without its costs: it is a most contentious policy, leading to divisive debates both within individual nations and between the members of the Alliance; it reduces NATO's preparedness for conventional war; and, as I have indicated, it increases the risk of nuclear war.

Preparing for tactical nuclear war limits NATO's ability to defend itself conventionally in several ways. Nuclear weapons are indeed "special" munitions. They require special command, control and communications arrangements. They require special security precautions. They limit the flexibility with which units can be deployed and military plans altered. Operations on a nuclear battlefield would be very different than those in a conventional conflict; NATO planning must take these differences into account.

Moreover, since most of the systems that would deliver NATO's nuclear munitions are dual-purpose, some number of aircraft and artillery must be reserved to be available for nuclear attacks early in a battle, if that became necessary, and are thus not available for delivering conventional munitions.

Most important, though, the reliance on NATO's nuclear threats for deterrence makes it more difficult to muster the political and financial support necessary to sustain an adequate conventional military force. Both publics and governments point to the nuclear force as the "real deterrent," thus explaining their reluctance to allocate even modest sums for greater conventional capabilities.

To the extent that the nuclear threat has deterrent value, it is because it in fact increases the risk of nuclear war. The location of nuclear weapons in what would be forward parts of the battlefield; the associated development of operational plans assuming the early use of nuclear weapons; the possibility that release authority would be delegated to field commanders prior to the outset of war—these factors and many others would lead to a higher probability that if war actually began in Europe, it would soon turn into a nuclear conflagration.

Soviet predictions of such a risk, in fact, could lead them to initiate nuclear war themselves. For one thing, preparing themselves for the possibility of NATO nuclear attacks means that they must avoid massing their offensive units. This would make it more difficult to mount a successful conventional attack, raising the incentives to initiate the war with a nuclear offensive. Moreover, if the Soviets believe that NATO would indeed carry out its nuclear threat once they decided to go to war— whether as a matter of deliberate choice or because the realities of the battlefield would give the Alliance no choice—the Soviets would have virtually no incentive not to initiate nuclear war themselves.

I repeat, this would only be the case if they had decided that war was imminent and believed there would be high risk that NATO's threats would be fulfilled. But if those two conditions were valid, the military advantages to the Warsaw Pact of preemptive nuclear strikes on NATO's nuclear storage sites, delivery systems, and support facilities could be compelling.

The costs of whatever deterrent value remains in NATO's nuclear strategy are, therfore, substantial. Could not equivalent deterrence be achieved at lesser "cost"? I believe the answer is yes. Compared to the huge risks which the Alliance now runs by relying on increasingly less credible nuclear threats, recent studies have pointed to ways by which the conventional forces may be strengthened at modest cost.

V

Writing in [*Foreign Affairs* in 1982] General Bernard Rogers, the present Supreme Allied Commander in Europe, stated that major improvements in NATO's conventional forces were feasible at a modest price.[4] These improvements, he said, would permit a shift from the present strategy requiring the early use of nuclear weapons to a strategy of "no early use of nuclear weapons." General Rogers estimated the cost to be approximately one percent per year greater than the three percent annual increase (in real terms) which the members of NATO, meeting in Washington, had agreed to in 1978.

An experienced Pentagon consultant, M.I.T. Professor William W. Kaufmann, has taken General Rogers' suggestions of four percent annual increases in NATO defense budgets and analyzed how those funds could best be allocated to improve the Alliance's conventional defenses. After an exhaustive analysis, he concluded that a conventional force could be acquired which would be sufficiently strong to give a high probability of deterring Soviet aggression without threatening the use of nuclear weapons.

Recently, an international study group also analyzed the possibilities for moving away from NATO's present nuclear reliance.[5] The steering committee of this "European Security Study" . . . concludes that NATO's conventional forces could be strengthened substantially at very modest cost—a total of approximately $20 billion which would be spent over a period of five or six years. For comparative purposes, note that the MX missile program is expected to cost $18 billion over the next five years.

The European Security Study stated that to constitute an effective deterrent, NATO's conventional forces did not have to match specific Soviet capabilities. Rather, these forces need only be strong enough to create serious concerns for Warsaw Pact planners whether or not their attack could succeed.

To accomplish this, the study concluded, NATO's conventional forces would have to be able to:

- stop the initial Warsaw Pact attack;
- erode the enemy's air power;
- interdict the follow-on and reinforcing armored formations which the Pact would attempt to bring up to the front-lines;
- disrupt the Pact's command, control, and communications network; and
- ensure its own secure, reliable, and effective communications.

The report outlines in detail how NATO could achieve these five objectives utilizing newly available technologies, and accomplishing with conventional weapons what previously had required nuclear munitions. These technological advances would permit the very accurate delivery of large numbers of conventional weapons, along with dramatic improvements in the ability to handle massive quantities of military information.

The effectiveness of the new technologies was testified to most recently by Senator Sam Nunn, a leading congressional expert on European defense issues:

> We now have at hand new conventional technologies capable of destroying the momentum of a Soviet invasion by means of isolating the first echelon of attacking forces from reinforcing follow-on echelons. These technologies . . . capitalize on three major advances. The first is the substantially improved lethality of improved conventional munitions. . . .The second is the . . . growing capability of microelectronics to enhance the rapid collection, processing, distribution, and ability to act upon information about the size, character, location, and movement of enemy units. . . . The third is improved ability to move and target quickly large quantities of improved conventional firepower against enemy force concentrations.[6]

The potential of these new conventional technologies is great. Unfortunately, they have not yet been accepted by any NATO nation for incorporation in its force structure and defense budget.

Moving from the present situation to revised strategic doctrines, war plans, and force structures to implement a conventional deterrent strategy could not be accomplished overnight. Still, over time, NATO's basic strategy could be modified within realistic political and financial constraints. . . .

In the meantime, immediate steps could be taken to reduce the risk of nuclear war. For example:

- Weapons modernization programs designed to support a strategy of early use of nuclear weapons—such as those to produce and deploy new generations of nuclear artillery shells—could be halted.
- The Alliance's tactical nuclear posture could be thoroughly overhauled, with an eye toward shifting to a posture intended solely to

deter the first use of nuclear weapons by the Warsaw Pact. Such a shift would permit major reductions in the number of nuclear weapons now deployed with NATO's forces in Europe; no more, and probably less, than 3,000 weapons would be sufficient. Those weapons which raise the most serious problems of release authority and pressures for early use—atomic demolition munitions and nuclear air defense systems—could be withdrawn immediately. Nuclear artillery could be withdrawn as the program to improve the conventional posture was implemented.

- The creation of a zone on both sides of the border in Europe, beginning in the Central Region, within which no nuclear munitions could be deployed, could be proposed to the Soviets.[7] The agreement to create such a zone could be verified by on-site inspections on a challenge basis. The Soviet Union has stated officially that it supports a nuclear-free zone, although it proposed that the width of the zone be far greater than is likely to be acceptable to NATO. If agreement could be reached on the size of the zone and adequate methods established to verify compliance with the agreement, such an agreement could build confidence on both sides that pressures for early use of nuclear weapons could be controlled. . . .

VI

. . .Having spent seven years as Secretary of Defense dealing with the problems unleashed by the initial nuclear chain reaction 40 years ago, I do not believe we can avoid serious and unacceptable risk of nuclear war until we recognize—and until we base all our military plans, defense budgets, weapon deployments, and arms negotiations on the recognition—that *nuclear weapons serve no military purpose whatsoever. They are totally useless—except only to deter one's opponent from using them.* . . .

. . . [I]f we are to reach a consensus within the Alliance on the military role of nuclear weapons—an issue that is fundamental to the peace and security of both the West and the East—we must face squarely and answer the following questions.

- Can we conceive of ways to utilize nuclear weapons, in response to Soviet aggression with conventional forces, which would be beneficial to NATO?

- Would any U.S. President be likely to authorize such use of nuclear weapons?

- If we cannot conceive of a beneficial use of nuclear weapons, and if we believe it unlikely that a U.S. President would authorize their use in such a situation, should we continue to accept the risks associated with basing NATO's strategy, war plans and nuclear warhead deployment on the assumption that the weapons would be used in the early hours of an East-West conflict?

- Would the types of conventional forces recommended by General Rogers, Professor William Kaufmann and the European Security Study, serve as an adequate deterrent to non-nuclear aggression by the U.S.S.R.? If so, are we not acting irresponsibly by continuing to accept the increased risks of nuclear war associated with present NATO strategy in place of the modest expenditures necessary to acquire and sustain such forces?

- Do we favor a world free of nuclear weapons? If so, should we not recognize that such a world would not provide a "nuclear deterrent" to Soviet conventional aggression? If we could live without such a deterrent then, why can't we do so now—thereby moving a step toward a non-nuclear world?

NOTES

1. A 100-kiloton tactical nuclear weapon would be needed to destroy approximately 50 to 100 armored fighting vehicles (e.g., tanks) in dispersed formation, the equivalent of a regiment. Such a weapon would create general destruction (of structures and people) in a circle with a diameter of 4.5 miles (an area of 15 square miles). A blast circle of this size, in typical Western European countries, would be likely to include two or three villages or towns of several thousand persons. In addition, depending on the nature of the weapon and height of burst, a much larger area could be affected by fallout. Several hundred of such tactical nuclear weapons would be required to counter an armored development in Europe. See Seymour J. Deitchman, *New Technology and Military Power*, Boulder (Colo.): Westview Press, 1979, p. 12.

2. Helmut Schmidt, *Defense or Retaliation?* New York: Praeger, 1962, p. 101; Schmidt's comment and the exercise result are cited in Jeffrey Record, *U.S. Nuclear Weapons in Europe*, Washington: Brookings, 1974.

3. *General and Complete Disarmament: A Comprehensive Study on Nuclear Weapons: Report of the Secretary General, Fall 1980*, New York: United Nations, 1981.

4. General Bernard W. Rogers, "The Atlantic Alliance: Prescriptions for a Difficult Decade," *Foreign Affairs*, Summer 1982, pp. 1145–56.

5. *Strengthening Conventional Deterrence in Europe*, Report of the European Security Study, New York: St. Martin's Press, 1983.

6. *Congressional Record*, 98th Cong., Ist sess., July 13, 1983, Washington: GPO, 1983, p. S 9853.

7. Such a proposal was made in the Report of the International Commission on Disarmament and Security Issues, *Common Security: A Program for Disarmament*, London: Pan Books, 1982.

14 LEAPING THE FIREBREAK
Michael T. Klare

Since the first atomic bombs were dropped on Hiroshima and Nagasaki in 1945, military theorists have recognized that there is a nuclear "firebreak"—a barrier that will prevent even the most intensive forms of conventional combat from escalating into nuclear war. Existence of the firebreak attests to the fundamental, qualitative difference between the most destructive forms of conventional warfare and the catastrophic potential of nuclear conflict. However violent a conflict on the conventional side of the barrier, it cannot annihilate the planet; once the firebreak is crossed, though, there can be no such assurances.

Preservation of the firebreak is, therefore, essential to continued human survival. And human survival is being jeopardized right now by developments in both conventional and nuclear weaponry that threaten to eliminate the firebreak.

The most basic function of the firebreak is to serve as a powerful psychological deterrent to escalation. By emphasizing the profound difference between conventional and nuclear war, it underscores the unique military and political risks a government would assume if it were to cross that line. The firebreak also plays a more direct role in preventing nuclear war: By interrupting the process of escalation, it provides maneuvering space within which warring parties can agree to limit the scale of hostilities.

With the deployment of ever more powerful nuclear weapons, that limiting function of the firebreak has assumed tremendous importance, for once the line is crossed, there will be little opportunity to control the process of retaliation and escalation.

"The 'firebreak' must be absolute," Swedish arms expert Alva Myrdal wrote in her classic study, *The Game of Disarmament*. "If the present distinction between nuclear and conventional weapons becomes blurred, it will be impossible . . . to avoid uncontrollable escalation."

Scientists have often warned of potential threats to the firebreak, but the discrepancy in destructive power between nuclear and conventional weapons has helped to preserve the gap. Recently, however, the development of new types of both conventional and nuclear munitions has begun to erode the firebreak. Modern conventional weapons employ explosive technologies that begin to approach the damage potential of the smallest nuclear weapons. And nuclear munitions now under development have the controlled destructive effects associated with conventional arms. The firebreak, in other words, is being encroached upon from *both* sides of the conventional-nuclear spectrum.

As conventional weapons become more destructive, it will become possible to escalate non-nuclear conflicts to levels of violence approximating those of a limited nuclear conflict. Once such levels are reached, tactical nuclear munitions could easily be perceived as essentially interchangeable with the most powerful conventional arms.

In these circumstances, there will be little inhibition against going "one step further" and substituting nuclear for conventional munitions. As Julian Perry Robinson of Sussex University's Science Policy Research Unit observed at a recent Pugwash Conference, "If the destructiveness of the one [class of munitions] in fact overlaps with that of the other, the threshold becomes merely symbolic. How strong and how permanent a bulwark against nuclear war can such an abstraction be?"

Unfortunately, Robinson's question has gone unanswered. The frightening potential of the new generation of intercontinental nuclear missiles and Eurostrategic nuclear arms has impelled national leaders, arms control specialists, and peace activists on both sides of the Atlantic to accord highest priority to the dangers posed by such nuclear weapons. These efforts are critically important, but they divert attention from the equally threatening trend to merge conventional and nuclear warfare. It is essential that we understand the threats to the firebreak and consider any new steps that may be needed to ensure its preservation.

In the past decade, military scientists in the United States, Europe, and the Soviet Union have developed new generations of conventional munitions that have greater range, accuracy, and destructive potential than anything previously available. These weapons, combining advanced guidance and target-detection systems with new explosive technologies, are capable of engaging targets with great precision and of saturating very large areas. As Senator Sam Nunn noted in a report to Congress [in 1982], "Long-range conventional weapons are now being developed that begin to approach the destructive potential of small-yield (two to three kiloton) battlefield nuclear weapons."

Weapons of the type cited by Nunn are being developed under the Pentagon's "Assault Breaker" program, designed to produce conventional arms capable of destroying enemy bases and attack formations deep inside Warsaw Pact territory. As now envisioned, the Assault Breaker system (also known as the Joint Tactical Missile System program) will consist of a short-range missile that will break open over the battlefield and spew out hundreds of terminally guided submunitions capable of seeking out and striking individual targets in the area. Distinct versions of these weapons are being designed for attacks on vehicles, fortifications, and personnel, so that each missile can be individually loaded for specific targets.

By dispersing the submunitions in a uniform pattern, the missile can ensure blanket coverage of sizable areas—as much as one square kilometer, approximately the same area destroyed by a one-kiloton neutron bomb. West German Defense Minister Manfred Woerner has acknowledged that "the effectiveness of these [conventional] weapons enters a dimension that heretofore was limited to nuclear weapons."

Some strategists suggest that deployment of such "near-nuclear" conventional weapons will strengthen deterrence and "raise the nuclear threshold" by enhancing NATO's capacity to repel a conventional Warsaw Pact attack with conventional weapons. "If NATO had those [improved conventional] capabilities," General Bernard W. Rogers, the NATO commander-in-chief, told the Association of the U.S. Army . . . "then the aggressor—should he attack conventionally and his attack be frustrated—would be forced either to withdraw or make the agonizing decision to be the first to escalate to nuclear weapons—[a situation in which] I do not believe Soviet leaders would attack."

This is the basis upon which many security analysts, including some who have endorsed a "no first use" nuclear policy, support the development of high-tech conventional weapons. But other analysts argue that the deployment of such conventional weapons by the West will almost inevitably be followed by similar action in the East—thereby forcing NATO to *increase* rather than decrease its reliance on the nuclear deterrent. "I question whether the development [of highly destructive conventional weapons] will raise the nuclear threshold," Colonel Trevor N. Dupuy, a military theorist, wrote in a recent issue of *Armed Forces Journal*. "I suspect . . . that the more effective and destructive conventional weapons have become, the inhibitions on using nuclear weapons are lowered correspondingly."

Introduction of high-tech, wide-area conventional arms will certainly produce a new and more lethal battlefield, where anything that moves or gives off heat or sound will be targetable by precision-guided munitions with near-total effectiveness. "The environment of future warfare is likely to differ greatly from any we have known in the past," the Pentagon noted in its *Defense Guidance* document for the fiscal years 1984–1988. "Combat against Soviet [and] Soviet-supplied forces will be of higher intensity and longer duration, with weapons of much greater accuracy and possibly higher rates of fire and mobility."

In his Pugwash presentation, Julian Robinson asked, "May it not be the case that, as more and more of the militarily valued effects available from nuclear weapons come to be provided by a variety of non-nuclear means, a non-nuclear battlefield may come closer and closer to resembling a nuclear one, even to the point where it would seem to make no great practical difference to initiate nuclear war?"

The risk of nuclear escalation may increase further because many of the proposed delivery systems for these new conventional weapons— including the Lance, Patriot, and cruise missiles—are also intended to carry nuclear warheads. Their use in battle, therefore, could prompt an enemy to order a nuclear strike in the belief he was being attacked with nuclear rather than conventional weapons.

"The firing of a cruise missile armed with a conventional warhead may send an ambiguous signal to the Soviets," Bradley Graham wrote in *The Washington Post*. "Though intended to postpone a nuclear engagement, the missile could be mistaken by the Soviets for one carrying a nuclear warhead, which could result in the nuclear escalation that NATO had intended to avoid."

Just as military scientists are being encouraged to "think big" to produce conventional weapons with damage potentials approaching nuclear arms, nuclear engineers are being encouraged to "think small" to produce nuclear munitions with "near-conventional" damage radii. According to recent Congressional testimony, scientists at the Energy Department's Los Alamos and Lawrence Livermore laboratories are developing a new generation of nuclear munitions with highly controlled blast, radiation, and heat effects.

These weapons, often described as "third generation" nuclear arms to distinguish them from the earliest fission and fusion devices (the "first generation") and the compact, high-yield warheads of current nuclear weapons (the "second generation"), could theoretically be used to attack military targets without producing widespread "collateral damage" to surrounding structures and populations. Some of these new weapons are intended for use as "defensive" weapons in space—to disable incoming enemy missiles—while others, such as the enhanced radiation or neutron warhead, are intended for use as "battlefield" weapons to attack enemy aircraft, warships, tank formations, and other front-line combat systems.

To be militarily effective in this second role, such battlefield munitions would have to produce relatively confined blast or radiation effects. They would, in other words, have to inflict damage not much greater than that of the most powerful conventional weapons. U.S. strategists have long advocated the development of battlefield nuclear arms with "near-conventional" damage radii for deployment in Western Europe, to replace the 6,000 or so first-generation and second-generation tactical nuclear munitions now stockpiled there.

Because these existing munitions would produce immense collateral damage, NATO officials might hesitate to use them in a crisis. Some analysts regard them, therefore, as a less effective deterrent against Soviet conventional attack than enhanced radiation warheads and other third-generation munitions. This view prompted former Secretary of Defense James R. Schlesinger to suggest in his fiscal 1976 report to Congress that NATO's deterrent would be strengthened by "replacing the existing stockpiles with nuclear weapons and delivery systems more appropriate to the European environment."

In accordance with this perspective, the United States has already begun to produce the W-79 neutron warhead for the eight-inch howitzers used by both the Army and the Marine Corps. A 155-millimeter enhanced radiation warhead, the W-82, is now in advanced development. Other warheads with equivalent or even smaller radii of destruction are in the planning stage at the Los Alamos and Lawrence Livermore labs.

According to U.S. military officials and some members of Congress, such weapons are a welcome improvement over existing tactical nuclear munitions because of their reduced collateral-damage effects. Critics suggest, however, that introduction of these weapons—while arguably less dangerous than the continued deployment of existing, higher-yield nuclear devices—could help erode the nuclear firebreak and thus increase the risk of nuclear war. If these low-yield nuclear weapons "become standard equipment," Alva Myrdal argued in *The Game of Disarmament*, "this would blur the distinction between nuclear and conventional weapons," making escalation across the firebreak more likely.

Both of these trends—the development of near-nuclear conventional munitions and near-conventional nuclear weapons—are working separately to undermine the firebreak. But it is also evident that they are acting *jointly* to alter the military equation. With the introduction of precision-guided munitions and third-generation nuclear weapons, even small combat forces are capable of destroying major enemy forces and installations. Any conflict fought with modern weapons is likely to escalate rapidly into a high-intensity conventional war that could spill over the firebreak and trigger a nuclear holocaust.

The danger was vividly demonstrated in 1982, when British forces carried tactical nuclear munitions into the South Atlantic war zone and Argentina engaged the British fleet with its French-made Exocet missiles. Although the ensuing battle did not precipitate a nuclear attack, the Falklands conflict showed just how intense such small-scale engagements can become. As high-tech conventional weapons are introduced in ever greater numbers into the world's arsenals, engagements of this sort are likely to become even more intense, and the risk of nuclear war will grow.

If this analysis is correct, the arms control and disarmament communities will have to develop entirely new strategies for the prevention of nuclear war. Clearly, any disarmament agreements that confine themselves to the most massive of strategic weapons will not, by themselves, diminish the long-term risk of nuclear war if the firebreak continues to be eroded. Similarly, adoption of a nuclear "freeze" or "no first use" policy based on the deployment of large quantities of high-tech conventional weapons—an approach favored by many Congressional backers of these proposals—may ultimately *increase* rather than decrease the risk of nuclear war. The only sure approach to nuclear peace is one that views protection of the firebreak as imperative.

Fortunately, there is still time to preserve the firebreak. Many of the weapons systems to which I have referred are not expected to become operational until the late 1980s. This means we have about five years to consider new arms control initiatives and other protective measures—including, if necessary, cancellation of the more threatening nuclear and conventional systems.

The expansion of the already crowded arms control agenda will not be easy to achieve. But as public concern over the risk of nuclear war grows, it should be possible to demonstrate the common stake we all have in the continued safety of the nuclear firebreak.

15 STRATEGIC BUILD-DOWN: A CONTEXT FOR RESTRAINT

Alton Frye

The search for national security is a dialectic of hope and fear. Fear of war spawns demand for weapons; hope for peace feeds demand to control those weapons. Judging by the rampant growth of weaponry in modern times, fear is more fruitful than hope. If foreign policy is the management of contradictions, national security policy requires a synthesis of hope and fear, a prudent blend of arms and arms control.

That synthesis has proved elusive. Now a new approach has emerged in the idea known as "build-down." In essence the build-down principle says that no new weapons should be deployed unless a larger number of existing weapons are destroyed. Conceived and refined over the last two years, the build-down seeks to apply a relatively simple principle to the complex realities of international competition in the development and deployment of weapons. . . .After months of intricate political dialogue with a congressional coalition led by Senators William Cohen (R.-Maine) and Sam Nunn (D.-Georgia), President Reagan adopted the build-down principle in October 1983 as a basic element in the U.S. proposals at the Strategic Arms Reduction Talks (START) in Geneva. . . .

. . . Mr. Reagan now offers to build down ballistic missile warhead inventories from the current 8,000–9,000 range on each side to 5,000 by eliminating more than one warhead for each warhead newly deployed.[1]

1. Each warhead installed on a new land-based missile (ICBM) with multiple independently targetable re-entry vehicles (MIRVs) would oblige a party to eliminate two existing warheads.

2. New warheads on submarine-launched ballistic missiles (SLBMs) or small, single-warhead ICBMs would force reductions at a lower ratio, perhaps three for two.

3. If a side were not modernizing and introducing new warheads—a highly unlikely contingency in the next few years—it would still have to make annual reductions at an agreed percentage rate, possibly five percent.

Note: Some footnotes have been deleted, and the others have been renumbered to appear in consecutive order.

4. The President would also apply the build-down principle to deployment of new bombers (though not directly to individual weapons carried on bombers), reducing bomber forces to levels well below those permitted under the 1979 strategic arms limitation [talks] treaty (SALT II).

5. The United States would also accept limits on the number of air-launched cruise missiles each aircraft could carry and on the aggregate number of such missiles deployed.

And finally:

6. The extent of reductions in missile throw-weight would be balanced against the reductions in bomber carrying capacity through a formula measuring potential destructive capacity. This feature of the proposed approach . . . is important. Since the two categories vary so basically from each other, and since the Soviet side would be more affected by the missile warhead reductions and the U.S. side more affected by the reductions in bomber-carried weapons, a measure integrating these force components is necessary to permit precise trade-offs between them.

In short, the new approach seeks major reductions in both missile-carried and bomber-carried weapons—through the build-down route—and also explicitly links the two. In announcing this basic shift in the U.S. START position, President Reagan stated the central objective: "We seek limits on the destructive capability of missiles and recognize that the Soviet Union would seek limits on bombers in exchange. There will have to be trade-offs and the United States is prepared to make them, so long as they result in a more stable balance of forces."

The last phrase should be underscored. Set alongside other statements by the President and top members of his Administration, it defines the U.S. objective in terms of "balance," not superiority, and in terms of stability, in which neither side has the capacity or incentive to launch a first strike against the other. . . .

II

. . . The build-down approach is not a magic panacea for all the problems that have piled up in the last 20 years. It accepts the continued existence of large numbers of nuclear weapons on both sides as a given, and assumes that the two countries will remain concerned, partly for political reasons, with both the substance and the appearance of parity. At root it addresses the goal endorsed by the Scowcroft Commission— moving toward reduced nuclear postures that are less vulnerable to a first strike. That goal requires a balanced melding of warhead reductions and selective modernization.

Build-down would retain the counting and verification provisions embodied in the SALT II Treaty while moving beyond it to bring about meaningful reductions in the arsenals on both sides. It would operate, not through rigid categories and subcategories (although previously agreed provisions would remain in effect), but through relatively free choice for the two military establishments to bring themselves within broadly defined warhead ceilings and other limits. And, as we have already noted, it would provide a trade-off in which reductions in the Soviet missile advantage would be balanced against reductions in the U.S. bomber advantage.

This article will consider each of these questions, dwelling especially (in *Section V*) on the kinds of choices that the two sides would be encouraged to make by the ground rules of a build-down. Following analysis of the potential merits (and difficulties) of the build-down approach (*Sections III–VII*), two concluding sections assess the implications of the build-down approach for the ongoing political debate in the United States, and the reasons why it ought to appeal to the Soviet Union.

But first let us take a hard look at an objection already being made to the build-down idea, namely that its focus on numbers and quantity leaves untouched the kind of qualitative improvements that are—it may be argued—an even more important component of the strategic arms race.

III

The build-down approach is indeed couched in terms of *numbers* of *offensive* weapons. It neither includes nor precludes possible arms control measures expressly aimed to halt improvements in the quality of such weapons—such as a comprehensive nuclear test ban (CTB), limits on ballistic missile testing, or the suspension of fissile material production. All these are elements of proposals for a nuclear freeze, usually defined as a comprehensive curb on both the quantitative and qualitative escalation of nuclear armaments. The build-down is not a substitute for or an alternative to the full range of limitations envisioned by the nuclear freeze movement. But, if successful, it can help arrest the deterioration in Soviet-American relations and pave the way for more ambitious restraints.

Moreover, the build-down approach does not address the problem of defensive systems. Now tightly limited by the 1972 ABM Treaty, this is an area in which President Reagan has excited new interest within his government and new worries in the Kremlin regarding a possible American movement toward strategic defense based in space. On its face, the sharp reduction in offensive warheads visualized under build-down might tend to reduce the incentive to seek some new "impregnable" defense—or conversely it might tend to make such a defense seem more attainable. In any case the problem is not within the scope of the build-down approach. One dragon at a time.

The fact that the build-down approach does not directly control modernization of strategic weapons is understandably a matter of concern to those who are dedicated to a total freeze. The build-down seeks not to prohibit modernization but to regulate it. It would do so not by elaborate categorical restriction, but by putting a price on modernization. That price would be stated in terms of force reductions. New weapons could not be deployed unless a greater number of existing weapons were phased out of the forces. In this way, each side could be assured that the process of modernization would not mean continued increases in the number of nuclear weapons being deployed. Indeed, the very momentum of modernization would compel unprecedented reductions in strategic offensive forces. And those reductions would simultaneously lower the level of lethal capabilities and improve the climate for more substantial arms control arrangements.

In short, as we shall see in greater detail in *Section V* below, the build-down approach *would* indirectly affect the qualitative character of the nuclear arsenals on both sides. And here it is important to stress that qualitative improvement in weapons and delivery systems *may* cut in either direction, toward or away from that "more stable balance" that is our main objective. Just as MIRVs have been deeply destabilizing, the progressive replacement of MIRVed missiles by single-warhead ones (in effect, a reduction in the ratio of warheads to missiles) would work in the opposite direction. For years the United States has sought, both by argument and example, to persuade the Soviet Union to reduce the proportion of ICBMs in favor of a higher proportion of SLBMs, which are less accurate and less vulnerable. Qualitative change may make matters worse—improvements in accuracy or explosive power almost automatically have this effect—but it may also make them better. Indiscriminate modernization and indiscriminate reductions can erode stability. The task of policy is to discriminate.

Finally, numbers *are* important in themselves. Quantitative increases on the scale in prospect greatly complicate either side's ability to plan and execute a program of force modernization which can yield significant improvements in stability. A larger number of weapons may add a kind of inertial stability, as each government recognizes the impossibility of destroying enough of the other's weapons to avoid a decimating retaliation. But that larger number also increases the risk of war through accident, terrorist theft or official lunacy. More important, expanding force levels generate pressures to compensate for new-felt insecurity by adopting reckless policies, e.g., launch-on-warning, and by structuring forces in ways which improve survivability at the cost of the verifiability necessary to reassure the parties that neither intends to use the weapons it deploys. In the latter regard, dual-purpose systems like cruise missiles, which could carry either conventional or nuclear munitions and which are likely to proliferate on land, sea and in the air, pose grave problems.

Moreover, numbers are the feature of the arms race most visible to other nations. Moscow and Washington share an interest in moderating their own competition as a prerequisite for convincing others to refrain from building independent nuclear capabilities. Non-proliferation, as well as the stability of the superpower balance, requires a renewed effort to dampen the Soviet-American arms race. . . .

IV

Our next question is the relationship of the build-down approach to the SALT II agreements. On the one hand, the scheme would preserve and strengthen the positive accomplishments of the SALT II treaty. In order for the build-down to operate, there would have to be an agreed data base identifying the forces to which the rules would apply. There would have to be counting rules to determine the number of warheads associated with specific missiles, and there would have to be tight controls to prevent circumvention of the reductions by secreting additional warheads on the missiles which remain. There would also have to be agreed procedures for monitoring new deployments and destruction of other systems. The SALT regime provides these, as well as a functioning institution to supervise the build-down, namely, the Standing Consultative Commission.

Perhaps most valuable is the SALT II rule for counting the number of warheads on a given ballistic missile type. The rule is simple: a missile is considered to have the maximum number of warheads with which it has been tested. Thus, a Soviet SS-18 is credited with ten warheads and an American Poseidon with 14. In fact, intelligence sources indicate that these missiles sometimes carry fewer warheads, but the counting rule provides an accurate estimate of the maximum number of weapons to which the country is entitled on such boosters. From these counting rules, one can derive a satisfactory baseline count from which the build-down would begin. There would be no distinctive verification problems, since actual launchers would have to be destroyed for the nation to receive credit for the warhead reductions. The Standing Consultative Commission has a decade's experience with monitoring launcher dismantlement, and national technical means of observation provide high confidence of compliance. Warheads removed from missiles might, of course, be stored, but they would have no strategic significance without means to deliver them.

Similarly, SALT II provides at least skeleton rules for the most important class of bomber weapons, the newly developed air-launched cruise missiles. It permits a side to field a force with an average of 28 cruise missiles per aircraft, but the number of ALCMs on existing types of heavy bombers like the U.S. B-52s and the Soviet Bears is limited to 20 each. (The higher average number grew out of U.S. interest in possible future deployments on wide-bodied ALCM carriers, an option not now seriously in view.) As we shall see in *Section VI*, however, these rules would need to be refined in order to weigh bomber forces systematically against missile forces.

Thus, build-down would build upon SALT II. But it would also improve upon it, in three key respects. First, whereas SALT II was based on counting launchers, the build-down approach . . . focuses explicitly on the number of warheads—using the counting rule just described for missiles. Second, build-down is a proposal for major reduction in warheads—whereas SALT II stabilized launcher totals at existing levels but left the sides free to add thousands of warheads. By reversing the trend toward additional warheads, build-down would cure the central weakness of SALT II, its relatively permissive treatment of new forces. In this way build-down would correct the allegedly fatal flaw which led some to doubt the value of that treaty. With warhead totals forced to decline, the real virtues of SALT II would survive and should win wider approval. Instead of 15,000 or more strategic warheads on each side in the 1990s, build-down could produce forces in the 8,000-warhead range for missiles and bombers combined.

And finally, build-down approaches reductions in a totally different way than SALT II did. No one who studies the tortuous negotiations that ran from 1973 to 1979 to produce the SALT II Accords can fail to see how much time and effort had to go into defining precise categories of weapons to be limited. By contrast, one dimension of build-down theory is the degree of flexibility it would permit defense planners in shaping their force postures. The scheme would retain previously agreed categorical limits, e.g., no new heavy ICBMs could be tested or deployed, and the various MIRV sub-limits and fractionation rules would remain in force. However, the build-down rule itself would focus not on altering the core of the two forces, but on adjusting the margins of total deployments. It would liberate negotiators from the intractable task of persuading their counterparts to accept basic restructuring of their forces as the condition of agreement. And it would grant broad discretion to military establishments to select their own forces, while enabling them to plan their defenses against a smaller threat than they now face.

V

What kinds of choices would be likely in a situation where, for every new warhead added to the official count, defense planners would have to dismantle more than one existing warhead? . . .

Two points seem fairly evident. First, build-down would compel attention to force survivability as the overriding requirement. The logic is straightforward. A planner who must rely on a smaller number of weapons for deterrence must make sure that enough of them can survive an enemy surprise attack. In theory, one can get by with fewer weapons if the opponent also has fewer, since the scale of the threat bears most directly on the size of one's own force requirements. But one must take every precaution to guarantee that moving to a smaller force does not expose a nation to increased risk of a successful first strike. Thus, there is a tremendous premium on making each component of a diminishing force less vulnerable. For example, as overall levels come down, it would be foolish to maintain a rising percentage of weapons in presumably vulnerable fixed silos.

Second, any introduction of new warheads on a large scale would involve major adjustments in existing deployments. The proposed build-down ratio is particularly high for ICBMs with multiple warheads.

Both points are deliberate and evident. In combination, these considerations should operate to reduce incentives for future generations of large MIRVed ICBMs. For the United States, they should advance the long-term strategic vision articulated by the Scowcroft Commission, part of which was that any MX deployment would be strictly limited as a transition to a more dispersed force of single-warhead ICBMs. The build-down process would heighten the urgency of moving on to small, single-warhead missiles as an element in a mixed force on land, sea and in the air. . . .

On the Soviet side, there is also an important point to be made. This is that the present Soviet ICBM posture is one of high concentration of warhead totals in a relatively few launching sites; in that respect Soviet ICBMs are relatively more vulnerable than U.S. land-based missiles, which carry fewer warheads. . . . Over 50 percent of all Soviet warheads now stand on about 650 ICBMs, while less than 23 percent of U.S. warheads are at risk on theoretically vulnerable ICBMs.

So far as concerns the instabilities which flow from mutual counterforce capabilities, the two countries are already subject to them. The MX and its Soviet counterparts could make the situation marginally worse, but merely interrupting their deployment will not cure the problem. While there remain opportunities to impede refinement of counterforce capabilities on submarine-launched ballistic missiles, the accuracy and lethality of ICBMs are now so great that only a combination of force reduction and adaptation can redress the instabilities associated with missiles that are at once potent and vulnerable. . . .

Since there is no longer the option of precluding ICBMs capable of counterforce missions, the best we can do unilaterally is to shift the force exchange ratios toward stability by deploying single-warhead missiles. Planners on both sides are bound to recognize this relationship and build-down would encourage them to act on it. Because they are farther along with development of a single-warhead missile, the Soviet Union may well pursue this path sooner than the United States.

On the Soviet side, we have just noted that build-down would tend to discourage or limit any new large-scale system, especially of MIRVed ICBMs. Moreover, under the proposed build-down regime, even if the Soviet (or U.S.) side did not modernize, it would have to reduce its warheads by five percent a year.[2]

Thus planners would face hard choices. They would have to judge the value of new systems in comparison to the larger number of currently deployed weapons they must dismantle. And, as the compulsory percentage reductions proceeded with or without new systems, they would have to decide which existing systems to retain and which to eliminate.

For example, at some point in the process of reductions and modernization, the Soviet Union would have to choose between reducing either its SS-18 heavy missiles (credited with ten warheads each under the counting system) or its SS-19 medium missiles (credited with six each). Would one prefer some multiple of three SS-18s or of five SS-19s? To an American analyst the choice seems clear. Retaining the SS-19s would provide a more survivable and more flexible force. The inclination to phase down the SS-18s should flow from the military logic of the case, but the Soviets might wish to disregard it for political or psychological reasons. If they did so, they would simplify U.S. targeting, although the consequences for stability could be worrisome. This kind of potential trade-off illustrates the way a build-down might induce changes that could not be negotiated directly. The Soviets would be free to retain the heavy SS-18s, but their objective interest should favor the more dispersed force of SS-19s. (By the same token, the United States could only achieve significant numbers of MX-type missiles by sacrificing twice as many warheads on the sea-based missiles it has consistently preferred as the backbone of its retaliatory posture.)

This kind of choice has a direct bearing, of course, on the difficult issue of throw-weight, which has been the subject of long and arcane disputation. While the two countries have rough parity in the number of missile warheads, the Soviets today have a three-to-one advantage in the throw-weight of their missiles. Their missiles are bigger, but, being liquid-fueled, there can be disagreement as to whether they are as versatile and reliable as U.S. solid-fuel systems. Some officials have insisted that even if the Soviets accept reductions in the number of missile warheads to a lower level, they must also agree to cut their throw-weight advantage by making those reductions in their larger ICBMs. That is the meaning of the longstanding U.S. demands in START for sub-limits on Soviet heavy missiles.

However one assesses the Soviet advantage in throw-weight, the crucial point in assessing the build-down approach is that *any agreement which cuts the number of warheads will itself tend to cut the throw-weight disparity.*

For instance, if the Soviets agreed to a 5,000-warhead limit for ballistic missiles, reaching that level would drop their missile throw-weight by more than 50 percent and lower the ratio of throw-weight between the two forces. That would be true even if Moscow elected to maximize its total throw-weight by holding onto its larger missiles, the SS-18s and SS-19s, in which case it would fill its permissible warhead quota with only about 650 missiles—and it would have no other missiles at all on land or sea. Obviously, that posture is preposterous; the realistic range of Soviet forces would presumably spread the warheads over more launchers with relatively less gross throw-weight. In addition, technological trends on both sides point toward relatively compact and portable warheads, meaning that a reduction in the number of warheads will mean concomitant cuts in throw-weight and megatonnage. The two countries have such vast power at their disposal that these changes will still leave them with extraordinarily high levels of destructive capability, but there is little doubt that, even with modernization, reducing the number of warheads in the two forces will trim the currently deployed explosive yield quite significantly. . . .

VI

We turn next to the question of trade-offs between missile capabilities and bomber capabilities, to which President Reagan has now committed the United States. It is a difficult and controversial issue. . . . The first problem is that of counting bombers and their loads. To devise a sensible counting rule for bombers one must deal with the crucial differences between weapons delivered by aircraft and those delivered by missiles. Aircraft cannot conduct a quick first strike and can be recalled after precautionary takeoffs—hence the Western view that they are more stabilizing systems. Furthermore, the alert rates for bombers are much lower than for missiles, so that at any given time a smaller proportion of bomber weapons is actually available for war. Most importantly, bombers face active defenses, as missiles will not, so long as the ABM Treaty is effective.

For all these reasons, bomber weapons are worth less than missile weapons in most strategic calculations. Their redeeming value is to enhance overall force survivability . . . by denying an attacker the opportunity to concentrate his strikes against other types of strategic forces. Bombers also have a quality other strategic forces lack. They can perform important conventional missions, a factor which argues for maintaining a reasonable number of them.

These diverse considerations complicate setting a satisfactory rule for bombers in the strategic nuclear equation. At the end, while elaborate quantitative assessments are interesting and helpful, any counting rule for bombers will be arbitrary. . . .

VII

Where, then, might the two sides emerge under the build-down approach? As we have noted, both the United States and the Soviet Union now have approximately 10,000 warheads in their strategic and INF forces. Programs now under way or projected point toward still higher force levels in the 1990s, approaching or surpassing 15,000 strategic warheads on each side. And these forces, left unchecked, would increasingly incorporate systems perplexing for arms control, including a varied array of cruise missiles and mobile ICBMs.

A build-down agreement would sharply change this prospect. The proposed target would be 5,000 missile-carried warheads, with a progressive tendency toward reducing the ratio of warheads to missiles. Assuming planners act rationally to distribute their reduced warhead quota over a reasonable number of launchers, the situation should be one of relatively greater strategic stability. To put the matter concretely, gradual introduction of perhaps 1,000 Midgetmen in the context of declining Soviet warhead totals should move the ratio of hard-target killers to ICBM targets from the present 5 to 1 toward less than 3 to 1, while evolutionary changes in the Soviet missile force would presumably move away from the dangerously skewed deployment now in evidence. It should indeed be, in President Reagan's key phrase, "a more stable balance of forces."

As to bomber-carried weapons, any viable agreement would almost certainly demand a curtailment in present U.S. plans. Speaking roughly . . . the U.S. bomber force might have a strength of 250 to 300 aircraft (compared to 576 in the SALT II data base) and approximately 3,000 warheads, including perhaps 2,000–2,500 ALCMs. It is possible to envisage an aggregate warhead ceiling for both bombers and missiles that would be at the level of 8,000 warheads and would provide major cutbacks in potential destructive capacity. If INF missiles were included, the aggregate ceiling might emerge at a level of approximately 8,500 warheads.

These levels would be dramatically below those now expected in the 1990s, but would leave ample scope for the two sides to modernize their way out of the vulnerabilities and unreliabilities now emerging. If it is possible to agree on a ballistic-missile warhead sub-limit of 5,000 to 6,000 within the aggregate, so much the better for stability. Because the Soviets have so many weapons on missiles, they may be reluctant to accept the missile reentry vehicle sublimit preferred by the United States. If, however, they do intend to deploy a sizable Blackjack force with cruise missiles (or long-range cruise missiles on Backfire, which would redefine those planes as "heavy bombers" in SALT II terms), they would consume a good fraction of their quota for that assignment. . . .

VIII

. . . From the beginning, the build-down was contrived to bridge the serious differences now evident among Americans. It seeks to mold a consensus among those who have campaigned for a nuclear freeze and those who have opposed it. Not all those on either side will find the compromise satisfactory, but they should understand its features. Those who say we must stop strategic modernization immediately and those who say we must not limit modernization at all will oppose any proposition aimed at mapping a middle ground between the contending factions.

Few Americans hold such extreme positions, and it would be a caricature to portray pro- and anti-freeze camps as polarized in this way. Many Americans endorse the freeze as a shorthand message to prod a reluctant Administration to get on with the business of negotiating with the Soviet regime it has chosen to confront. In that sense, the freeze movement is demand-side politics, a vehicle enabling apprehensive citizens to indicate their preference for comprehensive arms restraints rather than unbounded military competition. On examination, moreover, many freeze proponents acknowledge the need for some adjustments in the present U.S. forces. The dispute shades off into questions of what kinds of replacement forces should be allowed under a freeze; that, in turn, often leads to the conclusion that, if replacement is to occur, it would be better to emphasize systems thought to be more stabilizing (like bombers and sea-based missiles) instead of such destabilizing weapons as large missiles with multiple warheads in fixed silos. . . .

Similarly, reasonable advocates of force modernization accept the need to strive for effective arms accords. They do not contend that modernization should be totally unfettered. The assertion is that *selective* modernization is needed to correct or hedge against instabilities in the existing forces, for example, the rising threats to ICBM silos. Across a broad spectrum of American opinion, there is a greater basis for mutual accommodation than sometimes appears.

Making such an accommodation possible is, of course, a challenge to the American government, and one which it has found difficult to meet. . . . Yet it is almost axiomatic that a democratic foreign policy without domestic consensus leads to friction at home and failure abroad. Unless we can find common ground for Americans, we are not likely to find common ground with the Soviets.

IX

Not surprisingly, Moscow is the wariest of all. It is understandably suspicious of any proposal from an American Administration it considers the most hostile of modern times. . . .

If the Kremlin does not like reductions paced by the variable ratios, let it argue for exclusive reliance on a percentage rate of reductions. If it does not like the percentage rate approach, let it suggest an annual quota or other method. If it does not favor the 5,000 ballistic-missile warhead limit, let it make a case for some other number. If it does not like the proposed constraints on bomber and air-launched cruise missiles, let it formulate others for negotiation.

If it merely rejects out of hand the build-down and related initiatives, what evidence will there be that Moscow has any genuine interest in the reductions it professes to want? . . .

[Build-down] is not a complete solution or the only solution to the dilemmas of nuclear competition. But those who find merit in reducing strategic arms and in restraining strategic modernization should welcome build-down as a useful approach. Above all, a mutual commitment to build-down would testify to acceptance of the first fact of our age: the American and Soviet peoples must find safety from the nuclear menace together—or they will not find it at all.

NOTES

1. In this discussion, the terms "warheads" and "weapons" are used interchangeably; unless otherwise noted, estimates of warhead inventories are based on the maximum number of warheads permitted on individual missiles under the SALT II Treaty.

2. Some examples may help to clarify the subtle and potentially confusing interaction between reductions dictated by an annual percentage rate and those dictated by variable ratios. The basic point is that in determining the scale of reductions, the largest cutback—whether set by the percentage rate or the variable ratios—would govern.

Thus, a percentage rate of five percent would force cuts of more than 400 missile warheads on each side in the first year; reductions under the percentage rate would be smaller in later years, as the total warhead balance to which the rate applied declined. In order to come within the lower ceiling set by the net reduction goal, a country would have to eliminate *in addition to the first 400 weapons* one existing warhead for each warhead newly deployed. Thus, a country deploying 400 new warheads in a year when it had to make a net reduction of 400 warheads, would have to destroy 800 of its currently installed weapons. In effect, the percentage rate reduction creates *an implicit ratio* of warheads destroyed to warheads deployed that is never less than 2:1, so long as the number of newly deployed warheads does not exceed the net reduction total specified by the percentage.

At higher deployment rates, e.g., 600 new warheads in a year when a side must make a net reduction of 400, MIRVed ICBMs would always remain subject to the 2:1 penalty but marginal additions of SLBMs and single-warhead missiles would enjoy preferential ratios requiring smaller reductions. If the 600 new warheads were all on MIRVed ICBMs, the side would have to eliminate 1,200 existing warheads, meaning a *net* reduction in the force of 600 weapons. If 300 of the 600 were on SLBMs and single-warhead missiles, subject to a 3:2 ratio, the side would only have to eliminate 1,050 existing warheads (600 for the MIRVed ICBMs and 450 for the other warheads) for a net reduction of 450.

Projections of actual modernization programs by Lawrence J. Cavaiola and Bonita J. Dombey of the Congressional Budget Office suggest that, of the two build-down mechanisms, the percentage rate is likely to be more potent in the early years and the variable ratios are likely to grow in impact in the late 1980s. See *Modernizing U.S. Strategic Offensive Forces: The Administration's Program and Alternatives*, Washington: Congressional Budget Office, May 1983.

16 SUSTAINING THE NON-PROLIFERATION REGIME

Joseph S. Nye

. . .Whether the non-proliferation policy prospects are hopeless or not depends upon the policy objective. If the policy objective is defined as preventing another explosion of a nuclear device, then the prospects are indeed gloomy.[1] If the policy objective is to reduce the rate and degree of proliferation in order to be able to cope with the destabilizing effects, then the situation is by no means hopeless. What is remarkable from this second point of view is that the rate of proliferation has not been faster. Of the many states expected in 1960 to have exploded nuclear devices by now, most have not.

From an international perspective, the policy objective is to maintain the presumption against proliferation. The great danger is an acceleration of the rate of proliferation, with general restraints breaking down and decisions to forbear reconsidered because "everyone is doing it." Such scrambles have occurred in international politics—witness the rapid partition of Africa in the third quarter of the nineteenth century, or the rapid extension of coastal states' jurisdiction in the oceans during the past decade. Preventing such a breakdown in the restraints against nuclear proliferation is a feasible long-term objective, one that has been pursued with some success. . . . Ironically, these gains are currently threatened on one side by those who pursue a broader anti-nuclear agenda and assert it as anti-proliferation policy, and on the other side, by those whose satisfied view of the past leads them to belittle the risks of proliferation in the future.[2] This essay assesses the central gains and mistakes of the last few years, and outlines the major problems involved with maintaining a non-proliferation regime in the 1980s.

THE NON-PROLIFERATION REGIME: 1950s TO 1970s

The beginnings of the current non-proliferation regime date from December 1953, when President Eisenhower launched the "Atoms for Peace" Program. Realizing that the technology was spreading anyway,

Note: Some footnotes have been deleted, and the others have been renumbered to appear in consecutive order.

the United States offered to share the fruits of her then long technological lead, in return for the acceptance by other countries of conditions designed to control destabilizing effects from such sharing.

Specifically, the central accomplishment of the Atoms for Peace Program was the creation of a system of international safeguards and an institutional framework, in the form of the International Atomic Energy Agency (IAEA), established in Vienna in 1957. The safeguards system is central to the basic bargain of the international regime, in which other countries are assisted in their peaceful nuclear energy needs in return for accepting the intrusion of safeguards and inspection.[3] The initial acceptance of such intrusion was slow and halting, but the idea was successfully implanted in the 1950s.

The next step in the development of the regime was the formulation of the Non-Proliferation Treaty (NPT) during the 1960s. Eight significant states have refused to sign the NPT, usually on the grounds that it is a discriminatory treaty. But of the eight, France has indicated she would not undercut the purposes of the Treaty, and in Latin America the Treaty of Tlatelolco, a regional treaty limiting nuclear weapons, signed in February 1967, helps to fill the normative gap. Sceptics have dismissed the NPT as a modern equivalent of the Kellogg–Briand pact, since any state can quit on three months notice. Other detractors have argued that the treaty is imperfectly drafted and involves promises that cannot be fully kept. Nonetheless, by establishing a normative presumption against proliferation; and by creating procedures for verifying intentions, the NPT has helped to build confidence and a degree of predictability in the behavior of states. Like its regional counterparts, such as the Treaty of Tlatelolco, it helps to strengthen the international regime by symbolizing a common interest. . . .

By the early 1970s there was a degree of complacency about the nonproliferation regime that had been constructed. This complacency was shattered, however, by three events which occurred during 1974–5. One was the Indian explosion of a "peaceful" nuclear device using plutonium derived from a Canadian-supplied research reactor with US-supplied heavy water. The Canadian embargo on the export of uranium, which even included her allies, and the US Non-Proliferation Act of 1978, whose stringent conditions aroused resentment abroad, can both be traced back to this explosion.

The second event was the oil embargo and the four-fold increases in oil prices which created a widespread feeling of insecurity vis-à-vis energy supply. The oil crisis led to a sudden surge of exaggerated expectations about the importance of nuclear energy, and raised questions about whether there would be sufficient uranium to fuel all the reactors which had suddenly appeared on the drawing boards. The net effect was to accelerate governments' plans for early commercial use of plutonium fuel which, unlike the low enriched uranium currently used as fuel in most reactors, is a weapons-usable material. The IAEA projected that some 40 countries might be using plutonium fuels by the end of the 1980s. At the same time, safeguards and institutions for dealing with such a flood of weapons-usable materials had not been adequately developed.

The third set of events that shook the regime in the mid-1970s was the proposed sale of facilities for producing weapons-usable materials without regard to their economic justification or proliferation implications. In some cases, reprocessing plants were offered to countries that were only just building their first power reactors and lacked any serious economic justification for reprocessing. Subsequently, it was disclosed that, in at least two cases, the recipients were attempting to develop nuclear weapons programmes, and there would almost certainly have been violations or abrogation of safeguards. In such circumstances there was grave danger of collapse of the international regime so laboriously constructed over the previous decades and a further weakening of public support for nuclear energy (not to mention exports) in many of the advanced countries.

The threats to regime stability which came from the ambiguities of "peaceful" uses were reinforced by trends in the power position of the United States inside and outside the nuclear issue area. Outside the nuclear issue area, the United States had suffered her disastrous defeat in Vietnam, with an accompanying inward turn in her cycle of foreign policy attitudes. This heightened the sense of insecurity felt by a number of former client states, particularly in Asia, and weakened the credibility of security guarantees as an instrument that could be extended to less developed countries. While the US Congress showed strong concern about proliferation, for example passing the Symington Amendment in 1976 which mandated the withdrawal of military or economic aid to a country importing a reprocessing plant, simultaneous Congressional restrictions on aid and arms transfers emptied such sanctions of much of their supposed clout. The sticks were shrinking and the carrots were not growing!

Inside the nuclear issue area, US influence had begun to diminish. America's share of world exports began to decline as strong industrial competition for the sale of light water reactors developed in Europe. Equally important, however, was the erosion of the US near monopoly on provision of enrichment services. France, Germany, Britain, the Netherlands, Japan and South Africa had all begun projects to build their own enrichment capacity well before the more stringent non-proliferation policies of the late 1970s. Thus by the mid-1970s, US leverage over other countries' nuclear policies had begun to erode. The US was still the most important state in the peaceful nuclear arena, but she no longer held a hegemonic position. In any efforts to refurbish the regime, US leadership would be a necessary but not sufficient condition for success.

THE CARTER ADMINISTRATION APPROACH

In 1976 and 1977 there was a series of American initiatives in response to the fuel cycle events that had threatened the regime. A number of private studies were raising doubts about the economic need for rapid introduction of plutonium fuels. Congressional hearings and draft legislation called for a more stringent approach to exports, and the election campaign accentuated public and press attention to the non-proliferation issue.

Two important steps were taken by the Ford Administration. First, the Nuclear Suppliers Group was established in London. Seven (later fifteen) major suppliers came together to discuss guidelines for nuclear commerce that would prevent commercial competition from undercutting safeguards obligations. While the guidelines were not finally agreed upon until September 1977 and published through notes to the IAEA in January 1978, much of the basic work was done in 1976.

Second, in October 1976, President Ford announced a more cautious policy towards the use of plutonium in the US nuclear programme. Reprocessing was to be deferred pending a solution of proliferation and economic problems. The exact meaning of this deferral and how it was to be implemented was to be studied in a somewhat ambiguous Reprocessing Evaluation Program. Thus some of the main lines of response later identified with the Carter Administration actually preceded it, and one of the basic policy choices faced by the Carter Administration was what to do with the legacy of past policies. While the eventual choices stressed continuity with the past, then as now, there were strong pressures for more radical departures from previous policies.

The approach that was chosen was designed to reinforce the existing regime, but not to accept the eroding status quo. It was important to shake the other countries into attention and action to refurbish the regime, but to do so without coercion and with as little overt discrimination as possible. By its very nature, non-proliferation does involve a degree of discrimination. Yet the way in which that discrimination is handled can spell the difference between success and failure in a policy of regime maintenance. Thus the Carter Administration deferral of reprocessing at home was not expected to lead all other countries to follow suit. But it was felt that exaggerated projections of nuclear growth and spurious economic calculations were driving decisions in the United States and other countries. US diplomatic efforts to persuade others to look more carefully at their calculations and at the problems associated with plutonium would be undercut if America did not restructure her own domestic programmes to stop plans for thermal recycle and stretch out the timing of breeder research and development.

The strategy chosen was to focus strongly on the recycle of plutonium in thermal reactors as posing a clear and present proliferation danger that promised at best marginal economic and supply assurance gains. Breeder reactors, however, had a greater potential long-term energy significance. Moreover, certain key governments such as France, Britain, Japan and Germany were heavily committed to breeders. Thus the Administration did not oppose all breeder research and development programmes at home or abroad. It expressed reservations about their commercial deployment before proliferation-resistant technological and institutional alternatives had been explored. . . .

. . . [I]t became clear that maintaining and refurbishing the international regime would require a general approach around which a broad group of nations could rally. The process of rethinking the conditions of the regime had to be shared beyond the United States alone. . . .

The device the Carter Administration designed to meet these various policy needs was the International Nuclear Fuel Cycle Evaluation (INFCE), to expand the Ford Administration's Reprocessing Evaluation Program to include the whole cycle and to make participation international.

INFCE

INFCE has been described as a pioneering effort in international technology assessment. Officially, INFCE provided a 2-year period in which nations could re-examine assumptions and search for ways to reconcile their different assessments of the energy and non-proliferation risks involved in various aspects of the nuclear fuel cycle. While officially INFCE was given a predominantly technical rationale, this was a means of attracting broad participation into what was really part of a political process of stabilizing the basis for the international regime. The 66 countries and organizations that came together in Vienna after October 1977 included consumers and suppliers, East and West, and a dozen countries that had not signed the NPT. In all, 519 experts from 46 countries participated in 61 meetings of eight working groups, and produced 20,000 pages of documents.

As a diplomatic device, INFCE helped to re-establish a basis for consensus on a refurbished regime for the international nuclear fuel cycle. The very process of engaging in international technology assessment helped to heighten awareness of the non-proliferation problem and the threats to the regime. Nearly all countries gained some ground, including for the US the core points against the recycling of plutonium in the current thermal reactors. In turn, France and others won acceptance of exaggerated estimates of demand for breeder reactors, but this was qualified by statements denying the value of breeders to countries with small electrical or nuclear grids.

While no single fuel cycle emerged on its technical merits as indisputably more proliferation resistant, a general consensus was reached for more caution in introducing weapons-usable fuels. Working Group 1 agreed on a range of projected demands for uranium by the end of the century that was less than one half of the internationally accepted figures before INFCE started. This helped reduce the acrimony that characterized disputes over uranium resources, since it had the same effect as doubling uranium reserves.

As for the use of plutonium, Working Group 4 found that recycling in thermal reactors was not likely to have large economic advantages, and Working Groups 6 and 7 found that safe storage or disposal of spent fuel did not require reprocessing. Working Group 5 concluded that plutonium would be needed for breeder reactor programmes, but that successful breeder programmes would be based on large nuclear energy programmes where important economies of scale could be achieved. The net effect of these findings was to reduce the pressures for the widespread and premature use of plutonium that posed a clear and imminent danger to the international safeguards system. Instead, INFCE laid the foundation for a cautious introduction of plutonium use that could be guided by realistic development needs rather than by wasteful and dangerous imitation based on a spurious conventional wisdom and exaggerated projections.

To the extent that countries are guided by realistic energy concerns, the INFCE technical findings, combined with an evolutionary approach, provided a valuable seed from which a restored consensus could develop. For example, the INFCE technical findings help to reduce the tensions between Article 7 of the Suppliers Guidelines which urges restraint in sensitive exports and Article IV of the NPT which calls for "further development of the applications of nuclear energy for peaceful purposes, especially in the territories of the non-nuclear weapons states party to the treaty, with due consideration for the needs of the developing areas of the world." In fact at the 1980 NPT Review Conference Article IV was less the problem than Article VI, which calls on the nuclear weapons states to negotiate in good faith towards reductions in their nuclear arsenals. However, other aspects of policy relating to the fuel cycle issues were less successful.

Incentives

In 1977, President Carter announced incentives to help countries manage their fuel cycles in ways that would support non-proliferation interests. The US was willing both to contribute to an international fuel bank to provide security of supply for countries fulfilling their non-proliferation obligations and to offer to store limited amounts of foreign spent fuel, and to help explore sites for international spent fuel storage. Both these initiatives proceeded extremely slowly.

Export Legislation

Whatever its substantive merits or faults, the timing and tone of the Non-Proliferation Act of 1978 had an unfortunate effect on efforts to restore consensus over fuel cycle measures. It was widely regarded as a unilateral prejudging of the outcomes of INFCE; and an intrusion into other countries' nuclear programmes. Both the procedural role of the Nuclear Regulatory Commission and the various guillotine clauses threatening to cut off supply created a sense of confrontation and insecurity. . . .

Domestic Breeder Policy

In trying to direct world attention to the problems of too rapid a movement to weapons-usable fuels, the Administration altered the US domestic programme to stress a more gradual transition. This involved deferral of commercial reprocessing, and cancellation of the Clinch River Breeder Reactor which had been oriented towards demonstrating early commercialization. . . . [T]he idea was not to halt the breeder programme, but to restructure it to emphasize development of a safer fuel cycle over a longer time horizon rather than early commercialization.

There were a number of technical and budgetary reasons other than non-proliferation for opposing the Clinch River project. Unfortunately, too much of the decision was publicly attributed to non-proliferation reasons, thus obscuring the intrinsic economic weakness of the project, and implying a false trade-off between energy needs and non-proliferation concerns.

MAINTAINING THE REGIME IN THE 1980s

The policy responses of the late 1970s focused heavily on fuel cycle questions. Obviously there were other measures as well—for example, efforts to strengthen adherence to the NPT and to the Treaty of Tlatelolco; efforts to negotiate a Comprehensive Test Ban; and specific diplomatic responses in particular problem cases.[4] But the charge that policy focused on fuel cycle questions is largely correct. This was not because policy makers regarded the fuel cycle as the only source of proliferation. Rather it was because some of the most immediate threats to the regime arose out of fuel cycle questions, and because in the post-Vietnam period, other non-proliferation instruments were often difficult to use.

One of the problems for the 1980s will be keeping fuel cycle questions in a reasonable perspective. One might say these questions were half the source of the proliferation problems of the 1970s and that the policy responses of the 1970s provided half a solution to those fuel cycle problems. By any political arithmetic, to ameliorate a major social problem by one-quarter is not trivial. But it is not the solution to the whole problem. Lovins *et al.* overstate when they say that nuclear power is "the main driving force behind proliferation."[5] Important steps remain to be taken in the fuel cycle area, but they must not monopolize attention or create frictions with other key nations that will interfere with the overall maintenance of the non-proliferation regime.

After INFCE, a number of steps will be necessary to strengthen the fuel cycle aspects of the regime.

(a) *Safeguards.* The next steps are both technical and institutional. Of the latter, the most important is the agreement by the handful of states with unsafeguarded facilities to join in the comprehensive safeguard regime.

(b) *Plutonium and highly enriched uranium management.* The INFCE discussion acknowledged that weapons-usable fuels are not like other fuels, and require special procedures. New developments in fuel technology are reducing the need for weapons-usable uranium fuels in most research reactors. Equally important for the future are the IAEA discussions of plutonium storage. It is argued that international management cannot affect how re-exported plutonium is used. This may be true physically, but it is not necessarily true politically. A continuous international presence could reduce proliferation risk by raising the political costs of seizure or diversion. On this international basis, it may be possible to reconcile current divergences in national procedures for transfers of nuclear fuels.

(c) *International spent fuel storage.* Although spent fuel storage has been likened to plutonium "mines", radiation barriers remain and such sites are more amenable to international monitoring than are prematurely reprocessed plutonium "rivers." The international monitoring of national spent fuel storage could also be reinforced by the availability of international sites for spent fuel storage. In this way the evolutionary regime would be reinforced by a balance between a modest amount of breeder demand-oriented reprocessing and safer storage alternatives for excess supplies of spent fuel.

(d) *Fuel assurances*. The period of turmoil in nuclear commerce that followed the events of 1974–5 created insecurities in fuel supplies that added to incentives for premature use of plutonium. A useful way of strengthening the regime would be to reinforce national stockpile measures by an international institutional arrangement to insure vulnerable countries against interruptions in bilateral supplies. For large programmes in countries meeting non-proliferation standards, this might take the form of special agreements for long term supply. For small programmes, modest, internationally-controlled stockpiles of low enriched uranium could be helpful and are still worth further exploration.

The steps mentioned above represent modest but important ways to strengthen the fuel cycle aspects of the international regime begun in the 1950s and focused on the IAEA. They will not by themselves solve the problem of nuclear proliferation, in part because the fuel cycle is only part of the proliferation problem, and in part because there is always a temptation for some to remain outside the regime. None the less, the norms of the regime create a strong presumption against misuse of the fuel cycle and the institutions provide mechanisms that help ascertain that the norms are being observed.

THE PROBLEM OF PRIORITY

Non-proliferation is not a foreign policy; it is part of a foreign policy. Foreign policy always involves the adjustment of partly conflicting objectives in order to achieve as much as possible within the constraints of a refractory world. How non-proliferation fares in that adjustment process depends on the priority it receives. One of the effects of the attention given to the issue in the late 1970s was that a number of governments gave the issue greater priority.

As the 1980s [unfold], a number of sceptics inside and outside the bureaucracy urge a general lowering of the priority given to non-proliferation, on the grounds that its negative effects are exaggerated. Proliferation may be disastrous for the particular countries involved in a regional nuclear arms race, but they argue that such a race would have little effect on the rest of the world.

Another group of analysts goes even further and argues that proliferation would have beneficial and stabilizing effects on world politics.[6] Just as nuclear weapons have produced prudence in US–Soviet relations, they argue, so may nuclear weapons stabilize regional balances. This might be true if political conditions were similar. But the transferability of prudence assumes governments with stable command and control systems; the absence of serious civil wars; the absence of strong destabilizing motivations, such as irredentist passions; and discipline over the temptation for pre-emptive strikes during the early stages when new nuclear weapons capabilities are soft and vulnerable. Such assumptions are unrealistic in many parts of the world. On the contrary, rather than enhancing its security, the first effects of acquiring new nuclear capability in many circumstances may be to increase a state's vulnerability and insecurity. And even a local use of nuclear weaponry would be a serious breach of a 35-year global taboo.

The destabilizing aspects of proliferation are further complicated if one thinks of possible roles of non-state actors. Whatever the prospect of successful acquisition of a nuclear device by a terrorist group, even threats of such action may create severe civil difficulties. Moreover, the possible theft of weapons-usable materials and black market sale to maverick states means that the problems posed by non-state groups do not depend solely on their technological capabilities. Nor would the superpowers necessarily remain isolated from the effects.

Equally important is the way that the wide or rapid spread of nuclear capabilities could affect both the central strategic balance, and prospects for the gradual evolution of a peaceful world order. To illustrate both points, take the case of the Federal Republic of Germany and Japan. One of the striking and constructive features of the world since 1945 is that those two great powers of the pre-war period have been reintegrated into world coalitions and institutions as the third and fourth most powerful states in economic terms without their feeling it necessary to develop equivalent nuclear military power. This makes the central strategic balance more calculable and contributes to the stability of Europe and Asia.

Unfortunately, there can be no decisive answer in the debate over the effects of proliferation. Particular outcomes may differ. Some cases may start a disastrous chain of events; others may turn out to have benign effects. At the same time, a great power, particularly one that plays a critical role in maintaining a regime, must take a prudent and cautious approach to the assessment of risks both inside and outside a region. The consequences of guessing wrong about effects are not the same in both directions; a stable outcome may be a happy regional surprise; an unstable outcome that triggers a chain of proliferation events could have a disastrous effect on the global regime.[7]

RATE VS. DEGREE OF PROLIFERATION

Even if there is a high priority given to non-proliferation, difficult policy choices exist in relating the rate and degree. Proliferation is sometimes conceived in simple terms of a single explosion. Indeed that concept is enshrined in the NPT. But it can also be seen as a staircase, with many steps before and after a first nuclear test. A first explosion is politically important as a key landing in the staircase, but militarily, a single crude explosive device does not allow admission into some meaningful nuclear "club." The very idea of a nuclear club is very misleading. The difference between a single crude device and a modern nuclear arsenal is as stark as the difference between having one small apple and having an orchard. While the rate of proliferation refers to the politically symbolic event of a first explosion, the degree of proliferation refers to the size, military quality and deliverability of a country's nuclear arsenal.

As technology spreads and proliferation occurs, it will be necessary to direct more attention to these questions of advanced proliferation. Controls on information about laser fusion devices, technology with advanced weapons uses, launchers and other delivery systems will require more systematic analysis. Strategic and arms-control policies will also require attention from this perspective. Formulating sanctions that deter a quickening rate while creating fire-breaks after a first explosion will be a delicate balancing act.

Obviously there is a trade-off between the attitudes and measures that are taken to deter first explosions—the events that politically symbolize the rate of proliferation—and the measures taken to limit the degree of proliferation after the first explosion. Yet clearly there is a difference, for example, between a South Asia in which India and Pakistan engage in an escalating nuclear arms race, and a situation which stabilizes around the fiction of one-time "peaceful nuclear explosions." Measures to deal with the degree of proliferation will be difficult to announce in advance, but will require thought.[8] That thought must balance the effects of rate and degree, and of any measures both on the region and on the general regime. And the adequacy of the regime tends to be defined in terms of rate alone.

RELATIONS AMONG REGIMES

International regimes co-exist in different issue areas with a degree of autonomy from each other. None the less, they also exist within an overall political context and can have a net strengthening or weakening effect on each other. In one direction, the non-proliferation regime interacts with other nuclear weapons and arms-control regimes; in the other direction with international energy and economic regimes. A successful non-proliferation policy in the 1980s will require attention to the connections in both directions.

The relation between non-proliferation and other arms-control regimes is not as simple as it first appears. The usual connections are made by provisions like Article VI of the NPT, and by various UN Disarmament Committee resolutions calling for a halt to the "vertical proliferation" of the arms of the super-powers. This gives rise to certain paradoxes in non-proliferation policy. Ironically, calculability and stability of deterrence between the United States and the Soviet Union has occurred over time and at high levels of weaponry. By historical evolution this pattern has produced prudence in their relationship and extended deterrence to their allies who have thus been able to eschew the development of nuclear weaponry. Changes in the balance, which are perceived as weakening the credibility of deterrence, threaten not only the stability of the central relationship, but reduce the sense of security that permits allied states to forswear proliferation. It is paradoxical but true that under many circumstances the introduction of a single weapon in a new state may be more likely to lead to nuclear use than the introduction of an additional thousand each by the United States and the Soviet Union.[9]

On the other hand, to profess indifference to the super-power nuclear arms relationship can weaken the non-proliferation regime in two different ways. First, a disdain for the arms-control institutions and concerns expressed by non-weapons states can exacerbate the discrimination issue that is the central dilemma in non-proliferation policy. Second, nuclear doctrines and deployments which stress the usefulness of nuclear weapons in war-fighting situations may help to increase the credibility of deterrence, but they also tend to make nuclear weapons look more attractive to others. If states that have deliberately eschewed nuclear weapons see them treated increasingly like conventional defensive weapons, they may one day reconsider their decisions. In short, the relation between non-proliferation and the general nuclear arms-control regimes will require a sensitivity to both areas during what promises to be a difficult period in the super-power relationship.

In the realm of energy and economic regimes, it is important that the moderate restrictions of an evolutionary approach to the nuclear fuel cycle do not appear as a general posture of technology denial by advanced countries. Threats that poor countries will go nuclear to turn the terms of the North–South dialogue are not particularly credible because nuclear weapons are so ill-suited to such a purpose. But indifference to the energy and economic concerns of poor countries can weaken the non-proliferation regime. A forthcoming posture on energy and technology transfer, including the development of non-nuclear energy alternatives, and other measures to deal with energy insecurity, can help to defuse confrontations about status and attention rather than security.

While national security concerns are the dominant reason for most states to preserve and strengthen the non-proliferation regime, at the same time, it is important not to neglect the status and prestige interests of nations. Above all, it is important on prestige grounds that overt discriminatory solutions be avoided. Justifiable temporary differentiation and permanent discrimination are not the same thing. We must be careful not to reinforce the illusion that being a nuclear weapon state provides unusual privileges or position in international affairs.

CONCLUSION

[Four] decades have passed since the energy of the atom was used in warfare. Yet rather than nuclear doom, the world has seen a surprising nuclear stability—thus far. Equally remarkable is the fact that over the same period nuclear technology has spread to more than two score nations, yet only a small fraction have chosen to develop nuclear weaponry. A third notable point about the period has been the development of an international non-proliferation regime with a set of rules, norms and institutions which haltingly, and albeit imperfectly, has discouraged the proliferation of nuclear weapons capability. Can this situation last? Obviously there will be changes in political and technical trends, but the prospects that proliferation may be destabilizing in many instances; that nuclear weapons need not enhance the security position of states; and that super-powers cannot fully escape the effects, provide the common international interest upon which the non-proliferation regime is based. Under such conditions some inequality in weaponry is acceptable to most states because the alternative anarchic equality is more dangerous. So long as countries can be made better off without a bomb than with one, then a policy of slowing the spread of nuclear weapons technology rests on a realistic formulation of common interests, and there are serious prospects for maintaining a legitimate and stable international nuclear regime.

Realistically, an international regime does not need perfect adherence to have a significant constraining effect, any more than deviant behaviour means the irrelevance of domestic legal regimes. Nevertheless, there is a point beyond which violations lead to the breakdown of normative constraints. The police function is traditionally the domain of the great powers in international politics, but if their preponderance in the nuclear issue area erodes, and they become diverted by other issues, there is a danger that the gradual historical curve of proliferation could approach such a point.

Given the natural decline in American preponderance in the nuclear issue area, it was important that the burden of leadership in regime maintenance be more broadly shared. To a considerable extent, INFCE and the other initiatives of the late 1970s helped to accomplish this. For example, in sharp contrast to attitudes [only recently], key figures in

Japan warn against asserting only "our own position and lacking the wider perspective of anti-proliferation."[10] Or as one long term French official noted wryly and privately in Vienna near the end of the INFCE, 'we may encroach on your markets, but somehow we seem to have inherited your non-proliferation policy in the process'. Changed attitudes are reflected in many decisions such as the June 1977 German policy against the export of reprocessing plants; or the agreement about sanctions in 1978 Suppliers' Guidelines; or the French pressure on South Africa and restrained response to Brazilian inquiries about breeder technology, and other examples which have not yet been made public.

To a very considerable extent, leadership in the job of maintaining the non-proliferation regime is now shared. But collective leadership is difficult to manage. The US still has to adjust to sharing the process. The wrong policies in the 1980s could still sacrifice the current modest success in regime maintenance on the altars of either purism or cynicism. Unfortunately, there is no simple solution to the political problem of proliferation. But given the difficulty of constructing international institutions in a world of sovereign states, and the risks attendant upon the collapse of these institutions, political wisdom begins with efforts to maintain the existing regime with its presumption against proliferation.

NOTES

1. J. J. Weltman, 'Nuclear Devolution and World Order', *World Politics* XXXII (January 1980): 192.

2. See for example, Amory Lovins, L. Hunter Lovins, Leonard Ross, 'Nuclear Power and Nuclear Bombs', *Foreign Affairs* 58 (Summer 1980); and Kenneth Waltz, 'Nuclear Weapons and International Stability', Adelphi Paper forthcoming. Both articles make a number of good points. In my judgment each would be destructive as a guide to policy for reasons spelled out below.

3. Contrary to some opinions, safeguards need not be perfect to deter diversion and have a significant political effect. The necessary probability of detection is debatable, but thus far I am unaware of significant diversion of IAEA safeguarded materials.

4. See J. S. Nye, 'Non-Proliferation: A Long-Term Strategy', *Foreign Affairs*, (April 1978).

5. Lovins *et al.*, *op. cit.* in note 2, p. 1138 (though they are correct in its limited effectiveness in the displacing of the oil).

6. See for example, Kenneth Waltz, 'What Will the Spread of Nuclear Weapons Do to the World?', in John Kerry King (Ed), *International Political Effects of the Spread of Nuclear Weapons*, (Washington, GPO, 1979).

7. In my judgment these considerations are not adequately dealt with by Waltz, cited above.

8. See Lewis Dunn, 'After INFCE: Some Next Steps for Non-Proliferation Policy', Hudson Institute Paper, Vol. 33 (Autumn 1979).

9. George Quester, 'Nuclear Proliferation: Linkages and Solutions', *International Organization*, Vol. 33 (Autumn 1979).

10. Editorial, *Asahi Shinbun* 25 February 1980, Tokyo.

17 TOWARD BALLISTIC MISSILE DEFENSE

Keith B. Payne and Colin S. Gray

On March 23, 1983, President Reagan delivered a televised speech to the nation in which he initiated a potentially radical departure in U.S. strategic policy. The President suggested that the policy of nuclear deterrence through the threat of strategic nuclear retaliation is inadequate, and called upon the vast American technological community to examine the potential for effective defense against ballistic missiles. . . .

The central problem of nuclear deterrence is that no offensive deterrent, no matter how fearsome, is likely to work forever, and the consequences of its failure would be intolerable for civilization. The President's call was a direct challenge to the offensive concept of deterrence that has dominated U.S. strategic policy for decades. That concept is based upon the simple and still widely accepted argument that neither the United States nor the Soviet Union will launch a nuclear first strike or engage in other highly provocative actions if both sides are vulnerable to nuclear retaliation. The President's speech suggested that vulnerability to a Soviet nuclear attack is not an acceptable condition in the long term, and that the United States would examine avenues to counter the threat of nuclear missiles. . . .

Although a small core of strategic defense enthusiasts has always been present within the U.S. defense community, this level of officially expressed interest in strategic defense is an unprecedented development in recent U.S. strategic policy. The goal of actively defending the American homeland in the event of nuclear conflict has not received serious official endorsement since the 1960s. Also unprecedented is the fact that the President has set policy in front of technology. If the United States does, in fact, deploy a multilayered system for defense against ballistic missiles, it will be the result of policy leading technology, not the more familiar "technology creep" generating enthusiasm and a constituency for a weapons system which then "finds" a policy rationale as it is developed. . . .

Strategic defense has not been debated seriously since the antiballistic missile (ABM) debate of 1968–1971. Many of the technological, political

Note: Some footnotes have been deleted, and others have been renumbered to appear in consecutive order.

and strategic factors pertinent to the old debate have changed considerably since then, but the key issues remain unchanged. They are:

- What role is ballistic missile defense expected to play;
- What effect will a commitment to strategic defense have on stability;
- What is the role of strategic offensive forces during and after a defensive transition;
- How are the European allies likely to react;
- What is Soviet policy concerning ballistic missile defense, and how is the Soviet Union likely to respond to an American initiative; and finally,
- What are the arms control implications of a defensive transition?

II

The role that strategic defense might play in U.S. national security policy is now a contentious issue. Should it be expected to provide an "astrodome" covering American military forces and cities comprehensively, or is a more limited objective acceptable, such as only defending U.S. retaliatory weapons? The criteria for defense effectiveness have profound implications for the research programs to be pursued and the types of defensive systems to be deployed.

For example, if a comprehensive defense for the American homeland is the only objective deemed worthy of the cost, then "exotic" defensive technology such as space-based, directed-energy beam systems or hypervelocity guns will be essential—technology that may take many years to mature. If, however, a more limited defensive mission is endorsed, such as the defense of U.S. retaliatory forces against a Soviet first strike, then more conventional ground-based systems incorporating radars, infrared sensors, and rocket interceptors would be appropriate. Proponents of the "astrodome" approach fear that the diversion of attention toward less sophisticated and less effective systems could harm the chances for the deployment of any defensive forces. They feel that the promise of a comprehensive defense of cities by exotic systems and the transcending of offensive-oriented deterrence is a goal that will capture the imagination and support of the American people—support that should not be jeopardized by discussion of limited defenses for U.S. retaliatory forces.

A limited defense for U.S. retaliatory forces, however, need not be inconsistent with a future exotic defense of cities. Indeed, the two roles and systems would be highly compatible, perhaps essential to a stable defensive transition. A comprehensive BMD system would require multiple defensive layers, including conventional earth-based rocket interceptors as well as exotic beam technology. Such a system would use multiple tiers of defensive protection, intended to intercept Soviet missiles during different phases of flight: the boost and post-boost phase, early and late mid-course, and the terminal phase of flight. More or fewer defensive tiers could exist depending upon the number and types of systems deployed. The layering of defensive forces into multiple tiers of interceptors could provide an extremely capable system for defense. For example, five tiers of defensive interceptors achieving 85-percent effectiveness in each layer would reduce the overall attack to less than .01 percent of the original number of attacking weapons. If 10,000 nuclear warheads were launched at the United States with such a multi-layered defensive system in place, at most a single weapon would be likely to penetrate to its target.

Current, more conventional earth-based BMD technology is relevant to the interception of warheads at various points in the mid-course and terminal phases of missile flight, but it does not promise effectiveness in the boost phase, wherein an attacking missile would be intercepted prior to releasing its host of individually targetable warheads (MIRVs). Intercept during this stage exerts great defensive leverage over the attacking force because each missile destroyed eliminates all the warheads carried by that missile.

Nevertheless, near-term BMD technology could provide the means for the important lower tiers of conventional defense designed to defend U.S. intercontinental ballistic missiles (ICBMs), strategic bomber bases, and selected critical command, control and communication facilities. These ground-based defensive systems designed to intercept Soviet warheads in their mid-course and terminal phases of flight would likely be non-nuclear, i.e., they would not use nuclear-tipped interceptors, and could be available by late in this decade. The deployment of such near-term defenses for limited coverage would actually help to facilitate a subsequent commitment to a more comprehensive defensive system involving exotic space-based systems.

The period of transition to a comprehensive defense incorporating additional layers of more advanced defensive technology could require two decades or longer for full deployment of the systems. It must be recognized that this transition period could be dangerous if precautions were not taken to ensure political and strategic stability during that period. The Soviet Union, for example, is likely to achieve an initial temporary advantage in defensive capability given its existing extensive radar network and rapidly deployable ground-based BMD. A unilateral Soviet BMD system of even limited effectiveness could be highly destabilizing in the context of existing Soviet offensive first-strike capabilities and extensive air defense and civil defense preparations: the U.S. deterrent threat could be severely degraded by the combination of the

Soviet first-strike potential to destroy American strategic nuclear forces and a Soviet defense against surviving American forces.

This combination of Soviet offensive and defensive capabilities could increase first-strike incentives during a crisis if Soviet leaders were persuaded that the U.S.S.R.'s defenses might be capable of largely absorbing the much-diminished U.S. retaliatory capability. Admittedly, Soviet strategic defenses on a modest scale could do little to limit damage against a coordinated and large-scale attack by undamaged U.S. offensive forces; but alerted Soviet defenses could be very effective in defending against a U.S. force sharply reduced in size and impaired by a Soviet first strike.

Thus, early deployment by the United States of a ballistic missile defense for its retaliatory forces would not only help to ensure the survival of U.S. strategic weapons, but would also assist in preserving the credibility of the U.S. offensive deterrent during an otherwise potentially unstable transition period. Even such limited conventional defensive coverage for U.S. retaliatory forces would create enormous uncertainties for Soviet planners considering the effectiveness of a strategic first strike, in addition to those longstanding doubts pertaining to the calculated effectiveness of their offensive forces. In the context of Soviet defensive deployments, enhancing the survivability and potential effectiveness of U.S. retaliatory forces by means of both strategic defense and more immediate special "penetration aids" for offensive weapons would help to ensure that a transition to a comprehensive defensive capability could be pursued safely.

The crucial role played by U.S. retaliatory forces to safeguard stability during the initial phase of a defensive transition should also be clear. MX-Peacekeeper intercontinental ballistic missiles, a new small ICBM, B-1B bombers, cruise missiles, and Trident submarines are essential for deterrence stability during the decades of transition. New defensive weapons should not be considered a substitute for, or alternative to, the current modernization of strategic offensive forces; indeed, a strategic defensive initiative necessitates modernization of offensive forces to help sustain stability during the defensive transition. The leaders of the Soviet Union are likely to share this view.

Finally, a transition to a comprehensive defense for the American homeland would require the support of many Administrations and necessitate major technological advances. Completion of such a transition could be waylaid for technological or political reasons over the course of the decades that any such transition will require. As a result, each phase of a defensive transition must be valuable in and of itself, and should complement any subsequent investment in strategic defense. Early deployment of BMD coverage for U.S. retaliatory forces would constitute the first phase of a comprehensive defensive transition; it would safeguard the process of transition, and would be strategically valuabl₂ on its own merits, even if subsequent phases were delayed or terminated for political or technical reasons.

An important by-product of a ballistic missile defense system, even of limited effectiveness, is protection of the United States (and Soviet Union) from the accidental launch of a missile. For both sides to be protected against an accident would be far preferable to the current condition which carries a very high risk that disastrous consequences would follow from any such mishap. Further, limited BMD could help protect the United States against lightly armed nuclear powers of the future.

There are dozens of technical possibilities for future strategic efense systems; the debate over the proposed defense transition is not about the prospective effectiveness of one or two systems. Faced with the very rich menu of technical options for defense, it is simply untenable to assert that "they" (ground-based conventional interceptors and beam weapons, and space-based or deployable directed- and kinetic-energy weapons) will not work. . . .

All of recorded history has shown swings in the pendulum of technical advantage between offense and defense. For the strategic defense to achieve a very marked superiority over the offense over the next several decades would be an extraordinary trend in the light of the last 30 years, but not of the last hundred or thousand years. Military history is replete with examples of defensive technology and tactics dominating the offense.

In sum, different levels of defensive technology can make important, and distinct, contributions to strategic stability. The near-term role for limited ballistic missile defense suitable to the technology likely to be available soon would be to provide protection for the U.S. nuclear deterrent and perhaps protection of the nation against small or accidental attacks. As the initial phase in a transition to comprehensive BMD coverage, defense of U.S. retaliatory forces would help provide the stability necessary for the long-term development of the more effective systems needed for a comprehensive defense of U.S. cities. If the technology for effective city defense proves to be attainable, then strategic defense can expand in scope and depth to provide coverage for urban and industrial America. . . .

III

What is the likely effect of strategic defense on stability? If the Reagan Administration (or its successors) cannot answer critics who charge that strategic defense would be "destabilizing," it will have little hope of generating or sustaining the necessary congressional and public support. During the initial phase of a defensive transition, stability could be safeguarded by defending U.S. offensive forces and by enhancing their potential to penetrate Soviet ballistic missile defenses.

A more difficult question concerns how stability would be maintained during the later phases of a transition wherein, theoretically, neither side could pose a credible threat to inflict very widespread nuclear destruction upon the other's homeland. Deterrence in the nuclear age has come to be understood in terms of mutual threats of nuclear devastation varying only in kinds of targets, i.e., counter-military, counter-industrial, counter-city, or all of these. The nuclear missile age has so far been an age of defenselessness against these threats. The question now is: could stability be maintained if the current condition of mutual homeland vulnerability were to be altered drastically? . . .

If . . . one assumes a very high degree of confidence by U.S. and Soviet leaders in their defensive systems, deterrence should still function, but it would no longer be the long-familiar deterrence from mutual vulnerability. The U.S. deterrent would rest on a defensive capability to deny plausibility to any Soviet "theory of victory." That is, U.S. defenses would thwart Soviet strategy and deny the Soviet Union its requirements for military and political success. These include: the destruction of U.S. military potential such that the Soviet Union, though not escaping damage in nuclear war, would survive, recover, and continue to function; the destruction of opposing forces in Europe; and the seizure of critical strategic assets world-wide. Soviet military writers caution against any nuclear "adventurism" in the absence of a capability to meet these requirements for success.

This type of defensive deterrent is not totally removed from the current offensive-oriented deterrent. Currently the United States seeks to deny the Soviet Union its theory of victory by promising a devastating nuclear retaliation. In contrast, a defensive deterrent would deny the Soviet Union its theory of victory by ensuring its inability to defeat the United States—promising a long and potentially unwinnable war which could allow the vastly superior U.S., and U.S.-allied, military-industrial potential to come into play. Soviet leaders are acutely sensitive to the probable negative political consequences of such wars and are highly respectful of U.S. military-industrial potential. The prospect of waging a protracted war would be a deterring prospect for Soviet leaders. Perhaps most important, unlike the current condition, a defensive deterrent would combine the prospect for denial of Soviet victory with the avoidance of U.S. defeat and destruction. . . .

. . . While it is difficult to compare the relative efficacy of [offensive and defensive] types of deterrents, there is one critically important distinction. In the event deterrence fails, extremely effective defenses could enable the United States (and perhaps the Soviet Union) to avoid a nuclear holocaust, while a purely offensive approach to deterrence virtually ensures a holocaust.[1]

In short, a transition to strategic defense would not be inconsistent with deterrence. Rather it would introduce a different approach to deterrence, an approach that could reduce both the probability and the consequences of nuclear war.

IV

A defensive deterrent would thus present powerful disincentives against a Soviet nuclear first strike. It is likely, however, to be less appropriate for the current policy of extending deterrence coverage to allies and global interests. The U.S. strategic nuclear threat, which is integral to NATO's "flexible response" doctrine, would be less deterring in the presence of Soviet strategic defenses. Moreover, the Soviet Union might believe that the potential benefits of conventional conquest in Europe or the Persian Gulf would be worth the risk if there were a strategic defensive stalemate with the United States. Indeed, control and exploitation of the industrial and energy resources of Western Europe and the Gulf may be seen by Soviet leaders as the way of overcoming their otherwise long-term structural economic disadvantages in the global competition with the United States, notably in the production of military high-technology items.

A possible solution to this potential problem is the same as that suggested for the solution to NATO's current over-reliance upon the threat of nuclear retaliation, namely the enhancement of NATO's conventional forces. That solution has been understood and advocated by every U.S. Administration for the past two decades. The European allies, however, have long resisted incurring the social and economic costs associated with providing NATO with conventional forces sufficiently large, well equipped, and intelligently deployed to compel the Soviet Union to think in terms of a high-risk, high-cost nuclear attack. Instead, NATO Europe has preferred for years to rely heavily on a largely U.S.-provided nuclear deterrent. Should, however, the Soviets develop an effective strategic defense, the U.S. "nuclear umbrella" would appear much less fearsome to the U.S.S.R., compelling Western Europeans to seek an alternate means of preserving their security.

Thus, it is doubtful that America's European allies will ever be enthusiastic about a defensive transition in U.S. national security policy. They are likely to see it as a weakening of the U.S. commitment to provide a nuclear umbrella over Western Europe. Moreover, European countries confront a wider spectrum of threat than does the United

States. A BMD system that effectively protected the United States *and* its European allies from strategic nuclear attack would still leave the Europeans vulnerable to conventional and some kinds of tactical nuclear attack. This asymmetry in vulnerability, and hence the perception of an asymmetry in American and European interests, could be exacerbated by a new U.S. defensive deterrence policy.

A defensive transition by both superpowers would also degrade, perhaps nullify, the British and French independent strategic deterrents. It was clear during the SALT I negotiations that the British and French wanted BMD limited to very low levels so that their relatively small independent nuclear forces would retain effectiveness. There is little to indicate that the British or French have a different perspective today.

During a defensive transition, however, some of the allies might seek to parallel U.S. and Soviet efforts and acquire their own strategic defenses. . . . In the near- to mid-term, however, it would seem unlikely that independent European offensive or defensive capabilities could compete successfully with those of Soviet forces.

On an objective analysis, there are some respects in which a defensive transition could enhance security in Europe. First, U.S. BMD technologies could help protect the Western Europeans from Soviet long-range theater nuclear weapons (such as SS-4s, SS-5s, SS-20s, and variable-range ICBMs and submarine-launched ballistic missiles or SLBMs). . . .

Second, if America is defended, the President is likely to see a lower level of risk involved in responding to a Soviet invasion of Europe than if America were naked to Soviet nuclear attack. This fact alone should significantly reduce any Soviet inclination to attack NATO Europe. . . . Thus, the U.S. "extended deterrent" over Europe could still be effective to an important degree.

Nonetheless, the reaction of major NATO countries to a U.S. BMD program would be likely to reflect the concerns already noted, as well as a fundamental difference between American and European perspectives on security. NATO allies have long criticized what they identify as the U.S. penchant for a technological rather than a political solution to security concerns. No matter how sound the strategic case for a defensive transition, many Europeans will be more impressed by the effect a defensive transition might have on the political foundations of the familiar East-West security system. . . .

V

How would the Soviet Union respond to an American defensive transition? Would the Soviet Union cooperate, tacitly or explicitly, with a defensive transition, by negotiated reductions in offensive weapons to ease the defense burden, or would it choose to compete comprehensively in an offense-defense race?

First, it should be noted that the Soviet Union has exhibited much more enthusiasm for strategic defense over the past two decades than has the United States. Soviet strategic defensive activities were roughly five times U.S. outlays in 1970 and increased to 25 times U.S. outlays in 1979.[2] While the United States drastically reduced its number of interceptor aircraft and de-activated its air defense, surface-to-air missile (SAM) batteries during the 1960s . . . the Soviet Union modernized and increased its air defenses. While the United States reduced its commitment to civil defense to a marginal level, the Soviet Union expanded its civil defense efforts. Additionally, Soviet offensive-force modernization over the last decade has been directed toward achieving the capability to destroy U.S. retaliatory forces before they could be used—"active defense" in Soviet military parlance. It is apparent that the notion of defending the homeland is central to Soviet strategic thinking.

The Soviet Union has approached ballistic missile defense through two avenues. First, the Soviet Union has maintained, and is now modernizing, the world's only operational ballistic missile defense site around Moscow. Moreover, it has continued to upgrade its extensive network of air defense radars and interceptors . . . giving them some capability against strategic ballistic missiles and intermediate-range theater nuclear missiles such as the Pershing II. . . .

Second, the evolving Soviet ballistic missile defense research and development program accommodates directed-energy beam systems and a more conventional BMD system involving transportable radars and high- and low-altitude interceptors that could be deployed rapidly. The combination of an existing infrastructure of large battle management radars, rapidly deployable BMD interceptors, and transportable missile site radars has led some in the intelligence community to conclude either that the Soviet Union is preparing to "break out" of ABM Treaty constraints and initiate a defensive transition, or is engaged in a "creeping" break-out, to be followed by rapid deployment of BMD.

Yet there are several reasons why it is unlikely that the Soviet Union would be the first to withdraw formally from the ABM Treaty and initiate an overt transition to ballistic missile defense. While the Treaty is in effect, the Soviet Union can continue to pursue its gradual upgrading of air defense to achieve greater ballistic missile defense capability, with less likelihood that the United States will react strongly. . . .

Second, the Soviet Union obviously is aware that for the first time in two decades the United States is making a very serious commitment to explore the technical promise of strategic defense. Soviet leaders may suspect that the United States will petition for revision or withdrawal from the ABM Treaty within the decade. A prudent tactic for the Soviet

Union would be to wait for such a U.S. initiative, and then to insist on significant U.S. arms control concessions in return for Soviet endorsement of the revisions sought by the United States. In this case the Soviet Union could achieve a major propaganda success with the charge that it was the United States that had sought to weaken or terminate this important symbol of détente, indeed, this perceived monument to the mutual commitment to prevent nuclear war. Given the enduring West European commitment to 1970s-vintage détente, the Soviet Union could further its traditional objective of dividing NATO by presenting itself as the defender of the ABM Treaty.

Finally, if the Soviet Union should "break out" of the ABM Treaty in the near term, it is almost certain that the United States would respond with deployment of a system based upon current defensive technology. U.S. ballistic missile defense research and development has focused upon ICBM defense for almost two decades, and it is clear that the defense of ICBM silos is within our grasp. The Soviet Union, however, has spent billions of rubles deploying its fourth-generation ICBMs (particularly the SS-18s and SS-19s) for the purpose of putting U.S. ICBM silos at risk. . . . With MX-Peacekeeper ICBMs scheduled to go into silos in 1986, it seems unlikely that the Soviet Union would choose to surrender its ability to threaten U.S. ICBMs by abrogating the ABM Treaty. . . .

Given all of these considerations, it would appear unwise for the Soviet Union overtly to break out of the ABM Treaty regime. What then would be the likely Soviet responses to a U.S. defensive initiative? Our judgment is that the Soviet Union would be most likely to pursue a dual-track response—combining arms control and diplomatic initiatives with strong military programs. Such behavior would be in keeping with the traditional Soviet proclivity for pursuing arms control negotiations and a dynamic arms buildup simultaneously. . . .

VI

This brings us to the question of the impact on arms control of a determined U.S. BMD program and of the likely Soviet response to such a program. Here the first question is the impact on existing arms control agreements, notably the ABM Treaty.

The United States and Soviet Union would have to revise the ABM Treaty to permit deployment of BMD systems of even limited effectiveness. A comprehensive defense would likely necessitate withdrawal from the Treaty, which Article XV permits on six months' notice.

The United States certainly has sound strategic and arms control reasons to reconsider its continued endorsement of the ABM Treaty. At the time the Treaty was signed, the United States established a clear linkage between offensive and defensive arms control limitations. Such a linkage made good sense; the United States could accept severe constraints on BMD, which might defend U.S. ICBMs and strategic bomber bases, if the Soviet offensive threat to U.S. retaliatory forces could be constrained and reduced on a long-term basis through arms control. . . .

Unfortunately the standard thus set by the United States for continued support of the ABM Treaty has not been met. Indeed, the Soviet offensive threat to U.S. retaliatory forces has increased dramatically since the signing of SALT I, and the signed but unratified SALT II agreement would not have eased the problem of strategic force vulnerability given the types and numbers of weapons permitted.

Yet the strict prohibitions on BMD systems that could defend retaliatory forces remain intact in the form of the ABM Treaty. Since the signing of SALT I, the United States has, to a large degree, dismissed the sensible linkage between offensive and defensive limitations established at those negotiations.

Thus, the United States and the Soviet Union do have the legal right to withdraw from the ABM Treaty, given proper notice, and the United States does have a strategic and an arms control rationale for reconsidering the ABM Treaty. The Treaty should not be considered sacrosanct. . . .

In this broader context, there are several reasons why defense and arms control could be mutually beneficial. A defensive transition could establish a necessary basis for deep offensive force level reductions. First, even limited near-term defense systems designed to protect retaliatory forces could alleviate the verification difficulties associated with deep force level reductions. At current relatively high force levels a degree of ambiguity in the ability to verify an agreement is considered acceptable because only large-scale violations would have a "significant" impact upon the strategic balance, and such violations are likely to be noticed. Reducing U.S. and Soviet strategic arsenals to the level initially proposed by the United States at START . . . or lower, however, would place a higher premium on each delivery system. At much lower force levels even a relatively small level of noncompliance could have a significant impact upon the strategic balance, and thus be of great concern.

In the context of small numbers of U.S. retaliatory forces, the covert retention or deployment of even a few MIRVed ICBMs could be a threat to the survivability of an important fraction of U.S. deterrent forces, and thus provide the Soviet Union with an increased incentive to strike first. And the importance of very strict verification for deep reductions is incongruous with the increasing difficulty of totally monitoring the deployment of new types of nuclear weapons such as cruise missiles and mobile ballistic missiles. Consequently, in the absence of a defensive transition the U.S. insistence upon the ability to verify an agreement with very high confidence could reduce the chance for any deep arms reductions. A transition to strategic defense, however, would reestablish the condition wherein deception on a very large scale would be necessary before the strategic balance could be jeopardized by cheating. . . .

Second, it is clear that one reason for the Soviet commitment to large numbers of strategic weapons is to achieve a damage-limiting effect through offensive "counterforce" capabilities, i.e., the ability to disrupt U.S. command channels and to destroy U.S. retaliatory forces before they could be launched against the Soviet Union. It is likely that the Soviet Union has been so reluctant to agree to U.S. proposals for deep reductions in heavy MIRVed ICBMs because these weapons are the primary counterforce instruments in the Soviet arsenal. As noted above, damage limitation for national survival is a key objective of Soviet strategic doctrine, and that objective currently is pursued primarily through offensive counterforce preparations.

A defensive transition could provide the damage-limiting capability mandated by Soviet doctrine, with strategic defense replacing offensive forces as the principal means for limiting damage. Strategic defense could, in effect, take over the damage-limitation mission now given to offensive counterforce weapons. Such a development should reduce the long-noted reluctance of the Soviet Union to accept negotiated cuts in its large ICBM force.

Finally, if defensive technology proves to be extremely effective, it could reduce the incentives for the offensive arms competition by rendering it futile. The Soviet ballistic missile defense program of the 1960s probably was truncated because it became apparent that U.S. advances in MIRV technology would easily counter the Soviet defensive system. Thus, U.S. technological advances in offensive systems probably discouraged the Soviets from continuing to deploy what had become obsolete defensive technology. The development of highly effective defensive technology could, and logically should, have a similar impact upon offensive weapons programs.

Of course, a transition to defense could lead to a competition in the development and deployment of increasingly advanced defensive technologies. Nevertheless, restructuring the arms competition toward a "defense race" would have a benign impact upon the catastrophic potential of nuclear war, and would be far preferable to an indefinite continuation of the competition in offensive nuclear arms.

VII

In one other respect, related to arms control, a defensive transition could serve the interest of all mankind in a critically important fashion. A recent study on the "Global Consequences of Nuclear War" indicates that a relatively "small" nuclear war, involving between 500 and 2,000 detonations, could result in climatic changes that would trigger a global catastrophe.[3] That number of detonations would reflect the use of only a small fraction of the nuclear weapons in U.S. and Soviet arsenals. Strategic defense is the only candidate answer to this potential threat to humanity. Suggested alternatives simply are ineffective.

The most obvious and effective solution to this danger would be for nuclear weapons never to be used. However, it simply is not within the power of a U.S. President to determine whether a nuclear war will occur. Despite the best efforts of the United States to avoid nuclear war, the Soviet Union or another nuclear-armed country could employ nuclear weapons against the United States or a local foe. The first step in understanding this issue is to recognize that whatever the United States does, or does not do, cannot ensure the prevention of nuclear war. It is beyond reason to believe that all nuclear-armed powers would agree to ban the use of nuclear weapons and abide by that agreement under all conditions.

Equally incredible is the prospect for arms control to reduce the global arsenal of over 50,000 nuclear weapons to numbers below the threshold reportedly necessary to cause a climatic catastrophe. This does not mean that the arms control process has no value for the U.S. pursuit of strategic stability. Rather, what is suggested is that this avenue can hardly be relied on to prevent a climatic catastrophe that might stem from even a "small" nuclear exchange. . . .

VIII

. . . Unfortunately, though not unexpectedly, the debate that is shaping up promises to be yet another stale and unimaginative confrontation between those who judge homeland defense to be destabilizing and those who do not. Neither the government nor private commentators are well equipped at present with an understanding of how offense and defense can proceed together in complementary, synergistic fashion for the benefit of more stable deterrence. It is very desirable that those who are strongly committed to President Reagan's vision of an America defended against ballistic missile threats think constructively about the positive roles that U.S. offensive and near-term defensive forces can play both to safeguard the defensive transition and, perhaps, to help stabilize deterrence beyond the transition.

Neither superpower, at least in the early stages of an essentially competitive defense transition, is going to cooperate tacitly in assisting the defenses of the other side to achieve high effectiveness. The United States and Soviet Union have, after all, been involved in an arms competition expressing deep-rooted political rivalry. No matter how great the technical success of U.S. and Soviet defense transitions, the competition between offense and defense will not stop. Neither superpower is likely to abandon permanently all hope of gaining a major advantage by developing both effective offensive and defensive weapons.

One must assume that both the Soviet Union and the United States prefer a condition wherein *both* their offensive *and* their defensive capabilities are effective, to a condition wherein only their defensive weapons can perform as intended. Neither side, however, is likely to anticipate an enduring advantage in strategic offensive and defensive systems; both will be constrained to accept much more limited offensive targeting capabilities than now exist. Future missions for U.S. strategic offensive forces may include the following: guarding the defense transition; holding at risk so many high-value assets of the Soviet state that the Soviet leaders perceive a substantial net advantage in negotiating a major bilateral drawdown in offensive forces (thereby assisting the U.S. defense transition); providing an enduring hedge against sudden revelation of weaknesses in defensive systems; and providing some deterrent effect in order to help discourage gross misbehavior by third parties. . . .

Strategic defense should not be viewed in terms of an all-or-nothing "astrodome." "Star wars" defenses, no matter how great their promise, will not constitute the last move in high-technology arms competition, and strategic defensive technology will not solve the fundamental problems of political rivalry. But strategic defense, embracing a wide range of near-term and far-term weaponry, promises to strengthen the stability of deterrence by imposing major new uncertainties upon any potential attack. In the long run, it holds out the possibility of transforming, though not transcending, the Soviet-American deterrence relationship.

NOTES

1. The qualifier, "virtually," acknowledges the presence of the existing theory of damage control and limitation. To be specific, damage to the American homeland in war might be limited if the Soviet government chose to exercise restraint in its nuclear targeting.

2. Central Intelligence Agency, National Foreign Assessment Center, *Soviet and U.S. Defense Activities, 1970–1979: A Dollar Cost Comparison*, SR-80-10005, January 1980, p. 9.

3. See Carl Sagan, "Nuclear War and Climatic Catastrophe," *Foreign Affairs*, Winter 1983/84, pp. 257–292. [A portion of this article is reprinted in Part III of this book—eds.]

18 STAR WARS: A CRITIQUE

Union of Concerned Scientists

OVERVIEW

> I call upon the scientific community who gave us nuclear weapons to turn their great talents to the cause of mankind and world peace: to give us the means of rendering these nuclear weapons impotent and obsolete. (President Reagan, March 23, 1983)

These words unveiled the President's Strategic Defense Initiative, a "comprehensive and intensive effort" with the "ultimate goal of eliminating the threat posed by strategic nuclear missiles." It proposes to rely on unborn generations of sophisticated space weapons that the Secretary of Defense told *Meet the Press* would provide a "thoroughly reliable and total" defense. We shall adopt Mr. Weinberger's words, and refer to the President's goal as *total ballistic missile defense,* or *total BMD*—what in the vernacular is now called "Star Wars."

Every sane person yearns to escape from the specter of nuclear annihilation. But that consensus still leaves a host of unanswered questions: will these BMD systems, which still are just conceptual designs, provide a total defense of our civilization against the Soviet missile force? That force now carries 9,000 nuclear warheads, each far more powerful than the Hiroshima bomb, and able to arrive on US targets within thirty minutes. (The US arsenal is, of course, equally devastating.) If these defenses of the distant future could protect us totally against today's threat, could they cope with the Soviet strategic weapons of their own era?

What would the Soviets' response be? Would they devote themselves to a similar effort, and agree to reduce their offensive nuclear forces? Or would they perceive this new American program as an attempt to nullify Soviet nuclear forces—as a supplement to the emerging US capacity to destroy Soviet missiles in their silos? If so, would they not

Note: The members of the study panel that issued the report "Space-Based Missile Defense" excerpted here are Kurt Gottfried, Henry W. Kendall, Hans A. Bethe, Peter A. Clausen, Richard L. Garwin, Noel Gayler, Richard Ned Lebow, Carl Sagan, and Victor Weisskopf. The footnotes have been deleted. This selection is excerpted from an article that first appeared in *The New York Review of Books* on April 26, 1984, and was later updated and reprinted in *The Fallacy of Star Wars: Why Space Weapons Can't Protect Us* (Vintage, 1984).

respond with a missile buildup and "countermeasures" to confound our defenses, so that they could still destroy the United States (just as the US can destroy the USSR)? Or would the Soviets not have this option, because our defense would be truly total—robust enough to foil any offensive countermove?

. . . There is general agreement that a defense of our population is impossible unless the vast majority of Soviet missiles can be intercepted in the first phase of their flight, while their booster engines emit a brilliant flame and before their multiple warheads are released. Otherwise, the subsequent layers of the BMD system will not be able to cope with the attack. We therefore devote the bulk of our attention to "boost phase" defense.

All boost phase interception must be carried out at long distance. Hence it is essential to transmit a blow to the enemy booster with a weapon that can travel quickly. The highest velocity attainable is the speed of light (186,000 miles per second). For that reason, laser beams which move at that speed, and beams of atoms or electrons which are nearly that fast, would be ideal if they could be made intense enough to cause damage at such large distances. Such devices are called directed energy weapons.

A laser is a device that emits a beam of light composed of rays that are almost perfectly parallel. We shall consider several types of lasers: chemical lasers that emit infrared light, excimer lasers that emit ultraviolet light, and a laser that is pumped by a nuclear explosion and emits X-rays.

In a weapon, the beam from an infrared or ultraviolet laser is concentrated on the target by adopting the familiar trick of lighting a fire with a magnifying glass that focuses the sun's rays. In a space weapon, the task of focusing and aiming the laser beam is carried out by a suitably oriented and shaped mirror or system of mirrors. The laser itself could be in space or on the ground, but the mirror must be in space if it is to send the beam toward the booster.

In assessing each BMD system, we first assume that it will perform as well as the constraints imposed by scientific law permit—that targets can be found instantly and aiming is perfect, that the battle management software is never in error, that all mirrors are optically perfect, that lasers with the required power output will become available, etc. Above all, we assume that the Soviets' forces remain static—that they do not build more missiles or install any countermeasures. Hence, our initial optimistic appraisal ignores the critical question of whether BMD will eventually work as well as it possibly could, and does not depend on classified information.

Even in this utopian regime, our findings concerning the proposed BMD schemes are that:

- Chemical laser "battle stations" in low orbits, or "space trucks" carrying "kill vehicles," will have to number in the hundreds to give adequate coverage of the Soviet silo fields.
- Excimer lasers on the ground, whose beams would be reflected toward boosters by over a thousand orbiting mirrors, would require power plants which alone would cost some $40 billion.
- The atmosphere and the earth's magnetic field combine to make particle beam weapons implausible into the foreseeable future.

These cost estimates do not include research and development, or construction of space platforms, lasers, kill vehicles, mirrors, and command and control facilities. Just the R&D portion of this program has been described by Dr. Richard DeLauer, Under Secretary of Defense for Research and Engineering, as having at least eight components "every single one . . . equivalent to or greater than the Manhattan Project." Furthermore, all costs will climb rapidly should the mirrors be imperfect, the time for aiming exceed several seconds, redundancy be desired, etc. The full costs cannot even be estimated because the proposed technologies are still too immature, but it is clear that many hundreds of billions of dollars would be needed.

The proposal to launch X-ray lasers pumped by nuclear explosions at the time of an attack would require a new fleet of submarines, since there is no suitable base on land close enough to Soviet silos to allow interception in the time available. The laser's soft X-rays cannot penetrate the atmosphere, and they deliver a rather light blow from which the booster can readily be protected. These facts, when combined with the feasibility of shortening the boost so that it ends before the missile leaves the atmosphere, imply that the X-ray laser is not a viable BMD weapon.

These findings assume a minimal Soviet reaction to a US missile defense. But the Soviets have made it clear that they view the quest for a total BMD as an unacceptable threat. They fear that such a BMD system would give us the option to strike first—an understandable fear since Mr. Weinberger has said that he would view a similar Soviet system as "one of the most frightening prospects" imaginable. And they have heard Administration officials speak of space-based BMD as a lever for stressing the USSR's technologically less sophisticated economy.

In the real world we must therefore expect a determined Soviet reaction, unconstrained by all existing agreements, because the very testing of our defensive weapons would violate our obligations under the ratified Anti-Ballistic Missile (ABM) Treaty. The Soviet reaction is likely to include:

- Offensive missiles designed to circumvent BMD, such as cruise missiles that cannot be intercepted from space.

- Fitting ICBMs with more powerful engines so that the boosters would burn out quickly and inside the atmosphere, which would stress any BMD system, and eliminate interception by kill vehicles and X-ray lasers.
- Cheap decoy ICBMs—boosters without warheads in fake silos—to overwhelm boost phase interceptors.
- Weapons that would exploit the fact that even a battleship's armor could not protect a space station from quite primitive types of attack.
- A Pandora's box of largely developed countermeasures that would vastly complicate the problem of targeting boosters and warheads.

All these countermeasures would exploit off-the-shelf weapons and techniques that exist today, in contrast to the unproven and improbable technologies on which our proposed defenses would rely. Hence, the Soviet response will be cheaper and far more reliable than our defenses, and available as those defenses emerge.

While this quest for a total defense against nuclear missiles would be endless, the decision to embark would have immediate political repercussions. . . . The ABM Treaty could not survive the start of this endless journey, and with it all constraints on offensive forces would go overboard. The impact on NATO would be profound. Our allies in Europe would not be protected by an American BMD system, and this would inflame existing suspicion that the US intends to conduct nuclear operations in Europe without risk to itself. Alliance cohesion would erode because Europeans would hold the US responsible for exacerbating East-West tensions.

The risk to our survival would mount dramatically were we ever to begin erecting the BMD system. This budding system would be exceedingly vulnerable to attack. Nevertheless, its capabilities would be overvalued by our adversaries, and its installation could well be perceived as an attempt to disarm the Soviet Union. These circumstances could in themselves provoke open conflict.

If we get through this hazardous passage, will we have reached the promised land where nuclear weapons are "impotent and obsolete"? Obviously not. We would then have a defense of stupefying complexity, under the total control of a computer program whose proportions defy description, and whose performance will remain a deep mystery until the tragic moment when it would be called into action.

The President and his entourage occasionally argue that we must pursue this quest because the benefits of success outweigh the costs and risks. However, that is only an argument for a research program in strict conformity with the ABM Treaty. Such a program has always had our support. It is needed to protect us from Soviet surprises, and it might uncover concepts that could actually provide a viable defense. But there is an enormous gulf between such a program and a call from the ramparts for a national "experiment" to mount a defense based on untried technologies and provocative doctrines. We have delineated the costs and risks of such an "experiment." At best, the outcome would be a defense of precarious reliability, confronted by offensive nuclear forces designed to circumvent and overwhelm it, and a host of new "anti-BMD" weapons to attack our armada of space platforms which, in turn, would have to be defended by yet another fleet of anti-anti-BMD weapons.

It is difficult to imagine a more hazardous confrontation. And it is equally difficult to understand how anyone can believe that this is the path toward a less dangerous world. A direct and safe road is there for all to see—equitable and verifiable deep cuts in strategic offensive forces and immediate negotiations to ban all space weapons. If we are to take that road, we must abandon the misconception that nuclear explosives are military weapons, and the illusion that ever more sophisticated technology can, by itself, remove the perils that science and technology have created. We must, instead, recognize the overriding reality of the nuclear age—that we cannot regain safety by cleverly sawing off the thin, dry branch on which the Soviets are perched, for we cling to the same branch.

THE PROBLEM OF CRUISE MISSILES

A cruise missile is, in essence, a small ground-hugging pilotless airplane that can carry a nuclear warhead over distances of thousands of miles. It measures the altitude of the overflown terrain with an on-board radar and matches that altitude against a map stored in its computer's memory. An accuracy sufficient to threaten hard targets is therefore attainable, though the time from launch to impact is much greater than it is for ballistic missiles. Cruise missiles capable of penetrating into the Soviet Union are already on our B-52 strategic bombers and are being deployed on the ground by NATO. Both superpowers could develop cruise missiles for submarines that could strike both civilian and strategic targets far inside their adversary's borders from an unpredictable launch point.

None of the space-based defense systems that are under discussion can touch cruise missiles. That is not their purpose. But until a virtually perfect shield against cruise missiles is developed, there is no such thing as a *total* missile defense. . . . No one doubts that a significant number of US strategic bombers (*not* just their cruise missiles) could penetrate the highly touted Soviet air defense system to deliver their high-yield bombs on target; the experiences of two Korean airliners have shown that this is the case. Cruise missiles are far harder to detect with radar than much larger and higher-flying airplanes, and as the so-called STEALTH techniques develop, cruise missiles will become even more elusive. Since they are unmanned, a high attrition rate is quite accept-able. Given these facts, it is very difficult to envisage a shield against air- and sea-launched cruise missiles that would protect our population.

SYSTEMATIC PROBLEMS AND VULNERABILITIES

Defense Suppression

One of the most effective tactics that can be employed against a Ballistic Missile Defense is to attack the ground and space assets on which it depends. Some of these assets are of surprising vulnerability while at the same time being crucial to the defense. Nuclear explosions in space . . . can blind infrared sensors and blackout radars. Detonated ahead of the flight of reentry vehicles, at altitudes of 60–80 km, a single precursor burst will ionize a region of space some tens of kilometers across, hiding the vehicles for several minutes. Anti-radiation homing vehicles may be used to destroy radars in space and on the ground. Space mines or inert objects, including sand, may be used against fragile space-based lasers and mirrors. A variety of measures can be taken to jam, spoof, and confuse the data transfer links of the battle management system.

Submarine-launched ballistic missile and cruise missile attacks can be a key factor in defense suppression in consequence of the immense damage that they would do to their targets. Submarine-launched mis-siles have short flight times, allowing as little as 3–5 minutes' warning for near-coastal targets. They have unpredictable launch points, which can make viewing angles poor for the defense. Moreover they can be launched on depressed trajectories, low enough to allow the missiles to evade most defenses. Cruise missiles are air-breathing, low-flying, and nearly invisible to optical and radar trackers. The BMD system cannot defend itself against such attacks. In the future, if an extensive missile defense moves toward deployment, increasing attention would have to be paid to submarine missile attacks.

Some improvements in sea-launched ballistic missile defense can be expected, but it is difficult to see what can be done to mitigate substan-tially the cruise missile threat. Targets would include ground facilities for battle management, rockets and basing facilities associated with pop-up sensors and weaponry, and communications and control stations. Successful pop-up launches from silos inside the United States which had survived the disarming strikes could be forestalled by nearby exo-atmospheric explosions, or by bursts in the fringes of the atmosphere to destroy missiles in flight. Well-executed strikes of this sort, in advance of the main offensive missile launch, would in all likelihood disable the entire defense structure. There appears to be no way that this vulnerability can be adequately reduced.

Software and Algorithms

The battle management systems of a total BMD must deal with thousands to hundreds of thousands of objects. This requires computers with the capacity to carry out many hundreds of millions, if not billions, of arithmetic operations per second. Advances in computer technology suggest that the hardware to accomplish this monumental task may become available in the future. There are, however, several challenges whose solutions are doubtful. One is the problem of designing and writing the programs (software) required to guide the computers. Experience with earlier defense system software, as well as examples from nondefense experience, suggests that it will be exceedingly difficult, if not impossible, to construct software that would operate properly in the environment of a nuclear attack, for which it could never have been fully tested.

A related problem is that of developing algorithms for tracking and, especially, for discrimination and weapons assignment. Algorithms are the rules or criteria by which the sensor data on range, velocity, maneuvering, and other target properties are assessed, weapons commitments made, damage evaluated, and weapons reassigned and committed. There would be one or more algorithms, for example, to decide which objects were decoys and which were lethal objects. These algorithms must be prepared long in advance of conflict and embedded in software and, to some extent, hardware. They are critical to the performance of the defense. Not only must these algorithms cope with the opponent's countermeasures, whose nature and effectiveness could only be guessed at in advance, but they must be free of internal flaws.

As with the software, it would be extremely difficult to be confident that a fatal flaw was not embedded somewhere in these criteria which might, for example, guide far too many weapons toward unusual or unexpectedly outfitted decoys or away from warheads. They must not . . . direct interceptors through the empty centers of composite targets. The inability to fully test a ballistic missile defense system before it is employed makes the prospect of errors an unsettling one. It is with respect to the battle management system—the hardware, software, and the algorithms—that this deficiency can have some of its gravest consequences.

Confidence

Suppose for a moment that a total missile defense system without obvious flaws had been developed and deployed. This defense, in a time of confrontation and nuclear attack, would represent the only prospect of avoiding overwhelming ruin. Could there be enough confidence in this defense that the US could safely reduce its nuclear forces unilaterally or that it could, during a crisis, ignore Soviet nuclear threats with impunity? The confidence that is needed is not just that each component of the myriad array of parts—the sensors, the weapons, the computers—would, individually, perform as expected. More important is the need for confidence that the entire assembly would operate as a harmonious machine and capably blunt the attack. Consider the nature of the defensive system: an enormous, intricate, and complex assemblage, novel in design, pushing the limits of technology, intended to provide a defense against a threat and, under circumstances which will be fully defined only when the attack comes, forced to meet an uncommonly high standard of performance. And, remarkably enough, it cannot ever have been adequately tested.

No amount of testing under simulated battle conditions could confidently explore the response of the defensive system to an actual nuclear attack. This is only in part because the nature of the attack and of the attacker's countermeasures cannot be known in advance. One simply cannot simulate the stress and the demands on the system of the circumstances of war.

The matter of testing is crucial. The performance of complex devices can rarely be confidently predicted before they are set in realistic operation even when their tasks are well defined. Complex designs breed complex problems. And this is also the case with computer software. All large programs contain "bugs," hidden flaws, and while their number dwindles over time as the programs are used, no one can ever be certain that the bugs are gone. The testing establishes a widening range of confident operation, no more. New circumstances can bring new flaws to light. There is no known way to get around this. We conclude that even if an apparently effective total defense could be prepared, it is highly unlikely much trust could be placed in its working properly when needed.

NET ASSESSMENT OF TOTAL MISSILE DEFENSE

In this section, we pull together our technical assessments of total ballistic missile defense, taking into account the interdependence of the various elements and the fact that the vulnerabilities of one portion of the system critically affect the performance of others.

Basing

The requirement that a total BMD operate in large part in space creates an insoluble basing dilemma. On the one hand, orbiting stations, whether for weapons, sensors, or mirrors, are inherently fragile and vulnerable to attack by space mines and other anti-satellite (ASAT) techniques. This vulnerability would make them provocative targets during a developing crisis, and thus might actually help precipitate the outbreak of conflict. On the other hand, the alternatives to orbital basing—airborne, ground-based, or pop-up systems—are inferior in important respects in their ability to perform BMD functions in boost phase and midcourse. There has been no satisfactory scheme put forward for using the X-ray laser, the only directed-energy weapon that could in theory be popped-up, as a component of a BMD system. X-rays cannot penetrate the atmosphere and it is perfectly practical [for the Soviet Union] to reduce boost phase so burnout occurs inside the atmosphere. Furthermore, the impact of the X-ray beam is too weak to damage warheads following boost phase. The ground-based excimer laser, another prominent boost phase candidate, relies on orbiting mirrors that would be extremely vulnerable.

Sensors and Battle Management

Both active and passive tracking and discrimination systems and the associated battle management facilities can be seriously compromised by countermeasures and by the very large number of largely indistinguishable objects comprising the threat cloud. This is likely to be an insuperable problem in midcourse. It will be necessary to forego any attempt at tracking each individual object, making individual weapons assignments impossible. Having given up the unique assignment of interceptors to targets, it is necessary to allow the interceptors to home at random on all the objects in the threat cloud. But this is highly inefficient and would require on the order of one million homing vehicles for the expected Soviet threat.

Weapons

Particle beam weapons are the least promising of the potentially available types of weapons. The prospects of developing them to a satisfactory level of performance seem dim at best. Laser prospects, although better than those of the particle beams weapons, are very far from bright. The improvements that are required are of such magnitude that important technical breakthroughs appear to be needed. While we cannot categorically rule out the possibility of ultimate success, we do not expect it. All of the particle beam weapons, and most of the lasers, must be based in space with all the vulnerability that implies. The one exception, the excimer laser, is still not much more than a laboratory curiosity and no one can be sure what its future will be. Any ground-based laser system must use a large number of mirrors in space which are extremely vulnerable. In any case, the threat of countermeasures, such as atmospheric nuclear bursts in the beam path or attacks on the mirrors, will disable such weapons. At the present time, self-propelled homing weapons are the most fully developed potential BMD weapon. The anti-satellite Miniature Homing Vehicle is approaching deployable status. Technical improvements in speed, guidance accuracy, and maneuverability appear feasible. Whether a satisfactory defensive system could be built around them is highly doubtful, however.

Ground Assets

In the above assessments we did not factor in the consequences of defense suppression attacks against the ground assets, such as satellite communication stations, radars, and pop-up and ground-based weapons. The operability of the entire defense is totally dependent on their survival. The minute leakage [of reentry vehicles, i.e., warheads] that can be tolerated necessitates that the ground assets survive intact. Because the ground installations cannot be confidently defended against sea-launched ballistic missiles, and probably not against cruise missiles, we conclude that this vulnerability represents a major Achilles' heel in a prospective defense.

Summary

Our analysis makes clear that total ballistic missile defense—the protection of American society against the full weight of a Soviet nuclear attack—is unattainable if the Soviet Union exploits the many vulnerabilities intrinsic to all the schemes that have been proposed thus far. In none of the three phases of attack can one reasonably expect the success rates that would allow a layered BMD system to reduce the number of warheads arriving on US territory sufficiently to prevent unprecedented death and destruction. Instead, each phase presents intractable problems, and the resulting failure of the system compounds from one phase to the next.

A highly efficient boost phase intercept is a prerequisite of total BMD, but is doomed by the inherent limitations of the weapons, insoluble basing dilemmas, and an array of offensive countermeasures. As a result, the failure of midcourse systems is preordained. Midcourse BMD is plagued not so much by the laws of physics and geometry as by the sheer unmanageability of its task in the absence of a ruthless thinning out of the attack in boost phase.

Terminal phase BMD, finally, remains fundamentally unsuitable for area defense of population centers, as opposed to hard-point targets. There seems no way of defending soft targets on a continent-wide basis against the broad variety of attacks that could be tailored to circumvent and overwhelm terminal defenses.

POLITICAL AND STRATEGIC IMPLICATIONS

The political and strategic dangers raised by the "Star Wars" initiative are at least as important as its technical flaws. Indeed, these dangers would weigh heavily against development of ballistic missile defenses even if the technical prospects for such systems were much brighter than they are. A US commitment to BMD would precipitate Soviet responses and a chain of actions and reactions that would radically change the strategic environment to the detriment of both countries' security. The offensive arms race would be greatly accelerated, arms control treaties undermined, and the nuclear peace made more precarious.

Of course, the technical and political issues are not completely unconnected. If it were possible to put in place overnight a fully effective, invulnerable defense against nuclear weapons, there could hardly be serious objections to doing so. But, as the preceding analysis has shown, such a system cannot be built now or, in all likelihood, ever. In the real world, BMD systems will be imperfect. Even under very optimistic assumptions about their ultimate performance, the process of improvement would be incremental and prolonged. During this extended and highly unstable transition period the strategic and political implications of BMD become critical.

While the alleged benefits of BMD are distant and hypothetical, the dangers are near-term and predictable. The adverse consequences of a commitment to BMD would be felt long before the actual deployment of mature technological systems, and quite likely even while the ABM Treaty was still technically being observed. These consequences would follow the familiar anticipated reactions syndrome, driven by the highly threatening nature of BMD and the worst-case assumptions that would dominate nuclear planning amid large uncertainties about the effectiveness of BMD systems and ambiguities about the intentions behind them. Accordingly, the dangers posed by a US policy of ballistic missile defense would be virtually independent of the level of performance that BMD systems might, decades in the future, finally achieve.

Consequences for the Arms Race and Arms Control

A collapse of the ABM Treaty and the initiation of a BMD competition between the superpowers would have a devastating impact on the prospects for offensive arms control. Following an inevitable action-reaction pattern, the Soviets are certain to respond to an American BMD with new offensive measures. Both a quantitative and a qualitative escalation of the arms race would ensue. Adherence to the terms of the SALT II treaty—not ratified by the US but until now informally observed by both countries—would end, and hopes for new agreements would be undermined.

The enormously threatening character of the policy goal announced by President Reagan in his March 1983 speech guarantees a strong Soviet reaction. Despite presidential rhetoric that defenses might be in the mutual interest of the superpowers, the Soviet Union will certainly view a serious US commitment to BMD as an attempt to achieve military superiority by negating the Soviet deterrent. After all, it is Soviet weapons that would be rendered "impotent and obsolete" by an American BMD breakthrough.

The Soviets will interpret a US BMD program not in relation to some utopian future, but in the context of the ongoing US nuclear buildup, particularly the conversion of virtually all US strategic forces to a counterforce role, and the war-fighting doctrine that this buildup is meant to implement. From this standpoint, one can readily appreciate that the Soviet Union might view an American BMD as part of a larger US effort to acquire a first-strike capability—the ability to carry out an attack against Soviet nuclear forces and to defend effectively against a heavily degraded Soviet retaliatory strike. The Soviet Union is no more likely than the US to accept such a development.

In a world of BMD deployments, each superpower's first priority would be the maintenance of forces able to penetrate or circumvent the other's defenses. The resulting stimulus to the arms race would be aggravated by uncertainties about the effectiveness of defenses. Operating as usual on conservative, worst-case planning assumptions, each side would tend to exaggerate the effectiveness of the other's defense while discounting its own. As a result, offensive responses would tend to surpass the level actually needed to maintain second-strike or retaliatory capabilities. For example, US defenses assessed by American defense planners as 50 percent effective might elicit a Soviet buildup based on the assumption of 90 percent effectiveness, and vice versa. Each side would then perceive the other's reaction as excessive and threatening, and would respond in kind, creating a vicious cycle of escalation.

In these circumstances, the hope that BMD might improve the prospects for negotiated force reductions, as suggested by the Reagan Administration, is totally unrealistic. Even less plausible is the idea that a US BMD could be used as a lever, in the words of Dr. George Keyworth II, the President's Science Advisor, to "pressure the Soviets to take our arms reductions proposals more seriously than they do now."

Instead, BMD would be doubly fatal to the prospects for controlling offensive forces—raising fear and suspicion that would poison the political atmosphere for negotiations, and creating technical problems of comparison and verification far more complex than those associated with SALT or the Strategic Arms Reduction Talks (START). In effect, defenses function as a wild card, making the nuclear balance much less calculable than if only offensive forces need to be taken into account. Given the large uncertainties and controversy that already surround efforts to compare US and Soviet nuclear capabilities, the addition of BMD to the mix would place an unbearable strain on arms control. An arms control process healthy enough to support reductions in an environment of strategic defenses would be more than strong enough to produce such reductions in the absence of BMD systems. Conversely, an arms control process that is already faltering badly would be unlikely to survive at all in the face of BMD deployments by the two sides.

Ironically, the administration's own "build-down" proposal in the START negotiations would be directly undermined by a US BMD initiative. This approach emphasizes cuts in the heavy, multiple-warhead Soviet ICBMs that threaten American land-based missiles, and seeks an overall restructuring of strategic forces away from MIRV missiles toward smaller, single-warhead ones. However, missile defenses would place a premium on large ICBMs, which offer the most efficient means of delivering large numbers of warheads, decoys, and other penetration aids to overwhelm a BMD system. The US first developed MIRV, largely in response to the Soviet ABM program in the 1960s. More recently, the Scowcroft Commission on US Strategic Forces cited BMD penetration as an important rationale for US deployment of the 10-warhead MX missile.

Administration officials have sometimes suggested that a US-Soviet BMD competition would play to US technological strengths. Whether or not this is true, it is clear that a BMD-driven offensive arms race would give the Soviet Union important advantages. Due to its large advantage in missile throwweight, as well as the absence of political constraints comparable to those in the US, the Soviet Union is much better positioned than the US for a rapid offensive buildup. In particular, if SALT II becomes a dead letter, the Soviet Union has an option for a sudden breakout from the SALT limits on MIRVs that the US does not enjoy. The Soviets could, for example, double their ICBM warheads simply by additional MIRVing of their 308 SS-18 missiles, which are limited under SALT II to ten warheads each but could accommodate up to thirty.

In addition to offensive efforts to overwhelm US missile defenses, the Soviets can also be expected to invest in delivery systems that would circumvent those defenses. Cruise missiles and depressed-trajectory ballistic missiles have already been alluded to in this report. Unconventional approaches, including "predelivery" of atomic weapons by emplacing them clandestinely on US territory, can also be envisaged. In many cases these responses would not only foil US missile defenses but would result in reduced warning times and verifiability, thereby further undercutting nuclear stability and arms control.

Superpower BMD deployments would also have an adverse impact on the prospects for theater nuclear arms control involving British and French forces. Both countries, as well as China, would feel threatened by a Soviet missile defense that undercut their ability to penetrate Soviet territory, and as far as possible would modernize and increase their forces to maintain the standard of minimum deterrence on which their nuclear strategies rest. . . .

More generally, a US BMD would cause major political and strategic strains in the Atlantic Alliance, inspiring European fears of a US retreat into "Fortress America." Existing perceptions that the US is complacent about nuclear risks, and willing to contemplate a "limited" nuclear war confined to European territory, would be likely to grow.

Consequences for Deterrence and Crisis Stability

In addition to the arms race consequences discussed above, the administration's BMD proposal would have a profoundly destabilizing effect on the nuclear balance, increasing the risk of nuclear war at times of US-Soviet confrontation and reducing the chances of bringing hostilities under control if war did occur.

These consequences run directly counter to the arguments often made by BMD advocates that US defenses would strengthen deterrence and, in the event deterrence fails, play an important damage-limitation role. Such arguments, it should be emphasized, are attempts to construct strategic rationales for only modestly capable BMD systems. As such, they represent a very large retreat from President Reagan's vision of transcending (not reinforcing) the system of nuclear deterrence by making nuclear weapons "impotent and obsolete." Nevertheless, these justifications for imperfect BMD systems are important to address. As the President's original vision is increasingly understood to be illusory, a US BMD program is likely to be promoted primarily on grounds of deterrence and damage-limitation. Administration officials and supporters have already begun to argue in these terms during the year since President Reagan's speech. In this regard, a close link has often been noted between these more modest roles for BMD systems and the administration's nuclear war-fighting strategy—a link that will not be over-looked by the Soviet Union.

The argument that BMD would strengthen nuclear deterrence rests mainly on the claim that it would reduce the vulnerability of US land-based missiles to preemptive attack. By protecting the US ability to re-taliate, BMD would make a Soviet first strike less certain of success and therefore less likely. However, this is an argument for terminal, hard-point defense of US missile silos, not for the layered, area defenses being proposed by the administration. The administration's initiative is not only vastly more expensive and complex than is necessary for the protection of retaliatory forces, but it is provocative to the Soviet Union in a way that would reduce, not enhance, deterrent stability.

Area defenses undermine deterrence because they magnify the advantage of striking first. Indeed, the modest BMD systems likely to be attainable in the foreseeable future would be useful *only* to the attacker. They would be easily defeated by a well-executed first strike, but might perform with some effectiveness against a poorly coordinated and weakened retaliatory strike.

As a result, these systems are likely to be perceived as components of a first strike strategy rather than as deterrent weapons, and to create strong incentives for preemptive attacks during periods of high tension. At such times, the fact that a first strike would be complicated by the adversary's BMD would be judged less relevant than the fear that, if one fails to attack first, effective retaliation may be impossible.

BMD, then, would aggravate the dangerous "use them or lose them" pressures that are already increasing due to the trend toward offensive weapons designed for counterforce. The result would be a serious weakening of mutual deterrence precisely at those times when it is most needed.

The damage-limitation rationale for BMD is as dubious as the deterrence argument. This rationale has two variants. First, in the event deterrence fails and nuclear war occurs, it is argued that defenses could save lives, reducing the threat of "assured destruction" that exists in the present offense-dominated system. Second, we are told, this damage-limitation effect would strengthen deterrence by making the threat of nuclear retaliation more credible. BMD advocates who emphasize these points generally subscribe to the theory that credible deterrence requires forces designed for actual warfighting, and capable of being used in a selective, flexible manner. In this context, the damage-limitation role of a BMD system is seen as useful not only to limit population fatalities but also to protect nuclear command and control systems.

These arguments are implausible in light of the size and destructive power of superpower nuclear arsenals and the adjustments in targeting and nuclear strategy the BMD deployments would bring about.

The overkill capacity of both superpowers is such that only a near-perfect defense could hope to reduce fatalities appreciably in the event of major nuclear exchanges. For example, if the Soviet Union were to target its missiles to maximize damage to the US population—a likely response to a serious American attempt to protect cities—it would need only 5 percent of its *current* ballistic missile warheads to kill up to half of the US urban population immediately. . . . In other words, even a 95 percent effective BMD would leave the US with the prospect of tens of millions of prompt fatalities in a nuclear war, leaving aside all the subsequent deaths from fire, disease, and social disruption. Moreover, enough nuclear explosions would occur even in this very optimistic case to pose a serious danger of triggering a climatic catastrophe (the "nuclear winter" phenomenon). [See the article by Carl Sagan in Part III of this book—*eds.*]

The vulnerability of the US to destruction by Soviet nuclear forces, in short, cannot be mitigated by any foreseeable defensive shield as long as nuclear weapons exist in their current numbers. Only if offensive forces were radically reduced, to perhaps a tenth of their present size, could a moderately effective defense begin to make a dramatic difference in the vulnerability of populations to nuclear destruction. As we have seen, the prospect of negotiating such reductions would become virtually nonexistent amid a major US-Soviet BMD competition.

In the absence of radical cuts in offensive arsenals, damage-limitation could be achieved, in theory, only through deliberate strategies of controlled, limited nuclear strikes, with the bulk of each superpower's nuclear forces being held in reserve and cities being spared. The nearly unanimous conclusion of those who have studied this issue is that a nuclear war could not in practice be controlled in this manner. [See, for example, the article by Desmond Ball in Part III of this book—*eds.*] Furthermore, there is good reason to believe that strategic defenses would make this possibility even more remote.

Contrary to the assumptions of those who view BMD as a useful adjunct to a limited nuclear war strategy, it is likely that BMD deployments would reduce both the incentives and the capabilities of the two superpowers to contain nuclear war below the threshold of all-out exchanges. First, as noted above, to the extent that defenses pose a serious threat to the "assured destruction" capability of either side, they invite retargeting to retain such destructive capacity. The fewer warheads the Soviets can expect to arrive on US territory, the more likely these warheads are to be assigned to the softest and most valuable targets—major urban areas. Warhead accuracy would become less important, and sheer destruction, with maximum collateral damage, more important, thus reversing the priorities associated with limited war strategies. Targeting for strikes against cities would also be encouraged since missile defenses might be able to break up precisely timed attacks against hardened and defended targets.

Second, the space-based command and control systems necessary to limited war strategies would be put at risk if "Star Wars" defenses were deployed. Plans for controlled, protracted nuclear conflict depend critically on survivable satellites for communications, navigation, early warning, and reconnaissance. However, a growing vulnerability of these systems to antisatellite attacks would be an unavoidable side-effect of the development of space-based BMD. In a strategic environment characterized by space-based missile defenses and unrestricted ASAT competition, attacks on military space assets would occur in the early stages of a superpower conflict. This situation would not only exacerbate mutual fears of preemptive attack, but would create incentives to use nuclear forces in massive strikes at the outset of hostilities to take advantage of the capabilities of command and control systems before they are destroyed.

Far from contributing to a strategy of limited nuclear war, BMD points in the opposite direction—toward massive, indiscriminate exchanges and the erosion of control over strategic forces. Instead of damage limitation, a nuclear war fought under these circumstances could well produce higher numbers of fatalities than one fought in the absence of defenses.

Summary

The superficial attractions of a strategy of nuclear defense disappear when the overall consequences of BMD deployments are considered. More than any foreseeable offensive arms breakthrough, defenses would radically transform the context of US-Soviet nuclear relations, setting in motion a chain of events and reactions that would leave both superpowers much less secure. Deterrence would be weakened and crisis instability increased. Damage-limitation would be undermined by a greater emphasis on the targeting of cities and the increased vulnerability of command and control systems. And virtually the entire arms control process would be swept away by the abrogation of the ABM Treaty, the launching of a new offensive round of the arms race, and the extension of the arms race into space.

Part III: War

Nuclear war is possible. It may not be probable, but it is possible. This is the premise of the first selection in Part III of *The Nuclear Reader*. In it the six Harvard University associates making up the Harvard Nuclear Study Group examine alternative scenarios that might prompt the onset of nuclear war.

Six triggers or sequences of events leading to nuclear war are often discussed. One is a "bolt from the blue," a Pearl Harbor type of surprise attack by one superpower against the other (typically assumed by Americans to be a Soviet strike against the United States). Second, nuclear war might begin as a conventional conflict in Europe escalates to the point that the nuclear threshold is bridged, leading to an all-out nuclear exchange between the superpowers. Third, a regional conflict between Third World countries could draw in the superpowers, which once more may find the conflict escalating to the point that nuclear weapons are used. Fourth, war might occur by accident or miscalculation, as, for example, in a situation in which one nuclear power launches an attack on another after (mistakenly) concluding that the other had already launched a preemptive attack. Fifth, in yet another escalation scenario, a terrorist attack involving nuclear weapons could create a condition of such chaos and confusion that the superpowers decide to launch their weapons against each other. Finally, nuclear war could start following an accidental or unauthorized use of nuclear weapons.

The Harvard Nuclear Study Group examines variants of each of these possibilities and attaches rough probabilities to each. Interestingly, they conclude that the bolt-from-the-blue scenario, "commonly the most feared prospect," is also "a most unlikely scenario for the start of a nuclear war," *provided*, however, that "no Russian military leader could ever report to the Politburo that a Soviet victory in nuclear war was probable or that the damage from American nuclear retaliation could be reduced to acceptable limits." The conclusion that a surprise attack will be prevented if nuclear adversaries are convinced that the costs of war are greater than its rewards is simply another way of saying that war will be prevented if deterrence succeeds—and the authors do point toward the elements that could avert a situation so dangerous that it might tempt a surprise attack. Thus, the probability of nuclear war is closely related to the political strategies that policymakers have devised for nuclear weapons and to alternative means of managing them so that they serve political purposes rather than becoming the causes of conflict themselves.

Unfortunately, there are other sequences of events that could lead to nuclear war for which the conditions promoting deterrence are less easily identified. The slide from conventional to nuclear war would be harder to arrest because, as the Nuclear Study Group concludes, "once war begins, the balance between political and military considerations shifts decidedly toward the military side." In such situations, the principal need is to maintain the firebreak between conventional and nuclear weapons. But as the articles in Parts I and II of this book make clear, opinions differ widely on how this can best be done. Do the presence of battlefield or tactical nuclear weapons and the threat of their use make nuclear war less or more likely?

Should nuclear war break out, it is difficult to comprehend its destructive consequences. In August 1945 a single bomb dropped from a single plane killed an estimated 100,000 to 200,000 people. Yet by today's standards, the bomb that leveled Hiroshima was small indeed. "Little Boy," as the atomic or fission bomb was called, had a destructive force of thirteen kilotons (that is, thirteen thousand tons) of TNT. Today the thermonuclear or fusion (hydrogen) weapons in the superpowers' strategic arsenals are often measured in megatons (that is, millions of tons of TNT), and weapons in the kiloton range are frequently considered tactical. There are literally thousands of these spread throughout the world.

Figure 3.1, created by the antinuclear organization *Ground Zero*, shows the enormous destructive power of today's nuclear arsenals. The single dot in the center of the figure represents three million megatons—the equivalent of all the firepower used during World War II. The other dots represent the eighteen thousand megatons of firepower that now comprise the superpowers' nuclear arsenals—the equivalent of six thousand Second World Wars. Each U.S. Trident submarine alone carries the equivalent of eight times the force used in all of World War II. The destructive power represented by only two squares on the figure (three hundred megatons, or about that carried on twelve Trident submarines) is sufficient to destroy all large- and medium-sized cities in the world. It is little wonder that "overkill" is popularly used to describe what seems to be an unnecessarily large stockpile of weapons of mass destruction.

The presumption, of course, is that policymakers have no intention of using their arsenals. Indeed, there is a great distance between what is technologically possible and what is politically tolerable. As McGeorge

Figure 3.1. The Destructive Power of Nuclear Weapons

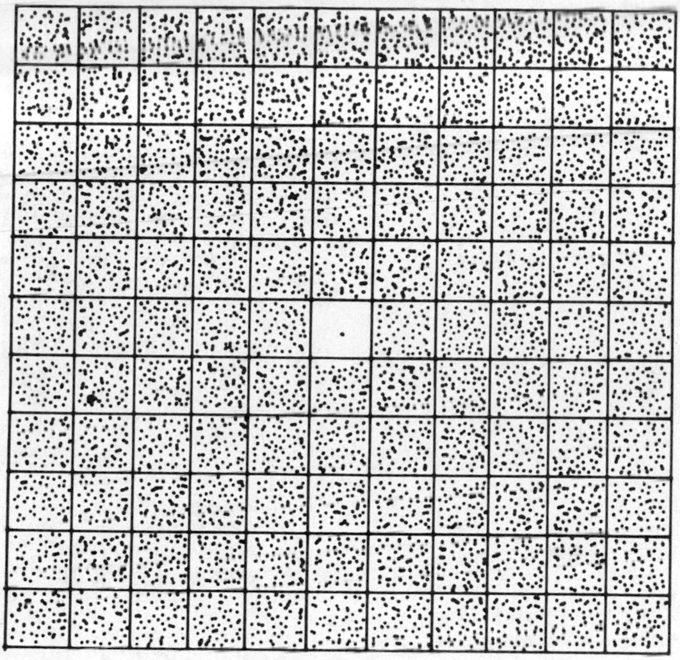

Note: Each dot represents three million megatons of explosive force.

Bundy, national security adviser to Presidents John F. Kennedy and Lyndon B. Johnson, observed:

> There is an enormous gulf between what political leaders really think about nuclear weapons and what is assumed in complex calculations of relative "advantage" in simulated strategic warfare. Think-tank analysts can set levels of "acceptable" damage well up in the hundreds of millions of lives. They can assume that the loss of a dozen cities is somehow a real choice for sane men. In the real world of real political leaders—whether here [in the United States] or in the Soviet Union—a decision that would bring even one hydrogen bomb on one city of one's own country would be recognized in advance as a catastrophic blunder; ten bombs on ten cities would be a disaster beyond history; and a hundred bombs on one hundred cities are unthinkable. Yet this unthinkable level of human incineration is the least that could be expected by either side in response to any first strike in the next ten years, no matter what happens to weapons systems in the meantime.[1]

Nuclear war is possible nonetheless. It may not be probable, but it is possible. What would its effects be? President Jimmy Carter's National Security Council estimated that in the event of a nuclear exchange between the superpowers, the toll in lives in the United States and the Soviet Union alone would be over 250 million. The catastrophic pro-

Figure 3.2. Estimated Soviet and American Deaths in a Nuclear War

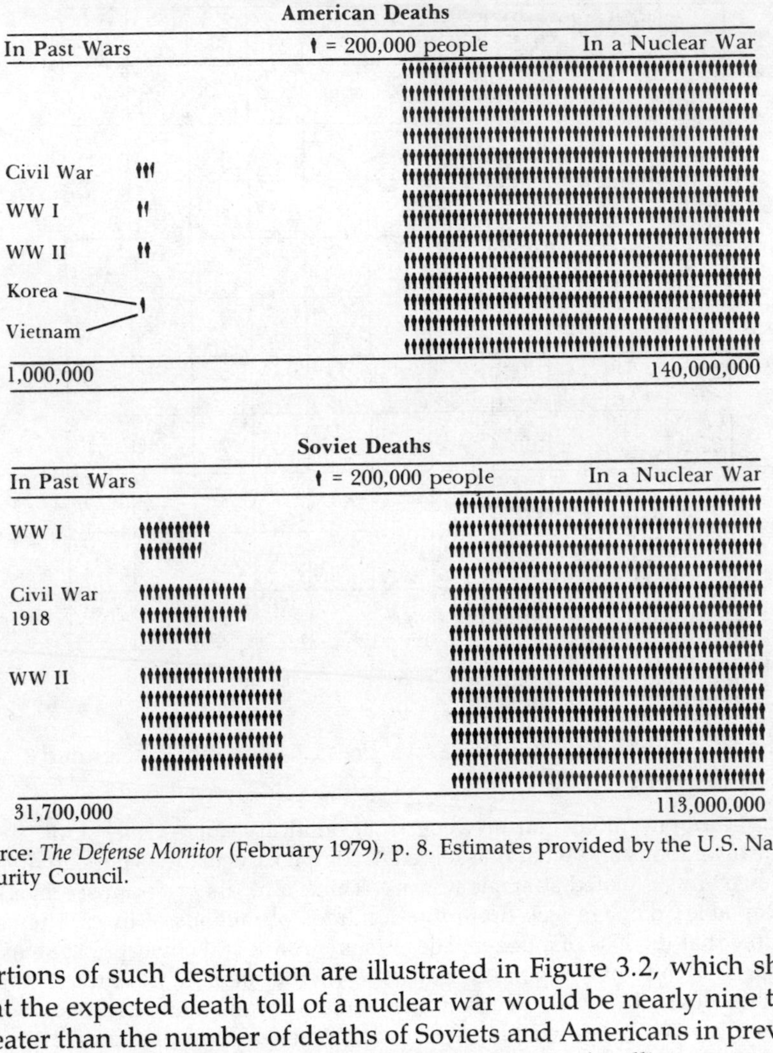

American Deaths

In Past Wars	† = 200,000 people	In a Nuclear War

Civil War †††
WW I ††
WW II ††
Korea —┐
Vietnam —┘†

1,000,000   140,000,000

Soviet Deaths

In Past Wars	† = 200,000 people	In a Nuclear War

WW I
Civil War
1918
WW II

31,700,000   113,000,000

Source: *The Defense Monitor* (February 1979), p. 8. Estimates provided by the U.S. National Security Council.

portions of such destruction are illustrated in Figure 3.2, which shows that the expected death toll of a nuclear war would be nearly nine times greater than the number of deaths of Soviets and Americans in previous wars. And these figures do not include the tens of millions more who would suffer the ravaging effects of radiation.

A nuclear blast produces two kinds of radiation. Direct radiation occurs at the time of a nuclear explosion and, though intense, is limited in range.[2] Fallout radiation, on the other hand, which is caused when particles thrown into the air by a nuclear blast become radioactive, can extend well beyond the immediate area of a nuclear explosion, with damaging effects lasting for comparatively long periods of time. Nuclear explosions at or near the ground create greater amounts of radioactive fallout than do airbursts.

In addition to radiation, nuclear weapons destroy through the effects of blast and thermal radiation, or heat. Most of the damage to cities, the U.S. Congressional Office of Technology Assessment concluded, would be caused by a nuclear weapon's explosive blast.

> The blast drives air away from the site of the explosion, producing sudden changes in air pressure (called static overpressure) that can crush objects, and high winds . . . that can move them suddenly or knock them down. In general, large buildings are destroyed by the overpressure, while people and objects such as trees and utility poles are destroyed by the wind.[3]

The energy released in the form of thermal radiation would cause "flash-blindness" among those who looked directly at the intense light that a nuclear explosion emits. Skin burns and fires caused by the thermal radiation's ignition of combustible materials would be extensive.

Jonathan Schell's "Nuclear Holocaust," from his popular book *The Fate of the Earth*, translates these stark figures and facts into the human tragedy they imply. He first uses the Hiroshima experience to dramatize the human horror of a nuclear holocaust. He then extrapolates from this experience, as well as from the results of U.S. nuclear tests in the years since 1945, to speculate about the consequences of a nuclear attack on New York City. Despite Schell's graphic descriptions, the extensiveness of the mass destruction is virtually impossible to comprehend. It is difficult to imagine millions of people being instantaneously vaporized, crushed, or maimed.

A counterforce attack, one directed on opposing military targets rather than on population and industrial centers, could conceivably avert the immediate level of carnage of a countervalue strike. To be sure, there would be collateral damage to the people and structures near the military installations, but it would doubtless be less than the destruction caused by a countervalue strike. In an odd sense, therefore, a counterforce nuclear attack or exchange may be preferable to a countervalue one. (A counterforce attack would likely produce more radioactive fallout, however, as groundbursts presumably would be required to destroy missiles protected by hardened silos.)

Would it be possible to control a counterforce nuclear exchange so that it did not escalate to the level of an all-out, countervalue nuclear spasm, thereby permitting a limited and quite protracted nuclear war to be fought? Our next two essays address this question, and both reach negative conclusions.

In the first, "Can Nuclear War Be Controlled?," Desmond Ball, a well-known strategic analyst, reasons that "it is most unrealistic to expect that there would be a relatively smooth and controlled progression from limited and selective strikes, through major counterforce exchanges, to termination of the conflict at some level short of urban-industrial attacks." A number of considerations lead to this conclusion, not the least of which is that the number of casualties on either side would be high, even if urban and industrial targets were not struck directly. The political pressures from any kind of nuclear exchange would be enormous, and the stress under which decision makers would have to operate would be unimaginable. Consider, for example, what Zbigniew Brzezinski, national security adviser to President Jimmy Carter, described as the "utterly dumbfounding . . . life-and-death decision tree" that a president of the United States might face when awakened in the middle of some night:

Time (in minutes)

0 Massive attack launched.

1 SLBMs detected.

2 ICBMs detected.

4–6 Confirmation of attack; uncertainty over scale; U.S. decision process begins.

6–10 First SLBMs detonate in High Altitude EMP attack; SAC launched preemptively; confirmation of scale of attack; final U.S. decision process.

10–12 U.S. decision needed: Ride-out or respond; first SLBMs detonate over U.S. SLBM bases and National Command Authority [political and military leaders responsible for the command of U.S. military forces].

12–14 Final window for initiating response; launch under attack.

16–20 [Soviet] Delta SLBMs launched from home ports hit SAC.

20–30 ICBM attack initiates possible X-ray pin-down and begins impact on targets.[4]

It is simply impossible to know how in such crisis circumstances American policymakers would respond either psychologically or operationally. Ball points out that the ability to respond at all will be seriously affected by the vulnerability of U.S. command, control, and communication (C^3) systems (the same is true of the Soviets' systems).

> The Soviet Union would need to expend thousands of warheads in any comprehensive counterforce attacks against US ICBM silos, bomber bases and . . . submarine facilities, and even then hundreds if not thousands of US warheads would still survive. On the other hand, it would require only about 50–100 warheads to destroy the fixed facilities of the national command system or to effectively impair the communication links between the National Command Authorities and the strategic forces.

Even if the C^3 systems were spared direct attack, the electromagnetic pulses (EMP, the pulses of electrical and magnetic energy released in a nuclear explosion) created by nuclear blasts on other targets would severely cripple, perhaps destroy, their capacity to function. As a consequence, "it is likely that beyond some relatively early stage in the conflict," the counterforce strikes "would become ragged, unco-ordinated, less precise and less discriminating, and the ability to reach an agreed settlement between the adversaries would soon become extremely problematical."

An attack on an adversary's command, control, and communication systems is often described as an attempt at nuclear "decapitation." Our second article on the question, "Invitation to a Nuclear Beheading," by Barry R. Schneider, considers whether it is possible to control a nuclear war and what would be required to avert the decapitation of the United States government, specifically to ensure the survival of its key policymakers. The physical problems of protecting the government from destruction are so great as to make protection seem impossible. The same is true, of course, of the Soviet Union, where, despite a limited antiballistic missile shield and a more extensive civil defense program, the task of avoiding decapitation is no less overwhelming. The conclusion, then, is straightforward; according to Schneider,

> the danger of decapitation attacks would seem to make a mockery of the idea of fighting limited nuclear wars, or protracted nuclear wars. Even if U.S. leaders somehow survived a first-wave Soviet attack, our command-control network is so perishable in a nuclear environment that a slow, tit-for-tat "walk" up and down the escalation ladder seems unlikely.

Furthermore, the vulnerability of both the United States and the Soviet Union to attacks against their leadership and command and control systems may mean that "negotiations to halt the slaughter might be impossible until both sides had expended their nuclear forces in a terrible agony of blow and counterblow."

Even if nuclear decapitation remains unavoidable, would a greater emphasis on civil defense systems protect domestic populations from nuclear annihilation? The Soviet Union has long pursued a more vigorous civil defense effort than the United States has, and the Reagan administration has sought funds from Congress that would enable it to decrease the gap with the Soviet Union somewhat on this dimension of the strategic competition.

Civil defense is appropriately considered an element of strategic competition since it is presumed by defense analysts to provide a glimpse of nuclear adversaries' intentions and expectations of nuclear war. For many analysts, the fact that the Soviet leadership has willingly pursued an active civil defense program is evidence that it expects to be able to fight and win a nuclear war. Thus one writer suggests that Soviet civil defense programs are designed to protect what are known as *cadres*, that is, the political and military leaders as well as industrial managers and skilled workers—those who could reestablish the political and economic system once the war was over. Judging by Soviet definitions, civil defense has as much to do with the proper functioning of the country during and immediately after the war as with holding down casualties.[5]

Civil defense has not been taken as seriously in the United States as it seems to have been in the Soviet Union. In part, perhaps, this is because the United States is a more urbanized society than the Soviet Union is, and so the prospects of building an effective defense against nuclear attack and paying for it seem beyond reach. Moreover, given the known destructive force of a nuclear blast, the positions adopted by some civil defense advocates appear ludicrous. T. K. Jones, deputy under secretary of defense in the Reagan administration, for example, in 1981 told a newspaper reporter

> that the United States could fully recover from an all-out nuclear war with the Soviet Union in just two to four years. T. K. . . . added that nuclear war was not nearly as devastating as we had been led to believe. He said, "If there are enough shovels to go around, everybody's going to make it." The shovels were for digging holes in the ground, which would be covered somehow or other with a couple of doors and with three feet of dirt thrown on top, thereby providing adequate fallout shelters for the millions who had been evacuated from America's cities to the countryside. "It's the dirt that does it," he said.[6]

John M. Weinstein explores the doctrinal and practical implications of civil defense efforts, with particular attention to the allegedly more sophisticated Soviet program, in "Civil Defense: Strategic Implications, Practical Problems." Although Weinstein believes that any government has a moral obligation to its citizens to seek to preserve life in the event of a nuclear war, he is not convinced that civil defense provides any meaningful protection against a concerted nuclear attack.

Certainly no amount of civil defense is likely to ease the catastrophic strains on the earth's ecosystem that a nuclear war would likely produce. Indeed, although it has long been asserted that a nuclear war could result in the extinction of the human species, there is now scientific evidence that lays out the path toward doomsday. The evidence is summarized in our concluding essay, "Nuclear War and Climatic Catastrophe: A Nuclear Winter," written by the distinguished astronomer Carl Sagan.

Based on studies of the atmosphere on the planet Mars, Sagan and his colleagues warn that a nuclear exchange—apart from the death and destruction caused by the blast, thermal radiation, and radioactivity—would spew so much dust, smoke, and poisonous gas into the atmosphere that the earth's surface would cool by tens of degrees, turning the earth into a dark, frozen wasteland incapable of sustaining humankind's delicate life-support systems.[7] Noteworthy is that the climatic catastrophe would occur worldwide, even if a nuclear exchange were confined to the Northern Hemisphere. Moreover, Sagan notes that "perhaps the most striking and unexpected consequence of our study is that even a comparatively small nuclear war can have devastating climatic consequences. . . ." The threshold arsenal for triggering a climatic catastrophe, Sagan estimates, is somewhere between five hundred and two thousand deliverable warheads—a fraction of the more than seventeen thousand strategic weapons already in both the Soviet and American arsenals. Indeed, the evidence suggests that only one hundred megatons of nuclear explosives would cause a nuclear winter. This is fewer than the dots contained in one single square in Figure 3.1. Thus every effort must be made to reduce the level of the world's nuclear arsenals below the threshold at which nuclear war would trigger a nuclear winter—and the possible extinction of humankind.

NOTES

1. Cited in *The Defense Monitor* 8 (February 1979): 5.
2. Our discussion of the effects of a nuclear explosion is based on Office of Technology Assessment, *The Effects of Nuclear War* (Washington, D.C.: U.S. Government Printing Office, 1979), pp. 15–23. This study examines the effects of various counterforce and countervalue nuclear attacks on the United States and the Soviet Union. See also Kevin N. Lewis, "The Prompt and Delayed Effects of Nuclear War," *Scientific American* 241 (July 1979): 35–47.
3. Office of Technology Assessment, p. 16.
4. "From Arms Control to Controlled Security," *Wall Street Journal*, July 10, 1984, p. 32.
5. Richard Pipes, "Why the Soviet Union Thinks It Could Fight and Win a Nuclear War," *Commentary* 64 (July 1977):33–34.
6. Robert Scheer, *With Enough Shovels: Reagan, Bush, and Nuclear War* (New York: Random House, 1982), p. 18.
7. These scientists' initial findings can be found in Richard P. Turco, Owen B. Toon, Thomas P. Ackerman, James B. Pollack, and Carl Sagan, "Nuclear Winter: Global Consequences of Multiple Nuclear Explosions," *Science* 222 (December 23, 1983), pp. 1283–1292. They have since been reaffirmed by the same authors in "The Climatic Effects of Nuclear War," *Scientific American* 251 (August 1984): 33–43.

19   HOW MIGHT A NUCLEAR WAR BEGIN?

The Harvard Nuclear Study Group: Albert Carnesale, Paul Doty, Stanley Hoffmann, Samuel P. Huntington, Joseph S. Nye, Jr., Scott D. Sagan

The question is grisly, but nonetheless it must be asked. Nuclear war cannot be avoided simply by refusing to think about it. Indeed, the task of reducing the likelihood of nuclear war should begin with an effort to understand how it might start.

When strategists in Washington or Moscow study the possible origins of nuclear war, they discuss "scenarios," imagined sequences of future events that could trigger the use of nuclear weaponry. Scenarios are, of course, speculative exercises. They often leave out the political developments that might lead to the use of force in order to focus on military dangers. That nuclear war scenarios are even more speculative than most is something for which we can be thankful, for it reflects humanity's fortunate lack of experience with atomic warfare since 1945. But imaginary as they are, nuclear scenarios can help to identify problems not understood or dangers not yet prevented because they have not been foreseen. . . .

Nuclear war would most probably begin for reasons similar to those which began wars in the past. Governments might see opportunities for quick and easy gains and, misjudging enemy reactions, could take steps toward nuclear war without being fully aware of the risks involved. Governments might, under other circumstances, believe that beginning a war was the lesser of two evils, a plausible belief if the other evil is the enemy striking first. These and many other causes have led to war in the past.

Nuclear war is possible. It could occur through purposeful choice, through miscalculation, or through a variety of accidents. It could be started by a political leader, by a military commander, or by a group of terrorists. It could come as a sudden surprise in a time of peace or as the seemingly inevitable culmination of a prolonged conflict between nuclear armed nations. We chose the following kinds of scenarios (some of which are more plausible than others) to illustrate a gamut of possibilities as well as to explore popular and current concerns: (1) surprise attack by one superpower on all or part of the nuclear forces of the other; (2) pre-emptive attacks launched in desperation in time of crisis because one side believes (rightly or wrongly) that the other intends soon to strike first; (3) escalation of conventional wars to nuclear ones; (4) accidental uses of nuclear weapons resulting from malfunctions of machines or of minds; and (5) nuclear wars initiated by other nuclear armed nations or by terrorist organizations. These categories are not unique; additional scenarios involving elements from two or more categories could easily be constructed. Nor is the list of scenarios exhaustive; not all the possible paths to nuclear war can be foreseen. Murphy's law— which states that if something can go wrong, it will—applies here as in all other human activities: military plans go awry, controls fail, misjudgments occur, and one mistake often seems to lead to another, in peacetime and in war. This should not breed despair; it should serve as a constant reminder of the need to control events so that events do not control us.

SCENARIOS

The Bolt from the Blue

Imagine the following conversation. The date is November 1, 1991; the location, inside the Kremlin.

General Secretary ———: "Comrade General, you have heard the debate. Some members of the Politburo favor your proposal for a surprise attack upon the United States. Others are highly opposed. We await your opinion. Can we go to war and win?"

General ———, Chief of Staff, Soviet Rocket Forces: "Yes! If war is to come, it must come soon, or all is lost. The counter-revolution in Eastern Europe has put our back against the wall. The American military buildup continues to threaten our socialist nation.

"But let me explain how we can triumph if we attack quickly, with all our power. The Americans suspect nothing. We have greatly improved our hunter-killer submarine force and now can closely follow all their submarines; our ballistic missile submarines can maintain adequate attack forces off the enemy's coast. In only seven minutes our submarine missiles could destroy American bombers on their runways, the American submarines in the ports, and, as importantly, American military and civilian command centers. Without orders from these command posts, the missiles in the United States will not be immediately launched and will be destroyed when our ICBMs arrive 23 minutes after the submarine missiles land on target.

"We have, of course, supreme confidence in our military strength. But if a small number of America's nuclear missiles and bombers escape destruction from our overwhelming attack, our ballistic missile defense system and our air defense system will shoot them down. We can end the capitalist threat forever. Let us decide now to end this intolerable situation, destroy them before they gain in strength and threaten us even more."

General Secretary ———: "Thank you. Comrades, the day of destiny may be upon us. How do you vote?"

Is this scenario possible? Yes. Is it likely? No. This bolt from the blue, commonly the most feared prospect, is a most unlikely scenario for the start of a nuclear war *as long as* no Russian military leader could ever report to the Politburo that a Soviet victory in nuclear war was probable or that the damage from American nuclear retaliation could be reduced to acceptable levels.

What military, political, and economic conditions would have to exist before Soviet leaders would seriously listen to the imagined general's proposal? First, nearly *all* American retaliatory forces and the entire command system would have to be highly vulnerable to a Soviet first strike. Currently, most of the Minutemen ICBMs (intercontinental ballistic missiles), U.S. bombers on airfields and submarines in port, and the American command, control, and communications network are theoretically vulnerable. But the forces that would survive a Soviet attack would still be enormously destructive. Most importantly, the American submarine force routinely at sea, which carries more nuclear warheads than does the entire Minuteman force, cannot now or in the foreseeable future be located or quickly destroyed by the Soviet navy.

Second, both Soviet ballistic missile defenses and air defenses would have to be improved greatly, perhaps beyond what is possible, before they could be expected to reduce the damage of the American retaliatory missile and bomber attacks to an acceptable level. Third, technical difficulties would plague the prospects of success in such a surprise Soviet attack: not only would it be enormously difficult to coordinate the actions of Soviet missile-bearing submarines, ICBMs, and anti-submarine warfare forces, but success would hinge on complete surprise being maintained. If Soviet strategic forces were put on full alert status, the possibility that the American intelligence network would miss the warning is exceedingly remote. Strategic Air Command bombers would be alerted and dispersed, American political leaders and military commanders could be sent to safer locations, and some submarines in port could be sent to sea. These actions would reduce still further the probability that a massive Soviet nuclear attack would be answered with only token nuclear retaliation. Finally, the United States could choose to launch its ICBMs on warning of the attack (i.e., while the attacking missiles were in flight toward their targets) or after the first attacking warheads had arrived.

The bolt from the blue is thus not likely now or any time in the fore-seeable future. This scenario is, indeed, so farfetched that it is useful to consider only in one sense: it points to a set of combined circumstances which, as a matter of long-range policy, the United States must seek to avoid. There is clearly no reason that such a dangerous combination of circumstances need ever develop. The bolt from the blue could become plausible only if there was a major deterioration of Soviet-American relations and if Soviet nuclear forces, defensive preparations, and antisubmarine capabilities were greatly enhanced, while American counter-measures were unilaterally restrained.

A Limited Attack on the Minuteman Missiles

Some defense specialists believe that while American nuclear retaliatory capabilities might successfully deter surprise attacks on American cities, as well as bolt-from-the-blue attacks on all of the nuclear forces, limited attacks on portions of America's nuclear arsenal are substantially more likely. This is one of the concerns that has fueled the debate over the basing mode for the MX missile, a replacement for the vulnerable Minuteman system. The feared scenario often runs something like this:

The decision in Moscow: In a deep crisis over the status of Berlin, the Politburo decides not to launch an all-out pre-emptive attack against American forces and command centers, but only to attack the Minuteman silos. A hot-line message is sent as soon as the warheads land: first, the Soviet Union will spare American cities if the United States refrains from retaliation and, second, the United States is urged to give in to Soviet demands in Europe.

The decision in Washington: The president asks the Joint Chiefs of Staff what military options exist, now that 90% of the Minuteman force is destroyed. They say that fifteen million Americans have just died in the Soviet attack and that an American response will likely trigger a Soviet attack on population centers. Should the president launch a retaliatory strike? Or should he give in to Soviet demands?

This Minuteman-only scenario rests upon a very questionable premise: that the Soviets would believe that the president of the United States would choose not to launch the ICBMs on warning or retaliate after 2,000 Soviet nuclear warheads have exploded here. The American submarines, moreover, could attack many Soviet military targets. A Soviet leader probably would assume that retaliation of some sort would be launched after 15 million Americans were killed. In such circumstances, it would be likely that the Soviets would try to reduce the American retaliation to whatever extent they could.

Thus, if the Soviets were to attack the United States on a large-scale basis, they would have great incentives to attack not only the land-based missiles, but also other American strategic forces and the American command, control, and communications network. There is little Soviet advantage to be gained by attacking the U.S. ICBMs alone, for they contain less than one-fourth of America's strategic nuclear warheads. It is not surprising that Soviet military doctrine, as far as American intelligence sources can determine, stresses that if nuclear war occurs, their nuclear forces would be used on a massive scale.

This Minuteman-only scenario, like the full-blown bolt from the blue, is far less likely than many other possible paths to nuclear war. These surprise attack scenarios preoccupy all too many defense analysts whose talents would be far better applied to preventing more likely dangers. And the attention of the public would be better directed to more realistic scenarios and more probable perils.

A Pre-Emptive War

Not all wars begin with coolly calculated decisions. Indeed, under certain circumstances, a nuclear war could originate from a series of hasty decisions made in the midst of uncertainty. In fact, a nuclear exchange could be precipitated by a mistaken action, originally intended to deter war, which could produce a counter-decision to launch a pre-emptive strike.

Consider the following scenario. It is the opening page of an imaginary historian's future best-seller, *The Missiles of August: The Origins of World War Three*:

> What was the cause of the war? The Greek historian Thucydides, in his history of the conflict between Athens and Sparta, differentiated between the immediate causes and the underlying causes of war. The latter can be compared to the mass of combustible material; the former is the match that sets the material ablaze.
>
> On August 2, 19——, none of the American leaders in Washington knew that they were lighting such a match. A number of years earlier, Soviet Premier Brezhnev had warned the United States that, if NATO deployed Pershing II and cruise missiles in Western Europe, the Soviet Union would "take retaliatory steps that would put the other side, including the United States itself, its own territory, in an analogous position." On the last day of July, American intelligence satellites spotted cruise missiles being unloaded onto Cuban soil from Soviet ships and on August 1 Premier Andropov announced that he

would remove the missiles only if the United States withdrew the NATO deployments.

The sole surviving member of the National Security Council later reported that the president's decision to attack the Cuban dockyard and the Soviet ships was taken overnight. "We had no choice. In a few days, those missiles—we didn't know how many—would have been scattered all over Cuba. This was the only way to get rid of the missiles. We told the Soviets that there would be no attack on Russia itself. Our nuclear alert was only meant to signal our strength."

This was not the view from Moscow. Two Soviet staff officers who survived reported that the Politburo was informed that the Americans must be about to launch a nuclear attack. The head of the KGB told the Politburo that if the Americans launched first, the vast majority of Soviet ICBMs would be destroyed and eventually up to 100 million Soviet citizens might die. But if the Soviet arsenal was used immediately to destroy American nuclear forces and command centers, the casualties after retaliation would probably be "only" between 10 and 20 million. He even told the group that there was a small chance that a pre-emptive attack would "decapitate" the American giant and that no response would come.

He was wrong. The Russians thought war was unavoidable and launched first in desperation and fear. Thirty-five million Americans were killed instantly. The retaliation was perhaps smaller than the first strike the Soviets feared, but it still left 25 million Russians dead.

Perhaps, however, it is misleading to start this history with the immediate cause of the war. The deeper causes go back to 1945. At the close of the Second World War, Soviet and American relations deteriorated rapidly . . .

How plausible is such a pre-emptive war scenario? Although no precise probabilities can be given, of course, it is at least a possibility that in a deep and apparently irresolvable crisis the Soviets (or the United States) might launch their nuclear weapons first with full knowledge that many of its citizens might die, but fearing far worse casualties if they allowed the other side to attack first. A desperate decision indeed, but a possible one.

What conditions would increase the likelihood of such a tragic decision being made by the leaders of a superpower? First, the leaders would have to believe that the other side intended to strike first, and soon. This would require that the adversary's forces be at or moving toward (or be perceived to be at) a high state of alert—a condition likely to be met only in times of crisis. Second, the leaders would have to believe that the other side could carry out a relatively successful disarming first strike—a judgment which would depend upon the capabilities of the adversary's forces and the vulnerabilities of their own. Lastly, the leaders must be convinced that by launching a pre-emptive attack against the other side's nuclear forces, they could substantially reduce the casualties and damage that would ultimately be suffered by their own nation.

The possibility that such a scenario might happen does not, by itself, mean that the United States should never put its forces on alert in a crisis or that we should always back down in dangerous circumstances. Nor does it mean that American nuclear forces should not be aimed at Soviet weaponry. But the possibility of such an occurrence should, at a minimum, promote great caution in times of crisis, highlight the importance of clear and unambiguous military orders, and stress the need for retaliatory forces that are invulnerable and are perceived as such by both sides. Moreover, it should serve as a constant reminder that the security of both sides is diminished by either side's fear of being struck first or by either side's temptation to strike first.

Escalation: Conventional Steps to Nuclear War

It is difficult, though clearly not impossible, to outline a credible scenario in which, during peacetime, a Soviet or an American leader would decide to launch an all-out nuclear attack. It is less difficult to imagine a war occurring between the conventional forces of the two superpowers. And once American and Soviet troops met in combat, the likelihood of the use of nuclear weapons would be increased.

The process by which a war becomes incrementally more violent, either through the plans of the combatants or unintentionally, is called escalation. Escalation from conventional fighting to nuclear war has been a continuing concern of defense planners since the Soviets developed their nuclear arsenal. This fear has, thus far, produced prudence: each superpower has been reluctant to use even conventional forces against the other. Can this prudence continue indefinitely? What would happen if Soviet and American conventional forces did clash somewhere?

We do not know. And this inability to know whether conventional war would escalate to a nuclear exchange both enhances prudence and perpetuates fear. Consider two possible scenarios for nuclear conflict developing through escalation:

War in Europe
Step 1: East German workers, organized by an underground labor union, go on strike, demanding political changes in the government of their country. Martial law is imposed and riots ensue throughout the country. Russian troops help in the "police action." East Germans flee across the border into West Germany.

Step 2: Fighting breaks out between West German military units, who are aiding the refugees, and East German security forces. Soon Soviet forces join in the fighting. Two days later Soviet divisions cross into West Germany and the Soviet premier publicly warns the United States to "refrain from self-defeating threats."

Step 3: Other NATO forces—American, British, and Dutch—become involved in the fighting as the Soviets advance further into West Germany. As the Allies are being pushed back by the superior numbers of Soviet divisions, NATO leaders gather to decide on further military action. They publicly warn the Soviets to withdraw immediately or "suffer the gravest consequences." Four airfields along the Polish-Soviet border are attacked with nuclear-tipped cruise missiles, a communiqué announces, "as a demonstration of NATO resolve."

Step 4: The Soviet Union immediately fires nuclear missiles to destroy nuclear weapons sites in West Germany.

Step 5: ?? Does the war escalate to a full nuclear exchange or is a settlement possible? What would the United States do? What would the Soviet Union do next?

War in the Persian Gulf

Step 1: The Iranian Communist party overthrows the increasingly unpopular government of Ayatollah Khomeini. Civil war breaks out throughout Iran and the new government requests that Soviet troops enter the country "to help restore order." Despite American warnings against such action Soviet forces cross into Iran and move toward Teheran.

Step 2: American troops are immediately sent to southwestern Iran to protect the West's oil supply sources. Advance parties of the two armies meet and engage in combat.

Step 3: As Soviet reinforcements begin to move into Iran, the president orders aircraft from an American aircraft carrier in the Indian Ocean to "close the mountain passes" along the Soviet supply route. Told that nuclear bombs might be needed, he refuses to give weapons release authority to the local commander, "The United States will not be the first to go nuclear," the president's message concludes.

Step 4: The American military commander orders six conventional air strikes against mountain passes in Iran. The next morning, Soviet bombers fly south and attack the American carrier task force with nuclear-tipped missiles. The aircraft carrier and many of its supporting ships are destroyed instantly.

Step 5: ?? Does the president escalate further? Does the Soviet Union stop fighting? What happens next? How does the war end?

These paths to nuclear conflict (or others like them) are more likely than the previous scenarios of initial homeland-to-homeland exchanges for an obvious reason: once war begins, the balance between political and military considerations shifts decidedly toward the military side. The leader of a government is far more likely to authorize use of a small number of nuclear weapons during a conventional war than to initiate a full-scale nuclear conflict. But unless the war is somehow terminated, there will be continued incentives for further escalation.

Once a conventional war began, there would be two other factors, in addition to possible decisions to take incremental escalatory steps, that could lead to nuclear war. First, there would be increased possibilities of miscalculation leading to nuclear war. It is possible that at some stage in a conventional conflict a field commander might be given "pre-delegation of authority," the president's option of allowing commanders to decide themselves when to use tactical nuclear weapons. Once this is done, the likelihood of use through miscalculation or mistake in the "fog of battle" would greatly increase. Second, the pressures for pre-emptive nuclear strikes would likely be enhanced after the line between superpower peace and superpower war was crossed. Once the fighting began, one or both governments might decide that full-scale use of nuclear weapons was inevitable or very nearly so; thus, despite the terrible risks involved, a pre-emptive attack might be chosen, on the basis that striking first is better than being stricken first, though both are worse than the unavailable option of no nuclear war at all.

The maintenance of a conventional-nuclear "firebreak"—an often used metaphor borrowed from forest fire-fighting techniques—is most strategists' goal here. If a conventional conflict between the superpowers does someday occur, every effort should be made to terminate the war without the use of nuclear weapons; escalation to full thermonuclear war should be avoided. Withdrawing tactical nuclear weapons from sites near borders, where they might be used quickly in a war, and keeping strict political control over weapons release authority widen the firebreak between conventional and nuclear war. It is not clear, however, exactly how wide such a firebreak should be because of . . . the "usability paradox": if nuclear weapons are too usable, they might be used when and in a manner not controllable by government leaders; yet if it is certain that weapons will not be used, might this not encourage conventional aggression?

Tragic Accidents

Could nuclear war begin purely by accident? Mechanical failures do occur, after all, even with (and perhaps especially with) the most sophisticated machinery. Human frailties always exist as well. And such frailties can produce highly irrational behavior at times, even when (and perhaps especially when) the psychological pressures to behave cautiously are enormous.

It is a common assumption that nuclear weapons are likely to be used, not through decisions of rational government leaders, but through mechanical or human accidents. Jonathan Schell, for example, has written that "the machinery of destruction is complete, poised on a hair trigger, waiting for a 'button' to be 'pushed' by some misguided or deranged human being or for some faulty computer chip to send out the instruction to fire."[1] Is this true? Are the following scenes possible?

The Faulty Computer Chip War
Deep inside a multimillion-dollar computer, used to process the military intelligence coming from American satellites, a 35-cent computer chip malfunctions. Suddenly the radar screens begin to flash. A thousand Soviet mis-

siles appear to be coming over the horizon. "Oh, my God," the radar screen operator says. "This is it."

In the White House, the president is informed of the warning, now ten minutes old. "In twenty minutes the missiles will destroy our retaliatory forces, sir," his military aide informs him. As the president leaves the White House for his specially equipped command post airplane, he orders that all land-based missiles be launched immediately.

"I am not going to let our missiles be destroyed on the ground," he says as he climbs aboard the helicopter. "We'll fight. But the Russians started this war. Let the history books record that fact."

The Strangelove Scenario

Individuals under pressure cannot always withstand the strain. Sometimes men snap. Late one night, a soviet submarine commander walks into the control room of his new *Typhoon*-class submarine and, before the astonished ensign can react, he pushes a button sending a single SLBM, with twelve nuclear warheads in the nose cone, on its way to the United States.

"What have you done?" the ensign cries as he tackles the commander, wrestling him to the floor.

The commander appears startled. Then he smiles, looks up, and says, "That missile is going to down a Nazi bomber. I'm teaching those fascists a lesson. Remember Stalingrad!"

Although such imaginative scenarios are often discussed, they are, fortunately, extremely unlikely if not impossible. This is not because the problem of accidental war is not a serious concern. Rather the opposite is the case: precisely because the possibility exists that nuclear weapons could be used accidentally, the United States government has devised numerous precautions to prevent such accidents. Indeed, contrary to a popular belief, the chances of an American weapon being used accidentally are probably much less today than they were in the 1950s. For along with more sophisticated and more numerous weapons, more sophisticated and more numerous precautionary policies have been developed.

Four kinds of measures intended to minimize the chances of unauthorized or accidental use are worth noting. First is the "two-man rule," which requires parallel actions by two or more individuals at several stages in the process of communicating and carrying out any order to use nuclear weapons. Second is the system of Permissive Action Links (PALs), including a highly secure coded signal which must be inserted in the weapons before they can be used. Third, devices internal to the weapon are designed to ensure that an attempt to bypass the PALs system will disarm the weapon. Finally, the nuclear warheads themselves are designed to preclude accidental detonation as a result of exposure to heat, blast, or radiation. The Soviets share our concern with unauthorized and accidental nuclear war, and there is reason to believe that they too have taken measures to prevent it.

In this light, how credible are the two scenarios outlined above? There have been, it is true, many false alarms in the American nuclear attack warning system. Some of them have been traced to such minuscule components as an inexpensive computer chip. But none of these false alerts has ever come close to leading the nation into war because the government has built redundancies into the system, precisely so that no president will ever have to rely on a single computer or single radar screen to make such important decisions. For this kind of accident to lead to war, several warning systems of different kinds (e.g., infrared sensors on satellites, and radars on land) would have to fail simultaneously. Even that by itself would be unlikely to cause the president to order an immediate launching of ICBMs. His incentives to do so might indeed be small if the missiles were relatively invulnerable and if he had other nuclear systems at sea, not under attack. It is even possible to maintain a policy of not launching missiles in a retaliatory strike until after the damage of the enemy's first strike is assessed.

Of course, it is possible that a military commander could go insane (although the stability of American officers with such responsibilities is carefully tested). An insane American officer could not, in peacetime by himself, arm and deliver the nuclear weapons under his command. In the submarine case, to give but one example, it would take the simultaneous insanity of a number of American submarine officers for an unauthorized American launch to be possible. Given the Soviets' strong propensity for tight political control of their nuclear weapons, there is no reason to believe that the chances of unauthorized Soviet use are any greater.

Thus it is a mistake to believe that a simple accident or an unstable commander could easily lead to a nuclear exchange. In reality, the probabilities of such an event are very low. This should not, however, breed complacency about the prospect of accidental war, for two reasons. First, it is only through continual concern that the likelihood of accidental use of weapons is kept so low. Second, mechanical accidents and human frailties could become increasingly dangerous in times of deep crisis or conventional war, during which time command centers could be threatened or destroyed.

There will continue to be an uneasy balance between the degree of control required to ensure that weapons are not used accidentally and the degree of "usability" required to ensure that the weapons can be used if needed. Preventing accidental use is an important goal, but it cannot be the only objective of a nuclear weapons policy. Nuclear weapons must be usable enough to provide credible deterrence, but not so usable as to invite unintended use.

Regional Nuclear War

One important reason why the world has seen nuclear peace since 1945 is that there has been no conventional war between the United States and the Soviet Union. In the future, if nuclear proliferation continues, there will be an increased danger of nuclear war breaking out between two nuclear armed Third World countries. Such an event might be more likely than nuclear war between the superpowers because many of the conditions that have led to the maintenance of nuclear peace—such as invulnerable second-strike forces, strong leadership control of nuclear weapons, and stable governments in nuclear weapons states—may be absent. The following is an imaginary future newspaper report of a nuclear war which neither Washington nor Moscow would be in a position to stop.

INDIA USES THE BOMB, PAKISTAN SUES FOR PEACE

New Delhi, India.—The Indian government this morning announced that four nuclear bombs were dropped on Pakistan late last night. At noon, a Defense Ministry spokesman in Islamabad read a declaration over the radio accepting "unconditional surrender" on behalf of the Revolutionary Islamic Council of Pakistan. Thus it appears that the week-long war between India and Pakistan has come to a sudden end.

Sources inside the Indian Ministry of Defense have revealed that India's entire nuclear arsenal was used in this morning's pre-emptive attack against Pakistan's three major military airfields and its nuclear weapons assembly facility. When the Pakistani forces crossed the Indian border last week, Radio Islamabad announced that any Indian use of nuclear weapons would be met in kind. After last year's Pakistani nuclear test, the government in New Delhi took the threat seriously, the Ministry of Defense officials reported, and only decided to attack pre-emptively when Indian intelligence warned that Pakistan's weapons were being readied for use. "We had no choice," an official said. "The enemy was preparing for an attack. Fortunately, we knew where the bombs were kept, and destroyed them and their bomber aircraft simultaneously."

Meanwhile, in New York, the UN Security Council met throughout the night and . . .

Somehow this scenario appears less farfetched than most of the previously outlined scenarios for superpower nuclear war. It also appears less apocalyptic (at least from a non-Pakistani perspective). Indeed, its less-than-apocalyptic nature may be precisely the characteristic that makes it less farfetched. The dangers of this kind of nuclear war may be comparatively small today, but they will increase in the future as more countries acquire nuclear weapons. . . .

It is tempting, but incorrect, to think that a nuclear conflict between any two countries would not affect other nations. There is the possibility that one government at war would be allied to the Soviet Union and the other government to the United States, thereby raising the specter of the superpowers becoming involved in the war. Moreover, there is a danger that a nuclear armed country could use a weapon, intentionally or not, against a superpower.

Catalytic War

There is yet another way in which the superpowers could be dragged into nuclear war by the actions of a third party. Imagine the two scenarios described below:

The French Connection

A conventional conflict between NATO and the Warsaw Pact erupts and, despite the imminent collapse of the NATO front, the United States does not use nuclear weapons. The French government, however, launches a small number of its nuclear-tipped submarine-launched ballistic missiles against military targets, hoping to bring a halt to the Soviet advance. The Soviets do not know who launched the missiles, and respond by launching a nuclear attack against NATO military targets throughout Europe. The American president orders that NATO's Pershing IIs be used against military targets in the USSR. . . .

Mistaken Identity

A war in the Persian Gulf has broken out between the United States and the Soviet Union. After a week of conventional fighting, nuclear-tipped cruise missiles are launched against the American carrier task force. The planes are Soviet models and bear Soviet markings; they are not manned by Soviet pilots nor are they otherwise under Soviet control. Some other country has intentionally and successfully disguised its aircraft, and the Americans mistakenly conclude that it is the Soviets who have initiated use of nuclear weapons. Does the American president escalate further? What might the Soviets do in the midst of this confusion? What happens next?

Clearly, such scenarios are possible. Under a number of circumstances another nuclear power might trigger a strategic nuclear exchange between the superpowers, a war that they had thus far avoided. The possibilities of such an event are greatly increased if conventional war occurs. Few strategists place the danger of catalytic war as high as nuclear war through escalation or pre-emption, but it still is a serious concern. Indeed, during the SALT I negotiations, the Soviet Union mentioned its concern that the growing Chinese nuclear arsenal might someday be used with such results.

Nuclear Terrorism

What if a terrorist organization gained possession of a nuclear bomb? Could nuclear war occur as a result? Consider the following scenario, which was invented in the best-selling novel *The Fifth Horseman:*[2]

On a snowy December evening, the President of the United States is told by his National Security Adviser that a tape recording in Arabic has just been delivered to the White House. It appears to be a message from Muammar al-Qaddafi, President of Libya, and claims that a nuclear weapon has been placed somewhere on Manhattan. Unless the United States forces Israel to withdraw to its 1967 borders, the bomb will be detonated.

"I must further inform you that, should you make this communication public or begin in any way to evacuate New York City, I shall feel obliged to instantly explode my weapon," the message concludes.

"A man like Qaddafi has got to know we have the capability to utterly destroy him and his entire nation in retaliation. He'd be mad to do something like that," the President tells his adviser.

But what should the president do? Is nuclear terrorism possible? How could it come about?

Terrorists might gain possession of an atomic bomb in one of several ways, including theft, purchase, or manufacture. If they were to steal it, and if it were of American origin, then the Permissive Action Links should frustrate any attempt to detonate it. But it is not at all clear just how confident a president might be in the ability of the PALs to resist a concerted attempt to bypass them, especially in light of the high stakes involved. And suppose the stolen bomb was not an American one. Other current and future nuclear weapons states may not have equipped their warheads with safety systems comparable to those developed by the United States.

A terrorist organization might purchase an atomic bomb from (or be given one by) a government that shares the terrorist group's goals. Indeed, this possibility is reason enough to work to inhibit the spread of nuclear weapons to additional countries.

Finally, terrorists might fashion their own nuclear explosive device. The highly enriched uranium or plutonium essential to the project might be stolen or bought, and a crude but workable bomb assembled. . . . The task would be difficult, but not impossible. In any event, how confident could a president be that the terrorists' bomb would not work? And against whom could he threaten retaliation?

CONCLUSION: CONTINUING ISSUES

How should one think about the various paths to war outlined in this chapter? Five points need to be stressed. First, the set of scenarios presented here is not exhaustive. Surely each reader can think of other ways in which a nuclear war might begin. How probable are such scenarios? What can be done to minimize the likelihood of their occurrence? Also, the dangers of these scenarios could be compounded. Suppose, to give but two examples, mechanical failures in warning systems developed during a deep superpower crisis, or human frailty produced unstable commanders during a conventional war. Thus, when thinking of the potential dangers to be avoided in the future, one must not assume that decisions will always be deliberate, or that accidents will always develop when they can do the least harm.

Second, this chapter suggests that it is usually misleading to concentrate one's attention on the number of nuclear weapons when analyzing the likelihood of war. It is widely assumed that changes in the numbers of weapons in the superpower arsenals—either upward or downward—are the major determinant of the risks of war. Sheer numbers, however, matter far less than factors such as the vulnerability of weapons, the credibility of commitments to allies, and imbalances in conventional forces. In the short run, to give but one example, making command and control systems less vulnerable can be as important, and probably more so, in reducing certain risks of war than would changes in the numbers of weapons: improved command and control could reduce an enemy's incentives for a "decapitating" attack, and could improve our ability to follow a policy of "no retaliation until specifically ordered." And the long-run risk of nuclear war is likely to depend more on our ability to stem proliferation than on any other single factor. The common fixation on numbers of weapons in the superpower arsenals misses such important issues.

Third, there is no reason to assume that an all-out nuclear exchange, certainly the most frightening scenario, is either the only kind of nuclear war possible or even the most likely type of nuclear war. Nuclear war occurring through the escalation of conventional conflict appears more probable. Avoiding conventional war is, therefore, one of the most important ways of avoiding nuclear war. And maintaining strong and credible conventional forces may thus be an important component of preventing nuclear war. One should never forget that, despite the incentives to keep a conventional was limited, once fighting begins it would be difficult to control escalation to the nuclear abyss. But escalation should not be considered inevitable, for that could prove to be a self-fulfilling prophecy.

Fourth, it is noted that in none of these scenarios do leaders of the United States or the Soviet Union act insanely. But departures from rationality are not inconceivable; they must be taken into account in the design of measures to prevent nuclear war.

Finally, this glimpse at the shattered crystal ball should breed neither complacency nor despair. A horrible nuclear future is not inevitable, but only because great efforts have been made in the past to decrease its likelihood. The good news for the present is, then, that nuclear war is not probable. The bad news is that nuclear war is, and will continue to be, possible. To make sure that the possible does not become more probable is the continuing task of nuclear policy.

NOTES

1. Jonathan Schell, *The Fate of the Earth* (New York: Knopf, 1982), p. 182.

2. Larry Collins and Dominique LaPierre, *The Fifth Horseman* (New York: Simon and Schuster, 1980), pp. 13–19.

20 NUCLEAR HOLOCAUST

Jonathan Schell

. . . Part of the horror of thinking about a holocaust lies in the fact that it leads us to supplant the human world with a statistical world; we seek a human truth and come up with a handful of figures. The only source that gives us a glimpse of that human truth is the testimony of the survivors of the Hiroshima and Nagasaki bombings. Because the bombing of Hiroshima has been more thoroughly investigated than the bombing of Nagasaki, and therefore more information about it is available, I shall restrict myself to a brief description of that catastrophe.

On August 6, 1945, at 8:16 A.M., a fission bomb with a yield of twelve and a half kilotons was detonated about nineteen hundred feet above the central section of Hiroshima. By present-day standards, the bomb was a small one, and in today's arsenals it would be classed among the merely tactical weapons. Nevertheless, it was large enough to transform a city of some three hundred and forty thousand people into hell in the space of a few seconds. "It is no exaggeration," the authors of "Hiroshima and Nagasaki" tell us, "to say that the whole city was ruined instantaneously." In that instant, tens of thousands of people were burned, blasted, and crushed to death. Other tens of thousands suffered injuries of every description or were doomed to die of radiation sickness. The center of the city was flattened, and every part of the city was damaged. The trunks of bamboo trees as far away as five miles from ground zero—the point on the ground directly under the center of the explosion—were charred. Almost half the trees within a mile and a quarter were knocked down. Windows nearly seventeen miles away were broken. Half an hour after the blast, fires set by the thermal pulse and by the collapse of the buildings began to coalesce into a firestorm, which lasted for six hours. Starting about 9 A.M. and lasting until late afternoon, a "black rain" generated by the bomb (otherwise, the day was fair) fell on the western portions of the city, carrying radioactive fallout from the blast to the ground. For four hours at midday, a violent whirlwind, born of the strange meteorological conditions produced by the explosion, further devastated the city. The number of people who were killed outright or who died of their injuries over the next three months is estimated to be a hundred and thirty thousand. Sixty-eight percent of the buildings in the city were either completely destroyed or damaged beyond repair, and the center of the city was turned into a flat, rubble-strewn plain dotted with the ruins of a few of the sturdier buildings.

In the minutes after the detonation, the day grew dark, as heavy clouds of dust and smoke filled the air. A whole city had fallen in a moment, and in and under its ruins were its people. Among those still living, most were injured, and of these most were burned or had in some way been battered or had suffered both kinds of injury. Those within a mile and a quarter of ground zero had also been subjected to intense nuclear radiation, often in lethal doses. When people revived enough from their unconsciousness or shock to see what was happening around them, they found that where a second before there had been a city getting ready to go about its daily business on a peaceful, warm August morning, now there was a heap of debris and corpses and a stunned mass of injured humanity. But at first, as they awakened and tried to find their bearings in the gathering darkness, many felt cut off and alone. In a recent volume of recollections by survivors called "Unforgettable Fire," in which the effects of the bombing are rendered in drawings as well as in words, Mrs. Haruko Ogasawara, a young girl on that August morning, recalls that she was at first knocked unconscious. She goes on to write:

> How many seconds or minutes had passed I could not tell, but, regaining consciousness, I found myself lying on the ground covered with pieces of wood. When I stood up in a frantic effort to look around, there was darkness. Terribly frightened, I thought I was alone in a world of death, and groped for any light. My fear was so great I did not think anyone would truly understand. When I came to my senses, I found my clothes in shreds, and I was without my wooden sandals.

Soon cries of pain and cries for help from the wounded filled the air. Survivors heard the voices of their families and their friends calling out in the gloom. Mrs. Ogasawara writes:

> Suddenly, I wondered what had happened to my mother and sister. My mother was then forty-five, and my sister five years old. When the darkness began to fade, I found that there was nothing around me. My house, the next door neighbor's house, and the next had all vanished. I was standing amid the ruins of my house. No one was around. It was quiet, very quiet—an eerie moment. I discovered my mother in a water tank. She had fainted. Crying out, "Mama, Mama," I shook her to bring her back to her senses. After coming to, my mother began to shout madly for my sister: "Eiko! Eiko!"
>
> I wondered how much time had passed when there were cries of searchers. Children were calling their parents' names, and parents were calling the names of their children. We were calling desperately for my sister and listening for her voice and looking to see her. Suddenly, Mother cried "Oh Eiko!" Four

or five meters away, my sister's head was sticking out and was calling my mother. . . . Mother and I worked desperately to remove the plaster and pillars and pulled her out with great effort. Her body had turned purple from the bruises, and her arm was so badly wounded that we could have placed two fingers in the wound.

Others were less fortunate in their searches and rescue attempts. In "Unforgettable Fire," a housewife describes a scene she saw:

A mother, driven half-mad while looking for her child, was calling his name. At last she found him. His head looked like a boiled octopus. His eyes were half-closed, and his mouth was white, pursed, and swollen.

Throughout the city, parents were discovering their wounded or dead children, and children were discovering their wounded or dead parents. Kikuno Segawa recalls seeing a little girl with her dead mother:

A woman who looked like an expectant mother was dead. At her side, a girl of about three years of age brought some water in an empty can she had found. She was trying to let her mother drink from it.

The sight of people in extremities of suffering was ubiquitous. Kinzo Nishida recalls:

While taking my severely wounded wife out to the riverbank by the side of the hill of Nakahiro-machi, I was horrified, indeed, at the sight of a stark naked man standing in the rain with his eyeball in his palm. He looked to be in great pain, but there was nothing that I could do for him.

Many people were astonished by the sheer sudden absence of the known world. The writer Yoko Ota later wrote:

I just could not understand why our surroundings had changed so greatly in one instant. . . . I thought it might have been something which had nothing to do with the war—the collapse of the earth, which it was said would take place at the end of the world, and which I had read about as a child.

And a history professor who looked back at the city after the explosion remarked later, "I saw that Hiroshima had disappeared."

As the fires sprang up in the ruins, many people, having found injured family members and friends, were now forced to abandon them to the flames or to lose their own lives in the firestorm. Those who left children, husbands, wives, friends, and strangers to burn often found these experiences the most awful of the entire ordeal. Mikio Inoue describes how one man, a professor, came to abandon his wife:

It was when I crossed Miyuki Bridge that I saw Professor Takenaka, standing at the foot of the bridge. He was almost naked, wearing nothing but shorts, and he had a ball of rice in his right hand. Beyond the streetcar line, the northern area was covered by red fire burning against the sky. Far away from the line, Ote-machi was also a sea of fire.

That day, Professor Takenaka had not gone to Hiroshima University, and the A-bomb exploded when he was at home. He tried to rescue his wife, who was trapped under a roofbeam, but all his efforts were in vain. The fire was threatening him also. His wife pleaded, "Run away, dear!" He was forced to desert his wife and escape from the fire. He was now at the foot of Miyuki Bridge.

But I wonder how he came to hold that ball of rice in his hand. His naked figure, standing there before the flames with that ball of rice, looked to me as a symbol of the modest hopes of human beings.

In "Hiroshima," John Hersey describes the flight of a group of German priests and their Japanese colleagues through a burning section of the city:

> The street was cluttered with parts of houses that had slid into it, and with fallen telephone poles and wires. From every second or third house came the voices of people buried and abandoned, who invariably screamed, with formal politeness, *"Tasukete kure*! Help, if you please!" The priests recognized several ruins from which these cries came as the homes of friends, but because of the fire it was too late to help.

And thus it happened that throughout Hiroshima all the ties of affection and respect that join human beings to one another were being pulled and rent by the spreading firestorm. Soon processions of the injured—processions of a kind that had never been seen before in history—began to file away from the center of the city toward its outskirts. Most of the people suffered from burns, which had often blackened their skin or caused it to sag off them. A grocer who joined one of these processions has described them in an interview with Robert Jay Lifton which appears in his book "Death in Life":

> They held their arms bent [forward] . . . and their skin—not only on their hands but on their faces and bodies, too—hung down. . . . If there had been only one or two such people . . . perhaps I would not have had such a strong impression. But wherever I walked, I met these people. . . . Many of them died along the road. I can still picture them in my mind—like walking ghosts. They didn't look like people of this world.

The grocer also recalls that because of people's injuries "you couldn't tell whether you were looking at them from in front or in back." People found it impossible to recognize one another. A woman who at the time was a girl of thirteen, and suffered disfiguring burns on her face, has recalled, "My face was so distorted and changed that people couldn't tell who I was. After a while I could call others' names but they couldn't recognize me." In addition to being injured, many people were vomiting—an early symptom of radiation sickness. For many, horrifying and unreal events occurred in a chaotic jumble. In "Unforgettable Fire," Torako Hironaka enumerates some of the things that she remembers:

1. Some burned work-clothes.
2. People crying for help with their heads, shoulders, or the soles of their feet injured by fragments of broken window glass. Glass fragments were scattered everywhere.
3. [A woman] crying, saying "Aigo! Aigo!" (a Korean expression of sorrow).
4. A burning pine tree.
5. A naked woman.
6. Naked girls crying, "Stupid America!"
7. I was crouching in a puddle, for fear of being shot by a machine gun. My breasts were torn.
8. Burned down electric power lines.
9. A telephone pole had burned and fallen down.
10. A field of watermelons.
11. A dead horse.
12. What with dead cats, pigs, and people, it was just a hell on earth.

Physical collapse brought emotional and spiritual collapse with it. The survivors were, on the whole, listless and stupefied. After the escapes, and the failures to escape, from the firestorm, a silence fell over the city and its remaining population. People suffered and died without speaking or otherwise making a sound. The processions of the injured, too, were soundless. Dr. Michihiko Hachiya has written in his book, "Hiroshima Diary":

> Those who were able walked silently toward the suburbs in the distant hills, their spirits broken, their initiative gone. When asked whence they had come, they pointed to the city and said, "That way," and when asked where they were going, pointed away from the city and said, "This way." They were so broken and confused that they moved and behaved like automatons.
>
> Their reactions had astonished outsiders, who reported with amazement the spectacle of long files of people holding stolidly to a narrow, rough path when close by was a smooth, easy road going in the same direction. The outsiders could not grasp the fact that they were witnessing the exodus of a people who walked in the realm of dreams.

Those who were still capable of action often acted in an absurd or an insane way. Some of them energetically pursued tasks that had made sense in the intact Hiroshima of a few minutes before but were now utterly inappropriate. Hersey relates that the German priests were bent on bringing to safety a suitcase, containing diocesan accounts and a sum of money, that they had rescued from the fire and were carrying around with them through the burning city. And Dr. Lifton describes a young soldier's punctilious efforts to find and preserve the ashes of a burned military code book while people around him were screaming for help. Other people simply lost their minds. For example, when the German priests were escaping from the firestorm, one of them, Father Wilhelm Kleinsorge, carried on his back a Mr. Fukai, who kept saying that he wanted to remain where he was. When Father Kleinsorge finally put Mr. Fukai down, he started running. Hersey writes:

> Father Kleinsorge shouted to a dozen soldiers, who were standing by the bridge, to stop him. As Father Kleinsorge started back to get Mr. Fukai, Father LaSalle called out, "Hurry! Don't waste time!" So Father Kleinsorge just requested the soldiers to take care of Mr. Fukai. They said they would, but the little, broken man got away from them, and the last the priests could see of him, he was running back toward the fire.

In the weeks after the bombing, many survivors began to notice the appearance of petechiae—small spots caused by hemorrhages—on their skin. These usually signalled the onset of the critical stage of radiation sickness. In the first stage, the victims characteristically vomited repeatedly, ran a fever, and developed an abnormal thirst. (The cry "Water! Water!" was one of the few sounds often heard in Hiroshima on the day of the bombing.) Then, after a few hours or days, there was a deceptively hopeful period of remission of symptoms, called the latency period, which lasted from about a week to about four weeks. Radiation attacks the reproductive function of cells, and those that reproduce most frequently are therefore the most vulnerable. Among these are the bone-marrow cells, which are responsible for the production of blood cells. During the latency period, the count of white blood cells, which are instrumental in fighting infections, and the count of platelets, which are instrumental in clotting, drop precipitously, so the body is poorly defended against infection and is liable to hemorrhaging. In the third, and final, stage, which may last for several weeks, the victim's hair may fall out and he may suffer from diarrhea and may bleed from the intestines, the mouth, or other parts of the body, and in the end he will either recover or die. Because the fireball of the Hiroshima bomb did not touch the ground, very little ground material was mixed with the fission products of the bomb, and therefore very little local fallout was generated. (What fallout there was descended in the black rain.) Therefore, the fatalities from radiation sickness were probably all caused by the initial nuclear radiation, and since this affected only people within a radius of a mile and a quarter of ground zero, most of the people who received lethal doses were killed more quickly by the thermal pulse and the blast wave. Thus, Hiroshima did not experience the mass radiation sickness that can be expected if a weapon is groundburst. Since the Nagasaki bomb was also burst in the air, the effect of widespread lethal fallout on large areas, causing the death by radiation sickness of whole populations in the hours, days, and weeks after the blast, is a form of nuclear horror that the world has not experienced.

In the months and years following the bombing of Hiroshima, after radiation sickness had run its course and most of the injured had either died of their wounds or recovered from them, the inhabitants of the city began to learn that the exposure to radiation they had experienced would bring about a wide variety of illnesses, many of them lethal, throughout the lifetimes of those who had been exposed. An early sign that the harm from radiation was not restricted to radiation sickness came in the months immediately following the bombing, when people found that their reproductive organs had been temporarily harmed, with men experiencing sterility and women experiencing abnormalities in their menstrual cycles. Then, over the years, other illnesses, including cataracts of the eye and leukemia and other forms of cancer, began to appear in larger than normally expected numbers among the exposed population. In all these illnesses, correlations have been found between nearness to the explosion and incidence of the disease. Also, fetuses exposed to the bomb's radiation in utero exhibited abnormalities and developmental retardation. Those exposed within the mile-and-a-quarter radius were seven times as likely as unexposed fetuses to die in utero, and were also seven times as likely to die at birth or in infancy. Surviving children who were exposed in utero tended to be shorter and lighter than other children, and were more often mentally retarded. One of the most serious abnormalities caused by exposure to the bomb's radiation was microcephaly—abnormal smallness of the head, which is often accompanied by mental retardation. In one study, thirty-three cases of microcephaly were found among a hundred and sixty-nine children exposed in utero.

What happened at Hiroshima was less than a millionth part of a holocaust at present levels of world nuclear armament. The more than millionfold difference amounts to more than a difference in magnitude; it is also a difference in kind. The authors of "Hiroshima and Nagasaki" observe that "an atomic bomb's massive destruction and indiscriminate slaughter involves the sweeping breakdown of all order and existence—in a word, the collapse of society itself," and that therefore "the essence of atomic destruction lies in the totality of its impact on man and society." This is true also of a holocaust, of course, except that the totalities in question are now not single cities but nations, ecosystems, and the earth's ecosphere. Yet with the exception of fallout, which was relatively light at Hiroshima and Nagasaki (because both the bombs were airburst), the immediate devastation caused by today's bombs would be of a sort similar to the devastation in those cities. The immediate effects of a twenty-megaton bomb are not different in kind from those of a twelve-and-a-half-kiloton bomb; they are only more extensive. . . . Therefore, while the total effect of a holocaust is qualitatively different from the total effect of a single bomb, the experience of individual people in a holocaust would be, in the short term (and again excepting the presence of lethal fallout wherever the bombs were ground-burst), very much like the experience of individual people in Hiroshima. The Hiroshima people's experience, accordingly, is of much more than historical interest. It is a picture of what our whole world is always poised to become—a backdrop of scarcely imaginable horror lying just behind the surface of our normal life, and capable of breaking through into that normal life at any second. Whether we choose to think about it or not, it is an omnipresent, inescapable truth about our lives today that at every single moment each one of us may suddenly become the deranged mother looking for her burned child; the professor with the ball of rice in his hand whose wife has just told him "Run away, dear!" and died in the fires; Mr. Fukai running back into the firestorm; the naked man standing on the blasted plain that was his city, holding his eyeball in his hand; or, more likely, one of millions of corpses. For whatever our "modest hopes" as human beings may be, every one of them can be nullified by a nuclear holocaust.

One way to begin to grasp the destructive power of present-day nuclear weapons is to describe the consequences of the detonation of a one-megaton bomb, which possesses eighty times the explosive power of the Hiroshima bomb, on a large city, such as New York. Burst some eighty-five hundred feet above the Empire State Building, a one-megaton bomb would gut or flatten almost every building between Battery Park and 125th Street, or within a radius of four and four-tenths miles, or in an area of sixty-one square miles, and would heavily damage buildings between the northern tip of Staten Island and the George Washington Bridge, or within a radius of about eight miles, or in an area of about two hundred square miles. A conventional explosive delivers a swift shock, like a slap, to whatever it hits, but the blast wave of a sizable nuclear weapon endures for several seconds and "can surround and destroy whole buildings." . . . People, of course, would be picked up and hurled away from the blast along with the rest of the debris. Within the sixty-one square miles, the walls, roofs, and floors of any buildings that had not been flattened would be collapsed, and the people and furniture inside would be swept down onto the street. (Technically, this zone would be hit by various overpressures of at least five pounds per square inch. Overpressure is defined as the pressure in excess of normal atmospheric pressure.) As far away as ten miles from ground zero, pieces of glass and other sharp objects would be hurled about by the blast wave at lethal velocities. In Hiroshima, where buildings were low and, outside the center of the city, were often constructed of light materials, injuries from falling buildings were often minor. But in New York, where the buildings are tall and are constructed of heavy materials, the physical collapse of the city would certainly kill millions of people. The streets of New York are narrow ravines running between the high walls of the city's buildings. In a nuclear attack, the walls would fall and the ravines would fill up. The people in the buildings would fall to the street with the debris of the buildings, and the people in the street would be crushed by this avalanche of people and buildings. At a distance of two miles or so from ground zero, winds would reach four hundred miles an hour, and another two miles away they would reach a hundred and eighty miles an hour. Meanwhile, the fireball would be growing, until it was more than a mile wide, and rocketing upward, to a height of over six miles. For ten seconds, it would broil the city below. Anyone caught in the open within nine miles of ground zero would receive third-degree burns and would probably be killed; closer to the explosion, people would be charred and killed instantly. . . .

If it were possible (as it would not be) for someone to stand at Fifth Avenue and Seventy-second Street (about two miles from ground zero) without being instantly killed, he would see the following sequence of events. A dazzling white light from the fireball would illumine the scene, continuing for perhaps thirty seconds. Simultaneously, searing heat would ignite everything flammable and start to melt windows, cars, buses, lampposts, and everything else made of metal or glass. People in the street would immediately catch fire, and would shortly be reduced to heavily charred corpses. About five seconds after the light appeared, the blast wave would strike, laden with the debris of a now nonexistent midtown. Some buildings might be crushed, as though a giant fist had squeezed them on all sides, and others might be picked up off their foundations and whirled uptown with the other debris. On the far side of Central Park, the West Side skyline would fall from south to north. The four-hundred-mile-an-hour wind would blow from south to north, die down after a few seconds, and then blow in the reverse direction with diminished intensity. While these things were happening, the fireball would be burning in the sky for the ten seconds of the thermal pulse. Soon huge, thick clouds of dust and smoke would envelop the scene, and as the mushroom cloud rushed overhead (it would have a diameter of about twelve miles) the light from the sun would be blotted out, and day would turn to night. Within minutes, fires, ignited both by the thermal pulse and by broken gas mains, tanks of gas and oil, and the like, would begin to spread in the darkness, and a strong, steady wind would begin to blow in the direction of the blast. As at Hiroshima, a whirlwind might be produced, which would sweep through the ruins, and radioactive rain, generated under the meteorological conditions created by the blast, might fall. Before long, the individual fires would coalesce into a mass fire, which, depending largely on the winds, would become either a conflagration or a firestorm. In a conflagration, prevailing winds spread a wall of fire as far as there is any combustible material to sustain it; in a firestorm, a vertical updraft caused by the fire itself sucks the surrounding air in toward a central point, and the fires therefore converge in a single fire of extreme heat. A mass fire of either kind renders shelters useless by burning up all the oxygen in the air and creating toxic gases, so that anyone inside the shelters is asphyxiated, and also by heating the ground to such high temperatures that the shelters turn, in effect, into ovens, cremating the people inside them. In Dresden, several days after the firestorm raised there by Allied conventional bombing, the interiors of some bomb shelters were still so hot that when they were opened the inrushing air caused the contents to burst into flame. Only those who had fled their shelters when the bombing started had any chance of surviving. (It is difficult to predict in a particular situation which form the fires will take. In actual experience, Hiroshima suffered a firestorm and Nagasaki suffered a conflagration.)

In this vast theatre of physical effects, all the scenes of agony and death that took place at Hiroshima would again take place, but now involving millions of people rather than hundreds of thousands. Like the people of Hiroshima, the people of New York would be burned, battered, crushed, and irradiated in every conceivable way. The city and its people would be mingled in a smoldering heap. And then, as the fires started, the survivors (most of whom would be on the periphery of the explosion) would be driven to abandon to the flames those family members and other people who were unable to flee, or else to die with them. Before long, while the ruins burned, the processions of injured, mute people would begin their slow progress out of the outskirts of the devastated zone. . . .

If instead of being burst in the air the bomb were burst on or near the ground in the vicinity of the Empire State Building, the overpressure would be very much greater near the center of the blast area but the range hit by a minimum of five pounds per square inch of overpressure would be less. The range of the thermal pulse would be about the same as that of the air burst. The fireball would be almost two miles across, and would engulf midtown Manhattan from Greenwich Village nearly to Central Park. Very little is known about what would happen to a city that was inside a fireball, but one would expect a good deal of what was there to be first pulverized and then melted or vaporized. Any human beings in the area would be reduced to smoke and ashes; they would simply disappear. A crater roughly three blocks in diameter and two hundred feet deep would open up. In addition, heavy radioactive fallout would be created as dust and debris from the city rose with the mushroom cloud and then fell back to the ground. . . . Exposure to radioactivity in human beings is measured in units called rems—an acronym for "roentgen equivalent in man." The roentgen is a standard measurement of gamma- and X-ray radiation, and the expression "equivalent in man" indicates that an adjustment has been made to take into account the differences in the degree of biological damage that is caused by radiation of different types. Many of the kinds of harm done to human beings by radiation—for example, the incidence of cancer and of genetic damage—depend on the dose accumulated over many years; but radiation sickness, capable of causing death, results from an "acute" dose, received in a period of anything from a few seconds to several days. Because almost ninety percent of the so-called "infinite-time dose" of radiation from fallout—that is, the dose from a given quantity of fallout that one would receive if one lived for many thousands of years—is emitted in the first week, the one-week accumulated dose is often used as a convenient measure for calculating the immediate harm from fallout. Doses in the thousands of rems, which could be expected throughout the city, would attack the central nervous system and would bring about death within a few hours. Doses of around a thousand rems, which would be delivered some tens of miles downwind from the blast, would kill within two weeks everyone who was exposed to them. Doses of around five hundred rems, which would be delivered as far as a hundred and fifty miles downwind (given a wind speed of fifteen miles per hour), would kill half of all exposed able-bodied young adults. At this level of exposure, radiation sickness proceeds in the three stages observed at Hiroshima. The plume of lethal fallout could descend, depending on the direction of the wind, on other parts of New York State and parts of New Jersey, Pennsylvania, Delaware, Maryland, Connecticut, Massachusetts, Rhode Island, Vermont, and New Hampshire, killing additional millions of people. The circumstances in heavily contaminated areas, in which millions of people were all declining together, over a period of weeks, toward painful deaths, are ones that, like so many of the consequences of nuclear explosions, have never been experienced.

A description of the effects of a one-megaton bomb on New York City gives some notion of the meaning in human terms of a megaton of nuclear explosive power, but a weapon that is more likely to be used against New York is the twenty-megaton bomb, which has one thousand six hundred times the yield of the Hiroshima bomb. The Soviet Union is estimated to have at least a hundred and thirteen twenty-megaton bombs in its nuclear arsenal, carried by Bear intercontinental bombers. In addition, some of the Soviet SS-18 missiles are capable of carrying bombs of this size, although the actual yields are not known. Since the explosive power of the twenty-megaton bombs greatly exceeds the amount necessary to destroy most military targets, it is reasonable to suppose that they are meant for use against large cities. If a twenty-megaton bomb were air-burst over the Empire State Building at an altitude of thirty thousand feet, the zone gutted or flattened by the blast

wave would have a radius of twelve miles . . . reaching from the middle
of Staten Island to the northern edge of the Bronx, the eastern edge of
Queens, and well into New Jersey, and the zone of heavy damage from
the blast wave (the zone hit by a minimum of two pounds of overpressure per square inch) would have a radius of twenty-one and a half
miles . . . reaching to the southernmost tip of Staten Island, north as
far as southern Rockland County, east into Nassau County, and west
to Morris County, New Jersey. The fireball would be about four and a
half miles in diameter and would radiate the thermal pulse for some
twenty seconds. People caught in the open twenty-three miles away
from ground zero, in Long Island, New Jersey, and southern New York
State, would be burned to death. . . . People hundreds of miles away
who looked at the burst would be temporarily blinded and would risk
permanent eye injury. . . . The mushroom cloud would be seventy miles
in diameter. New York City and its suburbs would be transformed into
a lifeless, flat, scorched desert in a few seconds.

If a twenty-megaton bomb were ground-burst on the Empire State
Building, the range of severe blast damage would, as with the one-
megaton ground blast, be reduced, but the fireball . . . would cover
Manhattan from Wall Street to northern Central Park and also parts of
New Jersey, Brooklyn, and Queens, and everyone within it would be
instantly killed, with most of them physically disappearing. Fallout
would again be generated, this time covering thousands of square miles
with lethal intensities of radiation. A fair portion of New York City and
its incinerated population, now radioactive dust, would have risen into
the mushroom cloud and would now be descending on the surrounding
territory. . . . [I]f the wind carried the fallout onto populated areas, then
this one bomb would probably doom upward of twenty million people,
or almost ten percent of the population of the United States.

21 CAN NUCLEAR WAR BE CONTROLLED?

Desmond Ball

For the greater part of the nuclear age, Western strategic thought focused on deterrence and other means of avoiding strategic nuclear war. The principal concerns of the strategic studies community were the conditions of viable mutual deterrence and crisis stability, the prevention of accidental nuclear war, and the promotion of nuclear non-proliferation to limit the danger of catalytic war. Virtually no consideration was given to the conduct of nuclear war in the event that deterrence failed or that, for whatever the reason, nuclear strikes were initiated. It was assumed, at least implicitly, that any significant use of nuclear weapons by either the United States or the Soviet Union against the territory or military forces of the other would inevitably develop into an all-out nuclear exchange limited only by the size of their respective nuclear arsenals.

During the last decade, however, there has been a radical shift in this thinking. Today, the principal concerns of the strategic studies community relate to the period *following* the initiation of a strategic nuclear exchange—i.e. to questions of nuclear war-fighting, such as targeting plans and policies, the dynamics of escalation during a strategic nuclear exchange, and the termination of any such exchange.

Controlled Escalation has become the central operational concept in current US strategic doctrine. This concept requires the US to be able to conduct very selective military operations, initially focussing on the protection of vital American interests immediately threatened, but also aimed at foreclosing opportunities for further enemy aggression; the intention is to "deter escalation and coerce the enemy into negotiating a war termination acceptable to the United States by maintaining our capability to effectively withhold attacks from additional hostage targets highly valued [or] vital to enemy leaders, thus limiting the level and scope of violence by threatening subsequent destruction."[1] Controlling escalation requires *both* adversaries to exercise restraint, and current US policy is to offer a combination of measures involving a mixture of self-interest and coercion.

Note: The footnotes have been renumbered to appear in consecutive order.

The capabilities for command and control, and the conditions which enable control to be exercised throughout a strategic nuclear exchange, are critical to the viability of the current US strategic doctrine. Without survivable command, control and communication (C^3) systems, for example, any limited nuclear operations involving control, selectivity, discrimination and precision would rapidly become infeasible. . . .

A strategic nuclear war between the United States and the Soviet Union would involve so many novel technical and emotional variables that predictions about its course—and especially about whether or not it could be controlled—must remain highly speculative.

To the extent that there is a typical lay image of a nuclear war, it is that any substantial use of nuclear weapons by either the United States or the Soviet Union against the other's forces or territory would inevitably and rapidly lead to all-out urban-industrial attacks and consequent mutual destruction. As Carl-Friedrich von Weiszacker recently wrote, "as soon as we use nuclear weapons, there are no limits."[2]

Among strategic analysts on the other hand, the ascendant view is that it is possible to conduct limited and quite protracted nuclear exchanges in such a way that escalation can be controlled and the war terminated at some less than all-out level. Some strategists actually visualize an escalation ladder, with a series of discrete and clearly identifiable steps of increasing levels of intensity of nuclear conflict, which the respective adversaries move up—and down—at will. Current US strategic policy, although extensively and carefully qualified, is closer to this second position: it is hoped that escalation could be controlled and that more survivable command-and-control capabilities should ensure dominance in the escalation process. Indeed, reliance on the ability to control escalation is an essential element of US efforts with respect to extended deterrence.

Escalation is neither autonomous and inevitable nor subject completely to the decisions of any one national command authority. Whether or not it can be controlled will depend very much on the circumstances at the time. The use of a few nuclear weapons for some clear demonstrative purposes, for example, could well not lead to further escalation. However, it is most unrealistic to expect that there would be a relatively smooth and controlled progression from limited and selective strikes, through major counterforce exchanges, to termination of the conflict at some level short of urban-industrial attacks. It is likely that beyond some relatively early stage in the conflict the strategic communications systems would suffer interference and disruption, the strikes would become ragged, unco-ordinated, less precise and less discriminating, and the ability to reach an agreed settlement between the adversaries would soon become extremely problematical.

There is of course no immutable point beyond which control is necessarily and irretrievably lost, but clearly the prospects of maintaining control depend to a very great extent on whether or not a decision is taken deliberately to attack strategic command-and-control capabilities.

Command-and-control systems are inherently relatively vulnerable, and concerted attacks on them would very rapidly destroy them, or at least render them inoperable. Despite the increased resources that the US is currently devoting to improving the survivability and endurance of command-and-control systems, the extent of their relative vulnerability remains enormous. The Soviet Union would need to expend thousands of warheads in any comprehensive counterforce attacks against US ICBM silos, bomber bases and . . . submarine facilities, and even then hundreds if not thousands of US warheads would still survive. On the other hand, it would require only about 50–100 warheads to destroy the fixed facilities of the national command system or to effectively impair the communication links between the National Command Authorities [political and military leaders responsible for commanding U.S. military forces] and the strategic forces.

This figure would permit attacks on the National Military Command Center, the major underground command posts (including the Alternative National Military Command Center and the NORAD [North American Defense] and SAC [Strategic Air Command] Command Posts), the critical satellite ground terminals and early-warning radar facilities, the VLF [very low frequency] communication stations, etc., as well as 10 or 20 high altitude detonations designed to disrupt HF [high frequency] communications and generate EMP [electromagnetic pulse] over millions of square miles. Any airborne command posts and communication links that survived the initial attack could probably not endure for more than a few days. Soviet military doctrine suggests that any comprehensive counterforce attack *would* include strikes of this sort. US strategic targeting plans involve a wide range of Soviet command-and-control facilities, and, while attacks on the Soviet national leadership would probably only be undertaken as part of an all-out exchange, it is likely that attempts would be made to destroy the command posts that control the strategic forces, or at least to sever the communication links between the Soviet NCA [National Command Authorities] and those forces at a much earlier stage in the conflict.

In fact, control of a nuclear exchange would become very difficult to maintain after several tens of strategic nuclear weapons had been used, even where deliberate attacks on command-and-control capabilities were avoided. Many command and control facilities, such as early-warning radars, radio antennae and satellite ground terminals would be destroyed, or at least rendered inoperable, by nuclear detonations designed to destroy nearby military forces and installations, while the widespread disturbance of the ionosphere and equally widespread generation of EMP would disrupt HF communications and impair electronic and electrical systems at great distances from the actual explosions. Hence, as John Steinbruner has argued, "regardless of the flexibility embodied in individual force components, the precariousness of command channels probably means that nuclear war would be uncontrollable, as a practical matter, shortly after the first tens of weapons are launched."[3] Moreover, any attack involving 100 nuclear weapons that was of any military or strategic significance (as opposed to demonstration strikes at isolated sites in northern Siberia) would produce substantial civilian casualties. Even if cities were avoided, 100 nuclear detonations on key military or war-supporting facilities (such as oil refineries) would probably cause prompt fatalities in excess of a million people.

The notion of controlled nuclear war-fighting is essentially astrategic in that it tends to ignore a number of the realities that would necessarily attend any nuclear exchange. The more significant of these include the particular origins of the given conflict and the nature of its progress to the point where the strategic nuclear exchange is initiated; the disparate objectives for which a limited nuclear exchange would be fought; the nature of the decision-making processes within the adversary governments; the political pressures that would be generated by a nuclear exchange; and the problems of terminating the exchange at some less than all-out level. Some of these considerations are so fundamental and so intemperate in their implications as to suggest that there can really be no possibility of controlling a nuclear war.

The origins of a nuclear exchange are relevant because, for example, a strategic nuclear strike by the United States or the Soviet Union against targets in the other's heartland—no matter how limited, precise, or controlled it might be—is most unlikely to be the first move in any conflict between them. Rather, it is likely to follow a period of large-scale military action, probably involving substantial use of tactical nuclear weapons, in an area of vital interest to both adversaries, and during which the dynamics of the escalation process have already been set in motion. Some command-and-control facilities, communications systems and intelligence posts that would be required to control a strategic nuclear exchange would almost certainly be destroyed or damaged in the conventional or tactical nuclear phases of a conflict. And casualties on both sides are already likely to be very high before any strategic nuclear exchange. In the case of a tactical nuclear war in Europe possible fatalities range from 2 to 20 million, assuming extensive use of nuclear weapons with some restraints, up to 100 million if there are no restraints at all.[4] The capabilities of the Warsaw Pact forces (using large and relatively 'dirty' warheads) and the Warsaw Pact targeting doctrine make it likely that the actual figure would lie at the higher end of this range.

A war involving such extensive use of nuclear weapons in Europe would almost inevitably involve attacks on targets within the Soviet Union. Indeed, it has long been US policy to use nuclear weapons against the Soviet Union even if the Soviet Union has attacked neither US forces nor US territory. As [U.S. Defense] Secretary [Harold] Brown expressed it in January 1980, "We could not want the Soviets to make the mistaken judgment, based on their understanding of our targeting practices, that they would be spared retaliatory attacks on their territory as long as they did not employ strategic weapons or attack US territory."[5] The US would attempt to destroy the Soviet theatre nuclear forces, including the MRBMs, IRBMs and bombers based in the western USSR, the reserve forces, and POL and logistic support facilities. Soviet casualties from these attacks could amount to several tens of millions. The prospects for controlling any subsequent strategic exchange would not be auspicious.

In addition to these technical and strategic considerations, the decision-making structures and processes of large national security establishments are quite unsuited to the control of escalatory military operations. The control of escalation requires extreme decisional flexibility: decision-makers must be able to adapt rapidly to changing situations and assessments, and must have the freedom to reverse direction as the unfolding of events dictates; their decisions must be presented clearly and coherently, leaving no room for misinterpretation either by subordinates charged with implementation or by the adversary leadership.

These are not attitudes that are generally found in large national security establishments. In neither the United States nor the Soviet Union are these establishments unitary organizations in which decisions are made and executive commands given on the basis of some rational calculation of the national interest. They are made up of a wide range of civilian and military individuals and groups, each with their own interests, preferences, views and perspectives, and each with their own quasi-autonomous political power bases; the decisions which emerge are a product of bargaining, negotiation and compromise between these groups and individuals, rather than of any more rational processes. The heterogeneous nature of the decision-making process leads, in the first instance, to a multiplicity of motives and objectives, not all of which are entirely compatible, and resolving them generally involves the acceptance of compromise language acceptable to each of the contending participants. The clarity of reception among the adversary leadership is consequently generally poor, and the reactions invariably different from the responses initially sought.

The 'fog of war' makes it extremely unlikely that the situation to which NCA believe themselves to be reacting will in fact correspond very closely to the true situation, or that there will be a high degree of shared perception between the respective adversary leaderships. In these circumstances it would be most difficult to terminate a nuclear exchange through mutual agreement between the adversaries at some point short of all-out urban-industrial attacks.

Of course, the pressures to which decision-makers are subject do not come only from within the national security establishment. In the event of a nuclear exchange, the national leadership would also be subject to the pressures of popular feelings and demands. The mood of horror, confusion and hatred that would develop among the population at large as bombs began falling on the Soviet Union and the United States and casualties rose through the millions would inevitably limit the national leaderships' freedom of maneuver. Whether the horror would force them to recoil from large-scale attacks on urban-industrial areas or the hatred would engender rapid escalation must remain an open question—but neither mood would be conducive to measured and considered actions.

The likelihood that effective control of a nuclear exchange would be lost at some relatively early point in a conflict calls into question the strategic utility of any preceding efforts to control the exchange. As Colin Gray has argued, it could be extremely dangerous for the United States "to plan a set of very selective targeting building blocks for prospective rounds one, two and three of strategic force application" while rounds four and five entailed massive urban-industrial strikes.[6] Implementation of such a plan, no matter how controlled the initial rounds, would amount "in practice, to suicide on the instalment plan."[7]

The allocation of further resources to improving the survivability and endurance of the strategic command-and-control capabilities cannot substantially alter this situation. Command-and-control systems are inherently more vulnerable than the strategic forces themselves, and, while basic retaliatory commands would always get to the forces eventually, the capability to exercise strict control and co-ordination would inevitably be lost relatively early in a nuclear exchange.

Furthermore, the technical and strategic uncertainties are such that, regardless of the care and tight control which they attempt to exercise, decision-makers could never be confident that escalation could be controlled. Uncertainties in weapons effects and the accuracy with which weapons can be delivered mean that collateral casualties can never be calculated precisely and that particular strikes could look much less discriminating to the recipient than to the attack planner. The uncertainties are especially great with respect to the operation of particular C^3 [command, control, and communication] systems in a nuclear environment. The effects of EMP and transient radiation on electrical and electronic equipment have been simulated on many components but rarely on large systems (such as airborne command posts). Moreover much of the simulation of nuclear effects derives from extrapolation of data generated in the period before atmospheric nuclear tests were banned in 1963.

Given the impossibility of developing capabilities for controlling a nuclear exchange through to favourable termination, or of removing the residual uncertainties relating to controlling the large-scale use of nuclear weapons, *it is likely that decision-makers would be deterred from initiating nuclear strikes no matter how limited or selective the options available to them.* The use of nuclear weapons for controlled escalation is therefore no less difficult to envisage than the use of nuclear weapons for massive retaliation.

Of course, national security policies and postures are not designed solely for the prosecution of war. In both the United States and the Soviet Union, deterring war remains a primary national objective. It is an axiom in the strategic literature that the criteria for deterrence are different from those for war-fighting, and capabilities which would be deficient for one purpose could well be satisfactory for the other.[8] The large-scale investment of resources in command-and-control capabilities, together with high-level official declarations that the United States would be prepared to conduct limited, selective and tightly controlled strategic nuclear strikes (perhaps in support of extended deterrence), could therefore be valuable because they suggest US determination to act in limited ways—the demonstrable problems of control notwithstanding. However, viable deterrent postures require both capabilities and credibility, and it would seem that neither can be assumed to the extent that would be necessary for the concept of controlled nuclear war-fighting to act as a deterrent. Rather than devoting further resources to pursuing the chimera of controlled nuclear war, relatively more attention might be accorded to another means of satisfying the objectives that limited nuclear options are intended to meet. This is likely, in practice, to mean greater attention to the conditions of conventional deterrence.

NOTES

1. Testimony of Dr William J. Perry, Under Secretary of Defense for Research and Engineering, in Hearings before the Senate Armed Services Committee, *Department of Defense Authorization for Appropriations for Fiscal Year 1980*, Part 3, March–May 1979, p. 1437.

2. Carl-Friedrich von Weiszacker, 'Can A Third World War be Prevented?', *International Security* (vol. 5, no. 1), Summer 1980, p. 205.

3. John Steinbruner, 'National Security and the Concept of Strategic Stability', *Journal of Conflict Resolution* (vol. 22, no. 1), September 1978, p. 421.

4. Alain C. Enthoven, 'US Forces in Europe: How Many? Doing What?', *Foreign Affairs* (vol. 53, no. 3), April 1975, p. 514; Alain C. Enthoven and K. Wayne Smith, *How Much Is Enough?: Shaping the Defense Program, 1961–1969*, (New York: Harper and Row, 1971), p. 128.

5. Harold Brown, *Department of Defense Annual Report Fiscal Year 1981* (29 January 1980), p. 92.

6. Colin S. Gray, 'Targeting Problems for Central War', *Naval War College Review* (vol. 33, no. 1), January–February 1980, p. 9.

7. *Ibid.*, p. 7.

8. See André Beaufre, *Deterrence & Strategy*, (London: Faber & Faber, 1965), p. 24; and Glenn H. Snyder, *Deterrence & Defense: Toward a Theory of National Security*, (Princeton, N.J.: Princeton University Press, 1961), pp. 3–6.

22 INVITATION TO A NUCLEAR BEHEADING

Barry R. Schneider

Soviet Yankee-class submarines regularly operating 600 nautical miles from the East Coast of the United States can destroy Washington, D.C., within 8 to 10 minutes of launching one of their nuclear missiles.

It might be five minutes or more before the President of the United States could be alerted to the missile launch, too late to board his helicopter for Andrews Air Force Base, too late to escape in his National Emergency Airborne Command Post (NEACP) aircraft.

A ballistic-missile attack by Soviet submarines would likely doom the President, the Vice President, Cabinet members, the Joint Chiefs of Staff, and members of Congress who were in Washington, D.C., at the time. On most days, the American government lives in the shadow of this threat of nuclear decapitation.

The Soviets have repeatedly stressed, in their military training and writings, the importance of using nuclear forces to strike early and often in order to create a favorable outcome to a nuclear war. One of their wartime strategic goals, outlined in the *Soviet Military Encyclopedia*, is "the disorganization of the enemy's system of political and military command and control." In any nuclear war, our political and military leaders and their communications links are likely to be among the Soviets' highest priority targets.

The political and military leaders who are designated members of the chain of command for U.S. forces—they are called National Command Authorities (NCA)—must be able to survive a surprise attack in order to guide the country and carry out retaliatory blows. If the Soviets or other adversaries know the U.S. can survive and respond, they are unlikely to consider an attack worth the risk.

Any nuclear attack on the United States would thus probably be an act of irrational desperation. It is highly probable that even a sudden and annihilating blow against Washington would not prevent a devastating, if uncoordinated, American retaliatory attack. In the event that communications with Washington are totally severed, military officers at command centers outside the capital may have orders to launch a counterstrike.

Nevertheless, if a major weakness exists in deterrence strategy, it is in the vulnerability of the President and his successors to a decapitation attack. If the near complete extermination of U.S. National Command Authorities occurred, and if communication links to the U.S. strategic forces were largely destroyed, a Soviet attack might prevent a coordinated and coherent U.S. retaliation.

To ensure that the U.S. could employ its nuclear forces effectively, we must guarantee the survivability of strategic command, control, and communications—the links between the parts of the system, which are generally labeled C^3 (and sometimes C^3I, to include intelligence activities). C^3 is the nervous system of U.S. military forces. The National Command Authorities are the brain. Kill the brain or paralyze the nervous system and the arms cannot be used effectively. It is clearly in the U.S. interest to convince the Soviets that a nuclear decapitation attack could not work.

In more than 200 years of U.S. history, eight Presidents died in office and another resigned. In each case the Vice President became President and served until the term of office expired. A smooth transition may be impossible, however, under the circumstances of a nuclear attack on Washington.

According to Department of Defense Directive 5100.30, issued December 2, 1971, the National Command Authorities shall consist "only of the President and the Secretary of Defense or their duly deputized alternatives or successors." This system lends itself to confusion because of the twin lines of succession, one for the Presidency (provided for in the Constitution) and the other for the top command of U.S. military forces. In the case of a sitting elected President these top roles are combined in one person, someone who everyone agrees holds the reins of power. However, in the case of a dead, disabled or missing President, the lines of authority are less clear.

For example, who is in charge if the President is dead, the Vice President cannot be located or certified as living, and military decisions have to be made immediately? The answer is (1) Thomas O'Neill, Speaker of the House of Representatives, if he is alive and can be found and briefed, or (2) the Secretary of Defense and his successors. Once a Presidential successor like Sen. Thurmond has been "designated" by a central locator system run by the Federal Emergency Management Agency, he becomes the ultimate authority. However, short of finding the next Presidential successor, U.S. military decisions will be made by the Secretary of Defense or his successors.

That this is confusing was demonstrated in the moments following John Hinckley Jr.'s attempted assassination of President Reagan. As many Americans recall, Secretary of State Alexander Haig went on television and declared, "I am in charge." The facts were that Vice President Bush was out of town and President Reagan was unable to make decisions during his operation and the beginning of his recovery at George Washington University Hospital. What Haig overlooked was that Thomas O'Neill, as Speaker of the House of Representatives, was next in line to succeed the President, and the Secretary of State was not. Nor was Haig in charge of U.S. military forces, since the Secretary of State is not one of the designated successors to National Command Authority. That power was held by Secretary of Defense Caspar Weinberger.

Should the President die or be declared incapable of performing his duties, his successors would take power in this order:

1. Vice President . . .
2. Speaker of the House of Representatives . . .
3. President pro tempore of the Senate . . .
4. Secretary of State . . .
5. Secretary of the Treasury . . .
6. Secretary of Defense . . .
7. The Attorney General . . .
8. Secretary of the Interior . . .
9. Secretary of Agriculture . . .
10. Secretary of Commerce . . .
11. Secretary of Labor . . .
12. Secretary of Health and Human Services . . .
13. Secretary of Housing and Urban Development . . .
14. Secretary of Transportation . . .
15. Secretary of Energy . . .
16. Secretary of Education . . .

If U.S. military decisions needed to be made immediately because the U.S. was under attack, and the President and his successors were dead, or could not be located, the Secretary of Defense or his successors have the authority to order military forces into action.

1. Deputy Secretary of Defense . . .
2. Secretary of the Army . . .
3. Secretary of the Navy . . .
4. Secretary of the Air Force . . .
5. Under Secretary of Defense for Policy . . .
6. Under Secretary of Defense for Research and Engineering . . .
7. Eight Assistant Secretaries of Defense and the General Counsel to the Defense Department, in order of their length of service.
8. Under Secretaries of the Army, Navy, and Air Force, in order of their length of service.
9. Ten Assistant Secretaries of the Army, Navy, and Air Forces, in order of their length of service.

Unfortunately, every one of these individuals, whose orders might guide the activities of U.S. military forces in a nuclear war, lives and works in the Washington, D.C., area; and neither the Pentagon nor the White House is designed to survive nuclear attack. Indeed, the Soviet Union could probably destroy any fixed structure in the U.S. above ground, unless some way were found of actively defending it (with planes, missiles, or directed energy beams) or hardening it (that is, insulating it against the effects of blast and heat). Compared with other hardened targets, the White House and the Pentagon are considered soft and easily destroyed.

The chaos that a Soviet nuclear decapitation attack might cause would be difficult to overstate. Perhaps the most difficult question to answer in the hours after an attack would be, "Who is in charge here?" With Washington destroyed and all or nearly all of the Presidential and National Command Authorities dead or dying, and with most C^3 linkages damaged or destroyed, it would be difficult for military commanders to know who the President or top civilian authority was at any given time after an attack began. As one Defense Department C^3I expert wonders, "How does the new President find out that he is President, and how does he convince the National Command Authority that he is the President?"

The job of sorting all this out is delegated to the Federal Emergency Management Agency. FEMA director Louis Giuffrida has said that "[o]ne of the things we discovered is that there was no authentication system. So that if [someone] got on the horn and said, 'I'm the successor,' and somebody said, 'prove it,' [no one could]. So we're working on that. FEMA will be the authenticating mechanism to say, 'Yeah, this guy is for real. The President's gone, and we don't know where the Vice President is . . . and this is the man.'"

FEMA operates the central locator system that keeps daily tabs on the whereabouts of the President and his 16 successors. FEMA also is responsible for briefing Presidential successors on plans for their dispersal during attack and on procedures for reporting their locations at all times. It is charged by Congress with carrying out drills of the Presidential Successor Dispersal Plans four times a year and for testing the central locator system. Each year it conducts two joint Presidential and Presidential Successor Emergency Support Exercises, in which both the locator systems and plans for evacuation of command authorities go through a trial run. FEMA continues to test and develop the Joint Emergency Evacuation Plan (JEEP) to provide for emergency dispersal of several thousand senior government officials.

One potential problem, however, is that the agency and much of its system of communications may be as vulnerable to nuclear decapitation as the rest of the U.S. government. FEMA headquarters is in downtown

Washington, just a dozen blocks from the White House and well within the lethal radius of any thermonuclear weapon exploded over the capital.

Even if the FEMA central locator and authenticator system worked perfectly, however, and even if several Presidential successors survived, they might be ill-suited to take command of an America reeling from a nuclear attack and of military forces engaged in the conflict. How many U.S. Cabinet members know the first thing about national security and military affairs? How many have any notion about the forces at hand, and the means needed to terminate or prosecute the conflict in a manner that would salvage the most for the United States?

At a time when the United States government and the nation's people would require strong and decisive leadership, a successor who might be virtually unknown to the public would be groping for solutions to problems he or she had never been prepared to solve. One can imagine a U.S. government on Day Two of World War III headed by [the] Secretary of Labor (successor No. 11), or by [the] Secretary of Education (successor No. 16). The problems of directing the war could be compounded by the deaths of the Joint Chiefs of Staff, the elimination of the Pentagon and all high Defense Department officials, and the destruction of Strategic Air Command headquarters (SAC) near Omaha and the North American Defense headquarters (NORAD) inside Cheyenne Mountain near Colorado Springs.

The nightmares of those concerned with National Command Authority protection are likely to reach a peak on certain key days of the political calendar: during a Presidential Inauguration, for example, or when the President delivers his State of the Union Message to a joint session of Congress. Not only are virtually all the NCA and their successors present in Washington on those occasions, but they are usually concentrated in the same place or in a single building.

Of course, the Russians have the same problems in defending their top command. Decapitation of the Soviet leadership is theoretically possible every time the Politburo assembles in a meeting or ceremony. May Day in Moscow, when the Kremlin's leaders watch from the same reviewing stand, is a potential decapitation day. Just as Soviet submarines off the Atlantic coastline threaten U.S. leaders in Washington, so too can Poseidon submarines operating in European waters launch missiles that within minutes can destroy Red Square or the Kremlin Palace. In nuclear arms negotiations, both sides should consider agreeing to a mutual redeployment of weapons that would take their two capitals out of range for a decapitation attack.

Fortunately, a bolt-from-the-blue Soviet nuclear attack is unlikely. First, a crisis or escalating conventional conflict in some region of the world is the most likely scenario for such a risky attack. Second, the

Soviet rocket forces, ballistic-missile submarines, and strategic bombers could not be brought to full readiness for attack without first giving a warning to the United States. Given their uncertainties about whether they could decapitate the U.S. government, and their inability to know what action U.S. military leaders might take if our top political leaders were killed, the Russians would have to be mad to order a strike on Washington without also trying to destroy our nuclear retaliatory forces. The Soviet action of bringing their forces to full alert could provide strategic warning to U.S. leaders prior to an attack.

To avoid the threat of decapitation, the U.S. government plans to evacuate the National Command Authorities from Washington to National Emergency Airborne Command Post aircraft and to 96 hardened command bunkers in the Federal Relocation Arc, 50 or more miles outside of the city. The 96 hardened command centers are scattered around the countryside and include sites in North Carolina, West Virginia, Virginia, Maryland, Pennsylvania and the District of Columbia.

Survival of our top officials depends upon their ability to rendezvous with the National Emergency Airborne Command Post and to take off by the time Soviet warheads hit Washington. The NEACP is based at Andrews Air Force Base, about 10 miles east of the White House, although the command authorities could also rendezvous with the aircraft at a number of other designated sites in the Eastern United States.

The President presumably would be transported to the rendezvous point by the Crown helicopter. Timing could be crucial if the crisis is sudden and there has been little advance warning. To fly from the White House to Andrews would take about eight minutes; it might be twice that before the President was safely aloft in the NEACP and away from the D.C. area.

During the "Ivy League" dispersion drill run in March 1982, President Reagan elected to stay in the White House and to send Vice President Bush aloft in NEACP. Earlier, President Carter also decided that in a crisis he would remain in the White House, and his National Security Adviser, Zbigniew Brzezinski, elected to do the same. Instead, Vice President Mondale and the Deputy Assistant for National Security, David Aaron, were designated for travel aloft in NEACP aircraft. In his recent book, *Power and Principle: Memoirs of the National Security Adviser 1977–1981*, Brzezinski related how his career (and life) almost came to an abrupt end on the evening of January 28, 1977, when he decided to test the Presidential emergency evacuation procedures:

"I called in the person responsible for evacuating the President in the event of a crisis. I obtained a detailed account on how long it actually would take to evacuate the President by helicopter. . . . I ordered him to run a simulated evacuation right now, turning on my stopwatch. The poor fellow's eyes . . . practically popped: He looked so surprised. He said, 'Right now?' And I said, 'Yes, right now.' He reached for the phone and could hardly speak coherently when he demanded that the helicopter immediately come for a drill. I took one of the secretaries . . . along to simulate Mrs. Carter, and we proceeded to the South Lawn to wait for the helicopter to arrive. It took roughly two and a half times as long to arrive as it was supposed to. We then flew to a special site from where another evacuation procedure would be followed. To make a long story short, the whole thing took roughly twice as long as it should have. Moreover, on our return we found that the drill somehow did not take into account the protective service and we were almost shot down."

The U.S. government has relocation plans for several thousand top officials who are considered vital to the continuity of government in a national emergency. All will be evacuated to sites in the Federal Relocation Arc or sent aloft in aircraft.

The most important alternative U.S. headquarters is the "underground White House," which is situated inside Raven Rock Mountain in Pennsylvania about 65 miles northwest of Washington and just five miles north of Camp David. This location is the home of the Alternative National Military Command Center and is equipped to house the President and other members of the National Command Authority. In the largest evacuation exercise to date, President Dwight Eisenhower and 1,500 top Federal officials moved the seat of power from Washington to Raven Rock Mountain for three days in 1955. In the same exercise, 13,500 other officials were dispersed to 30 different secret locations in the Arc.

Another important relocation center is a man-made cavern within Mount Weather, situated 50 miles northwest of Washington, just outside Bluemont, Virginia, along the Appalachian Trail. The official name for this command post is the Western Virginia Office of Controlled Conflict Operations.

Inside the mountain is a small city of multistoried buildings, including offices, apartments, dormitories, streets, sidewalks, cafeterias, hospitals, power plants, and a water purifying plant. This subterranean wartime capital is the product of 21 years of demolition, mining, excavation, and building by the U.S. Army Corps of Engineers. The Mount Weather complex contains detailed plans for running and rebuilding the U.S. economy and society, and for reconstituting the U.S. government in wartime conditions.

The sites of Federal Relocation Centers are probably well-known to Soviet war planners. Most were built before the Soviet Union had installed its very accurate fourth generation of intercontinental ballistic missiles. Now, Soviet SS-17s, SS-18s and SS-19s are capable of destroying virtually any hardened bunker. With the size and accuracy of these Soviet weapons, the military command posts at Raven Rock Mountain and Mount Weather could be reduced to radioactive ruins within a half hour.

Speaking of the Federal Relocation Centers, Bardyl Tirana, former head of the Defense Civil Preparedness Agency (now part of FEMA), has said, "You know where they are. Presumably if you do, the Soviet Union does. It's the last place I'd want to be."

If dispersion to fixed, hardened sites can no longer protect U.S. leaders from nuclear decapitation, airborne mobility at least provides a solution for the first 72 hours. With aerial refueling, the E4 evacuation aircraft need not land for three days.

But a decapitation attack does not have to kill the U.S. President and his successors to be effective. It must only sever the President's communication lines with the U.S. military and the rest of the government. As General Curtis LeMay, former head of the Strategic Air Command, used to say, "Without communications, the only thing I command is my desk." The same is true of the President or any National Command Authority. A Carnegie Institute for International Peace study recently noted:

"Strategic command, control, communications and intelligence is often characterized as the 'weakest link' in America's deterrent against Soviet attack. . . . Most experts say that major portions of the strategic C^3I system have been vulnerable for some time and that survivability of C^3I as a system sufficient to support our declared strategic nuclear policies is far more doubtful than is the survivability of the forces. At the same time that the C^3I system has been recognized as vulnerable to Soviet attack, shifts in American strategic nuclear doctrine have placed greater demands upon it. The challenge is not so much to transmit a single order for all-out attack—though some question even that—as to provide the endurance necessary for a controlled and flexible response."

John Steinbruner, director of foreign policy studies at the Brookings Institution, states the C^3I vulnerability problem in stark terms:

". . . The United States does not have a strategic command system that could survive deliberate attack of a sort that the Soviet Union could readily undertake. Fewer than 100 judiciously targeted nuclear weapons could so severely damage U.S. communications facilities and command centers that form the military chain of command that the actions of individual weapons commanders could no longer be controlled or coordinated. Some bomber crews, submarine officers, and ICBM silo launch officers could undertake very damaging retaliation and hence continue to pose a deterrence threat. Nonetheless, even 50 nuclear weapons are probably sufficient to eliminate the ability to direct U.S. strategic forces to coherent purposes."

The C^3I network has been neglected, partly because nuclear-weapons effects, notably from radiation, are not completely understood or easily calculated, and partly because protecting the network is both difficult and expensive. The present network was built ad hoc, piece by piece, each part tailored for a specific purpose, but without an authoritative provision for their overall coherent interaction.

The President and the strategic forces might be easier to protect than many of the links in the communications system. Early-warning radars, telephone lines, cables, relay stations, telephone exchanges, transmitters, receivers, and antennae are fixed, soft targets that cannot easily be moved. Some elements of the U.S. C^3I system can be dispersed and made mobile, but nearly all are vulnerable to different types of interruption, destruction, and interference. And, as Desmond Ball, an Australian command-control analyst, noted in a recent study published by the London-based International Institute for Strategic Studies:

"There will always be some critical nodal points—e.g., where communication links connect to the command posts and, most especially, where the chain of command and control originates at the national command level—which can neither be hardened nor duplicated. It is axiomatic that the chain of command is only as strong as its weakest link."

The C^3I network is vulnerable to nuclear blast, heat, and radiation effects, as well as attack by conventional weapons and sabotage. High-altitude nuclear explosions can block out radars, interfere with radio transmission, and short out electrical circuitry. A nuclear explosion emits an electromagnetic pulse (EMP), a large pulse of energy that can create chaos in a C^3I system. It can overload power lines, burn out telephone lines, short-circuit microprocessors, and render buried cables ineffective transmitters of messages. The new microchip semiconductors used in all kinds of mechanical, electrical, and communications devices are a million times more vulnerable to electromagnetic pulse than the older vacuum tubes that they have been replacing. EMP could erase computer memories and even change missile flight trajectories by altering internal missile electrical functions. EMP could also create power outages all over the U.S.

According to Daniel L. Stein, professor of physics at Princeton University: "A [one megaton] detonation at 500 kilometers above the central continental United States will effectively blanket the entire country, as well as parts of Canada and Mexico." Aside from military effects, Stein fears EMP from just a few detonations could cause a coast-to-coast power shutdown in the U.S.

At present, only one of the four National Emergency Airborne Command Post aircraft is hardened against EMP effects, although money is now being requested and spent to harden the others. Certainly the "Crown Helo" and even the NEACP might not withstand the EMP effects of nuclear detonations. Both types of aircraft are hardened by insulating wiring and sealing cracks that would otherwise permit entry of the EMP voltage. U.S. aircraft and weapons have been tested on an EMP simulator at Kirtland Air Force Base for their ability to withstand an electromagnetic pulse of 50,000 volts per meter. According to one report, even EMP-hardened systems might not survive.

The technical community is divided on this issue. "Some French physicists, among others, envision a pulse of about 100,000 volts per meter," writes science journalist William Broad. "If they are correct, the normal protections the Pentagon has tried to build into communications networks, missiles, aircraft, radars and radios would almost certainly be useless." If overloaded by the EMP pulse, NEACP could be disabled and might fall to the earth like a stone, with the President and his battle staff aboard.

EMP could have other impacts on U.S. C^3 aircraft. The so-called Take Charge and Move Out aircraft (TACAMO) used to relay the go-to-war message to U.S. ballistic-missile submarines are not yet EMP-hardened and just might be silenced in wartime before they could communicate the emergency action message to the submarine fleet.

Looking Glass, an airborne SAC EC-135 aircraft, is another important link between U.S. ICBM forces and the National Command Authority. This airborne post would operate as Strategic Airborne Command headquarters in the likely event that the ground-based SAC headquarters is destroyed in the attack. The importance of *Looking Glass* was illustrated by testimony by the late General John C. Meyers, former SAC Commander, who declared: "If SAC funding is reduced to the level that we can only keep one airplane flying, that plane will be the *Looking Glass*."

Unfortunately, *Looking Glass* could be vulnerable to EMP effects, too. So might other C^3I aircraft, such as planes of the Post-Attack Command and Control System (PACCS), which operate mainly out of Offutt Air Force Base and have maintained a constant airborne patrol over the past 22 years. These aircraft act as alternative command centers for SAC bombers and missile forces.

A U.S. nuclear test in the earth's atmosphere in 1962, code-named Starfish Prime, vividly demonstrated the effects of EMP on electronic circuits. In the test, a missile-borne package was launched from Johnston Atoll in the South Pacific, 820 miles southwest of Hawaii, and exploded 248 miles above the Earth's surface. EMP pulses traveling at the speed of light short-circuited 300 streetlights, disabled numerous power lines, and blew out other electric circuits on Oahu. The EMP pulse disrupted communications throughout Honolulu.

The Limited Test Ban Treaty in 1963 put an end to atmospheric nuclear tests before military physicists could explain the havoc created by EMP in Hawaii. Subsequent underground tests indicated the EMP problem was even worse than originally feared. More recently, the spread of solid-state integrated circuits has served to compound the danger.

The introduction of fiber optics to replace current materials is possibly the most effective means of blocking EMP pulses, since glass fibers do not pick up EMP or conduct electricity. But unless the entire U.S. C³I system could be so revised (at a prohibitive cost), the EMP danger will remain with us.

Ironically, the C³I vulnerability of U.S. and Soviet forces is a great equalizer. Both societies and both command networks are extremely vulnerable to disruption caused by just a few well-placed nuclear weapons.

As John Steinbruner of the Brookings Institution has noted: "The substantial superiority, for example, that the United States believed it possessed in the 1960s was sharply mitigated in reality by command vulnerability, which was particularly acute at the time. The then numerically and technically inferior Soviet forces could have done far more damage with judicious targeting than was ever acknowledged in official U.S. public reviews of the strategic situation.

"U.S. forces have always been seriously vulnerable to an initial attack, and the 1980s will not produce unusual dangers in this regard, as is often alleged."

The danger of decapitation attacks would seem to make a mockery of the idea of fighting limited nuclear wars, or protracted nuclear wars. Even if U.S. leaders somehow survived a first-wave Soviet attack, our command-control network is so perishable in a nuclear environment that a slow, tit-for-tat "walk" up and down the escalation ladder seems unlikely.

Such a conclusion belies the current official thinking that nuclear war might be kept limited, and that it might be winnable. For a graduated response to nuclear attack implies the survival of a communications-intelligence network to measure the precise response to each escalation. As one observer has concluded: ". . . the number of missiles launched in an attack must be determined immediately, damage assessment must occur within hours, and communications between warring parties must survive the initial strike."

The C³I technology simply is not there, nor will it likely be there even after the United States spends the planned $60 billion on modernizing the network over the next five years. The problems of adequately protecting the network and the leadership simply dwarf the available near-term solutions.

"The kinds of controlled nuclear options to which we're moving presume communication with the Soviet Union," notes Lt. General Brent Scowcroft, former National Security Adviser to President Ford. "And yet, from a military point of view, one of the most effective kinds of attack is against leadership and command and control systems."

Unfortunately, these vulnerabilities undermine our ability to deter war by less than all-out nuclear retaliation in the first minutes of attack.

The vulnerability on both sides after such an exchange of nuclear fusillades might preclude calling off the conflict. Indeed, negotiations to halt the slaughter might be impossible until both sides had expended their nuclear forces in a terrible agony of blow and counterblow. Once begun, a nuclear exchange between the superpowers is likely to be massive and virtually uncontrollable.

23 CIVIL DEFENSE: STRATEGIC IMPLICATIONS, PRACTICAL PROBLEMS

John M. Weinstein

INTRODUCTION

The cumulative effect of the massive expansion and modernization of the strategic and conventional forces of the Soviet Union has caused many to reevaluate the strategic balance between the superpowers. Specifically, there has been substantial concern about the Soviet development of a potent first-strike capability. This assessment, arrived at by the last two US administrations, reflects a number of technological improvements in the Soviet Strategic Rocket Forces (SRF) which appear ominous in light of Soviet strategic operational employment plans which stress seizing the strategic initiative through preemptive attacks against American ICBM launch silos, launch control facilities, support and maintenance facilities, strategic bomber bases, submarine berths and loading facilities, and nuclear storage and production facilities. . . .

Within this context, a number of civilian and military analysts take a particular ominous view of the Soviet Union's long-standing attention to civil defense. In light of America's inattention to civil defense since the aftermath of the Cuban missile crisis, numerous implications have been drawn from alleged Soviet plans and capabilities to undertake crisis relocation of urban populations, to disperse and harden industry, and to achieve rapid postattack recovery. Most serious among these implications is the potential effect of Soviet civil defense capabilities upon the real or perceived stability of deterrence. Specifically, some contend that the Soviet civil defense program threatens deterrence by upsetting the balance of mutual population vulnerability if, under certain conditions, Soviet civil defense measures might limit their fatalities to the low "tens of millions." According to 1979 projections by the Congressional Office of Technology Assessment and 1982 Congressional testimony, significant asymmetries exist in the number of US and Soviet fatalities that would occur in several nuclear warfighting scenarios. In most scenarios, the percentage of American casualties is double that of the Soviet Union

Note: Some footnotes have been deleted, and others have been renumbered to appear in consecutive order. An unedited version of the paper can be found in Robert Kennedy and John M. Weinstein, *The Defense of the West* (Boulder, Colo.: Westview Press, 1984).

and in an all-out Soviet attack upon the US population and its counterforce, military and economic targets, American fatalities might range as high as 88 percent of the population.

Furthermore, it is frequently argued that Soviet civil defense capabilities could threaten deterrence stability to the degree that they protect that country's economic power and recovery prospects relative to those of the United States. Such projected asymmetries are destabilizing because they suggest that under certain circumstances, the Soviet Union might emerge from a nuclear war in a better position than that of the United States. If the Soviet Union were to perceive nuclear war as potentially less costly and, thus, less frightening, they might feel more inclined in a crisis to launch a preemptive strike against the United States.

Those who are concerned about Soviet civil defense improvements are also frequently among those concerned over the comparative lack of US civil defense measures. Often these critics contend that there are several additional implications that result from the inability of the United States to protect its citizens or production base from nuclear assaults. First, America's allies would naturally have less confidence in the US nuclear umbrella if they could envision a situation in which the United States were facing a choice between sacrificing New York or assenting to Soviet coercion or occupation of Oslo or Bonn. Second, tactical nuclear weapons, whose use might escalate to a strategic exchange, might "no longer substitute for conventional strength as credibly as they did in the past."[1] Any resulting loosening of the bonds between the United States and its NATO allies might contribute ultimately to the disintegration of NATO and other US alliance systems. Such developments would constitute a major blow to US security and realize one of the principal Soviet postwar objectives. Finally, defensive inferiority might subject the United States to Soviet coercion with few alternatives to acquiescence, irrespective of raw, destructive power. . . .

This [selection] will (1) examine the effectiveness of the Soviet civil defense program, selected Soviet strategic vulnerabilities, and Soviet views of deterrence, and (2) evaluate the direction and scope of the current US civil defense program. . . .

SOVIET CIVIL DEFENSE: PLANS AND PROBLEMS

Population Protection

Protection of leadership is considered of paramount importance to Soviet civil defense planners. The CIA notes that sufficient blast-resistant shelter space exists to protect approximately 110,000 Soviet government and Party officials at all levels.[2] A second priority is the protection of workers at essential industrial installations. By current estimates, the Soviet Union has shelter space for 24–48 percent of the essential work force or 12 to 24 percent of the total work force that would be left behind in the event of crisis evacuation. Those most concerned about the estimated Soviet ability to protect much of their critical political and industrial populace point to several disquieting ramifications. First, while conceding the US ability to destroy shelters which are targetted directly, these shelters must first be identified, hardly an easy or assured task for intelligence. Second, the destruction of these shelters would require continued survival and connectivity of US strategic communications and missile installations as well as the expenditure of a disproportionately large percentage of land-based, hard target-killing warheads on these targets. Third, the survival of the Soviet political and military command and control systems might provide a capability to fight a protracted nuclear war designed to outlast the US adversary. Finally, the survival of key political and industrial cadres would facilitate rapid economic reconstruction vis-à-vis the United States.

Those who question the potential adverse impact of Soviet shelter capabilities counter with several points. First, a first-strike capability that exists on paper does not guarantee that it will exist under uncertain and confusing actual attack conditions. Second, the estimates of available Soviet shelter space are open to question. The CIA estimates that the space available for each person in a shelter would be only one-half to one square meter. This space allotment is inadequate according to most analyses of long-term survival requirements. In addition, the Oak Ridge Laboratories maintain that the shelters' ventilation systems are their most vulnerable aspect and that, even if a shelter were not destroyed by a nuclear blast, its inhabitants would risk suffocation and death from asphyxiation or heat exposure. Starvation also would prove to be a severe problem if shelter were required for more than a few days. Chronic Soviet food shortages make it unlikely that the Soviet Union would prestock shelters for more than a few days during peacetime. Furthermore, normal food distribution snarls, and the fact that Soviet citizens buy their food from day to day, are likely to prevent many from bringing additional supplies of food and water to the shelter. Even . . . Deputy Under Secretary of Defense for Strategic and Theater Nuclear Forces, T. K. Jones, an analyst who has written extensively on the dangerous implications of Soviet civil defense capabilities, concedes that inplace urban shelters "could not help much against a US attack designed to destroy populations." Thus, it is argued that the Soviet Union is likely to harbor few illusions about the potential success of its civil defense programs in a nuclear war with the United States. Furthermore, since urban shelters are not in place to protect the average Soviet citizen (assigned the lowest priority in the Soviet civil defense program), such citizens would be forced to build expedient shelters using "handy" materials and tools such as bricks, timber, boards, and shovels. Their plight would be compounded at night, during autumn when the ground is muddy, or winter when the ground is frozen, or during spring and summer when foodstuffs are depleted.

Finally, Leon Goure, author of numerous articles and studies of Soviet civil defense, described elaborate Soviet evacuation plans that are to be carried out by the urban populace within 72 hours after an evacuation order is issued. However, those who question the potential value of such an evacuation point out that the Soviet Union has never practiced full-scale evacuation of a major city; used more than one mode of transportation in their limited practice; conducted a drill without a long period of preparation; or carried out several evacuation exercises simultaneously.

The Soviet road network is one of the country's major strategic vulnerabilities. Because it has been constructed to accommodate travel within that country's cities, it would be hard pressed to support mass exoduses by motor transport or by foot from these cities. One report states that:

> [The Soviet Union] lacks a developed highway system to connect the outlying regions to its industrial hub. Less than 250,000 miles of paved roads exist in the entire nation. No two Soviet cities are connected by a divided highway. . . . In addition, Soviet severe weather conditions hamper what possible road travel exists. During the winter, spring thaw periods, and autumn rainy seasons, Soviet roads are virtually impassable. The Soviets describe their situation as *Rasputitsa* or roadlessness during those months.[3]

In addition to motor transport, Soviet evacuation plans depend heavily on railroads. Most railroads in the Soviet Union, however, are single track. To evacuate large cities by rail transportation, the Soviet Union would have to arrange that the trains were in their assigned evacuation locations and that they were not loaded with freight or allocated to carry troops or supplies to Eastern Europe. That so many logistical problems would be handled by a country whose transportation system is inefficient, at best, during calm and peaceful times is questionable.

Moreover, since most Soviet citizens do not have automobiles, Soviet evacuation plans also call for some 17 million urban residents to walk 30 miles (1.5 mph for 20 hours) and then build expedient protection. How the very young, the very old, and the sick are to make such formidable progress (while carrying two weeks' worth of food, water, and supplies) is not clear. Furthermore, how evacuees in expedient shelters would survive the higher levels of radioactive fallout that would result if the US retaliatory strike included ground bursts, is unclear and is seldom addressed by those who assert the effectiveness of Soviet civil defense.

The Soviet urban population, largely an apartment society, is more highly concentrated than the American urban population. This heavy concentration of urban citizens results in certain obstacles to successful evacuation. For instance, Moscow is surrounded on all sides by satellite industrial centers, and Leningrad is similarly bordered on three sides and by water on the fourth. Citizens from these population centers would face major problems evacuating to rural reception centers or areas suitable for the construction of expedient shelters.

Even if one disregards the logistical problems that would attend a decision to evacuate Soviet cities and assumes that such a momentous exodus could be executed, the Soviet Union would still face a major strategic dilemma. The declaratory policy of the United States . . . es-chew[s] the targeting of the Soviet population *per se*. Within this context, one may wonder what impact from a Soviet perspective the evacuation of its citizens would have on deterring an American retaliatory strike. Civilian evacuation serves certain humanitarian goals, but it has little effect upon the US ability to destroy critical Soviet military, industrial, and economic targets. The destruction of Soviet civilians would be an unintended effect of US plans to destroy Soviet military and economic infrastructures under certain retaliation scenarios. . . . [I]t could even be argued that the successful evacuation and survival of the Soviet Union's civilian population might prove detrimental to the country's long-term prospects for recovery. In the aftermath of a US retaliatory strike, one may wonder how the Soviet leadership plans to care for two hundred million survivors with the devastation of its economic, agri-cultural, medical, and transportation infrastructures.

With "strangelovian" logic, one could argue that rapid recovery in-deed might be more expeditious and effective with fewer rather than more survivors to drain scarce recovery materiel. The crucial element of civil defense revolves, then, around the ability of the Soviet Union to protect its economy and sustain survivors of a nuclear war.

The Protection of Soviet Industry

Traditionally, Soviet leadership has sought to protect their industry by two means: geographical dispersal and hardening against nuclear attack. Little is debated about the effectiveness of Soviet programs to protect their industry from the primary and collateral effects of a nuclear attack by means of the former. . . . More debate has concerned the effective-ness and implications of Soviet efforts to harden their industrial instal-lations. . . . [T]he Soviet leadership has opted for low-cost means of protecting vital equipment from secondary damage of nuclear explo-sives. These "engineering-technical" measures include rapid shutdown of equipment for protection against electromagnetic impulse; the use of expedient protective devices (e.g., wooden and metal bracing, covering equipment with sandbags, and the like), acknowledged by the Arms Control and Disarmament Agency (ACDA) as effective in areas on the periphery of a nuclear blast; contamination protection, and the protection of raw material supplies through underground storage. In a two-year study of the effectiveness of Soviet expedient measures, T. K. Jones concluded: "Russian methods could protect machinery within the three-day warning that would be provided by a Soviet evacuation. A full scale attack could be absorbed and production could renew in four to twelve weeks."[4] Such projections take on chilling importance if one posits that a Soviet preemptive strike knocked out as much as 90 percent of the accurate land-based US missiles, leaving the United States with less accurate SLBMs and its aging bomber fleet (which would have to penetrate increasingly sophisticated air defenses) to deliver the retaliatory strike. In such a scenario, the relatively limited destructiveness of the US response might seem tolerable to Soviet military planners.

Critics of this line of argumentation respond that a substantial gap exists between the theoretical and actual abilities to mount a successful first strike. They maintain that the Soviet leaders, who are normally cautious in military operations, would be loathe to gamble the survival of their state on the many unknown parameters relating to the coordination, timing, effects and consequences of so precipitous an action as a nuclear strike against the United States.

These same critics also point to the inability of the Soviet Union to harden many of the critical industries upon which their fragile economy and continued superpower status depend. These vulnerable industries include oil refineries; power plants; chemical storage plants; steel mills; pharmaceutical laboratories; component assembly factories; major truck, tractor, and rolling-stock plants; railheads and marshaling yards; major surface transshipment points and highway intersections; and pipelines. Because these targets cannot be hardened and their destruction does not require the pinpoint accuracy of ICBMs, they remain vulnerable to a US retaliatory strike. . . .

Third, these critics focus upon the observation . . . that after absorbing a first strike, the United States would be able to hit only a "few thousand aim points," precluding the infliction of unacceptable damage on the Soviet Union. Critics committed to an assured destruction philosophy contend that Soviet industry (50 percent of which is contained in 200 complexes) and the transportation and power infrastructure that support it are so concentrated in a narrow crescent stretching from Leningrad through Moscow, Sverdlovsk, Omsk, Novosibirsk and to Irkutsk that the United States would not require many weapons to achieve its Soviet industrial damage requirements. . . . Geoffrey Kemp[5] and Richard Garwin,[6] both prominent students of strategic studies, maintain respectively that as few as seven Poseidon submarines (one-third of the number normally on station at sea) could destroy 61 percent of the Soviet industrial base and that, even if only 10 percent of US ICBMs survived a Soviet preemptive strike, those 100-110 missiles could be retargetted (assuming the survival of American C^3 facilities) to deliver unacceptable damage to the Soviet Union. An ACDA estimate that recognizes the need for no more than 1300 warheads to destroy 70 percent of Soviet industry is consistent with these estimates.

Finally, and most crucial, is that even if one accepts the argument that the Soviet Union can protect individual pieces of industrial equipment from proximate nuclear detonations, it does not follow that the resumption of industrial production will be a near-term proposition. Industrial reconstitution and recovery will be hampered by a number of factors. For instance, how will production be resumed if the electrical infrastructure and available supplies of and transmission lines for diesel fuel, gasoline and petroleum are destroyed? How will industrial activity and recovery be realized if stocks of raw materials and the six rail transshipment points which load 80 percent of all empty railcars and are critical to the Soviet industrial supply and distribution are destroyed also? How will workers deal with residual radiation in targetted areas, especially in the absence of easy access to medical personnel and supplies? And who will feed, clothe and shelter workers and protect their equipment during the recovery phase?

Postattack Recovery

Absent effective protection measures, the significant and vulnerable concentration of Soviet industry . . . makes T. K. Jones' prediction that the Soviet Union could recover "within no more than 2 to 4 years from a US nuclear retaliatory attack"[7] appear optimistic at best.

The psychological condition of the survivors is critically important for postattack recovery. Yet those who examine nuclear attack/recovery scenarios say little about this variable, implicitly assuming that as a result of their civil defense training, (1) the survivors of Armageddon would calmly set about postattack reconstruction in a disciplined and effective manner; and (2) that the termination of the nuclear crisis and threat of continued exchanges would be unambiguous and evacuees would willingly return to their homes to aid their fellow citizens and begin reconstruction.

Such discipline and cooperative effort may not occur in the aftermath of nuclear war. The reactions of the survivors of Hiroshima and Nagasaki offer a limited, though imperfect, insight into what might be expected in the aftermath of a Soviet-American nuclear exchange. They expected that they were about to die. As a means of protection from the grotesque scenes around them, they closed their minds to the ubiquitous horror. This psychic numbing, causing profound blandness and insensitivity to the surrounding suffering, was temporary and dissipated as the outside world responded with aid to the victims of the disaster. A nuclear war, however, would result in unprecedented destruction and limit the amount of aid available from the "outside," especially if the war were massive in nature. Robert J. Lifton, a noted psychiatrist who has written extensively on the subject, concludes that the devastation that would attend a nuclear exchange would probably give rise to such extreme psychic numbing as described above that its effects would be irreversible.[8] . . .

According to Lifton, a major consequence of psychic shock could be the inability of the survivors to gather food, to bury their own dead, and perform other basic social rituals. Their behavior could be characterized by extreme suspiciousness and primitive forms of thought. Furthermore, Lifton argues that those from unscathed regions may not be willing to aid the survivors and share their horror. In light of these considerations, the prospects for the assured and disciplined recovery posited by Jones and others appear less certain.

Recovery from a nuclear attack depends heavily on the capability to rescue, feed, and care for the survivors and on the capability to provide repair parts and energy for capital reconstruction. Under certain strategic exchange scenarios . . . Soviet recovery efforts would be hampered severely by numerous obstacles. Massive urban areas could be too "hot"— too radioactive—to enter for several months. Depending upon the profile and scale of a US retaliatory strike, radiation sickness could be widespread, with 80 percent of the Soviet population, including the evacuees, having been exposed to at least 100 roentgens of radioactivity. In light of the coincidence of Soviet major food producing regions and its ICBM fields which would surely be targetted in a counterforce scenario, food would be in short supply. Half of the country's grazing livestock would be dead and, if the attack occurred during the growing season, 30 percent of all crops would be destroyed. Attempts to distribute surviving foodstuffs from farms and emergency storage sites could be delayed for several months, and this estimate is probably optimistic since the Soviet Union's 28 ICBM installations are interspersed throughout the heart of the rail network (See Figure 1). The ozone layer might be so depleted that outdoor activity beyond 30 minutes in duration would be hazardous for several years. As much as 80 percent of all medical personnel, supplies, and hospitals are likely to be destroyed. And, of course, a host of social and psychological problems would ensue. . . .

The most critical obstacle that would hamper Soviet efforts to achieve postwar recovery . . . relates to command and control (C^2). The pace and extent of recovery will depend heavily upon the ability of the na-

Figure 1

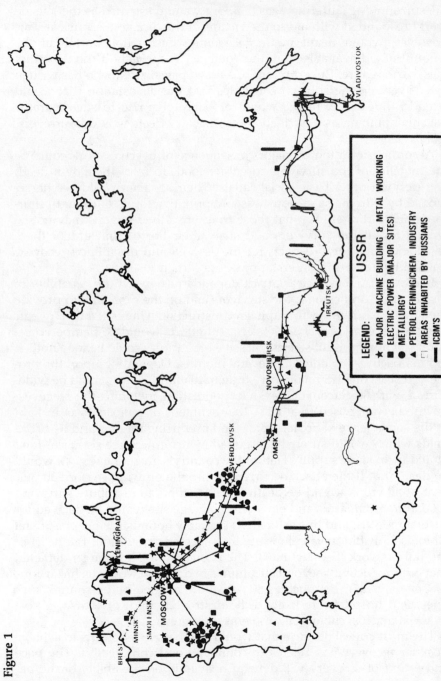

Source: Central Intelligence Agency, "USSR Summary Map," Department of Defense, *Soviet Military Power* (Washington, D.C.: U.S. Government Printing Office, 1983).

tional and regional political and party leaders to establish a consensus on national priorities, communicate their directives, and coordinate materiel supply and human effort. These recovery requisites, however, are likely to be affected adversely by the multinational nature of the Soviet society and the potential fragility of the various infrastructures of control. While many analysts have described (1) the polyglot composition of the Soviet Union; (2) the declining percentage of Great Russians and ethnic Slavs in the population relative to the rapidly increasing numbers of Moslems and Central Asians (who traditionally have resisted incorporation into the Russian empire); and (3) the ominous economic and political consequences of these developments for the Soviet policy, relatively few have recognized the Soviet state as multinational when the discussion turns to the matter of strategic deterrence and the requisites of postattack recovery. Indeed this consideration is paramount in Soviet strategic calculations. Recognizing the geographical coincidence of the majority of ICBM fields, key industrial installations and rail lines, and Great Russian population concentrations in a narrow Leningrad to Irkutsk crescent (See Figure 1) . . . even a limited American counterforce strike against the Soviet Union's missile and C^3 installations would affect most seriously the Great Russians who would perish in numbers disproportionately higher than their rapidly declining percentage (52 percent) of the total population. Whether they would be able to maintain control of the vast governmental, Communist Party, educational, and military hierarchies is questionable. Nuclear war might well usher in the decline of the Soviet empire in light of the current American interest in retaliatory targeting of the Russian dominated infrastructures of political and ethnic control, communication, and transportation in various escalation scenarios. . . .

Even if one assumes that the Soviet infrastructure of political control remained intact in the aftermath of a nuclear strike, it would still have to confront the problem of economic recovery. . . . During this period of incapacitation, could the Soviet leaders be confident that they could maintain the integrity of the Soviet Union? Is it likely that the Soviet-Moslem population might reaffirm religious and territorial ties to a Pan-Moslem movement? Would the nationalists in the Ukraine or the Baltic republics attempt to secede? And would the Russians have the wherewithal to prevent such centrifugal forces? Finally, would the East Europeans be inclined to maintain their political and economic ties to the Soviet Union? Assumptions and the role of uncertainty play heavily on the calculus of deterrence and one cannot be certain of the way leaders in the Kremlin arrive at their strategic estimates.

It is quite possible that, given the priority placed upon leadership survival in Soviet civil defense plans, the Russian leadership may view its own survival as a sufficient objective in its own right. If, however, the Russian leaders entertain uncertainties such as those described above, and in my opinion they do, and if they view civil defense as having a limited mitigating effect upon the problems outlined above, nuclear war necessarily would be viewed as counterproductive to their most basic national interests: the survival and integrity of the Soviet state, its rapid reconstitution and continuation of superpower status.

SOVIET CIVIL DEFENSE: IN SEARCH OF A BOTTOM LINE

The essential debate surrounding the Soviet civil defense program is the extent to which Soviet plans and goals could be translated into damage-limiting benefits in an actual nuclear exchange with the United States. . . . Civil defense, though admittedly imperfect, takes on substantial weight when viewed as a component of a Soviet warfighting strategy that also emphasizes other damage-limiting expedients such as a first strike against US warmaking capabilities and active (e.g., air and antisatellite) defense against actual US retaliatory strikes. If not, why would the Soviet leaders continue to spend increasingly scarce defense rubles on a civil defense program they consider ineffective? . . .

Skeptics of the Soviet civil defense program make several counter-arguments. Civil defense spending, they argue, continues due to a number of extraneous factors, such as bureaucratic inertia, legitimizing the continuation of the garrison state, Leninist ideological imperatives, and so forth. Also, to the skeptics, either the devastation of limited war is so great as to render it indistinguishable from unlimited war or there is little chance that a limited war would remain limited. Therefore, they liken Soviet (and US) civil defense efforts to the uneasy whistling of a frightened stroller in a cemetery at midnight. Surely, they argue, the normally cautious Soviet leaders recognize (1) the numerous, uncontrollable and uncertain nature of nuclear war, (2) the likelihood that the US deterrent will remain credible into the 1990's, and (3) that nuclear war between the superpowers will be an unprecedented disaster for each combatant—his civil defense preparations notwithstanding. . . .

. . . It is evident that the Soviet civil defense programs are imperfect and are beset most certainly with herculean problems. However, such programs are firmly in place and would probably reduce the number of deaths and contribute to economic recovery in the aftermath of a strategic exchange with the United States. The exact contributions of Soviet civil defense to their warfighting and war-survival capabilities as well as their perceptions of security are impossible to determine. The ambiguity of such speculation is illustrated in the "bottom line" of the CIA's 1978 study which, while stating that civil defense capabilities will not alter the Soviet leadership's evaluation of their efficacy, offers no insight into the actual level of those perceived capabilities. A conclusion of the CIA study was that:

> Present evidence does not suggest that in the foreseeable future there will be any significant change in the Soviet leaders' judgment that civil defense contributes to warfighting and war-survival capabilities, nor that their uncertainties about its effectiveness would be lessened. Thus we have no reason to believe that the Soviet leaders' perception of the contribution of civil defense to their capabilities for strategic nuclear conflict will change significantly.[9]

CIVIL DEFENSE PLANNING IN THE UNITED STATES

The Recent Initiatives

The increasing lethality of the Soviet nuclear threat, as well as asymmetries in the projected numbers of Soviet and American citizens that would survive a hypothetical major nuclear exchange in the mid-1980's, were major factors in the renewed emphasis upon civil defense in the United States.

This emphasis was made explicit in 1978 by the Carter Administration with the promulgation of Presidential Directive 41 (PD 41). Concerned that the absence of a credible civil defense program in the United States might destabilize deterrence if the Soviet leaders perceived nuclear war as less devastating to their own population and industry than to those of the United States, PD 41 committed the United States to a program of crisis relocation planning. The proponents of PD 41 argued that the planned ability to evacuate over 140 million Americans from more than 400 military and industrial high-risk areas would redress the asymmetry of superpower population vulnerability. Such an initiative would discourage the Soviet leaders from concluding that they enjoyed a decisive strategic advantage that could support attempts at coercion or greater risk-taking in a nuclear crisis. Moreover, it was argued that an increased civil defense capability would bolster the credibility of the US commitment to the nuclear defense of NATO. . . .

The Reagan Program

Early in 1982, President Reagan built upon President Carter's foundation with the signing of National Security Decision Directive Number 26 (NSDD 26). In this document, the President identified civil defense as "an essential ingredient of our nuclear forces." Noting that while the United States would continue to rely upon its strategic nuclear offensive forces (rather than civil defense) as the preponderant factor in maintaining deterrence, he observed that US civil defense efforts must contribute to "an improved basis for dealing with crises and carrying out eventual national recovery" in the event of the failure of deterrence. Specifically, he established the following goals for a revitalized civil defense program:

- Enhance deterrence and stability in conjunction with our strategic offensive and other strategic defensive forces. Civil defense, as an element of the strategic balance, should assist in maintaining perceptions that this balance is favorable to the US.
- Reduce the possibility that the US could be coerced in time of crisis.
- Provide for survival of a substantial portion of the US population in the event of nuclear attack preceded by strategic warning and for continuity of government, should deterrence and escalation control fail.
- Provide an improved ability to deal with natural disasters and other large-scale domestic emergencies.

. . . The most significant and immediate thrust of the President's civil defense program emphasizes population evacuation and protection. This emphasis distinguishes the population protection program . . . from the Soviet program which assigns to population protection the lowest priority of importance after the protection of the leadership and industry. . . .

The Administration has argued that the scope of its civil defense program is modest compared to that of the Soviet Union as well as to costly US offensive and defensive systems such as the MX, Trident and BMD. The scope . . . is consistent with the US view that modest civil defense expenditures "represent little more than insurance—insurance that in circumstances short of a central strategic exchange—some lives might be saved that would otherwise be lost.". . .

CIVIL DEFENSE AND CRISIS STABILITY

Two principal goals for civil defense planning by NSDD-26 were established: (1) to contribute together with strategic nuclear offensive forces to the deterrence of nuclear war between the superpowers and (2) to limit the number of casualties and amount of destruction should deterrence fail. While listed as separate objectives in NSDD-26, the contributions of civil defense to deterrence and to mitigating the effects of nuclear war cannot, in fact, be separated. Obviously, the effectiveness of civil defense plans and consequences as well as the credibility of the adversary's deterrent are important variables in the cost/benefit strategic calculus that leaders will assess in a crisis as they ponder the initiation of nuclear war.

In the absence of precise and unambiguous determinations of the damage-limiting effectiveness of civil defense plans or a clear understanding of an adversary's intent if civil defense plans are implemented during a crisis, it is impossible to ascertain the ultimate impact of these plans on the minds of Soviet and American strategic planners as they perceive their respective capabilities. Therefore, much debate has surrounded the issue of whether civil defense planning and the implementation of such plans would stabilize or destabilize superpower deterrence. To American proponents of civil defense who seek to redress the asymmetries of Soviet-American programs, the Soviet Union's unique possession of a defensive capability—assessed by its American evaluators as effective—destabilizes deterrence because it suggests to the Soviet leadership that nuclear war will be less destructive to the USSR than it will be to the United States. Such an assessment might make the Soviet leaders more, rather than less, inclined to institute a preemptive strike during a severe crisis in an attempt to limit further potential damage to the Soviet Union. Likewise, if the United States lacks an effective evacuation program and its leaders observe the initiation of a massive Soviet evacuation during a crisis (real or perceived by Soviet leaders but consistent with US interpretations of Soviet warfighting doctrine and capabilities), pressure might motivate an early, damage-limiting American strike. In either case, civil defense might be viewed as destabilizing.

Civil defense planning and implementation, however, during crises must not be viewed in a vacuum. Under almost any conceivable scenario the implementation of civil defense plans would take place in conjunction with a wide variety of other events, many of which would be observed by Soviet leaders and some of which would be specifically communicated to them in Moscow. For example, if the United States implemented its civil defense plans while simultaneously placing its forces on full alert and communicating to Moscow a desire to defuse the crisis along with a warning that any premature strike would fall on vacant US silos and vacated runways, would the Soviet leadership be inclined to execute a preemptive first strike for fear of a simultaneous US strike? Or, would Moscow believe any preemption now might more clearly result in risks which outweigh benefits? If such American events took place during an ongoing conflict in Europe, would the Soviet leaders believe that strategic nuclear war was inevitable and be inclined to preempt? Or, might they believe that further risks associated with war in Europe were not warranted and, thus, seek to de-escalate the conflict in Europe? Likewise, if the Soviet Union implemented its civil defense plans and commenced an evacuation, would the United States be inclined toward a preemptive nuclear strike? In short, much would depend upon who evacuated first, upon the relative abilities of each side to evacuate, and a number of complex and uncertain calculations made by US and Soviet decisionmakers relative to their independent perceptions of the intent of the other.

It would appear that civil defense plans and implementation during a crisis are likely to have less of an effect on the question of crisis stability than a host of other factors and signals during a crisis. Furthermore, there is reason to believe that their impact is not inalterably and unambiguously in the direction of instability.

CIVIL DEFENSE PLANNING IN AN UNCERTAIN ENVIRONMENT

. . . Whether . . . civil defense planning is a benign instrument of strategic policy or a provocative and destabilizing gesture which might result in the very war it seeks to avoid is, at present, an unanswerable question that has generated much debate. Furthermore, whether, and the extent to which, one can draw lessons from the strategic bombing survey of World War II or the 1979 evacuation of Three Mile Island which underlie certain assumptions about the effects of nuclear war and the consequences of relocation are questions similarly shrouded in uncertainty.

Nevertheless, even the casual observer of the nuclear war/civil defense issue can be fairly certain in at least one speculation: that in the event of a severe crisis between the United States and the Soviet Union, millions of Americans who perceive themselves to be in high-risk areas will evacuate to areas they believe to be safer. Moreover, in such a situation, one can expect them to look to their government for assistance. To the extent that such anticipations are valid, and short of an ability to guarantee the nonoccurrence of such crises, it becomes incumbent upon the government to identify safe host areas, designate appropriate travel routes, provide for the support of evacuees, and plan for the aftermath of the crisis.

This is the essential thrust of the current civil defense program being directed by the FEMA. Indeed, the ACDA has concluded that the United States is in a much superior position relative to the Soviet Union to mount such an ambitious and difficult program and at far less cost. This optimism is due to the following factors that favor the United States: (1) the US population is more dispersed than that of the USSR; (2) the United States has developed a superior rural infrastructure, an extensive highway system, plentiful food reserves, efficient distribution system, and a high degree of industrial redundance; and (3) the uniform belief of all Americans that the political integrity of the United States as currently constituted should continue to exist in the aftermath of a nuclear war.

. . . Certainly, many of the difficulties that bedevil the Soviet programs are also applicable to the United States. Let us consider some of the uncertainties and economic, social and political obstacles that might occur in a crisis scenario where the United States implemented the evacuation of its population from the more than 400 high-risk areas identified by FEMA. . . .

Evacuation/No War

Laurino, Trinkl, Miller, and Harker, authors of several computer simulations of the effects of crisis relocation (CR), have estimated that in a crisis, 13–26 million Americans would evacuate before any directions to do so were issued.[10] As a result of these evacuations, there would be a doubling of unemployment, and absenteeism would reduce industrial productivity by about 10 percent. Futhermore, individuals with reduced incomes and access to savings would engage in savings withdrawals, hoarding and panic buying. These effects on individuals in the pre-CR phase would ripple through the economy, greatly affecting businesses and banks and other financial institutions.

Upon the initiation of a preplanned CR, many of the problems noted above would be amplified and new ones would develop. For many individuals, income would cease, their checks and credit cards would be less acceptable in host areas and cash shortages would be experienced, all at a time when emergency costs would soar. Businesses would be confronted by general shutdowns (resulting in the unemployment of 60–70 percent of all nongovernment workers), freezes on assets and payment, unprecedented security problems, and distribution stoppages resulting in the need to find alternate supplies. This latter need would be difficult to satisfy due to the evacuation of central management and corporation headquarters, as well as to problems associated with re-routing goods in transit. Banks in high-risk areas, already forced to balance large withdrawals from domestic and foreign accounts with greatly reduced and delayed accounts receivable, deposits and interbank loans, would shut down and would face increased security problems. Meanwhile, banks in host areas would undergo extraordinarily high service demands, all at a time of reduced interbank transfers and the closing of financial exchanges.

As the CR's duration increased, the evacuees in the host areas would find it increasingly difficult to pay for services. Businesses in risk areas would remain shut down and would experience reduced accounts receivable, and businesses in host areas would face distribution problems and low support from essential industries. Banks would (1) receive reduced debt payments from individuals, businesses, and governments in high-risk areas and (2) be confronted by continued withdrawals, resulting in lower profitability and increases in their net borrowers' reserves. Local and state governments would continue to face greatly increased emergency costs, although restricted access to liquid credits, reduced revenue from intergovernment transfers, and reduced tax revenues would impede the discharge of their financial obligations.

Economic problems would not disappear with the end of the CR and the return of the evacuees to the high-risk areas. Citizens and businesses, with greatly reduced assets, would likely face overdue financial obligations. Businesses would need time to sort out their debts and financial situations (inadequate working credit, loss of asset values, and reduced access to credit) and reconcile their depleted inventories and resource imbalances with their production obligations. Hence, the buildup of production would be slow, and unemployment would be prolonged. The collapse of businesses which were marginal before the CR would aggravate an already bad situation. Banks would be required to undertake massive records updating and the clearing of backlogged checks. The maintenance of bank liquidity would be endangered by recent outflows, delayed revenues, a lowered savings rate and excessive credit demands. The developments might reduce further the prospects of numerous marginal economic concerns with effects that would ripple through the economy for some time. . . .

Particularly serious social problems would arise from a temporary or permanent evacuation as a result of the differences between urban and rural racial compositions and lifestyles. It may be optimistic to expect that in a moment of peril and uncertainty, host area residents will welcome a massive influx of these urban individuals. In addition, latent racial, cultural and religious prejudices may [militate] against the effective relocation of the evacuees in the host areas, especially if the evacuees are viewed by their hosts as interlopers, burdens and competitors for scarce provisions. Moreover, the tremendous overcrowding in many of the Eastern states would further intensify these hostilities and prejudices.

Ironically, even a decision *not* to evacuate the largest, high-risk metropolitan areas would be socially disruptive and politically dangerous since the urban poor and minorities would surmise that, at best, they were not welcome by their rural compatriots and, at worst, they were expendable. The social and political consequences of these perceptions would undermine the country's social cohesion and erode the legitimacy and support for future initiatives of the political leadership.

The sick, the very young and the very old—those groups requiring the most attention and care in society—would also suffer severely in the evacuation. These individuals would face numerous physical rigors in an evacuation, reduced attention and support services in the relocation centers and, possibly, death in many circumstances. Given all this suffering, the anger, remorse and recriminations among the host area individuals and the evacuees would be heightened at the end of a crisis in which a war did not occur.

Essential workers assigned to remain at their posts, yet who desire not to be separated from their families in time of crisis, will face incredible psychological strains. . . . [O]ne may expect that many essential workers will evacuate the risk areas with their families, irrespective of official procedures and pleas. It is uncertain that those who design CR plans can calculate accurately the effects of these pulls both into and away from the high-risk areas.

Hence, a CR could have numerous and severe social effects upon the young and the old, the sick, the poor, and the minority individual. Many of these effects could be translated into unprecedented political developments. Even if war did not occur, the government's assertion that it was the evacuation that helped to avoid Armageddon would be difficult to prove. . . .

NUCLEAR WAR AND POSTATTACK RECOVERY

This analysis suggests that even a logistically "successful" evacuation would have numerous and long-lasting deleterious economic, social, and political ramifications. Hence, the cumulative effects of the evacuation experience might well [militate] against *future* successful evacuations, irrespective of the prior evacuation's logistical success.

These effects of CR, however, would pale to insignificance if a nuclear exchange actually did ensue between the United States and the Soviet Union. . . . [W]hile the magnitude of death, physical destruction, social disruption, and psychological distress would vary with the size, timing and target selection of the attack, one should not believe that some proper mix of strategic retaliation against the Soviet Union and US civil defense preparation would make nuclear war anything less than a nightmare surpassing all comprehension. When one considers (1) the existence of scores of industrial and military targets in the United States; (2) the Soviet denigration of limited warfighting scenarios; (3) the easterly direction of the prevailing winds across the United States which will carry radioactive fallout to major population centers; (4) the location of many strategic targets in the country's breadbasket and especially along the populous seaboards; and (5) the highly interdependent nature of the U.S. economy, it becomes readily understandable why [one U.S. official] observed that:

> . . . a nuclear war [could] not be, in any intelligible sense of the word, won by either side. And no civil defense program that I could imagine would alter that sobering fact.[11]

Many of the problems for economic recovery that would confront the Soviet Union also would apply for the United States. According to the Stanford Research Institute's (SRI) input-output study of the United States, economic recovery from even a less than all-out nuclear attack would be most problematic, especially if the Soviet Union complemented its counterforce strikes with an economic "bottlenecking" target strategy. For instance, a Soviet attack of 750 warheads against the 15 major sectors of the US economy would require more than 9 years to engage fully the amount of initially surviving industrial capacity (67 percent). In other words, a substantial part of the surviving industrial capacity would not be used in the early years following an attack due, in part, to the loss of producers and consumers as well as capital investment and supporting infrastructures. Moreover, reflecting the sensitivity of econometric models to their assumed parameters and the difficulties involved in predicting far into the future, the SRI estimates depict nothing of how much time would be required to return to preattack GNP levels. SRI estimated that the GNP would remain only two-thirds to three-fourths of the preattack levels 9 years after Soviet attacks using 750–1250 warheads against US economic targets. During these years, one would expect that the experiences of infrastructural reconstitution would override investments in consumer goods. The result would be slow recovery of the quality of life at a time when the war's survivors would require much support and be at least able and willing to make sacrifices. . . .

Political and Social Problems

Many of the economic, political and social problems associated with a CR are germane to postattack scenarios because for many, a CR becomes permanent after a nuclear exchange. Those local, state and federal officials who survived would face a host of difficult problems. They would have to begin economic reconstruction without a once mighty industrial/financial infrastructure and thousands of skilled workers and consumers, along with massive regional imbalances, few prospects of international trade or aid and the threat of continued occasional nuclear attacks. Competing with economic reconstruction for scarce government resources would be incredible demands for social services and government intervention required by the millions of dead and injured. Certainly, the destruction of many hospitals, medical supplies, and trained personnel, along with the psychological trauma and numbing induced by the shock of war, would [militate] against the provision of orderly, rapid, and effective aid to the survivors. Whether the government chooses to emphasize the country's economic or social needs, it can expect significant opposition. When one considers that this decision would be made within the context of (1) the disruption of social, especially racial, stability due to the forced interaction of the country's rural and urban residents, (2) the government's allocation of the greatest recovery resources to some areas ahead of others; (3) confusion about jurisdictional authority among local, state and federal governments; and (4) the possibility that the government may be obligated to wage protracted war, thereby postponing any kind of reconstruction although not obviating the possibility of future destruction, it is quite possible the authority of past leaders would not be acknowledged and that the country's federal structure would disappear, being replaced by a confederated patchwork of quasi-feudal areas of association.

CONCLUSIONS

The relationship between Soviet offensive and defensive capabilities and the intentions of the Soviet Communist regime is speculative at best. In fact, the extent of Soviet civil defense effectiveness is a matter still debated with vigor by strategic analysts. The entire issue of civil defense and deterrence is arcane and necessarily dependent upon various assumptions, uncertainties and scenarios. Hence, it is unlikely that facile solutions or an unshakeable consensus will attend efforts to develop a civil defense policy that is militarily prudent and feasible politically as well as economically.

In this [selection], I have examined the arguments of those who fear and those who dismiss as ineffective the efforts of Soviet civil defense planners. The actual effectiveness of their programs probably lies somewhere in between. Those who criticize the Soviet program are likely correct in noting that such initiatives would not spare the Soviet Union from massive and unprecedented destruction. Their conclusion that these efforts would not contribute much to making nuclear war a more feasible policy option to the Soviet leadership is persuasive to this author. However, it is also probable that these, albeit imperfect, programs would reduce significantly the number of casualties in a nuclear war with the United States and contribute to postwar recovery. . . .

The attention directed to civil defense by the Carter and Reagan Administrations has been consistent and justified in light of even the limited capabilities ascribed to civil defense. . . .

Current US initiatives in civil defense planning are most accurately viewed as humanitarian and contributing little to a warfighting capability. In the first place, as is also the case with the Soviet Union, industry cannot be moved quickly or easily and, therefore, remains vulnerable to the increasingly accurate and destructive warheads found in the strategic arsenals of both superpowers. Moreover, it is not a particularly difficult objective for one superpower to destroy its adversary's industrial infrastructure, its civil defense efforts notwithstanding. Each superpower recognizes that the destruction of its adversary's population as an end in itself is neither desirable nor necessary to guarantee deterrence. Second, as John Troxall observed in his assessment of the US civil defense program: "There is no claim being made concerning the efficacy of such a program that would cause any leader to disregard the disasterous consequences of a nuclear exchange and thus lead to a greater willingness to initiate such an exchange."[12] Nevertheless, it remains an obligation of any government responsible to its citizens to plan for the preservation of life in the event of a nuclear war. The horror that would attend a strategic exchange and the imperfections of the civil defense plans do not relieve the government of this responsibility. Furthermore, if we assume that people will evacuate what they perceive as high-risk areas in a nuclear crisis, well coordinated plans identifying safe areas and assisting the populace in their efforts to relocate are prudent and necessary. While no amount of planning can ever mitigate the tragedy of nuclear war, there is no reason why efforts directed at reducing some of the economic and social dislocations described above should not be made. . . .

NOTES

1. [John Collins, *US-Soviet Military Balance*, New York: McGraw-Hill, 1980], p. 175.

2. [Central Intelligence Agency, *Soviet Civil Defense*, NI-78-1000 3, July 1978 (hereinafter referred to as CIA study)], pp. 1–3.

3. Keith A. Dunn, *Soviet Military Weaknesses and Vulnerabilities: A Critique of the Short War Advocates*, Strategic Issues Research Memorandum, Strategic Studies Institute, July 31, 1978, p. 12.

4. T. K. Jones and W. Scott Thompson, "Central War and Civil Defense," *Orbis*, Fall 1978, p. 699.

5. [See Geoffrey Kemp, *Nuclear Forces for Medium Powers*, Part II, Adelphi Paper No. 107, International Institute for Strategic Studies, 1974], pp. 5, 9.

6. Richard Garwin, Testimony Before Joint Committee on Defense Production, *Civil Preparedness and Limited Nuclear War*, April 28, 1976, p. 55.

7. [T. K. Jones, *Defense Industrial Base: Industrial Preparedness and Nuclear War Survival*, testimony before Joint Committee on Defense Production, Part I, November 17, 1976], p. 84.

8. Robert J. Lifton and Kai Erikson, "Nuclear War's Effect on the Mind," *The New York Times*, March 15, 1982, p. A17. Dr. Lifton's other publications which examine the psychiatric effects of nuclear war include *Death in Life: Survivors of Hiroshima* and a co-edited volume, *Last Aid: The Medical Dimensions of Nuclear War*, San Francisco: Freeman, 1982.

9. [CIA study], p. 13.

10. R. K. Laurino, F. Trinkl, C. F. Miller, and R. A. Harker, *Economic and Industrial Aspects of Crisis Relocation: An Overview*, DCPA 01-75-c-0279, Palo Alto: Center for Planning and Research, May 1977; and R. K. Laurino, F. Trinkl, R. Berry, R. Schnider, and W. MacDougell, *Impacts of Crisis Relocation on U.S. Economic and Industrial Activity*, DCPA 01-76-c-0331, Palo Alto: Center for Planning and Research, October 1978, pp. 5–11, also Arthur M. Katz, *Life After Nuclear War*, 1982, pp. 291–308.

11. [Richard Perle, "Statement to Subcommittee on Arms Control, Senate Foreign Relations Committee, Washington, March 31, 1982], p. 3.
12. [John Troxall, "Soviet Civil Defense and the American Response," *Military Review*, January 1983], p. 45.

24 NUCLEAR WAR AND CLIMATIC CATASTROPHE: A NUCLEAR WINTER

Carl Sagan

Apocalyptic predictions require, to be taken seriously, higher standards of evidence than do assertions on other matters where the stakes are not as great. Since the immediate effects of even a single thermonuclear weapon explosion are so devastating, it is natural to assume—even without considering detailed mechanisms—that the more or less simultaneous explosion of ten thousand such weapons all over the Northern Hemisphere might have unpredictable and catastrophic consequences.

And yet, while it is widely accepted that a full nuclear war might mean the end of civilization at least in the Northern Hemisphere, claims that nuclear war might imply a reversion of the human population to prehistoric levels, or even the extinction of the human species, have, among some policymakers at least, been dismissed as alarmist or, worse, irrelevant. Popular works that stress this theme, such as Nevil Shute's *On the Beach*, and Jonathan Schell's *The Fate of the Earth*, have been labeled disreputable. The apocalyptic claims are rejected as unproved and unlikely, and it is judged unwise to frighten the public with doomsday talk when nuclear weapons are needed, we are told, to preserve the peace. But . . . comparably dire warnings have been made by respectable scientists with diverse political inclinations, including many of the American and Soviet physicists who conceived, devised and constructed the world nuclear arsenals.

Part of the resistance to serious consideration of such apocalyptic pronouncements is their necessarily theoretical basis. Understanding the long-term consequences of nuclear war is not a problem amenable to experimental verification—at least not more than once. Another part of the resistance is psychological. Most people—recognizing nuclear war as a grave and terrifying prospect, and nuclear policy as immersed in technical complexities, official secrecy and bureaucratic inertia—tend to practice what psychiatrists call denial: putting the agonizing problem out of our heads, since there seems nothing we can do about it. Even policymakers must feel this temptation from time to time. But for policymakers there is another concern: if it turns out that nuclear war could

Note: Some footnotes have been deleted, and the others have been renumbered to appear in consecutive order.

312

end our civilization or our species, such a finding might be considered a retroactive rebuke to those responsible, actively or passively, in the past or in the present, for the global nuclear arms race.

The stakes are too high for us to permit any such factors to influence our assessment of the consequences of nuclear war. If nuclear war now seems significantly more catastrophic than has generally been believed in the military and policy communities, then serious consideration of the resulting implications is urgently called for.

It is in that spirit that this article seeks, first, to present a short summary, in lay terms, of the climatic and biological consequences of nuclear war that emerge from extensive scientific studies conducted over the past two years, the essential conclusions of which have now been endorsed by a large number of scientists. These findings were presented in detail at a special conference in Cambridge, Mass., involving almost 100 scientists on April 22–26, 1983, and were publicly announced at a conference in Washington, D.C., on October 31 and November 1, 1983. They have been reported in summary form in the press, and a detailed statement of the findings and their bases [has been] published in *Science*.[1] . . .

Following this summary, I explore the possible strategic and policy implications of the new findings. They point to one apparently inescapable conclusion: the necessity of moving as rapidly as possible to reduce the global nuclear arsenals below levels that could conceivably cause the kind of climatic catastrophe and cascading biological devastation predicted by the new studies. Such a reduction would have to be a small percentage of the present global strategic arsenals.

II

The central point of the new findings is that the long-term consequences of a nuclear war could constitute a global climatic catastrophe.

The immediate consequences of a single thermonuclear weapon explosion are well known and well documented—fireball radiation, prompt neutrons and gamma rays, blast, and fires. The Hiroshima bomb that killed between 100,000 and 200,000 people was a fission device of about 12 kilotons yield (the explosive equivalent of 12,000 tons of TNT). A modern thermonuclear warhead uses a device something like the Hiroshima bomb as the trigger—the "match" to light the fusion reaction. A typical thermonuclear weapon now has a yield of about 500 kilotons (or 0.5 megatons, a megaton being the explosive equivalent of a million tons of TNT). There are many weapons in the 9 to 20 megaton range in the strategic arsenals of the United States and the Soviet Union today. The highest-yield weapon ever exploded is 58 megatons.

Strategic nuclear weapons are those designed for delivery by ground-based or submarine-launched missiles, or by bombers, to targets in the adversary's homeland. Many weapons with yields roughly equal to that of the Hiroshima bomb are today assigned to "tactical" or "theater" military missions, or are designated "munitions" and relegated to ground-to-air and air-to-air missiles, torpedoes, depth charges and artillery. While strategic weapons often have higher yields than tactical weapons, this is not always the case. Modern tactical or theater missiles (e.g., Pershing II, SS-20) and air support weapons (e.g., those carried by F-15 or MiG-23 aircraft) have sufficient range to make the distinction between "strategic" and "tactical" or "theater" weapons increasingly artificial. Both categories of weapons can be delivered by land-based missiles, sea-based missiles, and aircraft; and by intermediate-range as well as intercontinental delivery systems. Nevertheless, by the usual accounting, there are around 18,000 strategic thermonuclear weapons (warheads) and the equivalent number of fission triggers in the American and Soviet strategic arsenals, with an aggregate yield of about 10,000 megatons.

The total number of nuclear weapons (strategic plus theater and tactical) in the arsenals of the two nations is close to 50,000, with an aggregate yield near 15,000 megatons. For convenience, we here collapse the distinction between strategic and theater weapons, and adopt, under the rubric "strategic," an aggregate yield of 13,000 megatons. The nuclear weapons of the rest of the world—mainly Britain, France and China—amount to many hundred warheads and a few hundred megatons of additional aggregate yield.

No one knows, of course, how many warheads with what aggregate yield would be detonated in a nuclear war. Because of attacks on strategic aircraft and missiles, and because of technological failures, it is clear that less than the entire world arsenal would be detonated. On the other hand, it is generally accepted, even among most military planners, that a "small" nuclear war would be almost impossible to contain before it escalated to include much of the world arsenals. (Precipitating factors include command and control malfunctions, communications failures, the necessity for instantaneous decisions on the fates of millions, fear, panic and other aspects of real nuclear war fought by real people.) For this reason alone, any serious attempt to examine the possible consequences of nuclear war must place major emphasis on large-scale exchanges in the five-to-seven-thousand-megaton range. . . . Many of the effects described below, however, can be triggered by much smaller wars.

The adversary's strategic airfields, missile silos, naval bases, submarines at sea, weapons manufacturing and storage locales, civilian and military command and control centers, attack assessment and early warning facilities, and the like are probable targets ("counterforce attack"). While it is often stated that cities are not targeted "per se," many of the above targets are very near or colocated with cities, especially in Europe. In addition, there is an industrial targeting category ("countervalue attack"). Modern nuclear doctrines require that "war-supporting" facilities be attacked. Many of these facilities are necessarily industrial in nature and engage a work force of considerable size. They are almost always situated near major transportation centers, so that raw materials and finished products can be efficiently transported to other industrial sectors, or to forces in the field. Thus, such facilities are, almost by definition, cities, or near or within cities. Other "war-supporting" targets may include the transportation systems themselves (roads, canals, rivers, railways, civilian airfields, etc.), petroleum refineries, storage sites and pipelines, hydroelectric plants, radio and television transmitters and the like. A major countervalue attack therefore might involve almost all large cities in the United States and the Soviet Union, and possibly most of the large cities in the Northern Hemisphere. There are fewer than 2,500 cities in the world with populations over 100,000 inhabitants, so the devastation of all such cities is well within the means of the world nuclear arsenals.

Recent estimates of the immediate deaths from blast, prompt radiation, and fires in a major exchange in which cities were targeted range from several hundred million to 1.1 billion people—the latter estimate is in a World Health Organization study in which targets were assumed not to be restricted entirely to NATO and Warsaw Pact countries. Serious injuries requiring immediate medical attention (which would be largely unavailable) would be suffered by a comparably large number of people, perhaps an additional 1.1 billion. Thus it is possible that something approaching half the human population on the planet would be killed or seriously injured by the direct effects of the nuclear war. Social disruption; the unavailability of electricity, fuel, transportation, food deliveries, communications and other civil services; the absence of medical care; the decline in sanitation measures; rampant disease and severe psychiatric disorders would doubtless collectively claim a significant number of further victims. But a range of additional effects—some unexpected, some inadequately treated in earlier studies, some uncovered only recently—now make the picture much more somber still.

Because of current limitations on missile accuracy, the destruction of missile silos, command and control facilities, and other hardened sites requires nuclear weapons of fairly high yield exploded as groundbursts or as low airbursts. High-yield groundbursts will vaporize, melt and pulverize the surface at the target area and propel large quantities of condensates and fine dust into the upper troposphere and stratosphere. The particles are chiefly entrained in the rising fireball; some ride up the stem of the mushroom cloud. Most military targets, however, are not very hard. The destruction of cities can be accomplished, as demonstrated at Hiroshima and Nagasaki, by lower-yield explosions less than a kilometer above the surface. Low-yield airbursts over cities or near forests will tend to produce massive fires, some of them over areas of 100,000 square kilometers or more. City fires generate enormous quantities of black oily smoke which rise at least into the upper part of the lower atmosphere, or troposphere. If firestorms occur, the smoke column rises vigorously, like the draft in a fireplace, and may carry some of the soot into the lower part of the upper atmosphere, or stratosphere. The smoke from forest and grassland fires would initially be restricted to the lower troposphere.

The fission of the (generally plutonium) trigger in every thermonuclear weapon and the reactions in the (generally uranium-238) casing added as a fission yield "booster" produce a witch's brew of radioactive products, which are also entrained in the cloud. Each such product, or radioisotope, has a characteristic "half-life" (defined as the time to decay to half its original level of radioactivity). Most of the radioisotopes have very short half-lives and decay in hours to days. Particles injected into the stratosphere, mainly by high-yield explosions, fall out very slowly—characteristically in about a year, by which time most of the fission products, even when concentrated, will have decayed to much safer levels. Particles injected into the troposphere by low-yield explosions and fires fall out more rapidly—by gravitational settling, rainout, convection, and other processes—before the radioactivity has decayed to moderately safe levels. Thus rapid fallout of tropospheric radioactive debris tends to produce larger doses of ionizing radiation than does the slower fallout of radioactive particles from the stratosphere.

Nuclear explosions of more than one-megaton yield generate a radiant fireball that rises through the troposphere into the stratosphere. The fireballs from weapons with yields between 100 kilotons and one megaton will partially extend into the stratosphere. The high temperatures in the fireball chemically ignite some of the nitrogen in the air, producing oxides of nitrogen, which in turn chemically attack and destroy the gas ozone in the middle stratosphere. But ozone absorbs the biologically dangerous ultraviolet radiation from the Sun. Thus, the partial depletion of the stratospheric ozone layer, or "ozonosphere," by high-yield nuclear explosions will increase the flux of solar ultraviolet radiation at the surface of the Earth (after the soot and dust have settled out). After a nuclear war in which thousands of high-yield weapons are detonated, the increase in biologically dangerous ultraviolet light might be several hundred percent. In the more dangerous shorter wavelengths, larger increases would occur. Nucleic acids and proteins, the fundamental molecules for life on Earth, are especially sensitive to ultraviolet radiation.

Thus, an increase of the solar ultraviolet flux at the surface of the Earth is potentially dangerous for life.

These four effects—obscuring smoke in the troposphere, obscuring dust in the stratosphere, the fallout of radioactive debris, and the partial destruction of the ozone layer—constitute the four known principal adverse environmental consequences that occur after a nuclear war is "over." There may be others about which we are still ignorant. The dust and, especially, the dark soot absorb ordinary visible light from the Sun, heating the atmosphere and cooling the Earth's surface.

All four of these effects have been treated in our recent scientific investigation. The study, known from the initials of its authors as TTAPS, for the first time demonstrates that severe and prolonged low temperatures would follow a nuclear war. (The study also explains the fact that no such climatic effects were detected after the detonation of hundreds of megatons during the period of U.S.-Soviet atmospheric testing of nuclear weapons, ended by treaty in 1963: the explosions were sequential over many years, not virtually simultaneous; and, occurring over scrub desert, coral atolls, tundra and wasteland, they set no fires.) The new results have been subjected to detailed scrutiny, and half a dozen confirmatory calculations have now been made. A special panel appointed by the National Academy of Sciences to examine this problem has come to similar conclusions.

Unlike many previous studies, the effects do not seem to be restricted to northern mid-latitudes, where the nuclear exchange would mainly take place. There is now substantial evidence that the heating by sunlight of atmospheric dust and soot over northern mid-latitude targets would profoundly change the global circulation. Fine particles would be transported across the equator in weeks, bringing the cold and the dark to the Southern Hemisphere. (In addition, some studies suggest that over 100 megatons would be dedicated to equatorial and Southern Hemisphere targets, thus generating fine particles locally.) While it would be less cold and less dark at the ground in the Southern Hemisphere than in the Northern, massive climatic and environmental disruptions may be triggered there as well.

In our studies, several dozen different scenarios were chosen, covering a wide range of possible wars, and the range of uncertainty in each key parameter was considered (e.g., to describe how many fine particles are injected into the atmosphere). Five representative cases are shown in Table 1, below, ranging from a small low-yield attack exclusively on cities, utilizing, in yield, only 0.8 percent of the world strategic arsenals, to a massive exchange involving 75 percent of the world arsenals. "Nominal" cases assume the most probable parameter choices; "severe" cases assume more adverse parameter choices, but still in the plausible range.

Table 1. Nuclear Exchange Scenarios

Case	Total Yield (MT)	% Yield Surface Bursts	% Yield Urban or Industrial Targets	Warhead Yield Range (MT)	Total Number of Explosions
1. Baseline Case, countervalue and counterforce[a]	5,000	57	20	0.1–10	10,400
11. 3,000 MT nominal, counterforce only[b]	3,000	50	0	1 – 10	2,250
14. 100 MT nominal, countervalue only[c]	100	0	100	0.1	1,000
16. 5000 MT "severe," counterforce only[b,d]	5,000	100	0	5 – 10	700
17. 10,000 MT "severe," countervalue and counterforce[c,d]	10,000	63	15	0.1–10	16,160

a. In the Baseline Case, 12,000 square kilometers of inner cities are burned; on every square centimeter an average of 10 grams of combustibles are burned, and 1.1% of the burned material rises as smoke. Also, 230,000 square kilometers of suburban areas burn, with 1.5 grams consumed at each square centimeter and 3.6% rising as smoke.
b. In this highly conservative case, it is assumed that no smoke emission occurs, that not a blade of grass is burned. Only 25,000 tons of the fine dust is raised into the upper atmosphere for every megaton exploded.
c. In contrast to the Baseline Case, only inner cities burn, but with 10 grams per square centimeter consumed and 3.3% rising as smoke into the high atmosphere.
d. Here, the fine (submicron) dust raised into the upper atmosphere is 150,000 tons per megaton exploded.

Predicted continental temperatures in the Northern Hemisphere vary after the nuclear war according to the curves shown in Figure 1. . . . The high heat-retention capacity of water guarantees that oceanic temperatures will fall at most by a few degrees. Because temperatures are moderated by the adjacent oceans, temperature effects in coastal regions will be less extreme than in continental interiors. The temperatures shown in Figure 1 are average values for Northern Hemisphere land areas.

Even much smaller temperature declines are known to have serious consequences. The explosion of the Tambora volcano in Indonesia in 1815 led to an average global temperature decline of only 1°C, due to the obscuration of sunlight by the fine dust propelled into the stratosphere; yet the hard freezes the following year were so severe that 1816 has been known in Europe and America as "the year without a summer." A 1°C cooling would nearly eliminate wheat growing in Canada.

Figure 1. Temperature Effects of Nuclear War Cases

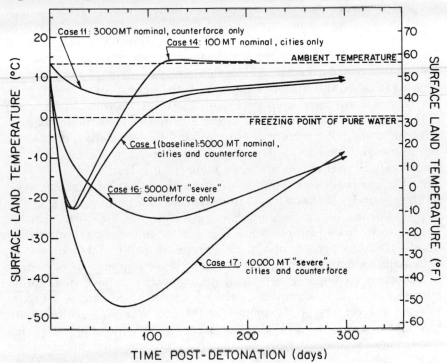

TIME POST-DETONATION (days)

Note: In this Figure, the average temperature of Northern Hemisphere land areas (away from coastlines) is shown varying with time after the five Cases of nuclear war defined in Table 1. The "ambient" temperature is the average in the Northern Hemisphere over all latitudes and seasons: thus, normal winter temperatures at north temperature latitudes are lower than is shown, and normal tropical temperatures are higher than shown. Cases described as "nominal" assume the most likely values of parameters (such as dust particle size or the frequency of firestorms) that are imperfectly known. Cases marked "severe" represent adverse but not implausible values of these parameters. In Case 14 the curve ends when the temperatures come within a degree of the ambient values. For the four other Cases the curves are shown ending after 300 days, but this is simply because the calculations were not extended further. In these four Cases the curves will continue to the directions they are headed.

In the last thousand years, the maximum global or Northern Hemisphere temperature deviations have been around 1°C. In an Ice Age, a typical long-term temperature decline from preexisting conditions is about 10°C. Even the most modest of the cases illustrated in Figure 1 give temporary temperature declines of this order. The Baseline Case is much more adverse. Unlike the situation in an Ice Age, however, the global temperatures after nuclear war plunge rapidly and take only months to a few years to recover, rather than thousands of years. No new Ice Age is likely to be induced by a Nuclear Winter.

Because of the obscuration of the Sun, the daytime light levels can fall to a twilit gloom or worse. For more than a week in the northern mid-latitude target zone, it might be much too dark to see, even at midday. In Cases 1 and 14 (Table 1), hemispherically averaged light levels fall to a few percent of normal values, comparable to those at the bottom of a dense overcast. At this illumination, many plants are close to what is called the compensation point, the light level at which photosynthesis can barely keep pace with plant metabolism. In Case 17, illumination, averaged over the entire Northern Hemisphere, falls in daytime to about 0.1 percent of normal, a light level at which plants will not photosynthesize at all. For Cases 1 and especially 17, full recovery to ordinary daylight takes a year or more (Figure 1).

As the fine particles fall out of the atmosphere, carrying radioactivity to the ground, the light levels increase and the surface warms. The depleted ozone layer now permits ultraviolet light to reach the Earth's surface in increased proportions. The relative timing of the multitude of adverse consequences of a nuclear war is shown in Table 2. . . .

Perhaps the most striking and unexpected consequence of our study is that even a comparatively small nuclear war can have devastating climatic consequences, provided cities are targeted (see Case 14 in Figure 1; here, the centers of 100 major NATO and Warsaw Pact cities are burning). There is an indication of a very rough threshold at which severe climatic consequences are triggered—around a few hundred nuclear explosions over cities, for smoke generation, or around 2,000 to 3,000 high-yield surface bursts at, e.g., missile silos, for dust generation and ancillary fires. Fine particles can be injected into the atmosphere at increasing rates with only minor effects until these thresholds are crossed. Thereafter, the effects rapidly increase in severity.[2]

As in all calculations of this complexity, there are uncertainties. Some factors tend to work towards more severe or more prolonged effects; others tend to ameliorate the effects.[3] The detailed TTAPS calculations described here are one-dimensional; that is, they assume the fine particles to move vertically by all the appropriate laws of physics, but neglect the spreading in latitude and longitude. When soot or dust is moved away from the reference locale, things get better there and worse elsewhere. In addition, fine particles can be transported by weather systems to other locales, where they are carried more rapidly down to the surface. That would ameliorate obscuration not just locally but globally. It is just this transport away from the northern mid-latitudes that involves the equatorial zone and the Southern Hemisphere in the effects of the nuclear war. It would be helpful to perform an accurate three-dimensional calculation on the general atmospheric circulation following a nuclear war. Preliminary estimates suggest that circulation might moderate the low temperatures in the Northern Hemisphere predicted in our calcu-

Table 2. Effects of the Baseline Nuclear War

Effect	Time After Nuclear War	U.S. / S.U. Population at risk	N.H. Population at risk	S.H. Population at risk	Casualty rate for those at risk	Potential global deaths
Blast		H	M	L	H	M - H
Thermal Radiation		H	M	L	M	M - H
Prompt Ionizing Radiation		L	L	L	H	L - M
Fires		M	M	L	M	M
Toxic Gases		M	M	L	L	L
Dark		H	H	M	L	L
Cold		H	H	H	H	M - H
Frozen Water Supplies		H	H	M	M	M
Fallout Ionizing Radiation		H	H	L - M	M	M - H
Food Shortages		H	H	H	H	H
Medical System Collapse		H	H	M	M	M
Contagious Diseases		M	M	L	H	M
Epidemics and Pandemics		H	H	M	M	M
Psychiatric Disorders		H	H	L	L	L - M
Increased Surface Ultraviolet Light		H	H	M	L	L
Synergisms	?	?	?	?	?	?

Note: This is a schematic representation of the time scale for the effects, which are most severe when the thickness of the horizontal bar is greatest. The columns at the right indicate the degree of risk of the populations of the United States and the Soviet Union, the Northern Hemisphere, and the Southern Hemisphere—with H, M, and L standing for High, Medium, and Low respectively.

lations by some 30 percent, lessening somewhat the severity of the effects, but still leaving them at catastrophic levels (e.g., a 30°C rather than a 40°C temperature drop). To provide a small margin of safety, we neglect this correction in our subsequent discussion.

There are also effects that tend to make the results much worse: for example, in our calculations we assumed that rainout of fine particles occurred through the entire troposphere. But under realistic circumstances, at least the upper troposphere may be very dry, and any dust or soot carried there initially may take much longer to fall out. There is also a very significant effect deriving from the drastically altered structure of the atmosphere, brought about by the heating of the clouds and the cooling of the surface. This produces a region in which the temperature is approximately constant with altitude in the lower atmosphere and topped by a massive temperature inversion. Particles throughout the atmosphere would then be transported vertically very slowly—as in the present stratosphere. This is a second reason why the lifetime of the clouds of soot and dust may be much longer than we have calculated. If so, the worst of the cold and the dark might be prolonged for considerable periods of time, conceivably for more than a year. We also neglect this effect in subsequent discussion.

Nuclear war scenarios are possible that are much worse than the ones we have presented. For example, if command and control capabilities are lost early in the war—by, say, "decapitation" (an early surprise attack on civilian and military headquarters and communications facilities)—then the war conceivably could be extended for weeks as local commanders make separate and uncoordinated decisions. At least some of the delayed missile launches could be retaliatory strikes against any remaining adversary cities. Generation of an additional smoke pall over a period of weeks or longer following the initiation of the war would extend the magnitude, but especially the duration of the climatic consequences. Or it is possible that more cities and forests would be ignited than we have assumed, or that smoke emissions would be larger, or that a greater fraction of the world arsenals would be committed. Less severe cases are of course possible as well.

These calculations therefore are not, and cannot be, assured prognostications of the full consequences of a nuclear war. Many refinements in them are possible and are being pursued. But there is general agreement on the overall conclusions: in the wake of a nuclear war there is likely to be a period, lasting at least for months, of extreme cold in a radioactive gloom, followed—after the soot and dust fall out—by an extended period of increased ultraviolet light reaching the surface.

We now explore the biological impact of such an assault on the global environment.

III

The immediate human consequences of nuclear explosions range from vaporization of populations near the hypocenter, to blast-generated trauma (from flying glass, falling beams, collapsing skyscrapers and the like), to burns, radiation sickness, shock and severe psychiatric disorders. But our concern here is with longer-term effects.

It is now a commonplace that in the burning of modern tall buildings, more people succumb to toxic gases than to fire. Ignition of many varieties of building materials, insulation and fabrics generates large amounts of such pyrotoxins, including carbon monoxide, cyanides, vinyl chlorides, oxides of nitrogen, ozone, dioxins, and furans. Because of differing practices in the use of such synthetics, the burning of cities in North America and Western Europe will probably generate more pyrotoxins than cities in the Soviet Union, and cities with substantial recent construction more than older, unreconstructed cities. In nuclear war scenarios in which a great many cities are burning, a significant pyrotoxin smog might persist for months. The magnitude of this danger is unknown.

The pyrotoxins, low light levels, radioactive fallout, subsequent ultraviolet light, and especially the cold are together likely to destroy almost all of Northern Hemisphere agriculture, even for the more modest Cases 11 and 14. A 12° to 15°C temperature reduction by itself would eliminate wheat and corn production in the United States, even if all civil systems and agricultural technology were intact. With unavoidable societal disruption, and with the other environmental stresses just mentioned, even a 3,000-megaton "pure" counterforce attack (Case 11) might suffice. Realistically, many fires would be set even in such an attack (see below), and a 3,000-megaton war is likely to wipe out U.S. grain production. This would represent by itself an unprecedented global catastrophe: North American grain is the principal reliable source of export food on the planet, as well as an essential component of U.S. prosperity. Wars just before harvesting of grain and other staples would be incrementally worse than wars after harvesting. For many scenarios, the effects will extend . . . into two or more growing seasons. Widespread fires and subsequent runoff of topsoil are among the many additional deleterious consequences extending for years after the war.

Something like three-quarters of the U.S. population lives in or near cities. In the cities themselves there is, on average, only about one week's supply of food. After a nuclear war it is conceivable that enough of present grain storage might survive to maintain, on some level, the present population for more than a year. But with the breakdown of civil order and transportation systems in the cold, the dark and the fallout, these stores would become largely inaccessible. Vast numbers of survivors would soon starve to death.

In addition, the sub-freezing temperatures imply, in many cases, the unavailability of fresh water. The ground will tend to be frozen to a depth of about a meter—incidentally making it unlikely that the hundreds of millions of dead bodies would be buried, even if the civil organization to do so existed. Fuel stores to melt snow and ice would be in short supply, and ice surfaces and freshly fallen snow would tend to be contaminated by radioactivity and pyrotoxins.

In the presence of excellent medical care, the average value of the acute lethal dose of ionizing radiation for healthy adults is about 450 rads. (As with many other effects, children, the infirm and the elderly tend to be more vulnerable.) Combined with the other assaults on survivors in the postwar environment, and in the probable absence of any significant medical care, the mean lethal acute dose is likely to decline to 350 rads or even lower. For many outdoor scenarios, doses within the fallout plumes that drift hundreds of kilometers downwind of targets are greater than the mean lethal dose. (For a 10,000-megaton war, this is true for more than 30 percent of northern mid-latitude land areas.) Far from targets, intermediate-timescale chronic doses from delayed radioactive fallout may be in excess of 100 rads for the baseline case. These calculations assume no detonations on nuclear reactors or fuel-reprocessing plants, which would increase the dose.

Thus, the combination of acute doses from prompt radioactive fallout, chronic doses from the delayed intermediate-timescale fallout, and internal doses from food and drink are together likely to kill many more by radiation sickness. Because of acute damage to bone marrow, survivors would have significantly increased vulnerability to infectious diseases. Most infants exposed to 100 rads as fetuses in the first two trimesters of pregnancy would suffer mental retardation and/or other serious birth defects. Radiation and some pyrotoxins would later produce neoplastic diseases and genetic damage. Livestock and domesticated animals, with fewer resources, vanishing food supplies and in many cases with greater sensitivity to the stresses of nuclear war than human beings, would also perish in large numbers.

These devastating consequences for humans and for agriculture would not be restricted to the locales in which the war would principally be "fought," but would extend throughout northern mid-latitudes and, with reduced but still significant severity, probably to the tropics and the Southern Hemisphere. The bulk of the world's grain exports originate in northern mid-latitudes. Many nations in the developing as well as the developed world depend on the import of food. Japan, for example, imports 75 percent of its food (and 99 percent of its fuel). Thus, even if there were no climatic and radiation stresses on tropical and Southern Hemisphere societies—many of them already at subsistence levels of nutrition—large numbers of people there would die of starvation.

As agriculture breaks down worldwide (possible initial exceptions might include Argentina, Australia and South Africa if the climatic impact on the Southern Hemisphere proved to be minimal), there will be increasing reliance on natural ecosystems—fruits, tubers, roots, nuts, etc. But wild foodstuffs will also have suffered from the effects of the war. At just the moment that surviving humans turn to the natural environment for the basis of life, that environment would be experiencing a devastation unprecedented in recent geological history.

Two-thirds of all species of plants, animals, and microorganisms on the Earth live within 25° of the equator. Because temperatures tend to vary with the seasons only minimally at tropical latitudes, species there are especially vulnerable to rapid temperature declines. In past major extinction events in the paleontological record, there has been a marked tendency for tropical organisms to show greater vulnerability than organisms living at more temperate latitudes.

The darkness alone may cause a collapse in the aquatic food chain in which sunlight is harvested by phytoplankton, phytoplankton by zooplankton, zooplankton by small fish, small fish by large fish, and, occasionally, large fish by humans. In many nuclear war scenarios, this food chain is likely to collapse at its base for at least a year and is significantly more imperiled in tropical waters. The increase in ultraviolet light available at the surface of the earth approximately a year after the war provides an additional major environmental stress that by itself has been described as having "profound consequences" for aquatic, terrestrial and other ecosystems.

The global ecosystem can be considered an intricately woven fabric composed of threads contributed by the millions of separate species that inhabit the planet and interact with the air, the water and the soil. The system has developed considerable resiliency, so that pulling a single thread is unlikely to unravel the entire fabric. Thus, most ordinary assaults on the biosphere are unlikely to have catastrophic consequences. For example, because of natural small changes in stratospheric ozone abundance, organisms have probably experienced, in the fairly recent geologic past, ten percent fluctuations in the solar near-ultraviolet flux (but not fluctuations by factors of two or more). Similarly, major continental temperature changes of the magnitude and extent addressed here may not have been experienced for tens of thousands and possibly not for millions of years. We have no experimental information, even for aquaria or terraria, on the simultaneous effects of cold, dark, pyrotoxins, ionizing radiation, and ultraviolet light as predicted in the TTAPS study.

Each of these factors, taken separately, may carry serious consequences for the global ecosystem: their interactions may be much more dire still. Extremely worrisome is the possibility of poorly understood or as yet entirely uncontemplated synergisms (where the net consequences of two or more assaults on the environment are much more than the sum of the component parts). For example, more than 100 rads (and possibly more than 200 rads) of external and ingested ionizing radiation is likely to be delivered in a very large nuclear war to all plants, animals and unprotected humans in densely populated regions of northern mid-latitudes. After the soot and dust clear, there can, for such wars, be a 200 to 400 percent increment in the solar ultraviolet flux that reaches the ground, with an increase of many orders of magnitude in the more dangerous shorter-wavelength radiation. Together, these radiation assaults are likely to suppress the immune systems of humans and other species, making them more vulnerable to disease. At the same time, the high ambient-radiation fluxes are likely to produce, through mutation, new varieties of microorganisms, some of which might become pathogenic. The preferential radiation sensitivity of birds and other insect predators would enhance the proliferation of herbivorous and pathogen-carrying insects. Carried by vectors with high radiation tolerance, it seems possible that epidemics and global pandemics would propagate with no hope of effective mitigation by medical care, even with reduced population sizes and greatly restricted human mobility. Plants, weakened by low temperatures and low light levels, and other animals would likewise be vulnerable to preexisting and newly arisen pathogens.

There are many other conceivable synergisms, all of them still poorly understood because of the complexity of the global ecosystem. Every synergism represents an additional assault, of unknown magnitude, on the global ecosystem and its support functions for humans. What the world would look like after a nuclear war depends in part upon the unknown synergistic interaction of these various adverse effects.

We do not and cannot know that the worst would happen after a nuclear war. Perhaps there is some as yet undiscovered compensating effect or saving grace—although in the past, the overlooked effects in studies of nuclear war have almost always tended toward the worst. But in an uncertain matter of such gravity, it is wise to contemplate the worst, especially when its probability is not extremely small. The summary of the findings of the group of 40 distinguished biologists who met in April 1983 to assess the TTAPS conclusions is worthy of careful consideration:[4]

> Species extinction could be expected for most tropical plants and animals, and for most terrestrial vertebrates of north temperate regions, a large number of plants, and numerous freshwater and some marine organisms. . . . Whether any people would be able to persist for long in the face of highly modified biological communities; novel climates; high levels of radiation; shattered agricultural, social, and economic systems; extraordinary psychological stresses; and a host of other difficulties is open to question. It is clear that the ecosystem effects *alone* resulting from a large-scale thermonuclear war could be enough to destroy the current civilization in at least the Northern Hemisphere. Coupled with the direct casualties of perhaps two billion people, the combined intermediate and long-term effects of nuclear war suggest that eventually there might be no human survivors in the Northern Hemisphere.

> Furthermore, the scenario described here is by no means the most severe that could be imagined with present world nuclear arsenals and those contemplated for the near future. In almost any realistic case involving nuclear exchanges between the superpowers, global environmental changes sufficient to cause an extinction event equal to or more severe than that at the close of the Cretaceous when the dinosaurs and many other species died out are likely. In that event, the possibility of the extinction of *Homo sapiens* cannot be excluded.

IV

The foregoing probable consequences of various nuclear war scenarios have implications for doctrine and policy. Some have argued that the difference between the deaths of several hundred million people in a nuclear war (as has been thought until recently to be a reasonable upper limit) and the death of every person on Earth (as now seems possible) is only a matter of one order of magnitude. For me, the difference is considerably greater. Restricting our attention only to those who die as a consequence of the war conceals its full impact.

If we are required to calibrate extinction in numerical terms, I would be sure to include the number of people in future generations who would not be born. A nuclear war imperils all of our descendants, for as long as there will be humans. Even if the population remains static, with an average lifetime of the order of 100 years, over a typical time period for the biological evolution of a successful species (roughly ten million years), we are talking about some 500 trillion people yet to come. By this criterion, the stakes are one million times greater for extinction than for the more modest nuclear wars that kill "only" hundreds of millions of people.

There are many other possible measures of the potential loss—including culture and science, the evolutionary history of the planet, and the significance of the lives of all of our ancestors who contributed to the future of their descendants. Extinction is the undoing of the human enterprise. . . . [At this point the author examines possible policy responses to avert a nuclear war–induced climatic catastrophe—eds.]

V

None of the foregoing possible strategic and policy responses to the prospect of a nuclear war-triggered climatic catastrophe seem adequate even for the security of the nuclear powers, much less for the rest of the world. The prospect reinforces, in the short run, the standard arguments for strategic confidence-building, especially between the United States and the Soviet Union; for tempering puerile rhetoric; for resisting the temptation to demonize the adversary; for reducing the likelihood of strategic confrontations arising from accident or miscalculation; for stabilizing old and new weapons systems—for example, by de-MIRVing missiles; for abandoning nuclear-war-fighting strategies and mistrusting the possibility of "containment" of a tactical or limited nuclear war; for considering safe unilateral steps, such as the retiring of some old weapons systems with very high-yield warheads; for improving communications at all levels, especially among general staffs and between heads of governments; and for public declarations of relevant policy changes. The United States might also contemplate ratification of SALT II and of the 1948 U.N. Convention on the Prevention and Punishment of the Crime of Genocide (ratified by 92 nations, including the Soviet Union).

Both nations might consider abandoning apocalyptic threats and doctrines. To the extent that these are not credible, they undermine deterrence; to the extent that they are credible, they set in motion events that tend toward apocalyptic conclusions.

In the long run, the prospect of climatic catastrophe raises real questions about what is meant by national and international security. To me, it seems clear that the species is in grave danger at least until the world arsenals are reduced below the threshold for climatic catastrophe; the nations and the global civilization would remain vulnerable even at lower inventories. It may even be that, now, the only credible arsenal is below threshold. George Kennan's celebrated proposal to reduce the world arsenals initially to 50 percent of their current numbers is recognized as hard enough to implement. But it would be only the first step toward what is now clearly and urgently needed—a more than 90-percent reduction . . . —adequate for strategic deterrence, if that is considered essential, but unlikely to trigger the nuclear winter. . . .

VI

We have, by slow and imperceptible steps, been constructing a Doomsday Machine. Until recently—and then, only by accident—no one even noticed. And we have distributed its triggers all over the Northern Hemisphere. Every American and Soviet leader since 1945 has made critical decisions regarding nuclear war in total ignorance of the climatic catastrophe. Perhaps this knowledge would have moderated the subsequent course of world events and, especially, the nuclear arms race. Today, at least, we have no excuse for failing to factor the catastrophe into long-term decisions on strategic policy.

Since it is the soot produced by urban fires that is the most sensitive trigger of the climatic catastrophe, and since such fires can be ignited even by low-yield strategic weapons, it appears that the most critical ready index of the world nuclear arsenals, in terms of climatic change, may be the total *number* of strategic warheads. . . .

Very roughly, the level of the world strategic arsenals necessary to induce the climatic catastrophe seems to be somewhere around 500 to 2,000 warheads—an estimate that may be somewhat high for airbursts over cities, and somewhat low for high-yield groundbursts. The intrinsic uncertainty in this number is itself of strategic importance, and prudent policy would assume a value below the low end of the plausible range.

National or global inventories above this rough threshold move the world arsenals into a region that might be called the "Doomsday Zone." If the world arsenals were well below this rough threshold, no concatenation of computer malfunction, carelessness, unauthorized acts, communications failure, miscalculation and madness in high office could unleash the nuclear winter. When global arsenals are above the threshold, such a catastrophe is at least possible. The further above threshold we are, the more likely it is that a major exchange would trigger the climatic catastrophe.

Traditional belief and childhood experience teach that more weapons buy more security. But since the advent of nuclear weapons and the acquisition of a capacity for "overkill," the possibility has arisen that, past a certain point, more nuclear weapons do not increase national security. I wish here to suggest that, beyond the climatic threshold, an increase in the number of strategic weapons leads to a pronounced *decline* in national (and global) security. National security is not a zero-sum game. Strategic insecurity of one adversary almost always means strategic insecurity for the other. Conventional pre-1945 wisdom, no matter how deeply felt, is not an adequate guide in an age of apocalyptic weapons.

If we are content with world inventories above the threshold, we are saying that it is safe to trust the fate of our global civilization and perhaps our species to all leaders, civilian and military, of all present and future major nuclear powers; and to the command and control efficiency and technical reliability in those nations now and in the indefinite future. For myself, I would far rather have a world in which the climatic catastrophe cannot happen, independent of the vicissitudes of leaders, institutions and machines. This seems to me elementary planetary hygiene, as well as elementary patriotism. . . . [At this point the author examines the growth of American and Soviet strategic inventories since World War II and discusses ways they might be reduced to a level below the threshold at which climatic catastrophe might be set in motion— *eds.*]

VII

In summary, cold, dark, radioactivity, pyrotoxins and ultraviolet light following a nuclear war—including some scenarios involving only a small fraction of the world strategic arsenals—would imperil every survivor on the planet. There is a real danger of the extinction of humanity. A threshold exists at which the climatic catastrophe could be triggered, very roughly around 500–2,000 strategic warheads. A major first strike may be an act of national suicide, even if no retaliation occurs. Given the magnitude of the potential loss, no policy declarations and no mechanical safeguards can adequately guarantee the safety of the human species. No national rivalry or ideological confrontation justifies putting the species at risk. Accordingly, there is a critical need for safe and verifiable reductions of the world strategic inventories to below threshold. At such levels, still adequate for deterrence, at least the worst could not happen should a nuclear war break out.

National security policies that seem prudent or even successful during a term of office or a tour of duty may work to endanger national—and global—security over longer periods of time. In many respects it is just such short-term thinking that is responsible for the present world crisis. The looming prospect of the climatic catastrophe makes short-term thinking even more dangerous. The past has been the enemy of the present, and the present the enemy of the future.

The problem cries out for an ecumenical perspective that rises above cant, doctrine and mutual recrimination, however apparently justified, and that at least partly transcends parochial fealties in time and space. What is urgently required is a coherent, mutually agreed upon, long-term policy for dramatic reductions in nuclear armaments, and a deep commitment, embracing decades, to carry it out.

Our talent, while imperfect, to foresee the future consequences of our present actions and to change our course appropriately is a hallmark of the human species, and one of the chief reasons for our success over the past million years. Our future depends entirely on how quickly and how broadly we can refine this talent. We should plan for and cherish our fragile world as we do our children and our grandchildren: there will be no other place for them to live. It is nowhere ordained that we must remain in bondage to nuclear weapons.

NOTES

1. R. P. Turco, O. B. Toon, T. P. Ackerman, J. B. Pollack and Carl Sagan [TTAPS], "Global Atmospheric Consequences of Nuclear War," *Science* [222 (December 23, 1983): 1283–1292]; P. R. Ehrlich, M. A. Harwell, Peter H. Raven, Carl Sagan, G. M. Woodwell, *et al.*, "The Long-Term Biological Consequences of Nuclear War," *Science* [222 (December 23, 1983): 1293–1300].

2. The climatic threshold for smoke in the troposphere is about 100 million metric tons, injected essentially all at once; for sub-micron fine dust in the stratosphere, about the same.

3. The slow warming of the Earth due to a CO_2 greenhouse effect attendant to the burning of fossil fuels should not be thought of as tempering the nuclear winter: the greenhouse temperature increments are too small and too slow.

4. P. Ehrlich, *et al.*, *loc. cit.* footnote 1.

"Nuclear Strategy and the Challenge of Peace: Ethical Principles and Policy Prescriptions." Excerpts from *The Challenge of Peace: God's Promise and Our Response*, copyright © 1983 by the United States Catholic Conference, Washington, D.C., are used with permission of the copyright owner. All rights reserved.

"Bishops, Statesmen, and Other Strategists on the Bombing of Innocents," by Albert Wohlstetter. Reprinted from *Commentary*, June 1983, by permission; all rights reserved.

"MAD is the Moral Position," by Paul M. Kattenburg, is an original contribution written for publication in *The Nuclear Reader*. Dr. Kattenburg, a retired U.S. Foreign Service Officer and author of numerous articles on international affairs, is presently Charles L. Jacobson Professor of Public Affairs at the University of South Carolina.

"The Madness Beyond MAD: Current American Nuclear Strategy," by Robert Jervis. Reprinted with permission from *PS*, Vol. 16, No. 1 (Winter 1984): 33–40.

"On Russians and Their Views of Nuclear Strategy," by Freeman J. Dyson. Pages 86–90, originally appeared in *The New Yorker*, from *Weapons and Hope* by Freeman J. Dyson. A Cornelia & Michael Bessie Book. Copyright © 1984 by Freeman J. Dyson. Reprinted by permission of Harper & Row, Publishers, Inc.

"When a Nuclear Strike is Thinkable," by Pierre Gallois and John Train. Reprinted by permission of *The Wall Street Journal*, © Dow Jones and Company, Inc., 1984. All rights reserved.

"Strategies for Making a Nuclear Strike Unthinkable," by Earl C. Ravenal. Abridged from Earl C. Ravenal, "Taking the Sting Out of the Nuclear War Threat," *Inquiry*, October 1983, pp. 20–24.

Part II: Weapons

"The Nuclear Balance, East and West," by the Harvard Nuclear Study Group. Reprinted by permission from *Living with Nuclear Weapons* (Toronto: Bantam Books, 1983), pp. 115–32. Copyright Harvard Nuclear Study Group, Harvard University Press.

"Arms Control in American Domestic Politics: Impediments to Progress," by Steven E. Miller. Reprinted from *International Security* (Spring 1984), pp. 67–90, and originally titled "Politics Over Promise: Domestic Impediments to Arms Control," by permission of The MIT Press, Cambridge, Massachusetts.

"The Irrelevance of a Nuclear Freeze," by Harold W. Lewis. Originally titled "Freeze on Nuclear Weapons Development: CON—The freeze—deep or shallow?" Reprinted with permission from *Physics Today* Vol. 36, No. 1, pp. 37–45 (1983). © American Institute of Physics.

"The Military Role of Nuclear Weapons: Perceptions and Misperceptions," by Robert S. McNamara. Reprinted with permission of the author from *Foreign Affairs*, Vol. 62 (Fall 1983), pp. 59–80.

"Leaping the Firebreak," by Michael T. Klare. Reprinted by permission from *The Progressive*, 409 East Main Street, Madison, Wisconsin 53703. Copyright © 1983, The Progressive, Inc.

"Strategic Build-Down: A Context for Restraint," by Alton Frye. Excerpted by permission of Foreign Affairs (Winter 1983/84). Copyright 1983 by the Council on Foreign Relations, Inc.

"Sustaining the Non-Proliferation Regime," by Joseph S. Nye. Reprinted by permission of The International Institute for Strategic Studies from *Survival* Vol. 23 (May/June 1981), pp. 98–107 and originally titled "Sustaining Non-Proliferation in the 1980s."

"Toward Ballistic Missile Defense," by Keith B. Payne and Colin S. Gray. Excerpted by permission of *Foreign Affairs* and originally titled "Nuclear Policy and the Defensive Transition" (Spring 1984). Copyright 1984 by the Council on Foreign Relations, Inc.

"Star Wars: A Critique," by the Union of Concerned Scientists. Excerpted by permission from *The Fallacy of Star Wars: Why Space Weapons Can't Protect Us* (Vintage, 1984).

Part III: War

"How Might a Nuclear War Begin?" by the Harvard Nuclear Study Group. Reprinted by permission from *Living with Nuclear Weapons* (Toronto: Bantam Books, 1983). Copyright Harvard Nuclear Study Group, Harvard University Press.

"Nuclear Holocaust," by Jonathan Schell. From *The Fate of the Earth*, by Jonathan Schell. Copyright © 1982 by Jonathan Schell. Reprinted by permission of Alfred A. Knopf, Inc. Originally appeared in *The New Yorker*.

"Can Nuclear War Be Controlled?" by Desmond Ball. Reprinted by permission from *Adelphi Papers* No. 161. London: International Institute for Strategic Studies, 1981.

"Invitation to a Nuclear Beheading," by Barry R. Schneider. Reprinted by permission of the author and The Conference Board from *Across the Board*, Vol. 20 (July/August 1983) pp. 9–16.

"Civil Defense: Strategic Implications, Practical Problems," by John M. Weinstein. Reprinted from Strategic Issues Research Memorandum, May 5, 1983, Strategic Studies Institute, U.S. Army War College, Carlisle Barracks, PA. 17013.

"Nuclear War and Climatic Castastrophe: A Nuclear Winter," by Carl Sagan. Reprinted by permission of the author and the author's agent, Scott Meredith Literary Agency, Inc., 845 Third Avenue, New York, New York 10022. Article appeared originally in *Foreign Affairs* 62 (Winter 1983/84): 257–292, as "Nuclear War and Climatic Catastrophe: Some Policy Implications."